Destructive Desires

Destructive Desires

Rhythm and Blues Culture and the Politics of Racial Equality

ROBERT J. PATTERSON

RUTGERS UNIVERSITY PRESS

NEW BRUNSWICK, CAMDEN, AND NEWARK, NEW JERSEY, AND LONDON

Library of Congress Cataloging-in-Publication Data

Names: Patterson, Robert J., author.
Title: Destructive desires : rhythm and blues culture and the politics
    of racial equality / Robert J. Patterson.
Description: New Brunswick : Rutgers University Press, [2019] | Includes
    bibliographical references and index.
Identifiers: LCCN 2018027677 | ISBN 9781978803596 (cloth) | ISBN 9781978803589 (pbk.)
Subjects: LCSH: Rhythm and blues music—Social aspects—United States—History. |
    Rhythm and blues music—Political aspects—United States—History. | Rhythm
    and blues music—History and criticism. | African Americans—Attitudes.
Classification: LCC ML3917.U6 P37 2019 | DDC 306.4/84243—dc23
LC record available at https://lccn.loc.gov/2018027677

A British Cataloging-in-Publication record for this book is available from
the British Library.

♾ The paper used in this publication meets the requirements of the American
National Standard for Information Sciences—Permanence of Paper for Printed Library
Materials, ANSI Z39.48-1992.

www.rutgersuniversitypress.org

Manufactured in the United States of America

A Song, for You

CONTENTS

PREFACE

RJP and the Rhythm and Blues Imagination

And I will give you my heart / And I will always be true to you / And I will love you forever / If I could just make love to you.

–Kenneth "Babyface" Edmonds and Toni Braxton, *Boomerang Soundtrack*, "Give You My Heart"

I'm telling you love / Boy makes things happen / You never know where it's coming from / You never know who you're gonna love / I'm telling you love makes things happen / You never know what you're gonna do / Whenever true love takes hold of you.

–Kenneth "Babyface" Edmonds and Pebbles, *A Closer Look*, "Love Makes Things Happen"

Cause this life is no good alone / Since we've become one, I've made a change / Everything I do now makes sense / All roads end / All I do is for you.

–Kenny Lattimore, *Kenny Lattimore*, "For You"

Background to the Foreground

Although too young to claim 8-tracks as a part of *my* generation, I am old enough to remember their significance in my household. Along with 45s and 33s, 8-tracks introduced me to a host of rhythm and blues artists who, through their voice and soulful musical renditions, narrated *love story* after love story gone awry. Songs about *love* dreams deferred (Brian McKnight's "One Last Cry," and Anita Baker's "Fairytales"), relationships never actualized fully (Teddy Pendergrass's "Love TKO"), affairs slowly dissipated (Shirley Murdock's "As We Lay" and "Husband"), and steamy relationships abruptly ended (Guy's "Goodbye Love") engendered curiosity and intrigue as much as did songs that told of love that never ended (Johnny Gill's "My, My, My," Natalie Cole's "Everlasting Love," and Jerry Butler and Brenda Lee's "Ain't Understanding Mellow"). As Atlantic Starr's "Secret

Lovers" played on our home stereo system or in my mother's Pontiac Grand Prix, fascination encapsulated me. Admittedly, I had yet to apprehend with certainty what a lover was, but the secret's significance had not eluded me. If the woman in the song was "hoping you call before anyone gets home" and "waiting anxiously, alone, by the phone," then whatever a lover was, it had to be good. At the same time, the tethering of secrecy and/or silence to sexuality was a forewarning about the moral, social, and libidinal complexities of love, sex, and monogamy: In the next verse, the man begs the question "how could something so wrong be so right?" and then affirms, "I wish we didn't have to keep our love out of sight."[1]

For a young boy, the song's evocation of right, wrong, secrecy, and wish fulfillment/deferral, delivered in crooning, enthralling voices, provoked what I would later learn to describe as cognitive dissonance. But in the late twentieth century, this critical acumen eluded me, and I had yet to develop the vocabulary or academic training to differentiate between the artist, the persona, and the performance, as contemporary scholarship in black music studies—Michael Awkward's *Soul Covers: Rhythm and Blues Remakes and the Struggle for Artistic Identity* in particular—wisely compels us to do.[2] I wondered then, and now, as I became more prepared to analyze these songs and rhythm and blues music more generally, what did these songs, and artists, and black cultural production more generally tell us about black citizens' desires, longings, and aspirations?

My early fascination with "Secret Lovers" precociously prophesied what would later become my philosophical, intellectual, and personal skepticism toward monogamy in general and the institution of marriage in particular—not only as a personal choice, but moreover, as a socially prescribed remedy for black inequality. I immediately grasped that the song stirred mixed emotions insofar as the tempo and melody *initially* seemed to contradict the lament of the secret. I subsequently came to understand (by experience and cognition) that "Secret Lovers" more so embodies a complication than it does a contradiction to the professed ideal of love. That is, the conflict between the lovers' inability to be together in socially recognized and valued ways functions as much as a critique of the norms of marriage and monogamy as it does as a lament about the lovers' unfulfilled desire to be together. More broadly, it attests to the complication that arises from our desires to have an all-encompassing, all-engaging romanticized love, with our experiential knowledge of the impossibility, impracticality, and improbability of finding and sustaining such a love. Even still, our desires and longings persist, and when we do not personally aspire to the norms, others project the desires onto us, then question why we in fact do not possess these longings. I began to wonder about the degree to which the desire for romantic love and monogamy undermined black people's abilities to thrive, and whether romantic love and monogamy were stand-ins as a metonym for an interconnected set of material and psychic desires. Rhythm and blues music and culture, for reasons *Destructive Desires: Rhythm and Blues Culture and the Politics of Racial Equality* clarifies, serve as crucial sites in which to imagine viable alternatives to romantic love and monogamy that can fulfill parallel psychic and material desires.

In this sense, "Secret Lovers" belongs to a robust set of songs, which include Mtume's "You, Me, and He," Cameo's "Single Life," Betty Wright's "I'll Be the Other Woman," Kenny Lattimore's "For You," and Adina Howard's "Freak Like Me" that upset conventional expectations of romance (including monogamy) to offer alternative ways of imagining kinship, relationship, and nonmonogamous affiliations.[3] *Upset* here signals how black cultural production can push against norms, even while leaving them intact, and the examinations throughout this book investigate these nuances. These alternative imaginings in turn force us to reimagine the relationships that exist between black inequality and its political and politicized discourses. Ad nauseam, we have heard in political discussions, public policy debates, scholarly papers, and everyday conversation that the black family remains under attack, that black marriage rates fall dismally low, and that the number of single-mother households skyrockets. Such discourses take for granted the nuclear family's stability as a pretext and prerequisite for black people to thrive; any configuration but the nuclear familial unit allegedly undermines the stability of black communities and threatens racial progress. Among many interventions, *Destructive Desires: Rhythm and Blues Culture and the Politics of Racial Equality* investigates how rhythm and blues culture reframes such conversations—shifting our attention away from conventional, individualistic, neoliberal, and familial-based paradigms for conceptualizing black inequality, and calling into question the usefulness and costs of the normative, nuclear family model. Perhaps unexpectedly, given its reputation for romantic cliché, I show how R&B helps us to think about how the focus on the nuclear family obfuscates how neoliberalism and post–civil rights era conservatism undermine black people's abilities to thrive; and how it imagines new possibilities for kinship organization that have potential to reshape our public policy discourses.

This study thus examines a constellation of discourses, cultural practices, industry factors, musical relationships, cultural influences, and interrelationships among texts (artists, music, musical performance) that demonstrate the complicated role that rhythm and blues culture has had in making and shaping black culture and politics. The examination both corrects and generates; it pushes back at formulations of progressive politics that valorize the respectable nuclear family; it instead poses new possibilities for how we think about choice, desire, and familial and social organizations. Beyond the songs and artists that this project examines, it also considers how entangled networks work across media sites to bolster the cultural work the art performs. Hence the book focuses on the broader culture in addition to the music. Although beyond the scope of this book's study, the sonic (the sound of the music) further contributes to music's meaning as the sonic performance also layers meaning that does not emerge fully, for example, in simply reading the lyrics. As Romans 10:17 reminds, "Consequently, faith comes from *hearing* the message and the message is *heard* through the word (of Christ)" (emphasis mine).

While I may have inherited 8-tracks, 45s, and 33s (many of which remain still in my mother's basement), I certainly owned more than my fair share of cassettes and compacts discs (many of which are currently in my basement, and some of which I have since resurrected in the process of working on this project). Both the compact disc and the cassette collections grew exponentially thanks to the era of BMG and Columbia House, where ten CDs could be mine for just $0.99 (plus shipping and handling) and the promise to buy one CD per month for the next six-months.[4] While I won't let memory, or lack thereof, overstate the effect that "Secret Lovers" had on me, I will note that I always had (and still do) an affinity toward love songs, and, going by a wide range of the listening public's classification, sad and romanticized ones. And so, when one of my older cousins would play Guy's "Goodbye Love," I once again found the soulful performances as moving as I found the failure of the promise to stay faithful in the love affair salacious and provocative. Even while Brian McKnight, who my older relatives and friends found to be as whiny as they did the original crooner, Keith Sweat, wanted to have his one last cry "before I put you out of my life," my sense was that we should not deprive this brother this prerogative. As did the group Hi-Five, I too liked when we played the "Kissing Game," though, for me, I imagined it. As did the newly introduced teenager Tevin Campbell, I too wanted to know "Can We Talk." His later song, "Shhh," made homework an entirely more enjoyable prospect. And, like "Secret Lovers," it referenced a silence and secrecy entangled in sex and desire that reinforced why sadness loomed and yet made more understandable Rick James and Teena Marie's "Fire and Desire." In both cases, social practices and cultural conventions were delimiting the boundaries of enjoyable, pleasurable, articulable sex. And as chapter 3's examination of Adina Howard proposes, the shift toward a more expansive notion of pleasurable and vibrant sex—sex positivity—expands the possibilities for black thriving and rejects conventional notions of black family and respectability—particularly as they relate to black thriving.

But even as I enjoyed the up-tempo, aspirational, celebratory love and loving songs, the woes of broken hearts, making up, and moving on (though not necessarily forward) especially fascinated me. Before I became old enough to be personally interested in, as Mary J. Blige's persona had been, searching for a "Real Love," one stumbled into my life; I distinctly remember watching the movie *Boomerang*, and actress Halle Berry declaring, "love shoulda brought your ass home last night," before slapping actor Eddie Murphy. As the scene faded, the strong vocals of an artist whom I had not encountered before belted out "our whole relationship is built on one lie." As the soundtrack, which, on its cover let the world know it was "introducing Toni Braxton," debuted "Love Should Have Brought You Home Last Night," it positioned Braxton as a new, rising, rhythm and blues artist, one whom I would follow closely for years to come and not solely because of my affinity toward her musical talents. More tellingly, the initial first half of the title to this book, *It's Just Another Sad Love Song*, nodded toward this signature track on her freshman album *Toni Braxton*. Although the book's shift in focus repositioned this title to the epilogue, Braxton, nonetheless, for reasons to be explained, remains a central figure in the rhythm and blues culture that this study pursues.

While completing this project, I had the opportunity to rediscover the vinyl, the 33 and 45 records that were becoming collector's items in my mother's basement, and to purchase a Christmas gift for myself, a Victrola record player. Undoubtedly, I cannot recall the number of times I have listened to Whitney Houston's "You Give Good Love." To hear Nippy sing that song amidst the "crackle" of the vinyl, however, transformed that listening experience, and reminded me of the indescribable pathos that black musical production captures and articulates. To discover records, such as Millie Jackson's "Leftovers," which would serve as intertexts to chapter 1's reference to Denise LaSalle's "Your Husband's Cheating on Us" and Betty Wright's "I'll Be the Other Woman" emphasized the reach of *Destructive Desires'* archive. As chapter 2 reveals, my examination of Babyface's archive also reminded me that songs and song performances speak across gender lines, that they resist the clear distinction that too often attempts to police and govern social relations. In January 2018, he performed "How Could an Angel Break My Heart," which he wrote for Toni Braxton, at the Kennedy Center for Performing arts. That he sang the song as Braxton, without changing the pronouns, (e.g., "I heard *he* sang a lullaby, I heard *he* sang it from *his* heart") struck me as a clear example of how rhythm and blues culture pushes against some of the very norms that it often in turn regulates.

This project, too, has provided me several opportunities to experience, in person, performances by rhythm and blues living legends, including Stephanie Mills, Gladys Knight, Patti Labelle, Kenneth "Babyface" Edmonds, Kenny Lattimore, Bell Biv Devoe, Chanté Moore, John Legend, Lenny Williams, Toni Braxton, Mint Condition, Tony Toni Tone, Melanie Fiona, SWV, and Jazmine Sullivan. While not exhaustive, this list possesses some of the most vocally gifted, lyrically rich, and dynamic performing artists to shape rhythm and blues culture's aesthetic, thematic, and political concerns. The range of artists also reflects the capaciousness of a genre that blends with soul music, crosses over to pop music, and incorporates elements of hip-hop music. Despite these genre mixings, their primary classification remains rhythm and blues. The delivery (the elusive soulfulness) and the subject matter (love/relationships) contribute to this classification, and my interest in what follows focuses on the subject matter, with some attention to the delivery.

Destructive Desires

Introduction

(Re)Reading Destructive Desires and Cultural Longings in Post–Civil Rights Era Rhythm and Blues Culture, Life, and Politics

Michael Jackson / Whitney Houston / Vesta Williams / Prince / Luther Vandross / Natalie Cole / Teddy Pendergrass / Eddie Levert / Aaliyah . . . and the list goes on.

TRACK 1

AN INTERLUDE

On June 25, 2009, I was in my apartment in Arlington, Virginia, and had just finished cutting my hair when I sent a text message to a friend of mine to ask, "What are your plans for tonight?" He responded, "Mourning the loss of MJ." "What in the world are you talking about?" I inquired and immediately turned the television to CNN. The headlines clarified what he had meant: "Michael Jackson has died" flashed across the screen in black and yellow. The looks on the commentators' faces revealed we shared a similar disbelief.

On February 12, 2012, I was sitting at my desk doing random stuff, talking on the phone to my friend Susana, and planning my departure for a late-evening house party. Midsentence, Susana interjected, "Oh, no!" "What?" I demanded. "Whitney," she replied. Running to the bedroom, I already knew what CNN—via Beverly Hills Police Lt. Mark Rosen—was confirming, "Whitney Houston has died." Houston's hits became the soundtrack for a party that the organizer certainly had not planned as a tribute.

On April 21, 2016, I was taking in my daily news digest on CNN.com when across the ticker it flashed, "Prince has died."

TRACK 2

THE OVERARCHING CLAIMS AND CONCERNS

Without a doubt, Houston's untimely death captivated me personally more than the others. Reading the early news reports and interviews about her "last days," watching the Oprah Winfrey special dedicated to her life and legacy, viewing her

1

three-plus hour funeral, and ultimately reading her autopsy report, I wanted to grasp better a variety of interrelated issues. In addition to the factual and contextual circumstances of Houston's life and death, I wanted to understand the public's response to the artist—from sympathy to empathy—to excoriation—as part of a larger conversation about blackness, black life, black aspirations, black desires, and black politics. How have public responses to Houston corroborated or contested racial norms? How did Houston's connections to dangerous or taboo love objects affect her public image and her artistic production? How does Houston's public circulation through her music and her iconography help us to understand her life and death? Representatively, these questions, a few of which chapter 4, "Didn't We Almost Have It All?: Reading Whitney Houston," undertakes, articulate the types of questions this book engages as it uncovers destructive desires, cultural longings, and entangled networks in post–civil rights era rhythm and blues culture.

Rhythm and blues music, artists, and, culture in general, and the areas of inquiry I raise in particular, have not received their due critical attention in scholarly studies of black music, popular music, black popular culture, sociology, or African American studies. This omission remains curious in light of the fact that rhythm and blues culture persists as a primary cultural site to imagine, contest, and reaffirm ideas about black intimate relations, and much discussion about black equality and progress returns to black intimate relations as a primary site for cause, effect, explanation, and solution. *Destructive Desires: Rhythm and Blues Culture and the Politics of Racial Equality* corrects this omission by analyzing how post–civil rights era rhythm and blues culture articulates competing and conflicting political, social, familial, and economic desires within and for African American communities. As an important form of black cultural production, rhythm and blues music helps us to understand black political and cultural desires and longings in light of neoliberalism's increased codification in America's racialized, gendered, and sexualized politics, policies, and economies since the 1970s. As Lisa Duggan explains of neoliberalism, "the politics of race, both overt and covert, have been particularly central to the entire project—but the politics of gender and sexuality have intertwined with race and class politics at every stage as well."[1] This analysis thus considers the mutually constituting features of race, gender, and sexuality as they intersect with and through social class to produce cultural longings (and destructive desires) for and by black people. Although themes emerging in post–civil rights era rhythm and blues culture have continuity with earlier eras, the neoliberal turn imbues the post–civil rights era cultural production with a distinct set of expectations, particularly as they relate to black inequality.

Whereas "rhythm and blues music" more narrowly describes how the music industry and society historically have classified certain sounds, performances, and themes within black music (and by black artists), the phrase "rhythm and blues culture" gestures toward a wider framework that foregrounds the interrelationship between music and other modes of black cultural expressivity. This framework supplements music to consider how music influences (and is influenced by) black modes of expressivity that include, for example, film (relationship to soundtracks), literature (cinematic adaptations that also have soundtracks), and personal stylings (adoption of an artist's aesthetic). It further considers how these same contexts shape the listening public's desires for and affinities to the culture and how those desires and affinities in turn reshape the culture. *Destructive Desires* thinks of these relationships as circular, dialogic, implicit, and explicit.

Cultural longings, as the book conceptualizes them, are not isolated psychological drives, but networks of representation, performance, and desires whose nodes include the following: the desires (psychic and material) to which black subjects aspire; the desires (psychic and material) that nonblack subjects project onto black subjects; the discursive contexts (political, sociological, artistic) that frame both sets of desires; and the imaginative possibilities that rhythm and blues culture provides to reimagine black subjectivity and black political desires outside of dominant, and often destructive, epistemologies. By analyzing the implicit and explicit cultural longings that rhythm and blues culture articulates, we can historicize the cultural production, theorize its aesthetic and discursive influences and possibilities, and extrapolate its "futurity" to reimagine black political possibilities.

More broadly, *Destructive Desires* (1) articulates the imaginative possibilities for blackness (as it intersects with gender, sexuality, and social class) and black politics that rhythm and blues culture provides in the ages of neoliberalism, postracialism, and post-Obama; (2) investigates how the historical and social demands for equality in the (late) post–civil rights era have repositioned rhythm and blues culture's roles vis-à-vis the civil rights movement and later-developing musical forms such as hip-hop; (3) explains how contemporary artists position themselves (and become positioned) within long-standing debates about what relationship(s), if any, black art and black artists have toward black politics; (4) corrects the tendency to privilege hip-hop music in scholarly examinations of black music, culture, and politics, while ignoring rhythm and blues culture; and (5) demonstrates how (black) popular culture has reinvigorated interest in rhythm and blues culture and how that interest expresses multiple cultural and political desires. To signify on VH1, *Destructive Desires* gets "behind the music" as it contextualizes and explicates rhythm and blues culture's relationship to racial politics. And it does so by juxtaposing a variety of texts and contexts, as well as disciplinary and subdisciplinary paradigms and methodologies, against and through each other, to better articulate the cultural, sociological, political, and historical import of rhythm and blues culture from the late twentieth century until the present.

To understand the complex processes through which rhythm and blues culture articulates cultural longings, we must also consider, analyze, and "read" the interdisciplinary cultural affiliations that entangle distinct networks and expand the discursive and material reach of rhythm and blues culture. The phrase "entangled networks," as *Destructive Desires* employs it, captures how rhythm and blues culture emerges, exists, expands, and produces meaning. The entangled networks operate through multiple, intersecting, and sometimes competing and even contradictory contexts: between artists, producers, and writers—who are sometimes one and the same; between cultural production mediums (movies—their accompanying soundtracks, and the literary text from which they are adapted); between implicit ways of shaping cultural values (musical production and consumption) and explicit ways of using one's brand and cultural cachet to engender more explicit activism (artist as spokesperson); musical influences (both as revisionary predecessor and as admiring newcomer); and musical production as politically charged cultural desire (instead of as detached, romanticized dreams). Each chapter deliberately produces its own set of entangled networks as its tracks unfold how rhythm and blues culture engenders cultural longings for racial equality vis-à-vis black intimate relations.

Although I could catalog the many artists whose musical talent compels, the main players in this book's musical interlude are Kenneth "Babyface" Edmonds, Adina Howard, Whitney Elizabeth Houston, and Toni Braxton. Edmonds's role as rhythm and blues father to a generation of songs, artists, and soundtracks reflects a broad influence that makes him indispensable to a study of rhythm and blues culture. Howard's innovation to the genre and expansion of black women's modes of cultural expressivity force us to examine her legacies. Whereas LaFace Records shows us a kind of centripetal force of rhythm and blues culture, Howard's innovation and expansion show us an influence from the margins. Houston's iconicity as "the voice" and her status as one of the best vocalists to live demand attention to her influence and influences. And Braxton's spanning of cultural modes of expressivity since Edmonds discovered her, alongside her musical talent and influence, position her as a central figure in ever-changing metrics of success in rhythm and blues culture. Individually and collectively, these cultural figures help us to articulate a scholarly story about rhythm and blues culture since the 1980s. Herein, I begin to weave together the cultural longings that the entangled networks produce by "reading," that is, analyzing and defamiliarizing, key moments in their careers, lives, and American culture and politics more generally, to uncover what these moments reveal about, in the words of W.E.B. DuBois, "our spiritual strivings."

Within these entangled networks, this book locates cultural longings that are destructive, counterproductive, and otherwise inhibitive to black people's ability to thrive. Despite their destructiveness, they persist in public policy as well as social, political, and economic discourses; sometimes black communities themselves also view them as viable solutions to and for black inequality. In fact, they are posited as necessary for and helpful to black thriving. The title of this book gestures toward this analytical tendency, yet frames these desires as oppositional to black progress. The book itself locates the imaginings of rhythm and blues culture, particularly as they aggregate around the topic of black intimate relations, as an important corrective to destructive cultural longings insofar as rhythm and blues culture engenders its own set of cultural longings that can advance a more progressive racial politics that tackles the sources of black inequality. Destructive desires thus functions as a two-faced construct where, on one face, the term illuminates the concealed destructiveness of normatively sanctioned desires (e.g., for a heteronuclear family, for monogamy, etc.). On the other face, the term turns an ironic/skeptical eye toward desires that are conventionally seen as destructive (having a mistress, being a freak, engaging in polygamy) to consider how they may in fact provide new ways to imagine black equality.

In its investigation, this book calls for a broad and diverse archive of cultural texts and interpretive tools, which together allow me to construct a cultural historiography of black rhythm and blues music, artists, and culture since the 1980s. Artists' interviews, including one I conduct and publish here for the first time, billboard ratings (including rhythm and blues and pop charts), magazine articles, biographies, memoirs, film, soundtracks, and the music lyrics constitute the primary archives from which this book begins the task of developing cultural longings' multidisciplinary theorization of this cultural production and its intersecting cultural milieus. To most fully excavate the archive, *Destructive Desires* calls upon a range of methodologies and theoretical paradigms that African American studies, literary studies, historical studies, gender and sexuality studies, black queer studies, black feminism studies, black music studies, and ethnomusicology have developed. In return, it also augments those paradigms and advances those intradisciplinary conversations about black cultural production in the process.

By foregrounding and reading across and through the multiple archives that shape rhythm and blues culture, *Destructive Desires* enacts a methodology of cultural analysis that emphasizes multidisciplinarity as a strategy for reading and interpreting rhythm and blues culture's ideological, social, musical, and political significances, and provides a method to decode the ignored and/or layered meanings of black cultural production more generally. Thought about another way, this book's methodology self-consciously mirrors the interdisciplinary questions and methodologies that African American studies—as an interdisciplinary field and discipline—asks and employs—and does so in light of the post–civil rights era concerns that inform black cultural production and culture as well as black life.

When chapter 2, for example, investigates Kenneth "Babyface" Edmonds's role as musical, lyrical, and entrepreneurial genius, it does so to demonstrate an interrelationship between gender relations, musical influences, black politics, and American cultural desires for and within black communities. These entangled networks articulate their cultural longings in light of neoliberal and post–civil rights era discourses about family and equality. To obtain the most penetrating analyses of the complexity of meaning, we must work through, against, and across the texts and paratexts. We thus are examining what Foucault phrases discursive formation, "and what makes it possible to delimit the group of concepts, disparate as they may be, that are specific to it, [and] the way in which different events are related to one another."[2] Because black cultural production has repeatedly embedded multiple artistic genres within it since its inception, the best excavations will upend the academic tendencies to reinforce disciplinarity by circumscribing the artistic production to a sole genre or the analysis to one methodology. The richness of W.E.B. DuBois's influential *The Souls of Black Folk*, for example, provides an instructive example;[3] not only does DuBois evidence the centrality of black music to America's cultural fabric, beginning each chapter with a "sorrow song," but the text itself also exemplifies how black cultural production relies upon multiple forms and multiple disciplines in staking out its claims and values.

Despite the rhetorical emphases on interdisciplinarity, multidisciplinarity, and transdisciplinarity in academia, disciplinary formations persist as privileged and desired forms of knowledge production, circulation, and consumption. In *Phonographies: Grooves in Sonic Afro-Modernity*, Alexander Weheliye laments, for example, the fact that "subdisciplines exist in quasi isolation, producing virtually identical insights."[4] In theory, academic pushes toward interdisciplinarity acknowledge that the production of cutting-edge knowledge best occurs when multiple disciplines bring together their methodological and theoretical paradigms to address a question, problem, issue, or challenge. In practice, the source of Weheliye's perturbation is his rightful perception that academic institutions—by and large—by way of organization and metrics of evaluation, lack the capacity to promote and evaluate interdisciplinarity in a meaningful way. Thus, Weheliye correlates that disciplinary interactions are just that—interactions at best—and not dialogues that produce more complicated models and more complex insights. This lack of "openings that facilitate fresh institutional configurations and imaginings of unorthodox intellectual endeavors" pose an opportunity for us to engage in transformative scholarly inquiry.[5] As Weheliye explains, it "presents a chance to leave behind old beliefs in order to invent nondisciplinary disciplines that are always in the throes of becoming, where limits are not preset but are negotiated within the contexts of the intellectual project in question."[6] Through the questions it asks, sources it analyzes, and methodologies it employs, *Destructive Desires* seizes the opportunity Weheliye identifies as it investigates rhythm and blues culture's fecund archive (figure I.1).

In its own right, the music itself merits consideration because, as Shana Redmond contends, "music is a method" that "allows us to do and imagine things that may otherwise be unimaginable or seem impossible."[7] From music's formal elements (tempo, tune, and notes), performative interpretations (pitch, inflections, bodily gesticulations), and thematic elements (subjects, allusions, referents), music and music culture function as a repository for cultural longings (past, present, and future), including black political desires. Redmond concurs with my argument insofar as her timely *Anthems: Social Movements and the Sound of Solidarity in the African Diaspora* articulates the transformative ways that *anthems* functioned to engender political consciousness, mobilize communities, and spark political activism that radically re-envisioned—vis-à-vis the imagination—black political possibilities across the black diaspora.

By analyzing the roles music plays in mobilizing groups politically, Redmond further demonstrates how "the lines delineating art and politics were blurred, often collapsing into each other as music, poetry, and drama vocalized the trials

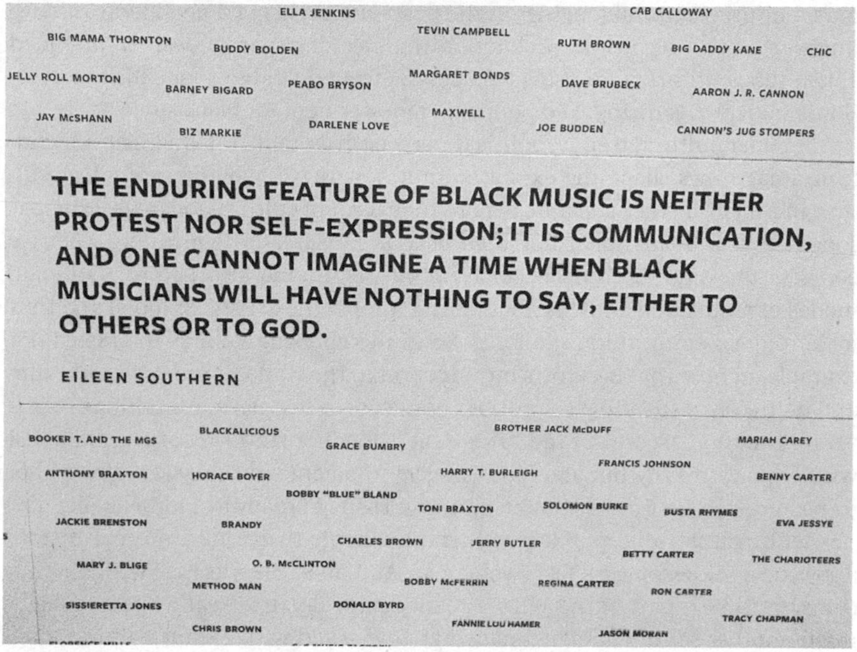

ELLA JENKINS   CAB CALLOWAY

BIG MAMA THORNTON   TEVIN CAMPBELL   RUTH BROWN   BIG DADDY KANE   CHIC
                BUDDY BOLDEN

JELLY ROLL MORTON   MARGARET BONDS   DAVE BRUBECK
            BARNEY BIGARD   PEABO BRYSON   AARON J. R. CANNON

JAY McSHANN   MAXWELL
            BIZ MARKIE   DARLENE LOVE   JOE BUDDEN   CANNON'S JUG STOMPERS

THE ENDURING FEATURE OF BLACK MUSIC IS NEITHER PROTEST NOR SELF-EXPRESSION; IT IS COMMUNICATION, AND ONE CANNOT IMAGINE A TIME WHEN BLACK MUSICIANS WILL HAVE NOTHING TO SAY, EITHER TO OTHERS OR TO GOD.

EILEEN SOUTHERN

BOOKER T. AND THE MGS   BLACKALICIOUS   BROTHER JACK McDUFF   MARIAH CAREY
                    GRACE BUMBRY
ANTHONY BRAXTON   HORACE BOYER   HARRY T. BURLEIGH   FRANCIS JOHNSON   BENNY CARTER
                BOBBY "BLUE" BLAND
JACKIE BRENSTON   BRANDY   TONI BRAXTON   SOLOMON BURKE   BUSTA RHYMES   EVA JESSYE
                    CHARLES BROWN   JERRY BUTLER
MARY J. BLIGE   O. B. McCLINTON   BETTY CARTER   THE CHARIOTEERS
            METHOD MAN   BOBBY McFERRIN   REGINA CARTER   RON CARTER
    SISSIERETTA JONES   DONALD BYRD
            CHRIS BROWN   FANNIE LOU HAMER   TRACY CHAPMAN
                                    JASON MORAN

FIGURE I.I. Names of artists whose cultural production reflects music's enduring significance. National Museum of African American History and Culture Museum, Musical Cross Roads Section, Washington, DC.

and triumphs."[8] This collapsing draws attention to this interweaving of art and politics. As important, it also emphasizes how micropolitics, or, as Gene Jarrett explains, informal politics, remain an important part of the constellation of activities that constitute black political activity. In other words, by analyzing rhythm and blues culture's direct and indirect engagements with these post–civil rights era and neoliberal cultural longings, this weaving of arts and politics maintains an important tension between informal politics, which "refers to the context of cultural representation, media representation, and subjectivity" and formal politics, which "refers to the context of governmental activity, public policy, and social formations."[9]

As *Destructive Desires* posits, formal and informal political activities also assist in the formation of black subjects, and, in more problematic ways, the subjection and subjectification of black people. *Destructive Desires* conceptualizes music culture at the interstices of informal and formal politics, and maintains a keen eye toward representation's potential to impact formal politics insofar as the music, artists, and culture can be thought to respond indirectly to formal politics, or the concerns that formal politics articulate. By analyzing destructive cultural longings in the cultural and political imaginations, we uncover personal, political, and other forms of abject desires that public policy and discourses enact and invoke to maintain black inequality. By analyzing rhythm and blues culture's cultural longings in the post–civil rights and neoliberal eras, we uncover how this cultural production remixes destructive desires' intended abject subjectification to instead articulate new possibilities for subject formation, political organizing, and political empowerment for black subjects.

Broader cultural trends, political perspectives, cultural longings, and cultural imaginings shape the extant cultural longings in rhythm and blues culture inasmuch as they generate a more robust set of cultural longings. Whereas songs themselves are important, their *imports* gain greater significance when we consider the ways that they become imbricated in and attached to additional modes of production and distribution that propel the artists' brand(s) and thus make them a cultural tour de force. So in the epilogue I am as interested, for example, in how Toni Braxton's introduction to the world in the *Boomerang* film and on the corresponding soundtrack connects to her platinum-selling records "Toni Braxton," "Secrets," and "The Heat"; how her status as one of the most vocally powerful rhythm and blues singers to emerge in the 1990s allowed her to become the first black woman star in a Disney Broadway play as Belle; how her willingness to be publicly vulnerable coupled with her musical history allowed her to become a spokeswoman for Autism Speaks, as I am with how her decision to be a part of the WE TV reality show *Braxton Family Values* inaugurated another set of entangled networks that toyed with extant cultural longings that reinforced destructive desires. The show jump-started her sister Tamar Braxton's music career; reinvigorated Toni Braxton's singing career (duet with Kenneth Edmonds, *Love, Marriage, and Divorce*); allowed her to achieve her authorial voice by co-writing *UnBreak My Heart: A Memoir* (and allowing for it to be produced as a biopic); and revived interest in her music career.[10] *Destructive Desires* insists that entangled networks implicitly and explicitly connect these moments in Braxton's career and that any analysis of rhythm and blues' cultural longings must contextualize more broadly cultural longings in music, culture, history, politics, society, and individuals. By probing these longings, *Destructive Desires* provides a more penetrating analysis of how rhythm and blues culture can act as a form of cultural revision that reshapes cultural expectations, and how these relationships shape cultural reception.

For the purposes of *Destructive Desires*, cultural expectations refer to demands—aesthetic, content, and ideological—that industries, individuals, and institutions place on black artists, and how black artistic production responds, and in some cases defies, these requests. Without a doubt, cultural expectations pay attention to how racial, gender, and sexual discourses inform not only the expectations but the imaginative possibilities for the *cultural reception*. Race, gender, sexuality, and social class individually and collectively inform cultural expectations to the degree that these intersecting subject, ideological, and discursive positions shape what rhythm and blues culture produces and how that production becomes interpreted, valued, and considered. As Stuart Hall contends, this encoding then, and corresponding decoding, "may not be symmetrical" because "the degrees of 'understanding' and 'misunderstanding' in the communicative exchange—depend on the degree of symmetry and asymmetry

(relations of equivalence) established between the positions of the 'personifica-
tions,' encoder-producer and decoder-receiver."[11] To that end, the black feminist
concept of intersectionality remains a critical heuristic in the analysis of both
cultural expectations—which often ask how these differing and competing subject positions inform, affect, circumscribe, and challenge cultural expectations—
and the dialogic similarity as to how the work itself informs, affects, circumscribes,
and challenges what we think we know about these subjects and subject positions and the power relations that produce ideologies.

As important as black feminist thinking remains to the argumentative arc
of *Destructive Desires*, the epistemologies of queer of color critique, quare studies, and black queer studies also become crucial interlocutors that expose the
significance of gender and sexual norms that the book denaturalizes. In some
ways, the emergence of black queer studies, which I am using here as the umbrella
term to capture the capacious thinking about black sexualities, emerged in ways
that parallel black feminism's origins.[12] The exclusion of blackness from (white)
queer studies necessitated thinking about blackness and materiality in ways that
white queer studies had not. In his proposal of a quare studies, for example, E.
Patrick Johnson notes the term *quare* "offers a way to critique stable notions of
identity and, at the same time, locate racialized and class knowledges."[13] This
knowledge, for Johnson, results from examining the "racialized bodies, experiences, and knowledges of transgendered people, lesbians, gays, and bisexuals of
color" in order to "foster contingent, fragile coalitions as it struggles against
common oppressive forms."[14] In offering the formative framework for what we
might now think of as queer of color critique, Johnson's proposition for quare
studies delineates how a turn to the nonnormative might in fact call into question the privileging of the normative, but also provides an analytical framework
for decoding the implicit ways race, sexuality, gender, and class reconstitute
social relations. As Roderick Ferguson explains, "queer of color critique
approaches culture as one site that compels identification with and antagonisms
to the normative ideals promoted by the state," and it "presumes that liberal ideology occludes the intersecting saliency of race, gender, sexuality and class in
forming social practices."[15] By calling into question the normativity of the nuclear
family and the presumed immutability of gender roles and gender performances,
Destructive Desires' thinking about how black cultural production revises cultural norms and expectations implicitly and explicitly calls upon these strands
of thinking in black sexuality studies.

To that end, cultural reception considers how and why the cultural production becomes situated within broader discourses and the implicit and explicit
significance of that production. This examination of reception moves beyond,
in the words of Michael Awkward, "a summary of surveys quantifying soul's
impact on its listeners" or "an approach that [seeks] to theorize, like reader
response criticism in vogue in the 1970s and 1980s, how listeners did, or ought to,
interact with the sounds, narratives, and ideologies of soul music."[16] Although
the social science tendency to rely on human data to generate and buttress its
theoretical premises demonstrates the potential usefulness for reader-response

criticism, this project instead traces the weaving of the imagination alongside sociopolitical and cultural sensibilities as cultural production expresses and cultural consumers might experience them. Put another way, it probes how the culture could be received, reinforces the epistemological and imaginative thrust of the cultural production, and uncovers how cultural longings bear the ideological and material markers of race class, gender, and sexuality.

Cultural expectations and cultural reception provide important contexts for understanding my premises, yet the argumentative thrust of *Destructive Desires* keeps a keen eye toward cultural revision insofar as it argues for how and why some forms of cultural production that rhythm and blues culture's cultural longings produce provide the discursive space to imagine politics outside of usual paradigms. It reframes cultural longings in a way that offers alternative epistemologies and narratives for those longings, and, in the process, produces newer, innovative, alternative cultural practices that afford the possibility for cultural revision, or the introduction of different ways of being, knowing, and understanding. It refutes binaries that reject the possibility for reinscribing a regressive politic while championing a progressive one to espouse the messiness of black intimate relations and their corresponding politics. Given the historical time frame this book spans, the attention to cultural revision eschews a contemporary presentism that might retroactively understate or overstate the significance and potential of the rebellion and revision. It instead contextualizes that moment to consider the potential then and now, continuing to blur the distinction between, and trace the commingling of, past, present, and future in black life, culture, and politics. This book describes the nuances of the ongoing negotiation between expectations and revision that reveals how cultural production potentially reconstitutes reception; foregrounds artists' roles in creating cultural epistemologies; explains the multiple relationships that exist among and between cultural longings; centralizes music culture's role in shaping black cultural politics; and recognizes cultural production, reception, and revision as circular processes.

TRACK 3
AESTHETIC CONCERNS: "KEEPING IT REAL"

Although nonscholarly texts have taken rhythm and blues culture more seriously than scholarly studies, none has exhausted the archive or questions that *Destructive Desires* takes up. One of the most notable and comprehensive examinations of rhythm and blues culture, Nelson George's *The Death of Rhythm and Blues*, for example, discusses the evolution of the genre, explains the histories of production studios and record labels, and details the key artists/groups/themes that representatively constitute the "tradition" at different historical moments. As the title suggests, George conceives of rhythm and blues culture as moribund (if not already dead), and attributes its demise to changing racial and economic politics of the post–civil rights, postintegration eras. Black intimate relations do not figure significantly into this discussion.

Sammy Davis Jr. performs at the NAACP Freedom
Spectacular, 1964 *Photo by David Gahr/Getty Images*

**THE POLITICS
OF CROSSOVER**

In an industry where musical categories
have been marketed by race, crossing over
from one genre to another had an artistic
and social impact. Artists like Ethel Waters,
Nat King Cole, and Sammy Davis Jr. defied

WE ARE AMERICANS TOO
Words and Music by
ANDY RAZAF, EUBIE BLAKE ...CHARLES L. COOKE
Featured in POWELL LINDSAY's
"THIS IS OUR
AMERICA"
presented by
PANORAMA
OF
PROGRESS

MUSICAL ADAPTATION BY
MAURICE KING
NARRATION BY
WILLIE BRYANT

FIGURE I.2. Sammy Davis Jr. and Nat King Cole perform as crossover artists during
the mid-twentieth century. National Museum of African American History and
Culture Museum, Musical Cross Roads Section, Washington, DC.

Shifts in the distribution and technical production of rhythm and blues
music impacted the cultural consumption of it insofar as the move away from
"race records" after World War II, and the continued commercialization of black
culture in the post–civil rights era, repositioned rhythm and blues culture's status in American culture. Prior to the 1970s and 1980s, for example, marketing
strategies targeted race music and race records primarily toward black audiences, and black (independent) distribution labels made the music available to
black consumers. Compounding the transformations in culture (and technology
and politics) that George explains was the desire among producers to generate
more mainstream interest (i.e., crossover appeal, of black rhythm and blues artists), and to use the larger, mainstream labels, including CBS, for distribution
(figure I.2). The consequence was more assimilationist music that supposedly
downplayed the blackness of the artist's physical characteristics (appearance)
and music performance (tone and style). Brian Ward's discussion of how James
Brown, who people had thought of as an exemplar of rhythm and blues protest
music, later becomes a spokesperson to quell black dissent and promote the
State's interest (and behavioral solutions to black equality) amplifies Nelson's
point.[17] If, as George contends, the continued success of *true* rhythm and blues
music necessitated artists and music "to break away from, ignore, or battle the
crossover consciousness and remain true to the strength of R&B," it appears

market forces too factor into the marginalization of this music.[18] While George's desire for artists to "remain true to the strength of R&B" gestures toward a more contentious debate about racial authenticity and realist aesthetics, George's study usefully points to the ways that race, economics, and gender (implicitly) inform the production, reception, and consumption of rhythm and blues culture, and this broader context becomes an important paratext for the analyses in which *Destructive Desires* engages.

About a decade after George publishes *The Death*, rhythm and blues resurrects and begins to take center stage, as a background singer, in academic discussions. To the degree that rhythm and blues music and culture function as a form of black popular music, the general discussion about black popular music's roles and theoretical challenges the genre presents for analyzing black life that Mark Anthony Neal undertakes in *What the Music Said: Black Popular Music and Black Public Culture* inaugurates a forthcoming more sustained analysis of rhythm and blues music and culture in scholarly inquiry. As is the case with select background singers who show promise, rhythm and blues music and culture get the opportunity to have the stage alone in Neal's *Songs in the Key of Black Life: A Rhythm and Blues Nation.* In this text, Neal, the most prolific, conscientious, and thorough scholar of black popular culture *and* rhythm and blues music, explains the neglect of rhythm and blues music (and artists) as a consequence of two concurrent historical and sociocultural forces. First, the cultural perception of rhythm and blues music as *nothing more than* a bunch of sad love songs has rendered rhythm and blues music, artists, and culture unworthy of serious inquiry. Second, the widely held and theoretically myopic idea that hip-hop, which the listening public views as more politically informed, motivated, and responsive, offers a more *authentic* representation and critique of the *real* conditions (substantive issues and not that love bullshit) that thwart black people from thriving also has marginalized rhythm and blues music's social and cultural significance.

The first point of view underappreciates how discourses about love become politicized as well as how political discourses shape representations, conceptualizations, and policies that govern expressions of love.[19] This disjunction between love and politics persists alongside and in spite of its dissonance with the consistent conjunction of love as a metonym for family and marriage in discourses that position the latter as the solution for black inequality. As contemporary debates about same-sex marriage in religious organizations, activist groups, and political caucuses should further clarify, the politics of love and love politics remain entangled and are not so odd bedfellows.[20] These debates also inform representations of love, thus reaffirming the intricate relationship that informal and formal politics have to each other. The second point of view posits an abject point of view about black life—that it is most authentic when black suffering, poverty, and nihilism prevail or are the subjects of critique. It neglects the specific ways that rhythm and blues culture engages the prevailing sociological discourses, while attempting to upset the ideologies that privilege black deviance as the cause of and explanation for black inequality. That is, the assumed opposition between rhythm and blues and hip-hop is based on their corresponding *literary* genres of romance and realism, and, in recent years, romance has increasingly, if tacitly, been dismissed as an irrelevant genre for black life.

Destructive Desires lays bare how rhythm and blues culture performs this intervention, drawing attention to how it shares a commonality with hip-hop culture. That is, the discussion of hip-hop here does not detract from its critical and cultural force but instead turns attention to how the dismissal of rhythm and blues music and culture ignores the role black intimate relations have in how we understand black life, black culture, black politics, and black equality. This latter claim remains underasserted. These concurrent moves have led, in the words of Neal, "to large numbers of volumes written about jazz, the blues, and hip-hop music," while "few of these efforts [scholarly inquiry] have taken seriously contemporary rhythm and blues."[21]

To summarily dismiss rhythm and blues music as apolitical, socially and culturally irrelevant, or otherwise unworthy of scholarly inquiry requires us to suspend for a moment the following facts: love is political and politicized; hip-hop is at best only a *representation* of some aspects of a putatively believable "black life"; a capitalist, racist marketplace often mediates cultural productions; and race politics in rhythm and blues music operate outside or beyond the context of musical production. Only this suspension of belief would allow us to arrive at a commonly shared scholarly and popular perspective—much more can be learned about black life, black experience, black culture, black (political) longings, black motivations, and black innovation from listening to and apprehending Tupac Shakur's "Brenda's Got a Baby" than can be learned from Keith Sweat (with Kut Klose) *whining* about this woman who won't give him the time of day, despite his having what she needs, and thus "got him 'Twisted.'"[22] The belief that undergirds this hierarchy is that what is authentic to black life is suffering, abjection, violence, and sexual aggression, not interiority, individuated desire, interpersonal connection, or sexual intimacy. Perhaps Shakur becomes more authentic than Sweat because critics and consumers imagine Shakur's depiction as an unmediated portrait of black life, while insisting that Sweat's is escapist, inconsistent with the *real* challenges of being black in America.

Then what fantasies about race, gender, sexuality, and class, for example, make hip-hop an authentic representation of black life more than other forms of "black music"? What does this fantasy, this cultural longing, as imagined fantasy and perceived fact, tell us about racial-gendered longing? What entangled networks—ideological and material—propel hip-hop culture into the heart of scholarly inquiry while suspending interest in rhythm and blues culture? In light of expectations and reception, what possibilities for cultural revision become available for and from both forms of music? Questions such as these frame the study, to varying degrees, of rhythm and blues music and culture throughout *Destructive Desires*.

Even while hip-hop has figured more prominently in academic conferences, plenary sessions, and scholarly journals, it remains enshrined in philosophical, aesthetic, and ideological controversies as to whether it is in fact an art form, which Imani Perry's *Prophets of the Hood: Politics and Poetics in Hip Hop* and Michael Eric Dyson's *Know What I Mean?: Reflections on Hip Hop* examine;[23] whether the politicization of hip-hop, within both academic and nonacademic contexts echo W.E.B. DuBois's notion of what black art's political efficacy should be;[24] whether hip-hop's glorification of ideals (materialism, sex, violence) that seem to undermine black communal thriving cuts short its effectiveness and validity as a form of cultural criticism (Tracey Sharpley-Whitting's *Pimps Up, Ho's Down)*; whether the represented and received images of blackness accord with expansive or restrictive notions of black subjectivities.[25] These very debates have not only catapulted hip-hop to the center of contemporary analyses of black music, but have also shifted conversation toward "to what degree it represents authentic black culture?" The elevation of hip-hop in black music studies also reveals the long-standing tradition to which black artistic production seems tethered: [sociological] realism.

In *Abstractionist Aesthetics: Artistic Form and Social Critique in African American Culture*, Phillip Brian Harper traces the history of realist aesthetics, and foregrounds how several black artists diverge from this trend in order to provide more capacious notions of blackness. He gestures toward the long-standing correlative thought that black people could prove their humanity and "earn" their civil rights through art and personal choices (behaviors). He rightfully suggests that realist aesthetics demand that black art "casts racial blackness in overridingly 'positive' terms" when he argues that "such positivity more fundamentally entails an empiricist demand that racialized representations perceptibly mirror real-world phenomena, however favorable—or not—any particular portrayal may be."[26] Too often the distinctions between reflection (mirror-like), representation (the art form), and life (lived experience) become blurred; conversations about hip-hop's *realness* and *authenticity* perpetuate the tendency, in the words of Stuart Hall, "to privilege experience itself, as if black life is lived experience outside of representation."[27] Such conversations ignore or diminish the representational and aesthetic aspects of hip-hop and instead treat it as either a direct reflection of black life or, even more problematically, as black life itself (figure I.3).

In *Prophets of the Hood*, Perry counters "the primacy of historical and sociological interpretations of hip hop and concentrates instead on the aesthetic, artistic, theoretical, and ideological aspects of the music, working from the premise that it has been undervalued as an art per se, even as its cultural influence has often been noted."[28] The tendency to focus on hip-hop's cultural influences and to treat the art form as black life lived outside of representation not only ignores hip-hop's formal and aesthetic attributes. As ethnomusicologist Kyra Gaunt and hip-hop feminist Gwendolyn Pough also argue, these historical and sociological analytical perspectives treat the black heterosexual male subject as the embodiment of black identity and thus ignore the wide range of experiences—black women's in particular—that constitute black lives.[29]

These debates about the relationships that black cultural production have to art, aesthetics, and politics have a long-standing history, and in the

FIGURE I.3. Hip-hop originated in the Bronx in the early 1970s, and this display captures the people, equipment, and conditions that made hip-hop a cultural force. National Museum of African American History and Culture Museum, Musical Cross Roads Section, Washington, DC.

twentieth century, emerge clearly in conversations among artists and critics during the Harlem Renaissance, the Black Arts Movement, and the post–civil rights era. Langston Hughes's paradigmatic essay, "The Negro Artist and the Racial Mountain," essentially ruminates on the responsibilities black artists have toward their race, considering the types of representation they should undertake and the purposes for which those representations might be used.[30] While Hughes ultimately concludes that a range of artistic representations *should* be available to black artistic production, the dominating opinion prescribed that artistic production's main purpose was to uplift the race. As DuBois had previously averred, art for art's sake (he perhaps questions if such a thing as pure art exists) was not a privilege that black artists could afford to employ, and even in the twenty-first century, this contention, and the debate surrounding it, persists.

For some artists, racial uplift had specific, and perhaps even overdetermined, criteria. When Richard Wright, for example, chides Zora Neale Hurston for writing a "love story" when she pens *Their Eyes Were Watching God* (1937), he not only suggests that love is both apolitical and deracialized,[31] but he also reinforces the expectation that the protest novel (mirrorlike, vis-à-vis Harper) and its tenets/protocols remained the desired and privileged form of *literary and artistic* expression of the era. For Wright and others, black artists and artistic production bore the responsibility to critique the social conditions that nurtured black inequality. The failure to do so meant shirking one's civic and political duties. James Baldwin's "Notes of a Native Son: Everybody's Protest Novel" calls into question the protest novel's privileging of abjection as the primary characteristic of black life, and usefully emphasizes the imaginative space that black art can provide even in the context of black suffering.[32] This corrective admonition supplements Hurston's earlier "Characteristics of Negro Expression," which itself articulated a descriptive set of characteristics that scoffed at sociological realism.[33] This brief overview sets the realist stage upon which black cultural production repeatedly finds itself performing an encore, even as the civil and post–civil rights eras worked to extend the ranges of black aesthetic modes of production.

Well into the 1960s and 1970s, these arguments persist, often coalescing in the manifestoes that the Black Arts movement offers for black art and artists alike. The artistic relative of the Black Power movement, the Black Arts movement, in its desire to promote positive, uplifting images of black people and black life, foregrounded representation as an important catalyst in shaping black politics and rising black political consciousness. In many respects, the establishment of a black aesthetic, as Larry Neal's "The Black Arts Movement" and Addison Gayle's "Cultural Strangulation: Black Literature and the White Aesthetic" exemplify, contests white aesthetics, which ignored or otherwise devalued black cultural production and black people.[34] In articulating the criteria for a black aesthetic, these black aestheticians necessarily produced exclusionary and sometimes myopic notions of black life and black art, even as they demanded more robust notions of blackness. As several critics have clarified, this myopia and exclusion often clustered around nonnormative expressions of gender and sexuality. If, as *Destructive Desires* contends, black intimate relations become increasingly conjoined with discourses about black (in)equality, this demand for "positive," "nuclear," and "strong black family" representations and configurations, for example, does not appear as surprising.[35]

And yet, as Gershun Avilez notes, this myopia and exclusion "upheld conventional conceptions of identity [blackness]," and on the other, "it pushed away from values of respectability that buttress such conventional understandings."[36] As several scholarly examinations of black feminism have shown, we are illuminating the both/and while shifting away from either/or understandings of the progressive/regressive politics of black cultural production. This examination of rhythm and blues culture considers the imaginative and material possibilities that become available even as we recognize how "cultural and revolutionary nationalist formations suppress the critical gender and sexual heterogeneity of minority communities," and turn away from respectability politics and black intimate relations as the primary sites for understanding black political progress.[37] In the twenty-first century, this turn may help us to arrive at a clearer understanding of what Margo Natalie Crawford refers to as "black post-blackness," or "the circular inseparability of the lived experience of blackness and the translation of that lived experience into the world opening possibilities of art."[38] *Destructive Desires* insists that rhythm and blues culture can provide another venue to demonstrate how black cultural production expands our ways of imagining and living.

The development of second-wave white feminism and the expansion of black feminism further call into question the *representative image* of black identity, black political interests and desires, and the goals and meanings of black liberation. The movement "away from values of respectability," for example, also works to displace the heterosexual black middle-class man as representative of black communities, and his political enfranchisement as most important. The intertwining of political concerns and identity politics continued to fragment during the 1960s and 1970s as the activists, theoreticians, theories, and paradigms upended this image of black men as the necessary and desired exemplars of black life and politics. The politicization of identity politics intensified and mapped itself (and continues to map itself) onto the relationship between artistic production, artistic freedom, and political uplift; this relationship reflects a tension that more generally ensconces black cultural production—the expectation that black cultural production be authentic, that it (re)presents a real, quantifiable/qualifying (singular) black experience. It also reflects a broader context of cultural expectation that governs black cultural products' reception and production. In other words, the emergence and rapid ascendancy of hip-hop, at the same time that rhythm and blues music and artists languish, occurs alongside these trends and within this historical scope of aesthetic debates.

The gendering of hip-hop—as hard, masculine, and manly—relative to rhythm and blues as soft, not masculine, and not manly—further relegates rhythm and blues music and culture to the periphery of academic studies in general and black music and African American studies in particular. Setting aside temporarily the expectations for *real, authentic, identifiable* "positive" images, we also witness the explicit rise in black masculinity studies and the more general heteronormative focus on African American political enfranchisement as crucial contexts for understanding why hip-hop ascends. On the one hand, hip-hop's perceived verisimilitude provides access to, critique of, and possible solutions for the structural vicissitudes that stunt black life. It becomes a vehicle through which to critique structural racism, give a voice to unheard impoverished black masses, and demand solutions to that inequality. On the other, as L. H. Stallings persuasively claims, "the academic industrial complex's pathologizing and privileging of the crisis of black masculinity resulted in a new field of knowledge now apparently termed *hip-hop* scholarship that would overwhelmingly favor specific cultural forms and institutional knowledge of those forms rooted in hegemonic black masculinities and femininities."[39] An emphasis on achieving and/or reaffirming hegemonic black masculinities and black femininities functions to maintain black inequality insofar as these roles perpetuate and reflect destructive desires. Yet a cultural longing for hip-hop persists, and its representation of hegemonic masculinities and femininities serves as a springboard to engage black inequality. For black music studies, Paul Gilroy illuminates the pitfalls of this thinking when he asks, "what special analytical problems arise if a style, genre, or particular performance of music is identified as being expressive of the absolute essence of the group that produced it?"[40] From this vantage point, there emerges a double-feminization that contextualizes rhythm and blues culture's relegation in scholarly studies.

First, the feminization of rhythm and blues music relative to hip-hop culture explains its marginalization in black music studies and African American studies; its concerns were not central or representative (read masculine) enough to warrant serious, substantive attention. Second, the feminization within rhythm and blues culture gestures toward how *within* the culture cultural expectations for black women artists required particular types of conformity to respectability politics, heteronormativity, and patriarchy more generally. Paradoxically, the post–civil rights era also provides women artists more access to and opportunities within rhythm and blues culture, where the same sexism that circumscribes their production within the genre ironically facilitates their incorporation within it too.

To this point, *Destructive Desires* offers an intersectional racial–gender–sexual analysis, as the examination in chapter 3 evidences, to make sense of why artists such as Adina Howard experience censorship while Robert Kelly's career soars during the early and mid-1990s. A double feminization emerges for and within the genre. Whereas hip-hop might have displaced further the (un)real, feminized rhythm and blues music in black music studies, the examination here contrastingly foregrounds its imaginative possibilities for black life, black culture, and even black politics and politicized desires as they implicitly and explicitly rebel against hegemonic masculinities and femininities.

TRACK 4
RHYTHM AND BLUES MUSIC: CONTEXTS AND CULTURAL TRENDS

As *Destructive Desires* stakes its claims about rhythm and blues culture, cultural longings, destructive desires, and entangled networks, it acknowledges and builds upon important scholarly and popular studies that thoughtfully historicize and adeptly analyze and theorize rhythm and blues music and culture produced during the late twentieth and early twenty-first centuries. Michael Awkward's *Rhythm and Blues Remakes and the Struggle for Artistic Identity* (2007), Mark Anthony Neal's *Songs in the Key of Black Life: A Rhythm and Blues Nation* (2002) and *What the Music Said: Black Popular Music and Black Popular Culture* (1998), Nelson George's *The Death of Rhythm and Blues* (1988), and Brian Ward's *Just My Soul Responding: Rhythm and Blues, Black Consciousness, and Race Relations* (1988) exemplify the tendencies to historicize the rise and mainstreaming of rhythm and blues music in the twentieth century (George), examine rhythm and blues music as a form of social critique (Neal and Awkward), examine the relationships that artists have to their musical precursors and how the politics of race and gender govern and inform those relationships (Awkward), foreground the politics of gender and gender politics in rhythm and blues culture (Awkward and Neal), and articulate the complex relationships that exist between social movements, artists, and rhythm and blues music and culture (Ward).[41] Throughout, *Destructive Desires* returns to these conversations, at times converging with and at times diverging from the premises, in order to augment our understanding of rhythm and blues culture's significance in black cultural production and politics.

Rhythm and blues music overlaps with and is perhaps sometimes indistinguishable from soul music, such that examinations of Motown usefully amplify the analytical archive that shapes rhythm and blues culture's history and import. Nelson George's *Where Did Our Love Go? The Rise and Fall of the Motown Sound* (1987, 2007) and Suzanne Smith's *Dancing in the Street: Motown and the Cultural Politics of Detroit* (1999) historicize Motown and its role in shaping black music and black entertainment, and artists' understanding of their roles in shaping black politics.[42] All of these discourses are crucial to, and for, the interdisciplinary analysis in which *Destructive Desires* engages and the scholarly interventions it makes. That is, music history and culture must be understood alongside the seismic waves rippling through popular culture.

Rhythm and blues culture, like other modes of black cultural expressivity, has engaged repeatedly how the legislative achievements of the modern civil rights movement have impacted black life, black culture, and black politics. Black popular culture in the post–civil rights era exemplifies what Neal refers to as a "post-soul aesthetic," which "describe[s] the political, social, and cultural experiences of the African-American community since the end of the civil rights and Black Power movements."[43] Implicitly, the turn to popular black genres of the 1970s and '80s may be linked to the desire to understand how the post–civil rights era remade opportunities, desires, and norms. This remaking occurs in light of persistent structural inequalities and racism that mask themselves by accusing that black people's culture and individual behaviors maintain inequality. Rhythm and blues culture's position as the "arbiter of love" and its consistent thinking about black intimate relations situate it uniquely as a site to examine how black cultural production engages and imagines these concerns. Unlike the world of scholarly production, popular culture has developed a significant interest in rhythm and blues culture so that turning to it may be useful in our investigation of the cultural longings and destructive desires it produces, provides, and reshapes.

By investigating rhythm and blues culture of the late twentieth century, and Kenny "Babyface" Edmonds, Adina Howard, Whitney Elizabeth Houston, and Toni Braxton in particular, I want to obtain a deeper and more nuanced understanding of the intersections of identity (race, gender, and sexuality), obstructions to and solutions for black (in)equality, and the material and psychic roles black music has in shaping the limits and powers of the black cultural imagination. In the second decade of the twenty-first century, when notions of new blackness, postblackness, and postracialism dominate, it might appear retrograde to return to the 1980s and 1990s to locate seemingly elusive ties to a difficult-to-define racialized culture. And yet, as Stuart Hall reminds in "What Is This 'Black' in Black Popular Culture," black "is not a category of essence" yet "there is, of course, a very profound set of distinctive, historically defined black experiences," and "it is to that diversity, not the homogeneity, of black experience that we must now give our undivided creative attention."[44] Noteworthy here, Hall contends we must turn attention to a plurality of black experiences in order to understand the multiple ways of experiencing black identity.

That undivided creative attention pertains to both the cultural products produced and the critical attention we devote toward our examination of them. In black music and popular culture studies, earlier hip-hop studies reinforced a homogeneity of black culture, although feminist hip-hop studies undercut this tendency by demonstrating how women hip-hop artists, in some instances, produced art that defied the masculinist discourses dominating hip-hop culture.[45] In a similar way, the shift to examining rhythm and blues culture allows us the opportunity to think through how black popular culture and cultural producers have generated multiple ways of being black, (re)imagined romantic love as it relates to black inequality, and placed black life in front of and beyond DuBois's metaphorical veil, oftentimes in the specter of white racism and black respectability politics. These innovative ways of conceiving of blackness, especially when we consider the historical moments in which they emerge, inform contemporary understandings and expressions of race and race politics, and perhaps even enrich our understanding and development of, vis-à-vis Thelma Golden's idea of postblack, new blackness.[46]

My examination and approach, even while locating transgressive and transformative moments and possibilities, eschew the tendencies to suggest that black popular culture necessarily transgresses and transforms, bucks hegemonic epistemologies, dissociates itself wholly from *high* culture, belongs solely to lower classes and/or *low* culture, or represents *authentic* blackness. In general, black popular culture reproduces some of the most conservative thoughts and values, which, while widely *accepted* by black people, widely *harm* black people's ability to thrive. The book title's "destructive desires" aims to keep this point in the forefront of these conversations. Michael Awkward's characterization of soul music's paradoxes extends to rhythm and blues music too: "It is ideologically engaged *and* relatively indifferent to sociopolitical concerns, it is forward-thinking with respect to representation of race and gender and hence, to changing ideas about acceptable social interactions (including in the realm of romance) *and* aggressively resistant to such changes[47] (emphasis in original)." Awkward's characterization embodies a persistent theme that emerges between conflicting desires to challenge political disempowerment on one hand, and to appeal to or appease the ideologies that undergird this disempowerment on the other. Across modes of black cultural expressivity this trend persists and provides one of the more fascinating aspects of black cultural production to examine.

These tensions (which are not contradictions) exemplify why popular culture remains an important site of inquiry: in the words of Stuart Hall, "popular culture, commodified and stereotyped as it often is, is not at all, as we sometimes think of it, the arena where we find who we really are, the truth of our experience. It is an arena that is *profoundly* mythic. It is a theater of popular

FIGURE I.4. Mack Wilds, Yolanda Sangweni, Melonie Fiona, Amanda Seales, Bridget Kelly, Brande Victorian, and Damon Williams attend Music Choice Celebrates Black History Month with the Next Generation of R&B Divas at MIST Harlem on January 29, 2014, in New York City.

desires, a theater of popular fantasies. It is where we discover and play with the identification of ourselves, where we are imagined, where we are represented, not only to the audiences out there who do not get the message, but to ourselves for the first time."[48] Instructively, Hall conceives of popular culture as an important site of cultural imagination, of cultural possibility that reorients our understandings of how we see ourselves in the context of how we are seen—a DuBoisian double-consciousness.[49] An examination of popular culture in general, and rhythm and blues culture in particular, thus helps us to understand not only the fantasies and myths (cultural longings) upon which their cultural productions rely, reinterpret, and revise. It also allows us to consider and imagine what desires and fantasies animate, and are resolved through, our consumption of popular culture.

In *Cruel Optimism*, Lauren Berlant employs the titular phrase to theorize the process under which people desire objects that are in fact detrimental to their thriving or perceive said detrimental objects as necessary for their survival. This intertext helps to frame my understanding of destructive desires' detrimental face, and recognizes that cruel optimism may be better than none at all (nihilism and afropessimism). In Berlant's own words, "cruel optimism: a relation of attachment to compromised conditions of possibility whose realization is discovered either to be impossible, sheer fantasy, or too possible, and toxic. What's cruel about these attachments, and not merely inconvenient or tragic, is that the subjects who have x in their lives might not well endure the loss of their object/ scene of desire even though its presence threatens their well-being."[50] *Destructive Desires* provides another lens through which to access some of black people's most persistent cultural longings and aspirations—even those that are cruelly optimistic. To reemphasize, cultural longings refer to those desires black people themselves possess, as well as those that are externally thrust upon them, even if not necessarily internalized by them. The imaginative possibilities of rhythm and blues culture unnerve the cruel optimism of black intimate relations as a solution to black inequality and illuminate how black intimate relations discourses function as destructive desires. They also at times provide possibilities for black intimate relations that exceed the normative, and that *excess* (an idea that typically is thought of as problematic) reframes our possibilities for black sociopolitical organization and longings.

TRACK 5

TV ONE AND THE RESURRECTION OF RHYTHM AND BLUES MUSIC

Within the last decade, TV One's influx of programming focusing on black music has reinvigorated interest in black popular music, musicians, and culture; foregrounded the importance of rhythm and blues music as both a cultural product and a form of social commentary; and popularized an often understudied and lesser-known history of black music, including its industry forces and interpersonal workings and relationships (figure I.4). In 2008, four years after Radio One launched this "lifestyle and entertainment" network geared toward "African American adults," TV One premiered the series *Unsung*, which has ensured that several forgotten, underexposed, or briefly exposed soul, hip-hop, rap, and rhythm and blues artists and music become enshrined in black cultural memory and musical history.[51] Debuting with a four-episode "mini" season, *Unsung* has become one of TV One's more highly anticipated and viewed programs, boasting of a predominantly black viewership that in 2009 "show[ed] an increase in 43% growth to previous season."[52] As of January 2016, *Unsung* had aired more than one hundred episodes, featuring only four artists who appear in any other documentary.[53] Featuring individual artists, including Jennifer Holiday, Otis Redding, Donnie Hathaway, Deborah Cox, Avant, Ike Turner, Chanté Moore, Al B. Sure, Teddy Pendergrass, Regina Belle—as well as groups, including Xscape, H-Town, Ready for the World, the Spinners, Jagged Edge, Silk, 702, Atlantic Starr, Shalamar, and Kylmaxx, *Unsung* offers an untapped archive from which scholars, critics, artists, and viewers can understand, contextualize, and historicize black artists, black music, and black cultural production.

According to executive producer Mark Rowland, *Unsung* "puts the songs and music in a larger context, and a personal context, [and] also in a kind of musical history context . . . [and thus] touches on social, cultural, and sometimes even political history."[54] Rowland's "sometimes even political history" statement diverges from this argument's contention that music and culture *very much* constitute "political history," and at the same time acknowledges black music's broader significances. The *Unsung* archives amplify the study of the entangled networks insofar as they gesture toward behind-the-scenes inner workings of a complicated and complex industry, and provide a strategy for documenting and understanding competing and conflicting dynamics in investigating other artists and groups. Beyond the multiple contexts that the documentary uses to narrate histories, the artists themselves enhance the episodes because their presence "gives them the freedom to basically tell their story from the inside."[55] They in essence help to *write* themselves into a history that would otherwise occlude their voices, if not overlook them altogether.

Insofar as the series "chronicles the rise, fall—and sometimes resurrection—of black performers from the 1960s to the 1990s who've either been done wrong, done-in or self-destructed," the artists' own voices clarify, correct, or, in several instances, provide the first time public account of how they became unsung.[56] This desire for black voices to speak and be heard has deep historical roots and reflects a broader cultural practice of writing and speaking oneself into and through history. While studies in autobiography of course have reminded us that narrative frames our understanding of the autobiographical self, that autobiographies too reflect mediated representations of a *constructed* self, the artist's perspective nonetheless provides another important set of data to our interpretive matrix, particularly as cultural expectations require an authorial voice to authenticate a type of "realness." Not all artists, however, have welcomed the opportunity to participate in the series. Stephanie Mills, for example, believes the moniker "unsung" pejoratively mischaracterizes her career, and the reframing of the series' introduction gestures toward the possibility that other artists shared this perspective. When *Unsung* first aired in 2009, the beginning of each episode introduced the artists by noting, "uncompromised, unrecognized, unparalleled, unsung, the story of . . ." As of 2017, each episode began explaining, "unparalleled, untold, unsung, the story of . . ." The removal of *uncompromised*, and *unrecognized* in particular, can demonstrate an awareness of concerns that artists such as Mills raise. As important, the new introduction refocuses the series' desire to emphasize the artist's significance and achievements within the context of black musical production and the wider sociopolitical contexts.

Unsung conscientiously underscores how autobiography, biography, social and political contexts, industry practices, and intergroup and intragroup dynamics embody *entangled networks* of their own that operate alongside the cultural longings and exist among and between cultural expectations, social practices, and historical processes. Anyone who watches an episode of *Unsung* on television, or an advertisement online, can comprehend why *Unsung* seems more like a phenomenon than a television show or music documentary; in addition to the hour-long episodes themselves, TV One has developed online quizzes and trivia and placed unaired footage on its website to encourage viewers to explore the robustness of this archive. In addition to *Unsung*, TV One featured a short *Unsung Hollywood* (2013–2015, 2017–), which operated on the same premise as *Unsung*, as well as the series *Life After* (2009–2013), which also featured rhythm and blues artists, including Ginuwine (Life after "Pony," 2011), Adina Howard (Life after "Freak Like Me," 2013), Shirley Murdock (Life after "As We Lay," 2013), Karyn White (Life after "Superwoman," 2012), and Christopher Williams (Life after "New Jack City," 2011). TV One's investment in black music culture reflects its recognition of black music's centrality to the development of many "American" music genres and American culture more generally, as well as the degree to which network programming responds to audiences' tastes and support. It also illuminates the black public's desire for and interest in black music culture.

Unsung's documentary style historicizes black music's cultural significance, and the interest that viewers have demonstrated toward black music culture by their participation in the *Unsung* phenomena evidences—the viewing and the online participation—has resulted in reality television–based shows that focus specifically on black women rhythm and blues artists. If *Unsung* uses the documentary genre to historicize black music's social, cultural, and political significance, the *R & B Divas* series uses the reality television format to contextualize the cultural significance of artists' personal and professional lives. Unlike *Unsung, R & B Divas Atlanta* (2012–2014), which aired for five seasons and ended abruptly, and *R & B Divas Los Angeles* (2013–2015), which aired for three seasons, the *R & B Divas* series eschews the documentary classification, despite its documentary moments/elements (figure I.5). Instead, this series, like reality television shows, provides viewers access into artists' personal space and putatively private moments (but for the fact that those moments are broadcast publicly). As Brenda Weber explains in the introduction to *Reality Gendervision: Sexuality and Gender on Transatlantic Reality Television*, even though reality television is by no means real, "the obvious performances encapsulated in a television format called 'reality' do not serve to bankrupt the medium on the grounds of hypocrisy. Instead, they heighten both the complexity of the context and the pleasures that viewers report experiencing as they hold the 'paradoxical positions' of performance and authenticity in creative juxtaposition with one another."[57] Thus part of the appeal of *R & B Divas* lies in the belief that the show provides access to the "real," the "essence" of the artists (returning us to aesthetic demands of black art), while simultaneously (and hopefully) recognizing that that representation remains always already mediated. Yet the documentary and the reality show give viewers a level of intimacy that provides a type of truth even if not a fact.

By featuring these artists within the highly acclaimed and highly consumed genre of the reality television show, *R & B Divas* also demonstrates how black popular culture remains deeply invested in and intrigued by rhythm and blues music and artists from the post–civil rights era. The original cast of *R & B Divas Los Angeles*, Kelly Price, Chanté Moore, Dawn Robinson (of En Vogue), Claudette Ortiz, and Michel'le; and the original cast of *R & B Divas Atlanta*, Monifah Carter, Syleena Johnson, Nicci Gilbert (of Brownstone), Faith Evans, and Keke Wyatt include artists who came of age or had major career milestones during the late twentieth century. Their emergence on *R & B Divas* reproduces and reinvents a cultural longing that has (re)invigorated interest in their music, cauterized their

FIGURE I.5. Executive producer Adam Reed, R & B Artists Syleena Johnson, Monifah Carter, Keke Wyatt, Nicci Gilbert, and Faith Evans from the show *R & B Divas* attend the TV One 2012 Summer Television Critics Association tour at the Beverly Hilton Hotel on August 1, 2012, in Los Angeles, California.

personal struggles, and, in some instances, reset their careers, providing a welcomed reentrance into the black music scene. *R & B Divas* encapsulates the relationship between the late twentieth century and the contemporary moment that *Destructive Desires* offers insofar as it insists upon the temporal blending that transpires between the postsoul aesthetic as it traverses the post–civil rights 1980s and 1990s eras.

TRACK 6

THE ORGANIZATION OF THIS BOOK

First, *Destructive Desires* provides a thorough examination of four specific individual artists—Edmonds, Howard, Houston, and Braxton—to examine black cultural longings and destructive desires by demonstrating how our *readings* of specific moments in their lives, careers, and/or performances serve as metacommentaries for broader issues in black culture and politics. Reading thus signifies a critical analysis, a hermeneutic that at once defamiliarizes and uncovers hidden meaning and then connects it to broader contexts, themes, and practices. The cultural studies methodologies of close reading and defamiliarization will assist in this process. Related, the analyses insist that we move beyond the music but through the music to other cultural media because those additional contexts and entangled networks help us to read, analyze, and interpret their significance—aesthetically, culturally, and politically. One challenge in writing a book such as this one is that readers' familiarity with the artists and culture will bring a set of expectations, particularly the desires for an extended biography of the artists or close readings of their songs and discographies. While *Destructive Desires* engages autobiographical elements about its artists, and exegetes isolated songs, the book neither purports to provide a biography nor to analyze the artists' repertoire. *Destructive Desires* instead situates these moments within entangled networks to uncover interrelated meanings. Second, the book thus *decidedly* moves beyond the music and artists to articulate the inner workings of history, culture, and imagination and how these processes shape black political, social, and cultural discourses. Third, a range of concerns animate the chapters and propel the book's scope of considerations, yet each chapter explains why the particular artist or artists become necessary for this study, how the corpus of work and life intersect with the entangled network and produce and upset cultural longings, and what the stakes are for the broader conversation surrounding black intimate relations and black inequality and their relationships to destructive desires. The respective parts of the book relate to the whole, and the chapters provide a coherent narrative, even while the chapters themselves study different subjects, artists, and concerns. These different issues, which the chapters sometimes compare, consider how these different "issues" in music and culture provide insights into the production and consumption of rhythm and blues music during the late twentieth and early twenty-first centuries.

The first chapter begins with an analysis of 1970s politics and culture to set the stage for how 1980s and 1990s rhythm and blues culture provides imaginative space to reject neoliberal and personal responsibility philosophies that root black inequality in black people's choices in general and in nonnormative family structures in particular. The chapter juxtaposes R&B music's discourses about love, marriage, and family—what it more generally phrases "black intimate relations"—against sociopolitical explanations for and solutions to black inequality to disrupt the tendency to privilege behavioral explanations of inequality and to diminish/ignore how structural barriers impede black people from achieving equality. In making this claim, the chapter analyzes how rhythm and blues culture reimagines possibilities for kinship that necessarily upset behavioral solutions to black inequality. This reimagining, I insist, upends neoliberal policies and logics (fair, open markets) insofar as it unmasks the ubiquity and persistence of structural inequalities (e.g., wage discrimination, lack of affordable housing, and redlining) and opens up space for us to consider alternative possibilities for black thriving. Jean Carne's "Shortage of Black Men," the O'Jays' "Family Reunion," Mtume's "You, Me, and He," and Cameo's "Single Life" are primary texts through which the chapter reads, and the chapter sets the discursive stage upon which the subsequent analyses perform. That is, this analysis sets the stage for the ensuing examination of the entangled networks, cultural longings, and destructive desires that animate rhythm and blues music and culture to the degree that rhythm and blues culture is in fact the arbiter of love (in terms of ideas and aspirations) and intersects with many trends and conversations about black intimate relations that black cultural production engenders.

Chapter 2 builds upon chapter 1 as it reads Kenneth "Babyface" Edmonds, one of the most accomplished rhythm and blues artists emerging in the 1980s, and positions him as one of *the* late twentieth-century black cultural producers and standard-bearers because of his multifaceted roles in shaping the cultural longings and entangled networks of rhythm and blues. That is, his roles as songwriter and producer (of both music and film) influenced a generation of artists and consumers from the 1980s to the present, and Edmonds creates and becomes an entangled network through which many artists express, reinforce, and contest cultural longings. A prolific song writer, he has written and produced songs that artists ranging from Toni Braxton to Whitney Houston, Mary J. Blige, Boyz II Men, and Bobby Brown (the disputable bad boy of R&B) have performed. As a music producer and with his business partner L. Antonio Reid, he has launched the careers of several well-noted artists, including Toni Braxton and TLC. With his then wife Tracey Edmonds, he produced a signature film celebrating black family, culture, and life in the 1990s, *Soul Food*, for which he also produced the soundtrack. Indeed, Edmonds has shaped a cross-generational public's attitudes about black intimate relationships and their possibilities and politics, and this chapter reads the meanings within several of these contexts. By examining Edmonds's multitudinous roles in the music industry, alongside the discourses that chapter 1 engages, the chapter's analysis of cultural longings and destructive desires begins with a brief historiography of Edmonds's own career to demonstrate his centrality in black musical studies. It isolates three issues: (1) Edmonds's scoring and writing of the *Waiting to Exhale* soundtrack, (2) the autobiographical elements of his life that inform his lyrical production, and (3) his roles in creating opportunities for other artists, specifically through his music production (writing lyrics) and distribution (record label). By situating this argument within the emergence of black male feminist praxis, I demonstrate how Edmonds's work, including its radical, progressive, and traditional perspectives on black gender relations, calls for more nuanced understandings of how gender, gender roles, and their respective performances index the different possibilities for re(imagining) black subjectivities outside of the normative face of destructive desires. I argue that Edmonds's cultural production, like Howard's (chapter 3), demonstrates the messiness of black sexual politics as he both contests and promotes destructive desires' investment in respectability politics and normative gender roles. This messiness, I insist, reveals a politics of racial liberation that enjoins the renouncement of hegemonic masculinities as necessary for black thriving, even as the messiness at times reinforces hegemonic gender performances.

Expanding some of the concepts that chapters 1 and 2 foreground and engage, chapter 3 disrupts the tendency in black musical studies and black popular cultural studies to think of love as "apolitical" and in black feminist studies to think about popular depictions of love as primarily reaffirming static, heterosexist, patriarchal formulations of love that undermine black thriving. My reading of Adina Howard's engagement with black intimate relations discourses considers how rhythm and blues artists and music utilized cultural rebellion and cultural revision to reimagine the possibilities for black love, sex, and relationships—black intimate relations—in the context of the 1980s and 1990s. The analysis follows trends in recent scholarship about gender and sexuality in African American studies that rethinks the messiness of radical black sexual politics. It thus locates agency and desire in the midst of seeming abjection and commodification. The analysis isolates four issues: (1) Howard's rise to stardom with her freshman album *Freak Like Me*; (2) respectability politics and its revisiting by way of her album cover, and subsequent "unsung" works; (3) her performances in the twenty-first century and the continued perceived threat of black women's sexuality; and (4) her personal branding and self-perceived role in rhythm and blues culture. The chapter provides historically grounded and culturally contextualized analyses of music, artists, and culture to demonstrate how their work imagines a place for black sexual and gender expression that extends beyond the binary trappings of European domination that still too often circumscribe popular and scholarly expectations for representations of black gender, sexuality, love, and relationships. Building on the concept of the television series *Unsung*, this chapter examines interviews (including one I conducted with Howard in March 2018), music, magazine articles, and gossip blogs to read and theorize Adina Howard as a paradigmatic unsung diva to chart out rhythm and blues' corrective vision to arresting gender and sexual ideologies in black culture. It argues that Howard's cultural production calls into question the normative face of destructive desires in order to destigmatize the assumed destructiveness of nonnormative desires, and does so to center black women's sexual pleasure as constitutive to black liberation and freedom.

Chapter 4's examination of Whitney Houston considers how the famed singer's life and career reflect cultural longings about blackness in general and black women's sexuality in particular that, while different from those desired for Howard, function within similar discursive contexts about black intimate relations. Whereas chapter 3 deploys black feminist thinking and theories to consider how gender and sexuality inform the racialization of Howard, chapter 4 assumes these arguments to emphasize how post–civil rights era racialization informs Houston's life and career, and how the rise of neoliberalism in American culture provides an important context for reading Houston. The chapter isolates four issues: (1) Houston's rise to stardom, including the branding of her "respectable" image; (2) Rumors about her sexuality and her marriage to Bobby Brown, including her appearance on *Being Bobby Brown*; (3) her Diane Sawyer (2002) and Oprah Winfrey (2009) interviews; and (4) her death on February 12, 2012. Building on some of the key concepts presented in chapter 3, chapter 4 insists that the fascination with a "pure" Houston and then an "ailing" Houston metonymically represents the cultural desire to contain race and gender—and black intimate relations—within a distillable and palatable form for dominant culture in the post–civil rights era. It insists that nonnormative sexuality and nonauthentic racial performances mutually constitute a nonnormative face of destructive desires that Houston faces and argues that her life and death demonstrate the stakes of resisting destructive desires' normative face. The chapter also identifies where her life provides possible examples to imagine these alternatives.

The brief epilogue begins with Toni Braxton's stunning 2013 announcement that she was retiring from singing and performing, prior to Edmonds convincing her to return and collaborating on their duet album *Love, Marriage, and Divorce* (2014), to chart out how cultural longings and cultural expectations create and occlude professional, personal, and political possibilities for rhythm and blues artists. It briefly references three issues: (1) the beginning of her music career, vis-à-vis her *Boomerang* soundtrack; (2) her filing for bankruptcy and suing of her record label; and (3) the publication of her memoir, *UnBreak My Heart*, and participation on *The Braxton Family Values*. By analyzing these representative elements of Braxton's career, the epilogue examines the more general trends of artists blurring genres and crossing over into other performance genres (reality television, memoir writer, foundation spokeswoman). In the process, it considers how destructive desires, entangled networks, and cultural longings continue to inform (and be informed by) the contemporary state of black politics and black aspirations.

Collectively, the chapters and epilogue demonstrate how entangled networks articulate black cultural longings and destructive desires, how black cultural longings become reframed in the process, and how the reframing of black cultural longings offer new possibilities—imagined or otherwise—for black intimate relations, destructive desires, black politics, and black culture. The arguments stage the relationship between the material and discursive, the explicit and implicit, and the imagined and yet to be imagined to demonstrate how black cultural production in general, and rhythm and blues culture in particular, articulates, contests, and invigorates discourses about what black people desire and what is desired for them in American culture, life, and politics.

1

Reading Race, Gender, and Sex

Black Intimate Relations, Black Inequality, and the Rhythm and Blues Imagination

Came into my life a stranger / You captured my heart / Now I've got to face the danger, I'm ready to start / Thought that I could make it on my own / All alone I tried too hard to fake it / Now the truth must be known / Two hearts are always better / Together, forever.

–Teddy Pendergrass and Stephanie Mills, *Stephanie*, "Two Hearts"

What's the sense in sharing this one and only life / Ending up just another lost and lonely wife / You count up the years / And they will be filled with tears.

–Candi Staton, *Young Hearts Run Free*, "Young Hearts Run Free"

TRACK 1

BLACK FEMINIST THINKING AND STRUCTURAL INEQUALITY

Released one year after Natalie Cole's "I'm Catching Hell" (1977) and two years after Candi Staton's "Young Hearts Run Free" (1976), Jean Carne's "There's a Shortage of Good Men" (1978) (re)focuses conversations about black intimate relationships toward the multilayered, interconnected, and persistent institutional factors that thwart black individuals, relationships, and communities from thriving. Unnerving the increasingly persistent post–civil rights era explanations for black inequality that locate black people's putative inability and unwillingness to enter long-term, monogamous marriages as the cause of and explanation for black inequality, Carne's persona attributes the shortage of good (black) men to economic, personal, and political deprivations that war, subemployment, unemployment, and imprisonment cause for black men in particular. If black intimate relations must shore up black inequality, and, as the persona laments, "brothers in jail" because "the system makes them fail," Carne's song leaves us to question: How might black intimate relationships thrive in this context where antiblack racism systemically colludes to erode black progress by removing black men from black households? If black men "can't find no job nowhere," how then are they to fulfill the patriarchal breadwinner model that organized American nuclear families? If even the good men become "strung out with drugs" and thus contribute to the "broken home" phenomenon, what options do heterosexual black women have available to improve their social location if the primary means for improvement is marriage?

Carne's lyrics thus demonstrate the pervasive and persistent cultural longing in public policy and the wider public's imaginary that views heterosexual marriage as the solution to black people's economic and political inequalities. Yet this destructive desire fails to consider the institutional and structural factors—historical and contemporary—that limit access to this model for black people, and instead situates any nonfulfillment of this model as a consequence of black people's lack of motivation or desire for monogamy. This (destructive) desire for black marriages, which I later refer to as the marriage panacea thesis, calls forth black behaviors, or, as is the case here, the failure to engage in norm-accruing behaviors, as the primary cause for black inequality. This cultural longing, which both nonblack and black people accept, seductively obfuscates how the persistence of racism undercuts the possibility for racial equality, how the institution of marriage itself masks and maintains inequality, and how the institution of marriage becomes a mechanism through which the welfare state can shirk its responsibility to ensure the welfare of its citizens.

Carne's lyrics, however, resist this cultural logic by revising the centrality of the mutually constitutive relationship between black intimate relationships and black behaviors: black behaviors do not necessarily produce or ameliorate black inequality (figure 1.1). And, the lyrics do so, as the aforementioned discussion of the song illuminates, by pointing to a myriad of institutional factors that impede black people and black relationships from thriving. With regard to black music culture more generally, and rhythm and blues and soul music more specifically, this revision to the cultural longings for black intimate relations diverges from the familial narratives emerging early in the 1970s that cherish the nuclear family model. As my forthcoming analysis of The O'Jays' 1975 album *Family Reunion* and Sly and the Family Stone's hit single "Family Affair" (1971) accentuates, by calling forth black familial organization as the key to black political enfranchisement, albums and songs like these reinforce the importance of black intimate relationships in forging and building black communities, as well as of the relationships themselves as becoming institutions to reshape black political and economic aspirations. Coming on the heels of the now (in)famous Moynihan Report, Carne's song discursively takes up the claims the report makes, usefully accentuating the structural impediments to black equality that, while present in the report, get subsumed by the behavioral explanations. To examine Carne's song then is to arrive at a more nuanced understanding of the complexities of black intimate relationships, how black intimate relationships explain black inequality, and how those explanations fall short in grasping the complexities of black inequality in the post–civil rights era. This knowledge then requires us to think about and propose solutions for black inequality that do not center intimate relations in traditional ways.

FIGURE 1.1. Jean Carne performs during the 17th Annual Long Beach Jazz Festival on August 14, 2004, at The Lagoon at the Long Beach Convention Center in Long Beach, California.

Rejecting the persona of Cole's song, who laments "that female liberation stuff" may in fact not be "worth it," "Shortage" instead also admonishes that a "strong woman needs a strong man," that "there's no time to be weak and insecure." "Shortage" thus counters the related notion that *out of place* black women also contribute to the dissolution of black intimate relationships, the failure of black men to achieve an empowered masculinity, and the overall problems attributed to black communities' inability to succeed without assistance from the government. Recall that it was in 1979 that Michele Wallace published *The Black Macho and the Myth of the Superwoman*, a groundbreaking black feminist manifesto that upended the matriarchy thesis, challenged a black machismo that lacked the capaciousness to appreciate black feminist politics, and foregrounded the elevation of black womanhood's status to that of black manhood.[1] This discursive context informs the cultural revision in which Carne's song engages as it rejects the notion that black men's liberation comes at the expense of black women by refusing to elevate and normalize black heteropatriarchy. The context also calls attention to the corrective analytical lens that black feminist theory and praxis brought to black empowerment conversations in that black feminism opened up the possibilities for revising cultural expectations about black intimate relationships and their political efficacy that would become more pronounced in the following eras; black feminism demanded what might now be called a nontoxic (black) masculinity.

Less demure than Cole's persona, Carne's rejects the notion that empowered black womanhood (the infamous variations of the matriarchy thesis) undermines empowered black manhood, while calling on (black) men to rise to the occasion. Whereas Cole's persona performs an ambivalent reading of (black) feminist thinking's effect on black intimate relationships, Staton's, by contrast, articulates the ways that the institution of marriage adversely affects black women's happiness and life chances. By asking, for example, "What's the use of sharing this one and only life" and further admonishing women that "you'll count up the years and they will be filled with tears," "Young Hearts" neither pictures marriage as a solution to the black community's problems nor as a prerequisite for women's personal fulfilment. At the nexus of these discourses, "Shortage" similarly extends this logic to examine how institutional racism impedes black men's abilities to fulfill the roles that society (and black women) would expect of them in heterosexual marriage, especially when structural racism curtails their abilities to fulfill those roles. The issues these songs raise provide the opportunity for us to think about how black cultural production becomes a discursive site to (re)imagine the causes of and solutions to black inequality by displacing black intimate relations from the *center* of those conversations.

Rhythm and blues music and culture since the 1960s have provided fertile cultural space to examine how African American cultural production and producers have imagined the possibilities for black love, relationships, marriage, and couplings, but black music studies have been conspicuously absent in these conversations. Indeed, cultural criticism has privileged African American literary production as a primary, if not preferred, site to investigate this issue, and two trends explain this phenomenon. First, the rise and institutionalization of black feminism increased the sustained examinations of black intimate relations' relationships to black political desire and empowerment. Second, a significant portion of black academic feminism emerged from and grew within black literary culture. Candace Jenkins's *Proper Lives, Proper Relations: Regulating Black Intimacy*, which *Destructive Desires* views as a crucial interlocutor, evidences this point as she examines black intimacy in twentieth-century black women's writing, thinking, and culture. *Yet*, given music's widespread reach, mass appeal, and cultural significance, as well as rhythm and blues culture's status as a *voice for intimate relations* in black cultural production, this turn to rhythm and blues music offers an opportunity to investigate the myriad of ways that black music intervenes in debates about black intimate relations and revises cultural expectations about how black intimate relations can shore up black political interests.

Through an analysis of rhythm and blues music produced during the 1970s and 1980s, this chapter examines what I theorize as the *marriage panacea thesis* to consider how aesthetic, political, and social conditions of the post–civil rights era contribute to the rejection of this thesis. The marriage panacea thesis refers to an interrelated set of cultural logics which insist that the institution of marriage will ameliorate black inequality, and fits more broadly within the rubric of behavioral explanations for black inequality, such as the culture of poverty.[2] The persistence of the marriage panacea thesis in social discourse, public policy, and everyday conversation positions the cause of and solution for black inequality on black people's behaviors, reinforces the supremacy of monogamy, and displaces and diminishes the state's role in providing for its citizens. Insofar as American culture widely believes marriage increases educational attainment, economic prosperity, and overall stability, it simultaneously insists that marriage reduces criminality and disrupts cycles of poverty for black communities. Yet, as "Shortage" intimates, it is important to shift attention from black people's behaviors to illuminate how behavioral explanations often ignore, or at least diminish, the structural and historical forces that entrench inequality for black people (even within their intimate relationships). This chapter thus sets the stage for a set of cultural longings that cohere in the 1970s, become more pronouncedly disrupted during the 1980s, and even more fragmented during the 1990s and beyond.

The trifecta of the rise of neoliberalism, the institutionalization of Reaganomics, and the decline of the welfare state collude to sediment black inequality and posit black people's behaviors as the cause of and solution to their political, economic, and social disparities. This discursive context crucially situates the cultural longings that frame black political desire and desire for black politics, and also becomes an entangled network through which rhythm and blues culture provides alternative epistemologies to reshape black politics. Whereas the beginning of this chapter analyzes Carne's "Shortage of Black Men" to demonstrate how it engages extant discourses about black intimate relationships and black inequality, the argument here (and throughout) emphasizes how the music and culture potentially reframe how we think, imagine, and act. Put another way, cultural revision and cultural rebellion focus on the discursive and epistemo-logical, and while they acknowledge their important relationships to the material, they consider the implicit, unspecific, un(measurable), and unquantifiable. The argument therefore does not predict that the music culture always, intention-ally, explicitly, engaged a policy, idea, or discourse to produce a specific, measur-able, quantifiable transformation.

To be clear, my work here and elsewhere rejects the problematic premise that the nuclear family is the best familial configuration and the related notion that monogamous heteronormative marriage will solve black people's political problems.[3] In fact, the two-faced meaning of destructive desires calls attention to this claim. Yet, given the persistence of the marriage panacea thesis, it is worth debunking the (il)logics and mythologies that undergird these cultural longings to demonstrate where they fall short in explaining black inequality and why they are in fact destructive desires. Moreover, and this point remains cru-cial, this argument demonstrates how the thesis fails to explain why—even when black people do marry, and conform to the expectations of marriage—their eco-nomic outcomes lag behind those of other groups (and white people in particu-lar). The turn to black music affords us the opportunity to understand how it provides alternative epistemologies that can help us reimagine black intimate relationships, and, in this innovative reimagining, articulate newer and more robust ways to address black inequality.

In *Soul Covers: Rhythm and Blues Remakes and the Struggle for Artistic Identity*, Michael Awkward posits that black popular music's "mass distribution enabled it to saturate and, indeed, reshape mainstream popular musical and sociocul-tural sensibilities" to account for black music's role in imagining and reimagin-ing some of the very ideas that influence its cultural production.[4] Moving beyond the critique of ideas, this chapter also sketches some of the ways that black music responded to "sociocultural sensibilities" about black intimate relationships in order to articulate new possibilities for both intimate relations and political empowerment, while rejecting the marriage panacea thesis. In other words, even if the songs are a bunch of love songs, their engagement with and construction of notions of love connect to broader political and politicized discourses about love, relationships, and family that remain sutured to conversations and discourses about (in)equality. By examining the political import of the cultural production, the chapter complements Brian Ward's *Just My Soul Responding: Rhythm and Blues, Black Consciousness, and Race Relations* (1996), which argues that rhythm and blues music intentionally and unintentionally engaged anti–civil rights move-ments that aimed to suppress black political advancement during the late 1960s.[5]

TRACK 2
BLACK FAMILIAL DISCOURSES AND AFRICAN AMERICAN MARRIAGES

Although the Moynihan Report's claims did little to support the amelioration of black inequality in terms of how the government responded to its proposi-tions, the sting of the report lies in the fact that its publication—at the height of the civil rights movement—also coincided with the onset of the decline of the welfare state's scope, the emerging anti–civil rights backlash, and the social and political transformation of "personal responsibility" philosophies in political discourses. That the black family was in a "crisis" was not an argument new to the 1960s, nor were the arguments that Senator Daniel Patrick Moynihan proffered in his now (in)famous report, *The Negro Family: A Case for National Action*, particularly novel.[6] Notwithstanding the argument's problematic assumptions—including a limited data sample that Moynihan himself acknowledges—the report seems at least to suggest, however cursorily, that institutional structures impede black people's ability to experience upward mobility (or even to conform to the nuclear family model). Although often dismissed or otherwise subordinated to more behavioral explanations for black inequality, the institutional barriers become significant—in terms of his acknowledgment and in terms of their impact. Rather than disrupt the cultural longing for the marriage panacea thesis by clarifying how discrimination in the workforce inhibits black families' abilities to thrive in a nuclear model, the report instead increased longing for black people to self-correct their familial configurations, thus reinforcing the idea that black intimate relations could and should rectify black inequality.

As William Julius Wilson explains of Moynihan and others who had analyzed the black family (e.g., E. Franklin Frazier), their reports *also identified* "structural conditions in the larger society, including economic relations [a]nd they underlined the need to address these programs that would attack structural inequality in American society."[7] That is, Moynihan notes how discriminatory employment practices against black men and women, as well as governmental policies, including Aid to Families with Dependent Children (AFDC), positioned African Americans at a disadvantage within American society. Moynihan concludes that the government—through policy and enforcement—also needed to intervene to correct these patterns of inequity. But even as Wilson clarifies this point, he reasserts the normativity of heterosexuality and binds class mobility to heterosexual marriage. As Ferguson explains, "In making the problem of joblessness of black men and therefore their ineligibility for marriage, any recommendation for correcting joblessness automatically becomes an attempt to recuperate heteropatriarchy and implicitly demands the gendered and sexual regulation of nonheteronormative racial difference of African American lower-class women."[8] A responsible analysis of Moynihan's report reasonably concludes that changes to family structure in and of themselves will not ameliorate black inequality because the roots of racial disenfranchisement, while historically enacted through the family, extend well beyond the purview of the familial unit. Rather than emphasize the multipronged approach needed to transform fundamentally America's institutions, the marriage panacea thesis privileged the familial explanations, extending for the next several decades the sense that black people's inability and unwillingness to conform to the nuclear family model explained and enabled black inequality.

Without a doubt, Moynihan argues that black families must be strengthened in order to sustain themselves, and maintains that such sustainability emerges from state support: "national effort towards the problems of Negro Americans must be directed towards the question of family structure," and the government must help "to strengthen the Negro family so as to enable it to raise and support its members as do other [white] families."[9] Even if the Negro family were to pull itself up by its bootstraps—as behavioral explanations of inequality demand by insisting that the one experiencing inequality transforms his/her own inequality—"national efforts" must *first* be made. In other words, the persistence of labor and wage discrimination, for example, inhibits black people from supporting and sustaining their families in general, and black men from becoming the head of household vis-à-vis his role as breadwinner. Beyond morality arguments that stigmatize high out-of-wedlock birth rates, the interventions must address the historical and ongoing forms of discrimination of which labor discrimination is one of several. Wilson views one of the greatest shortcomings in Moynihan's proposed solutions to structural deficiencies as his lack of consideration for how black men's lack of employment opportunities (conjoined with discrimination in existing opportunities) factors into this discussion.[10]

Yet Moynihan does understand how the lack of viable employment opportunities—in terms of actual jobs, quality of jobs, and wages within jobs—inflects these discussions: "Employment in turn reflects educational achievement, which depends in large part on family stability, which reflects employment. Where we should break this cycle, and how, are the most difficult domestic questions facing the United States."[11] Inasmuch as the report posits that the Negro family exists in a tangle of pathology, it surmises that there is a tangle of interrelated structural racial pathologies too. This issue is difficult because the solutions require reparative and ongoing sustained resources to undo the cumulative effects that structural racism has had on black individuals and communities, and the government does not appear committed to this process. Moynihan's discussion usefully points out the structural barriers that reproduce inequality, even within the putatively "private" space of the familial. This point confirms his earlier contention that the familial unit sets the foundation upon which many of the child's opportunities (or lack thereof) are built. Critical analyses of Moynihan often dismiss the discussion of structural racism and how it contributes to inequality, notwithstanding Moynihan's engagement. By accentuating this aspect of his argument, we usefully unsettle the behavioral explanation of inequality that lies at the heart of the marriage panacea thesis, and that more generally explains the cause of and solution for black inequality.

TRACK 3

WHY MARRY AT THIS JUNCTURE: THE SHIFTING
TERRAIN OF AMERICAN MARRIAGES

This discussion of Moynihan's attention to the structural barriers that impede black advancement opens up a forceful and tugging tension—between structural and behavioral explanations of black inequality—that continues to haunt public, popular, and scholarly discourses on black cultural advancement in general,

and the role that marriage plays in this process in particular. The marriage panacea thesis for African Americans becomes increasingly curious when we consider the more general skepticism toward the efficacy of the institution of
marriage that more broadly emerged in American society between the 1950s and
1970s. As Patricia Dixon explains in *African American Marriages and Relationships*,
the third-wave feminist movement, the sexual revolution, and the gay and lesbian movement worked collectively to decrease marriage rates in American society more generally.[12] By culturally sanctioning different expressions of sexual
desire—which included decoupling marriage and reproduction and destigmatizing same sex couplings—these movements repositioned marriage as an optional,
and so less expected, marker of adulthood. They made it more socially acceptable for sexuality to be expressed outside the norms that heretofore circumscribed individual subjects' notions of "proper sexual expression," and thus
foregrounded sexual choice, pleasure, and fulfilment as central to coupling experiences. For black rhythm and blues artists and culture in the 1980s, these more
expansive notions would prove crucial for the cultural longings they engender.
Furthermore, as Stephanie Coontz contends in *Marriage, a History: How Love Conquered Marriage*, women's increased access to economic independence not only
decreased the need for them to marry for economic security, this freedom also
encouraged them to pursue educational and social opportunities that marriage
at an earlier age (for financial reasons) would have prevented or delayed.

As the institution of marriage changed for women, it also morphed for men
by deferring the age at which they would marry, which, in many respects,
increased their financial stability when they did wed, and by foregrounding happiness as a constitutive reason to marry. The social and cultural shifts of the
1950s and 1960s helped to upend strict adherence to the breadwinner model of
marriage[13]—which positioned men as financial providers and women as home-
makers. This transformation changed the roles women and men played within
their respective marriages by introducing an increased amount of "role choice"
in how they performed gender roles. While these shifts remain noteworthy, marriage did, for the most part, remain especially patriarchal, if not always in practice, certainly within the cultural imagination. And so increased emphasis for
African American marriages carried the expectation that they would *finally* conform to a traditional model, one that was proving increasingly difficult for
groups who historically had had access to one of the primary resources—
employment—that made it viable. The logic assumed that if black men espoused
their putatively rightful roles as heads of households, they would disrupt the
matriarchal tangles of pathology that Moynihan described. They would restore
cultural, social, and, in turn, political order to black families, and, by extension,
black communities. By fixing their own ailing black familial structures, black
people could fully access and enjoy the opportunities that the civil rights movement had made possible.

This argument nonetheless ignores how institutional decimation (impris-
oning, murdering, or otherwise removing black men from black communities),
and institutional subsidization (requiring black women to be dependent on the

state for economic subsidy because of economic exploitation), and institutional deprivation (lack of viable employment opportunities) decrease the amount of African American men eligible for marriage and partnership. Moreover, the failure to acknowledge the material impact that institutional deprivation has on black intimate relationships conveniently ignores how the marriage panacea thesis falls short of addressing the structural inequalities that damage black relationships that do in fact conform to the nuclear family model. As Dixon explains, "institutional deprivation is the 'involuntary,' under-, sub-, and unemployment of African American males [which] makes it difficult for many to make adequate financial contributions to the development and maintenance of relationships, marriages, and families."[14] The shortage of good men that "Shortage" describes also results from a lack of employment opportunities that, in the 1970s, automation and suburbanization both augmented. By either displacing blue collar, manufacturing work with technology or incentivizing businesses to move to suburban locations that black men could not reach through public transportation, automation and suburbanization collaborated to position black men outside the formal economy.

The breadwinner model and expectations of gender role performance within relationships place black marriages in a precarious position; racism and discrimination within employment impact wages and wage disparities for black women and men, especially when black women earn more than black men, thus adversely impacting relationships. It might be useful to consider, for example, how institutional deprivation (and decimation) adversely impacts the formation of "strong" families; why, we might question, do black married couples and "strong" black families lag behind their white peer groups in terms of financial standing—including wealth and income—even when married? The question emphasizes that the causes of black inequality cannot be parceled off to black people's behaviors. Low wages, amplified by labor discrimination, still make it difficult for African American families to sustain themselves "as other [white] families do."

That the post–civil rights era would consider marriage an effective solution to the social and political inequalities African Americans experienced remains curious and vexed not only because of the transformations that the institution of marriage itself underwent but also because marriage could not uproot the institutional barriers that still impeded economic (and cultural and political) advancement. Even when African American men and women marry, there still exist economic, educational, employment, and health disparities within African American communities, and between white and black communities, that marriage, in and of itself, does not redress. On the issues of income and wealth, Melvin Oliver and Thomas Shapiro point out a troubling disparity in *Black Wealth, White Wealth: A New Perspective on Racial Inequality*:

> In most of the married-couples we interviewed both adults worked. We have already noted how increasingly important it is for families to send two wage earners into the work force if they desire to attain or maintain middle-class status, or even to survive. . . . Black household incomes

consistently trail those of white households with an equal number of earners by amounts ranging from $8,000 to $13,000. Turning to wealth, we find that the average household increases its wealth with additional workers. Adding a second member to the work force brings an extra $16,000 of net worth to white households but only about $5,000 to black ones. . . . Our data suggest that for blacks to procure white household income levels, one additional household member must enter the paid labor force; two extra members must do so to realize white net worth levels. The information we have uncovered on wealth and work experience fortifies our conviction that traditional occupation status and class approaches obscure the institutional and historical structuring of racial inequality.[15]

Why, we might question, when black people do marry, do their economic fates lag behind those of their white peers? What factors undermine their best efforts to achieve equality and close economic (as well as social and political) gaps within and outside of African America, and how does *race* (and racism) remain central to these discussions? Whereas Oliver and Shapiro disrupt the standard theories of how occupation, economic detours, family structure, and children affect wealth and income disparities, this analysis foregrounds the impacts of institutional deprivation, institutional decimation, and institutional subsidization.[16]

TRACK 4

THE 1970S TO THE 1980S: PERSONAL RESPONSIBILITY AND NEOLIBERALISM

The resistance toward the marriage panacea thesis that becomes legible in the late 1970s occurs alongside an increasing skepticism that conforming to societal norms would allow black people to achieve equality in the post–civil rights era. Recall that since the late nineteenth century black people had espoused respectability politics as a strategy to demonstrate their worthiness of citizenship and civil rights. This understandable strategy nonetheless reinforced the notion of a causal relationship between black behavior and black progress; black people could prove their deservedness of citizenship rights by following moral social norms and legal codes. The eradication of Jim Crow segregation during the modern civil rights movement enhanced the appeal of behavioral explanations of inequality in the post–civil rights era. Theoretically, the civil rights movement granted black people equal access to the same opportunities that white people had. As a consequence of this alleged *equal* access, attitudes towards post–civil rights era inequality ignored how discrimination against black people historically, along with its cumulative effects, continued to shape black inequality. If black people did not progress, the popular and political imaginations assumed the fault lay with black individuals and black culture's (misplaced) values. Apparently, some believed the civil rights acts of the 1960s had: (1) substantially improved black people's material conditions, (2) diminished white

FIGURE 1.2. Protesters in the March for Peace, Jobs, and Freedom march up Constitution Avenue in Washington on August 27, 1983, when an estimated 200,000 people commemorated the 1963 March on Washington for Jobs and Freedom.

people's emotional investments in racism, and (3) solved the historical problem of race relations and racial inequality.

But the late 1960s had begun to clarify that the legal gains African Americans won through the hallmark legislative achievements of the Civil Rights Act of 1964 and the Voting Rights Act of 1965 had not inspired broader popular investments in sustaining racial equality in the coming decades. The election of Richard Nixon in 1968, for example, served as a referendum on civil rights and racial equality movements and echoed a growing sentiment that national investments in civil rights equality was waning. The idea that "the government should do less, not more, and that strong civil rights enforcement threatened white liberty" both animated the presidential election, and also shaped public policy and cultural discourses for decades to follow.[17] In fact, as the documentary *13th* reveals, the Nixon and Reagan governments effectively targeted civil rights gains, employed the "southern strategy," cut welfare state programs, and criminalized drug use all to disempower black communities.[18] If the government were not to intervene in public policy, enforce civil rights gains, or ensure that equality of access and opportunity the laws provided translated into material outcomes, who would? Black people themselves, so the logic goes (figure 1.2).

In *The Age of Responsibility: Luck, Choice, and the Welfare State*, Yascha Mounk charts how a shift in philosophies about personal responsibility contributes to and coincides with the decline of the welfare state. This context importantly explains the increase in discourses that privilege black self-help philosophies as

the stand-in solution to ameliorate black inequality. Although self-help philosophies manifested themselves in a variety of contexts, including black nationalist discourses that championed black-owned, operated, and sustained businesses,
the broader trend toward self-help for black communities foregrounded black
people's individual behaviors, communal practices, and social organizations as
aspects of life over which they should exercise their control to gain greater equality. Black nationalist self-help philosophies recognized the fundamental intractability of antiblack racism in American institutions, and therefore employed
self-help philosophies in order to provide black communities a path to make economic and political gains in society. America's more generic self-help philosophies for black people, by contrast, absolved white people from their historical
and contemporary responsibilities to counter racism. Moreover, they also
ensured that the institutional and individual barriers toward black access,
achievement, and continued success remained intact. Correlatively, the sense
that the civil rights movement had removed all barriers to equality and leveled
the playing field for black people conjoined with an idea that the state's willingness to provide for its citizens became more dependent upon the choices the citizens had (or had not) made.

The sense that the government should provide basic rights to its citizens
waned between the 1940s and 1970s, as the idea that the choices citizens made
should impact whether the government assisted them become more prominent.
As Mounk explains, "In the post war years, there was a broad societal consen-
sus that many of the duties the state owes its citizens are largely independent of
the choices those citizens have made."[19] Society increasingly stigmatized individuals who make bad choices, for example, and deemed them unworthy of
deserving assistance. The welfare state instead preferred to help those who
had demonstrated "good" and "responsible" behavior, or people whose dire life
circumstances resulted from situations that were perceived as beyond their
control or individual choices. The political and cultural imaginations often
positioned black people's inequality outside these paradigms. Black inequality
consistently emerged as a consequence of black people's behaviors, bad choices,
and irresponsible actions. If black people were poor, they should stop having
children. Unwed black mothers should have fewer children and should marry
the black fathers of their children. If black families lived in poverty, they should
save their money, move to a better neighborhood, allow their children to attend
better schools, and thus disrupt the intergenerational transfer of poverty that
likely awaits their children. In political lingo, black people must be increasingly
personally responsible for their choices and fates, not relying on the government
to support them. At the heart of these claims emerges the need to regulate black
intimate relations.

Mounk notes that some who support personal responsibility discourses
"emphasize the structural changes and deliberate political decisions, not the
aggregate choices of individuals," but that they ultimately fall into the same trap
as "victim blamers," that is, those who point toward "the aggregate choices of
individuals." As Mounk explains, conversations around personal responsibility

obfuscate the more substantive, structural issues lurking beneath the surface. Mounk identifies three challenges the idea of personal responsibility poses: "It remains silent on all values other than responsibility; it distracts our attention from the structural factors that drive many economic outcomes; and it patronizes the very people whose equal status it is supposedly helping to uphold."[20] Emerging more pronouncedly as phase one of the modern civil rights movement yielded to phase two, the personal responsibility discourses in American culture more broadly served several purposes: it (1) gave the state a shield to diminish its responsibility to ensure that the equality of access legally guaranteed by civil rights acts translated into an equality of outcome; (2) presupposed that the removal of Jim Crow segregation necessarily leveled the playing field for black people and placed them on equal social and political standing with white people; (3) treated black people's inequality as a consequence of their own (lack of) efforts; (4) justified black and white inequality by maintaining that structural barriers neither existed nor had caused, or presently held responsibility for, black inequality; and (5) made black culture and behaviors a more heightened, policed, and stigmatized site of black life in American culture.

If the age of personal responsibility provided one discursive context to stage the unraveling of an already precariously stitched black progress social fabric, neoliberal economic and governmental policies conjoined to rip apart that which remained. In "The Spirit of Neoliberalism: From Racial Liberalism to Neoliberal Multiculturalism," Jodi Melamed charts how changes in attitudes toward racial equality occurred alongside changes in attitudes toward economic markets to demonstrate the processes that help "neoliberalism to appear just, while obscuring the racial antagonisms and inequalities on which the neoliberal project begins."[21] To Melamed's estimation, racial liberalism, which really began to shape America's attitudes toward race during the 1950s and 1960s, undergirded the government's involvement in civil rights movements. It also simultaneously worked to quell dissent among disenfranchised black people by integrating them into the U.S. body politic (at least symbolically) and providing them legal rights and protection. Roderick Ferguson echoes this point in *The Reorder of Things: The University and Its Pedagogies of Minority Difference*, where he specifically locates the roles institutions of higher education have had in quelling black dissent vis-à-vis integration and incorporation into the university's overall nonprogressive agenda.

As Melamed explains, "At racial liberalism's core was a geopolitical race narrative: African American integration within U.S. society and advancement toward equality defined through a liberal framework of legal rights and inclusive nationalism would establish the moral legitimacy of U.S. global leadership. Evidence that liberal antiracism was taking hold in the United States—civil rights legal victories, black American professional achievement, waning prejudice—was to prove the superiority of American democracy over Communist imposition."[22] By tying nationalism (Americanness) to achievement (successful integration), the racial liberalism paradigm helps to distinguish between upwardly mobile successful black people (who presumably succeed primarily because of their own doing) and downwardly spiraling black people (who presumably do not succeed because of their own doing).

Racial liberalism frameworks thus work mutually constitutively with developing personal responsibility philosophies to mask capitalism's pernicious effects against racial equality; that is, both discourses obscure how capitalism functions to perpetuate inequality, and, more insidiously altogether conceal capitalism's presence (which neoliberalism does even more so through its free-market notions). With racial liberalism frameworks in particular, "Black politics, culture, experience, and analysis incompatible with American cultural norms and nationalist sentiment (notably black socialist internationalism) become signs of black pathology, alongside poverty and underachievement. Racial liberalism's culture model for race thus worked to restrict racial meanings and politics to comply with 'official' liberal antiracism and to foreclose discussions of African American political and cultural autonomy and the dynamics of race and racism in the postwar expansion of transnational capitalism."[23] Within this logic, the legal eradication of segregation becomes the sine qua non for racial equality; black people succeed because of their own action; black people fail because of their own inaction.

Yet the explanation of black failure, when considering it alongside the explanation of black success, draws attention to the limits of the behavioral claim. The black success story, while tied to black behaviors, depends upon the notion that the structures themselves changed, thus allowing the possibility for black success. If this claim holds true, black failure, too, would seem tied to the structures, even as the behavioral explanations predominate discussions about black inequality. In other words, the structural changes that allow *some* to succeed do not mean those very changes allow *all* to succeed. Conversely, slight institutional changes can leave intact other, related structures that facilitate, promote, and amplify black failure. The interrelationship between structure and behavior that holds for success narratives rings true for failure narratives too. Neoliberalism of course functions best when it conceals the very structures through which it operates, and instead naturalizes inequality as fair, indiscriminate, and ordinary.

Although neoliberalism typically refers to a broad set of economic practices and principles, more expansive definitions recognize how economic and social practices more broadly shape American social, cultural, and political life. On the one hand, neoliberalism "most commonly refers to a set of economic regulatory policies including the privatization of public resources, financial liberalization (deregulation of interest rates), market liberalization (opening of domestic markets), and global economic management." On the other, to truly grasp neoliberalism's reach, we also have to understand it as a "world historic organization of economy, governance, and biological and social life."[24] This expanded definition of neoliberalism reveals the appeal of black intimate relations as a tool to explain, justify, and maintain black inequality.

By diverting attention away from how capitalism exploits nonwhite bodies, neoliberalism ignores that capitalism succeeds only through exploitation, and masks this fact to stitch economic success to one's ability to take advantage of the economic opportunity neoliberalism presents. This economic opportunity presumably avails itself to everyone and anyone who seeks it, but for the fact that it does not. As a cost, neoliberalism exacts a "violence that individuals and communities have had to absorb with social and economic restructuring for neoliberalism."[25] For black communities, this violence manifests itself through personal responsibility philosophies, black self-help urgings, and behavioral explanations of black inequality that render material and ideological violence to black people. Collectively, these forces and discourses threatened the conditions under which black individuals, communities, and families could thrive, even as the rhetoric of personal, familial, and communal responsibility became increasingly more popular. As the rhetoric of individual effort and merit continued to undermine the notion that the federal government—vis-à-vis the welfare state—had a responsibility to ensure the theoretical promise of equality translated into equality of outcome, behavioral explanations of inequality gained traction and became more intractable. Those behavioral explanations returned to black intimate relations in general, and the marriage panacea thesis more specifically.

In some respects, Carne's "Shortage" pushes back against the marriage panacea thesis to the degree that it locates putatively non-norm-accruing behavior such as low marriage rates among black people as a consequence of structural barriers and not simply individual choices and behaviors. At the same time, the song never calls into question how the institution of marriage itself, vis-à-vis the logics that built it, necessarily replicates patterns of inequality that thwart black thriving (for men and women). In other words, Carne's persona helps us to understand the cultural longing for black marriages, and provides a cultural revision to that longing, but falls short of casting marriage as a destructive desire. In the 1980s, however, a discernible skepticism toward monogamy and coupledom emerges. This chapter insists that this suspicion becomes a locus for imaginative possibility for both black intimate relationships and solutions for black inequality. In these songs, and the surrounding culture, more pronounced cultural rebellion emerges.

That this chapter that examines imaginative possibilities for black intimate relationships that extend beyond heteropatriarchal configurations would begin with Cole, Staton, and Carne lacks coincidence when we consider the role that black women's cultural production has had in the project of dismantling black heteropatriarchy in the quest to empower black communities more generally (an argument that chapter 3 takes up more fully). This claim acknowledges that both black men's and black women's cultural production championed and resisted nuclear family configurations, and differentiates that black women's productions did it more systematically, intentionally, and consistently. Whereas black men's musical productions of the 1970s that foregrounded family as their points of engagement or departure offered a variety of topics, one of the pervasive politicized themes emerging in the songs centered on unifying or strengthening the familial unit. By affirming the importance of marriage and biological kinship, these family-oriented songs for the most part perpetuated the marriage panacea thesis, notwithstanding at times offering more capacious notions of "choice" in gender roles.

TRACK 5
BLACK (MASCULINE?) FAMILIAL DISCOURSES AFFIRMED IN THE 1970S

Sly and the Family Stone's "Family Affair" (1971), for example, details the range of character traits found within a family, and endorses strong, cohesive familial units as necessary and desired for a thriving social fabric: "One child grows up to be / Somebody that just loves to learn / And another child grows up to be / Somebody you'd just love to burn." Regardless of the personal challenges, disagreements, and failures within a family, "Family Affair" emphasizes that biological families should strive for unity. This song typifies a more implicit nod toward the importance of building and maintaining "cohesive" familial units that value problematic children (the one they'd like to burn) as much as the one who loved to learn. By reminding that "blood's thicker than mud," the song characterizes biological kinship as a force that an individual family member's shortcomings cannot upset. Resonant of popular ideas that family (biological and not necessarily fictive) comes before and above all else, this message, in the post–civil rights era, further demonstrates how black behavior and family values become the focal points for explaining the persistence of black inequality. If black people can get their literal and metaphorical houses in order, their social and political ones will fall in line.

As a multiracial group, Sly and the Family Stone produced music that appealed across racial lines, though my reading of "Family Affair" homes in on how the song's meaning for blackness and black communities functions within the context of black intimate relations' putative unique position for shoring up black inequality. That *Rolling Stone* magazine later ranked the song number 138 on their list of 500 Greatest Songs of All Time, and the song peaked at number 1 on the Billboard Hot 100 for three weeks, and ranked number 1 on the Billboard R&B Singles chart for five weeks reveal the degree to which the song enjoyed popularity in American and African American culture.[26] Songs such as "Family Affair" foreground the importance of building strong familial bonds, and, in the process, perhaps misdirects the ways institutional, systemic, and systematic inequalities undermine black familial thriving. If, as some sources have speculated, the album on which this song appeared conveyed a more pervasive hopelessness that African Americans felt during the 1970s, this song at best provides only a partial solution to black inequality, even while it understandably promotes familial unity.

Music scholar Simon Frith rightly cautions us not to *overstate* how a song's sales, ratings, and other markers of "popularity" necessarily correlate with the aesthetic value of music specifically and cultural production more generally. In Frith's estimation, these markers "provide no evidence as to why such goods are chosen by their consumers nor whether they are actually enjoyed or valued by them (it is a common enough experience to go to a blockbuster film, watch a high-rated TV program, read a best-selling book, or buy a chart record that turns out to be quite uninteresting)."[27] Frith's distinction between what sells and how consumers use the product warns us against taking ratings, sales, and other markers of consumption as evidence par excellence of a song's cultural reach. Agreeing with Frith's admonition, I also insist that the imaginative possibilities the song provides remain important, and that consumption does provide insights into the potential for transformation; the song's broader reach increases the potential that its ideas can reshape the cultural imagination. Notwithstanding this group's popularity, the more well-known group, The O'Jays, also produced music that foregrounded family as central to its thematic concerns, and more explicitly extended the concerns that emerge in "Family Affair."

The O'Jays' song "Family Reunion" (1975), for example, explicitly reinforces the marriage panacea thesis insofar as it champions respectability politics and promotes marriage (and the nuclear family) as *the* solution to black suffering.[28] The title "Family Reunion" explicitly refers to the song's main subject, and simultaneously gestures toward the *traditional* values the family will celebrate as it reunites. The joyous event occasions the gathering of the extended family, and, while the grandmother and grandfather are absent (deceased), their descendants (as the song's personas manifest) remark that the grandparents would be proud to see their family "come together, to get together."[29] While the majority of the song reflects the melodic rhythm and blues voices of the group singing collectively, toward the end of the song an instructive shift happens: the background music fades, and the lead singer (Eddie Levert) begins a monologue. Here, the persona explicates the significance of the familial unit and exerts energy to outline the roles members of the nuclear family *should* have. In the process, he lays out how fulfilling those roles strengthens the familial units and, in turn, black communities. The roles conform to decidedly heteropatriarchal ideas of gender, affirm the marriage panacea thesis, and locate the solution to black suffering and inequality within black people's behaviors.

Beyond happiness, familial unit unification provides the personal stability required for political advancement and social transformation, reaffirming the notion that black familial instability plays a key role in black dispossession. As the persona explains, "You know the family is the solution to the world's problems today / Now let's take a look at the family / In the family the father is like the head, the leader, the director / Not domineering, but showing love, guidance / For everyone else in the family / Now if we could get all the fathers of the world / To stand up and be fathers / That would be great."[30] In several ways, these lyrics reflect an understanding of how the political and social upheaval of the 1960s had shifted roles for men within marriage. For example, while the song calls men to "lead households," it clarifies that they should do so lovingly, without the "domineering" (and dominating) ideas and practices that had been so central to the "reclamation of black manhood" discourses emerging in the civil rights and Black Power movements.[31]

The lyrics' portrayal of black women as "the right arm of the father" who are "supposed to do the cooking / Raise the children, do the sewing / And help the father to guide and direct," however, also construct women's roles within traditional domestic-sphere paradigms. More to the point, the song notes that black futurity depends on the mother and father adopting these roles: children learn from parents and then propagate roles to subsequent generations. This song thus portrays the parents effectually untangling, in Moynihan's words, the tangle of pathology. As Mark Anthony Neal confirms, "At the time of its release in 1975, lyricist Kenneth Gamble wrote that 'the generation gap is another evil plan. The result of which divided the family structure . . . being of truth and understanding of all things, we must recapture the family structure—Mother, Father, Sister, and Brother.'"[32] While not conflating the roles between the lyricist and performer, or overstating the significance of authorial intent, the lyricist's admission does further contextualize the broader discourses that inform the song's creation and/or reception.

By promoting the nuclear family as the right and preferred form of kinship organization, this song works with and against Moynihan's *The Negro Family* by demonstrating black families' desires not to be matriarchal tangles of pathology. At the same time, the song provides a more delicate, although no less encumbering, picture of black heteropatriarchy insofar as the relative position of the mother to the father is not one of complete subordination or subservience. Yet, if we interpret the lyrics as responding to Moynihan's claims, the song reinforces Moynihan's notions about the familial unit as it foregrounds the familial unit's role in reducing structural barriers to black equality. That is, it never calls into question, as the final section of this chapter does, how the nuclear family structure, and the logics upon which it functions, sometimes prevents black people from thriving. This, recall, becomes the two-faced nature of destructive desires. In other words, why is it that the (nuclear) family is the solution to the world's problems? In what ways does this point of view distort how the nuclear family historically has been used to perpetuate the world's problems, particularly as they relate to gender and class inequalities? In what ways do ideas about reclaiming black manhood in society function to reinforce the need to put black men and women into their "rightful" places within the nuclear family? The focus on black intimate relations and black behavior renders invisible how the nuclear family structure becomes a tool to reinforce black inequality by not calling into question how its material and discursive elements thrive upon and reinforce black inequality.

In the two songs that I analyze from the 1980s, I contend that their persona's adoption of nonnuclear intimate relationships attenuates the nuclear family's privileged position, and that this side-stepping of the nuclear family sets in motion other paradigms in which to address black inequality. In the absence of the nuclear family, for example, what would equality look like? Why should equality remain tethered to one's relationship to a nuclear family structure? To be clear, this argument asks for a more nuanced understanding of how structural inequalities become masked and otherwise obfuscated vis-à-vis these explanations for black inequality that foreground individual behaviors and choices as the causes of and solutions to black inequality. It would be a gross misinterpretation and misconstruing of this argument to suggest that this book rejects the notion of familial stability or even personal responsibility, even as it demands a more complex analysis of each. It instead asks us to think more energetically about the multiple forms that family, stability, and responsibility can and should take.

By foregrounding this discussion of structural inequality, *Destructive Desires* aims to disrupt two increasingly popular and alarming trends; the first maintains that black inequality persists because black people's behaviors and values prevent them from engaging in normative, norm-accruing activities. The second overstates the degree to which the eradication of Jim Crow during the modern civil rights movement has removed all structural barriers to equal access and outcomes for black people.[33] Whereas the first claim ignores altogether the presence and persistence of structural racism, the second miscalculates the degree to which the removal of Jim Crow has produced equal access and outcomes for black people. The consequence of both analytical moves is the same; it accuses black people of not living up to American ideals and standards, and positions them as the cause of and solution to their problems.

TRACK 6

1980S RHYTHM AND BLUES CULTURE: RESHAPING AN ERA OF THOUGHT

Rhythm and blues music and culture produced during the 1980s provide a wide range of attitudes that challenge the centrality of the marriage panacea thesis, while offering alternative forms of coupling and singlehood that defy the sociological, political, and cultural expectations for marriage and long-term monogamous relationships. Whether our own investment in marriage and the marriage panacea thesis precludes us from accepting the alternative modes of coupling the songs imagine, these arrangements force us to in turn (re)imagine solutions to black inequality that do not depend on the couple unit for their effectiveness. The songs disrupt an ongoing and increasingly more pronounced focus on black intimate relations, and this decentering of monogamy and heterosexual relationships provides an occasion to rethink social, political, and economic "policies" toward black inequality that depend upon these kinship relations. My exploration thus begins to think through the implications of this music, and the broader culture within which it circulates, rejecting (or at least pushing back at) some of the ideas that govern black intimate relationship discourses. These pushbacks in rhythm and blues music and culture afford the opportunity to develop more robust and complicated "fixes" to the problems of black inequality in social practice and public policy. Recognizing the wide range of music and groups that fit within the rubric of rhythm and blues, I am as focused on the circulation of the culture within black cultural spaces as I necessarily am on the racial composition of the group (Mtume, for example). That is, if we take Awkward's argument about Phoebe Snow in *Soul Covers* seriously, we understand cultural production and consumption around blackness as complicated, direct, and indirect.

This track's analysis therefore of Mtume's "You, Me, and He," and Cameo's "Single Life" argues that by positing polyamory and singlehood as viable and thriving alternatives to marriage in African American communities, these songs representatively diverge from the more common message that emerges in songs such as Al Green's "Let's Get Married," (1973) and Stephanie Mills and Teddy Pendergrass's "Two Hearts Are Better Than One" (1982). These alternatives to coupling usefully trouble the marriage/nuclear family model's status as *the* desired (and morally right) form of coupling, and help to destabilize the marriage panacea thesis. That is, by taking seriously the possibility of these arrangements, we decenter the marriage panacea thesis and can invigorate conversations about how to address economic, social, political, educational, health, and other disparities within African American communities without suturing empowerment to heteronormative marriage arrangements. This reconfiguration shifts solutions for black inequality away from behavioral *solutions*, while reconsidering how African American expressive culture refuted and affirmed dominant discourses about black intimate relationships by offering different, and no less complicated, nontraditional coupling/singling. Stated another way, we see how black artistic and cultural production revises cultural expectations about black art, politics, and intimate relations.

Many rhythm and blues songs released during the 1980s championed monogamous relationships between one man and one woman as the most desired form of coupling, yet several artists and groups challenged this coupling by introducing "triangulated" relationships as viable alternatives. Originally a funk and soul group that James Mtume founded in the late 1970s, the group Mtume achieved its prominence on the rhythm and blues charts with the release of its second album *Juicy Fruit* in 1982. This album, and its titular song, "Juicy Fruit," maintained the number one spot on the U.S. R&B chart for eight weeks, increasing the group's popularity and appeal. Two years later, they released *You, Me, and He*, with the titular song charting a coupling arrangement that diverged from the nuclear family model by foregrounding polyandry as a viable possibility. The song both disrupts the nuclear family model, and traditional portrayals of triangulated relationships, as it challenges women's typical roles.

For several rhythm and blues artists, the woman persona, for example, presents the triangulated relationship often in at least three representative forms: (1) a commitment-seeking other woman, as is the case in Betty Wright's "I'll Be the Other Woman," (1988), which itself ironically champions a monogamous commitment to and for the "other woman";[34] (2) a resigned (though not necessarily saddened) other woman who accepts her status as "other," yet laments it, as is the case in Shirley Murdock's "As We Lay" (1986); (3) or a revenge-seeking scorned other woman, who, upon finding out she is not the *sole* other woman, threatens to reveal her lover's infidelity to his wife, as is the case in Denise LaSalle's "Your Husband Is Cheating On Us" (1985). "You, Me, and He," however, upends these trends not only by disrupting this woman–man–woman configuration and replacing it with a man–woman–man relationship; its tone also pensively imagines the future possibilities for the relationship(s). That is, it accepts

FIGURE 1.3. Members of the group Mtume, James Mtume (back left), Raymond Jackson (front left), Philip Fields (back right), Tawatha Agee (front right) appear on the album cover for the release of the album *Juicy Fruit* (1982).

the triangulated relationship as "here-to-stay" and then considers how all might thrive in light of this reconfiguration of what had heretofore been a twosome (figure 1.3).

As a dialogue between a married couple, "You, Me, and He," presents two personas who reason through what it means to reject monogamy and to explore a polyandrous (and not polygynous) relationship. The song opens with the wife informing the husband that there's "something I wanna say" and implores the husband to "try and understand" her disloyalty to heterosexual monogamy. From the beginning, "You, Me, and He" notably defies tradition by presenting a woman persona who is not engaging in an extramarital relationship with a married man, and one who is not repenting for her participation in an adulterous affair. Rather, she states as fact that there's "another man in my life; he's my lover and I'm your wife." She follows her declaration with a question; "You, Me, and He, what we gonna do, baby?" The persona thus clarifies that the institution of marriage neither precludes her from possessing another man nor compels her husband to wholly possess her. As the song figures marriage, it does not consign women to a monogamous relationship, nor does it require her to channel all of her sexual energies through it. Nor does the presence of an extramarital relationship necessarily have to disrupt the stability of her marriage; here the song calls attention to the other face of destructive desires, and recognizes the value in and feasibility of the cultural practice that social norms presume to be problematic. In other words, the question invites the opportunity for the husband and wife to consider, to imagine, how they might proceed now that the wife has another lover, whom she does not intend to relinquish. In essence, they are renegotiating the terms of their marriage contract even if their initial one did not include nonmonogamy. The song participates in a broader cultural project of, in the words of L. H. Stallings, "countering the dispossession and displacement that happens through privatization and politicization of love and intimacy via monogamy and marriage."[35] While cross-cultural analyses of marriage from historical and contemporary perspectives demonstrate that monogamy is not a key feature of marriage in many cultures and geographical locations, in the United States it remains the norm.[36] This norm masks systems of oppression by placing on vulnerable citizens the responsibility to provide for themselves, and, in the process, diminishes the role of the welfare state. In this particular regard, marriage becomes a destructive desire.

By entertaining the possibility of this love triangle as a viable configuration for a relationship for the three of them, the song begs the question of how might the marriage panacea model work, in this scenario, to alleviate black political disenfranchisement. The persona, for example, asks, "can we give it [polyandry?] a try?" My argument does indeed account for how patriarchal principles operate more generally—that the man persona admits that he "was too blind, never thought it could happen to him." This admission reflects a more generalized notion of women's presumed faithfulness in a heterosexual coupling, despite a culture that sanctions and promotes men's infidelity. More to the point, however, the relationship poses a provocative consideration: if the triad were to remain intact, what possibilities for empowerment—especially financial—might emerge? Polygamy, or a nonmonogamous arrangement, can provide the familial unit more economic stability (even if the state does not have the mechanisms by which to acknowledge or validate the union) insofar as the consolidation of households and resources can increase the triad's and individual's respective capitals.

This type of marital configuration certainly defies the one the marriage panacea thesis suggests, yet by considering its potential impacts we can challenge the premises of the thesis (cause of and solution to black inequality). Here, nonconformity becomes a calculated choice and not necessarily an inability or unwillingness to adhere to norms. This decision, too, can financially benefit this triad's economic and political capitals that emerge from economic empowerment. Indeed, they will not wear what Ralph Banks refers to as the "ultimate merit badge" because monogamy remains a championed form of interpersonal arrangements in the United States.[37] But as Dixon and Coontz demonstrate, several contemporary and historical societies adopt(ed) nonmonogamous forms of coupling as the very strategy by which to increase individuals' abilities to thrive economically. To this point, recall the discussion on track two where Oliver and Shapiro found that because of racism (structural inequality) black households require a third adult worker to achieve income parity, and a fourth to achieve wealth parity, with two-person white households.

If we turn back to Carne's invocation of institutional deprivation, and recall the persistence of black men's unemployment and subemployment, the income that results from a relationship consisting of two black men and one black woman could approximate that of a two person white dyad. This point also reinforces the need to end economic discrimination, provide livable wages, and construct affordable housing. This choice for black intimate relations, while not shoring up structural inequality in its institutional forms, could provide the individuals with opportunities that actually do improve their material conditions. "You, Me, and He" perhaps invites listeners to imagine, in the words of L. H. Stallings, "radical reconfigurations of family, love, and relationships where monogamy and marriage are not situated as the ideal praxis."[38] This reimagining, I insist, in turn allows us to also reject the marriage panacea thesis and adopt alternative solutions that do not center black intimate relations and black behaviors when trying to address black inequality.

TRACK 7
CAMEO'S "SINGLE LIFE": WHAT TYPE OF LIFE IS THE SINGLE LIFE?

Some artists championed monogamy and marriage, and others eschewed those relationships for less socially acceptable arrangements, including implicitly and explicitly open relationships. Cameo's "Single Life" turns our attention to the detested "single" figure by repositioning him as a socially acceptable individual who can thrive in the absence of a steady girlfriend or wife. The single black man image threatens the marriage panacea thesis insofar as these actual men decrease the presumed population available for black women to marry, thus rendering the possibility for economic disparities more of a reality. Cameo's persona calls into question the viability of this claim, while more broadly displacing society's general concerns about the "single" figure. While encouraging both single guys and single ladies to "clap your hands," "Single Life" depicts the single as vibrant, not bereft of significance by lack of attachment to a value-accruing other. The persona's encouragement of single ladies to clap their hands undermines the broader culture's tendency to especially disdain women's singleness. Similar to Mtume, Cameo began as a funk band, although its horn-driven style positioned it as more similar to groups such as Earth, Wind, & Fire, the Commodores, and Parliament/Funkadelic. Cameo's music transformed between the 1970s and 1980s, becoming increasingly popular in dance halls and on dance charts. When "Single Life" debuted in 1985, for example, the song peaked at number 26 on the Dance Music/Club Play Singles Chart, number 28 on the Hot Dance Music/Maxi-Singles Sales Chart, and number 2 on the R&B Albums chart.[39]

By promoting the persona's status as a single man, "Single Life" challenges the notions that people should limit sexual expression to a single, monogamous relationship, that people prefer coupledom to singlehood, and that people achieve adulthood primarily through coupledom. Notwithstanding marriage's putative benefits, including the economic and social capital it produces (the ultimate merit badge), as well as the companionship it provides, within the context of American patriarchal culture, marriage remains an oppressive system that systematically privileges men and masculinist ideas, motivations, concerns, and ideologies. Although marriage may provide some benefits to women, it primarily does so to the degree that, as David Ikard has argued, patriarchy rewards women for remaining within the boundaries it delimits for them.[40] This view of marriage, while perhaps more pervasive within academic discourses, has eluded most popular engagements with and intuitions about it.

However difficult, constricting, outdated, and one sided the institution may seem, broader culture prefers it over the imagined alternative: the single, whom society deems not only as irresponsible or unsettled but also as a threat to the idealized couple. Michael Cobb's incisive polemical *Single: Arguments for the Uncoupled* echoes this claim, outlining marriage's specific political benefits and social capital. As Cobb explains, "if you belong to a couple, on sliding scales of social and legal legitimacy, you occupy a not-so-frivolous status."[41] Differentiations between the single and the coupled work to remind us how, in social discourses and the social imagination, the single may be just one step from being socially and politically "dead." Black intimate relations discourses map the single figure onto a host of other discourses about black inequality that produce and/or sustain social and political death. The single black mother and father, for example, in these contexts also become evidence par excellence to explain poverty and irresponsibility (think of how images of black women as "welfare queens" have legitimized welfare reform). The logic thus becomes: when singles marry, they decrease the chances of giving birth out-of-wedlock, as well as the chances of the mother and child living in poverty. The significant population of married, poor, black couples might call into question the absoluteness of this claim and reveal the fallacies within its logic.

One thus might read "Single Life" as a representative example of a black man persona's refusal to accept the responsibilities of a relationship and the commitment of monogamy (to become the strong black man that a strong black woman needs—if we think of Carne). Yet such a reading ignores how the song decidedly rejects monogamy and antisingle discourses. This complicated representation of course does not completely repudiate these ideas or the broader patriarchal discourses they reflect. Indeed, the song pays much tribute to heterosexist, sexist, and otherwise heteronormative issues that patriarchal constructions of relationships and gender roles symptomize, both of which shape the marriage panacea thesis. For example, the persona immediately declares that

"If I had my way, baby / I'd tie you up for a while," reinforcing both a literal and metaphorical fantasy of male sexual dominance and prowess (though my analysis in chapter 3 allows for the possibility for a woman to enjoy being tied up without that desire solely reinforcing patriarchy). The later declaration, "Just like a car, I'll drive you / Out of your mind," while perhaps foreshadowing R. Kelly's "You Remind Me," builds upon this principle of dominance yet foregrounds mental stimulation as prerequisite for sexual arousal.[42] As the next verse reminds, "It's always the first step / In us having a good time."

The music video for the song, which proves quite instructive in interpreting the song's possible meanings, casts this mental stimulation in physical terms; as the lead singer sits in the bar, he caresses and sings sensually to his date, thus suggesting that the mental stimulation is erotic. And finally, the persona notes, "I don't want nobody to get the wrong idea about me / I don't have nothing to hide / I want the world to see." These lines, within the context of the song as a whole, acknowledge not only how social discourses stigmatize the single figure by characterizing singlehood as socially and personally deviant; more specifically, it here points toward a sexual deviancy too that the persona rejects by reaffirming heterosexual identity. If as Angela Willey contends in *Undoing Monogamy: The Politics of Science and the Possibility of Biology*, "homophobia, biphobia, and transphobia function to reinforce compulsory monogamy," the declaration of "Single Life's" persona gains more traction[43]: to be clear, the reason that he prefers singlehood has everything to do with the assertion of heteronormative desire and not the concealment of nonheteronormative practices. Compulsory heterosexuality and compulsory monogamy discourses mutually constitute and reinforce each other.

Yet the song characterizes the single life as one replete with pleasure, including sexual pleasure, and consequently destigmatizes the single figure as someone solely irresponsible or otherwise unable to commit. As Cobb explains, the presence of another in the form of the couple provides a raison d'être: "not merely an activity [becoming a couple] one adds to a list of things to get done in this life . . . not life's primary obsession but life itself—life in which important feelings, work, and understandings are permitted to be accomplished because you have a witness."[44] Cobb's book *Single: Arguments for the Uncoupled* calls into question "the miscasting of singles as a terrible condition worth our pity and obfuscation" to demonstrate that "singleness is currently not compatible with a society in western Europe, North America, and probably other locations, that wants people to feel desperate, lonely, fearful of death, and ready for toxic forms of sociality."[45] Cobb's analysis unearths institutions, practices, and policies that reward the couple and penalize the single. As an obstruction to a necessary element of the marriage panacea thesis, the single figure becomes yet another scapegoat to avoid addressing the nuanced systemic contours of structural inequality. From marriage incentives, to tax credits, to health insurance, to social security benefits, to hospital visitation rights, our social structures and public policies explicitly and implicitly valorize and reward heterosexual marriage. Within this context, it is no surprise that American culture idealizes monogamy, vis-à-vis marriage, as the social arrangement by which society defines its core values and distinguishes between the social, political, and economic values of its citizens. The suturing of monogamy to economic stability masks how capitalism in neoliberal formulations or free enterprise and privatization become layered onto intimate relations. Contrary to popular discourse, this intertwining prolongs inequality rather than cuts it short.

By championing singlehood, the song not only resists the marriage panacea thesis but also challenges the fundamental ways that the thesis proposes addressing the persistence of black inequality. For example, as feminists compellingly have argued, justifications for wage inequality historically presumed that men need higher wages to support their families, and that women's work held less value (if any at all). Patriarchy thus poses a sleight of hand, wherein it encourages women to pursue monogamous heterosexual marriages, even if they desire otherwise, by binding women's abilities to thrive economically to men. Experience and research nonetheless reveal that the hierarchies replicated in these types of relationships, where men are the primary breadwinners, while perhaps improving women's financial lots, fall short of improving their overall quality of life, emotionally and otherwise. As Willey explains, "Women's overinvestment in a single relationship, emotionally and in terms of their labor, typically works to men's advantage, providing them with the support and free time to focus energies on career, personal growth, and/or other relationships."[46] The extrapolation of women's labor, literally and metaphorically, coupled with the stigmatization of the single figure, make coupledom a preferred though not necessarily ideal alternative for women and men, albeit for different reasons.

In positing behavior and (poor) choices as the explanatory force for inequality, social discourses and public policy obfuscate the menacing ways that capitalism, for example, intersects with racism and sexism to produce, maintain, and perpetuate, into perpetuity, inequality. If we disentangle, for example, personal responsibility discourses from capitalist exploitation, we would realize that despite the good choices people do make they end up impoverished. More importantly, when black individuals couple their economic strength, it lags that of their white peers. We might ask, under what systems can individuals, coupled or not, thrive economically? Rhythm and blues imaginings clarify that whatever system that is, or may become, it is not capitalism as we know it.

By disrupting discourses on singlehood that posit it as "the most despised position," "Single Life" occasions the opportunity to think about the conditions necessary for the single figure to prosper in a society in which social, economic, and cultural privileges exalt coupledom as the necessary and desired form of interpersonal social arrangements. If the single life remains viable, we must articulate how to develop more capacious understandings of singlehood and the opportunities available to singles. The single life forces us to consider ways to structure society that promote the thriving of all individuals—those within and outside of the couple dyad. We could, for example, pay everyone a livable wage and thus increase economic independence. If we did, would the marriage panacea thesis maintain its cultural weight, moralizing authority, and political cachet? We could reduce housing costs, which absorb significant portions of an individual's income. If we did, would the consolidation of resources, despite how that move might otherwise adversely impact one's life, appeal in the same ways that it does now? Although I am not conflating capital with political power, a relationship between the two exists. That relationship gains meaning in the context of black intimate relations' explanatory force as a cause of and solution to black inequality.

Marriage, therefore, does not solve structural economic inequality even if the consolidation of resources and reduction of expenses provide an individual upward economic mobility. The privatization of education, housing, and other economic systems under neoliberalism, for example, undermines the capacity for upward mobility to be a broader reality outside the select group of people who can exploit its appeal. Cobb's point that society invests (too) heavily in the dyad of the couple resonates well with the fact that, as the chapter points out previously, much of public policy and law privilege the couple as the ideal and desired social unit. For this reason, cultural longings that encourage African Americans to conform to this social ideal do not surprise—if for no other reason, marriage bestows several economic and political benefits that historically they have not experienced as a consequence of racism and its intersection with other "isms."

The promotion of the marriage panacea thesis continues to miss how President George W. Bush's investment in "state programs that promote and maintain healthy marriage," and programs like it, fail because racial disparities in housing, education, and health care, for example, undermine any advantages that marriage might bestow.[47] In other words, more general assaults on black life through institutional and structural racism undercut whatever effectiveness such a program might have by limiting the ability for black people, life, and culture to thrive economically. And as Dixon has shown (and this point remains significant), because of institutional deprivation, even when African American couples do marry, they still trail behind their white peers because structural (and not behavioral) etiologies overdetermine black people's disproportionate representation among the poor, underemployed, undereducated, overdiseased, and overimprisoned. Accounting for this fact seems requisite for anyone who desires to create viable solutions to black inequality. Rhythm and blues culture's imaginings provide us another entry point to understand solutions to black inequality that extend the scope of the explanatory power that black intimate relations discourses have had in our culture.

TRACK 8

BEYOND TRADITIONAL BLACK INTIMATE RELATIONS DISCOURSES

Although broader social and cultural shifts of the 1950s and 1960s helped to diminish strict adherence to the breadwinner model of marriage in general, the cultural longings for black relationships in particular continued to articulate the desire for black men to earn a (white) man's wage and become a bread winner (even if the wife also worked).[48] This desire for conformity articulates not only the social capital of the institution of marriage but also the more pernicious effects of racism and racial segregation that for too long had accused black people's behaviors and choices as the cause of their disenfranchisement (and not an effect per se). As Anastasia Curwood explains in *Stormy Weather: Middle-Class African American Marriages between the Two World Wars*, "African Americans responded by turning inward and focusing on domesticity: poor households plagued with illness and illegitimate children should be replaced with morally upright ones containing patriarchal gender relations and well-raised offspring. Middle-class blacks also believed that the marital relationship itself helped lift the race: it demonstrated moral values and provided support that each spouse needed to perform different forms of race work."[49] Although the black cultural longings for black intimate relations persisted for blacks and nonblacks alike, the underlying motive in both instances places the responsibility for upward mobility and political enfranchisement on black people.

Jim Crow segregation's depression of wages made thriving single-parent households nearly impossible, and instead bound a family for poverty—and an intergenerational one at that. This fact—the effects of wage and employment discrimination vis-à-vis institutional racism—is one of the significant yet under accentuated points that Moynihan's report articulates well. Yet popular and scholarly discussions about two-parent households often suggest children thrive because of the morals and values they learn within this configuration. These debates ignore the way economic systems privilege the nuclear family model to create access to opportunities that increase one's chances to thrive. We must investigate how and why capitalist principles thrive through the nuclear family's structure, and keep a keen eye focused on how arguments that focus on "strong family structures" maintain inequality, diminish the role of the welfare state, and encourage behavioral explanations as the cause of and solution to black inequality.

Although feminists have demonstrated compellingly how the institution of marriage impedes women's ability to thrive by exploiting their material and symbolic values, Roderick Ferguson has extended this argument to claim that states used marriage as a mechanism to deter and defer black political and economic progress. His argument rightfully insists that the success of the nuclear family model depends on exploitative capitalist principles that—contrary to most popular and scholarly discourses—undercut black people's progress; and, in the process, reinforce behavioral explanations of inequality to understand black economic inequalities. In *Aberrations in Black*, Ferguson argues that during Reconstruction, the state encouraged black people to marry as a way to shirk its responsibility for providing aid (welfare) to the formerly enslaved and otherwise disenfranchised African Americans. Because the state viewed "nonmonogamous and fluid intimate arrangements elaborated by slaves as evidence of their ineligibility for citizenship" it ultimately "attempted to rationalize African American sexuality by imposing heterosexual marriage upon the freedmen through the rule of law and as a condition for citizenship."[50] The attempt to curtail differences in sexual coupling arrangements allowed the state to regulate black sexual practices by tying citizenship rights and economic benefits to normative sexual couplings (and marriage in particular). That is, "those freed African Americans who rejected marriage and monogamy were imprisoned and/or denied pension payments."[51] It is no surprise that respectability politics, as Evelyn Higginbotham notes black women enacted at the turn of the twentieth century, become most entrenched in racial uplift ideology, as they become viewed as necessary to gain citizenship rights.[52]

A consequence of this practice was that "future material contradictions could be displaced onto African American intimate relations as the state regulated heterosexual marriage, making the husband legally responsible for the function and care of the household."[53] For a resonant example, recall that in the 1930s Aid to Families with Dependent Children (AFDC) refused to provide financial relief to indigent black families if an able-bodied black man who could obtain employment resided in the household. This repositioning of the husband as the primary "head of household" and "breadwinner" becomes increasingly problematic as institutional deprivation, which excludes or otherwise limits black men's access within the labor market, effectually puts the fate of the black family and its thriving on black people (men). The state's role in creating (through slavery) and perpetuating (through white men's wages and Jim Crow segregation) a system of inequality becomes erased; the explanation for and causation of black people's inability to succeed within American society are the same: the familial unit. Ferguson rightfully shifts this conversation that foregrounds behavioral explanations of inequality to understand how the familial unit, as experienced in the racialized context of the United States, reproduces a structural inequality that its adherence to claims to repudiate. This obfuscation clarifies how and why *Destructive Desires* posits marriage as a destructive desire.

Moreover, the belief that the "marriage relationship itself" helped uplift the race not only reinforces behavioral solutions to fix systemic black inequality, but it also, as Ferguson reminds us, fails to question whether and how the nuclear family structure itself may produce inequality. Certainly the perception exists that marriage is essential for black thriving—personal and political—and that one who does not marry, as Berlant reminds, "may not well endure the loss of" that marriage (actual or desired).[54] Yet this chapter has insisted that marriage, as a panacea for inequality, does in fact "threaten their well-being" insofar as it produces destructive desires and obfuscates how the institutions that produce inequality for black people remain intact, even after black people have married.

By contrasting how 1970s and 1980s rhythm and blues music and culture think differently and seriously about black intimate relations as a site for political redress, this chapter considers how that body of work provides a cultural space to refute the marriage panacea thesis and imagine alternative solutions to black inequality and models for black coupling. Whereas Brian Ward skillfully examines the implicit and explicit ways that rhythm and blues artists during the 1960s used their music (as well as how their music was later appropriated) to challenge black inequality, the analysis herein begins to sketch out the ways that rhythm and blues culture during the 1970s and 1980s implicitly and explicitly challenged the marriage panacea thesis. The goal has been to continue conversations that unearth the structural impediments to black inequality even as behavioral explanations persist, as well as to foreground the transformative role of rhythm and blues in imagining black futurity. While the issue of black intimate relations remains central to conversations about black inequality throughout *Destructive Desires*, the subsequent chapters keep this chapter's framework in mind as a discursive point of departure. That is, while the chapters do reference black intimate relations, they explore rhythm and blues culture's engagement with cultural longings and destructive desires vis-à-vis related and competing discourses that emerge in the cultural milieus and entangled networks in which the artistic production performs. Inasmuch as chapter 2's examination of Kenneth "Babyface" Edmonds considers his role as a musical force, for example, it binds that role to black cinematic production during the 1990s and situates it within the debates about black masculinity and black feminist inquiry to examine his multiple engagements with black intimate relations discourses.

2

"Whip Appeal"

Reading Kenneth "Babyface" Edmonds

When we go to work / How the day seems so long / The only thing I think about / Can't wait 'til we get home / 'Cause we got a way of talking / And it's better than words.

—Babyface, *Tender Lover*, "Whip Appeal"

We fell in love and who can blame us / The word was we were just beside ourselves / And everybody said it wouldn't last / Now they wonder / Why we didn't last.

—Babyface, *For the Cool in You*, "And Our Feelings"

I thank God that I'm me / To know that you love me / To know that you care / To know that you give up yourself and yet still ask of nothing / From me / Your love is exceptional.

—Babyface, *The Return of the Tender Lover*, "Exceptional"

TRACK 1

INTRO: KENNETH EDMONDS AND THE SHAPING OF AN ERA

On January 19, 2018, Kenneth "Babyface" Edmonds appeared at the John F. Kennedy Center for the Performing Arts in Washington, DC, where he, along with the Duke Ellington School of the Arts Show Choir, and in conjunction with the National Symphony Orchestra, reminded audiences of why *Destructive Desires* situates him as a principal architect, a founding parent, of late twentieth-century rhythm and blues culture. In its opening tribute to Edmonds, the Duke Ellington Choir transitioned through several songs, including "Count on Me" (Cece Winans and Whitney Houston), "Water Runs Dry" (Boyz II Men), "I'm Ready" (Tevin Campbell), "I'm Your Baby Tonight" (Whitney Houston), and "There Goes My Lady" (Charlie Wilson). This medley, covering a twenty-year stretch of Edmonds's career—"I'm Your Baby" (1989) to "There Goes" (2009)—recalled that Edmonds's appeal has as much to do with his own musical repertoire as it does with the voluminous songs he has penned for other artists. More precisely, the

Duke Ellington choir's selections implicitly and explicitly marked different, important, and distinct aspects of Edmonds and the respective performers' careers. For example, "Count on Me" appears on the *Waiting to Exhale* (1995) soundtrack; Edmonds scored and produced the fourteen songs for Forrest Whittaker's adaptation of Terry McMillan's titular novel (1992). As tracks 5 and 8 of this chapter explain, Edmonds's roles for this soundtrack solidified his status in the rhythm and blues imagination as the one (and perhaps only) man whose artistic imagination could tap into and help to convey *authentic* emotion for women performers. The then-burgeoning academic field of black male feminism, I insist, helps us to analyze the significance of such a role and consider how Edmonds consequently expands sociopolitical possibilities for black intimate relations during the 1990s (and beyond).

The performance of "Water Runs Dry" summons Edmonds's role as a *hit maker* for the group Boyz II Men, and draws attention to Edmonds's own entangled network, where, by writing songs and distributing them widely, he influences a generation's perspective on black intimate relations, love, and intimacy. Carolyn Bingham captures his global influence, concurring that "Babyface has made pop history as both an artist and writer/producer with his impeccable explorations of romance and relationships which have left an indelible imprint on the evolution of rhythm and blues throughout the world."[1] The expansion of black cinema during the 1990s increased Edmonds's reach because production companies often relied upon soundtracks to market films. While Edmonds penned "Water Runs Dry," he also had written "End of the Road," which broke billboard chart records by maintaining the number one spot for thirteen consecutive weeks. "End of the Road" catapulted the group's success, showcased Edmonds's talents, and previewed his role as a culture shaper. "End of the Road" *simultaneously* calls forth the film *Boomerang* (1992), and how it, along with its soundtrack, inaugurated a seismic wave in black cultural production that focused on black intimate relations.

Rhythm and blues music and culture amplified the cinematic construction of cultural longings and destructive desires by creating songs whose meanings cohered vis-à-vis interconnected and mutually reinforcing entangled networks. Edmonds's contributions to the *Boomerang* soundtrack paved the way for the more expansive role he played on *Waiting to Exhale*'s; his introduction of Toni Braxton on *Boomerang* helped to cultivate a listening public for Toni Braxton, the rhythm and blues sensation who became known as the first lady of LaFace Records, which Edmonds co-started vis-à-vis Arista Records. While the cultural significance of these interrelationships bears elaboration, Braxton's status as first lady of LaFace captures three resonant issues. First, it underscores how she became the label's first black woman artist to amass fame, wealth, and industry-wide recognition. Second, the title invokes a marriage metaphor, which, rather than grasping Edmonds and Braxton's professional relationship, works as a metonym for a broader relationship theme that would animate Braxton's corpus of songs, and the theme that underwrites their first and only duet album (*Love,*

Marriage, and Divorce, 2014). At the musical relationship's core, black intimate relations discourses become a framing and reframed narrative. Edmonds becomes a centripetal force in molding perspectives for which Braxton became a mouthpiece and disseminated them to a broader public. Third, the title *first lady* points toward a gender hierarchy in which Edmonds possesses the authority in producing and legitimatizing Braxton's public image and role in consolidating the respectability of LaFace Records.

If Kenneth Edmonds's primary talent were solely his voice, which critics, pundits, and everyday citizens have claimed is true about his contemporary—the late Whitney Elizabeth Houston (1963–2012)—his sonic deliveries, including his physical staging, intonations, crescendos, and vocal range would provide musicologists and performance theorists ample evidence to delineate a "Babyface aesthetic."[2] Such an aesthetic, I argue, would examine the following: What formal and informal strategies does Edmonds employ when performing his music live? In what ways do different elements of his performance converge and diverge to produce a multisensory musical experience for listeners? How does the notion of a multisensory listening experience decenter the aural as the best way to understand music's impact on the imagination? What feelings do the musical performances engender, and how do those feelings inform how listeners embrace and/or eschew the song's multiple meanings and imaginative possibilities for destructive desires? Yet Edmonds's role as singer, while significant, emerges as but one among a catalog of other positions that he occupies and negotiates. By adding writer, music producer, performer, talent scout, entrepreneur, film producer, and spokesperson to his list of "work," critics can begin to approximate the complexity of Edmonds's roles in shaping black cultural production and black personal and political desires (figure 2.1).

Although this chapter begins with a discussion of Edmonds's performance, it intentionally diverges to demonstrate that, despite his own voluminous oeuvre, Edmonds considers himself primarily a song*writer*.[3] By drawing attention to the historical, autobiographical, and sociocultural experiences that shape his song production, I foreground the ways that Edmonds uses his song writing to (re) shape black intimate relations discourses. Building on the arguments chapter 1 makes, this chapter reads Kenneth "Babyface" Edmonds, one of the most accomplished rhythm and blues artists emerging in the 1980s, and positions him as one of *the* late twentieth-century black cultural producers and standard bearers because of his multifaceted roles in shaping rhythm and blues' cultural longings, destructive desires, and entangled networks. His roles as songwriter and producer (of both music and film) influenced a generation of artists and consumers from the 1980s to the present. Edmonds creates and becomes an entangled network through which many artists express, reinforce, and contest cultural longings and their attendant destructive desires. Reviewer Kimberly Roberts, for example, insists that his "creativity and respect for the legacy of Black music almost single-handedly inspired the current R&B renaissance."[4] As a prolific songwriter, he has written and produced songs that a range of artists, including

FIGURE 2.1. Kenneth "Babyface" Edmonds accepts his award at the 48th Annual Songwriters Hall of Fame Induction and Awards Gala at the New York Marriott Marquis Hotel on Thursday, June 15, 2017, in New York City.

Toni Braxton, Whitney Houston, Mary J. Blige, Boyz II Men, and Bobby Brown have later performed. Whereas this analysis of Edmonds homes in on his contributions to black music, his influence emerges in country music, pop music, and other non–rhythm and blues or soul forms.[5] As music producer with his business partner L. Antonio Reid, he has launched the careers of several well-noted artists, including Toni Braxton and TLC; with his then wife Tracey Edmonds, he produced a signature film celebrating black family, culture, and life in the 1990s, *Soul Food*, for which he also produced the soundtrack. Indeed, Edmonds has shaped cross-generational publics' attitudes about black intimate relationships and their possibilities and politics, and this chapter reads the meanings within several of these contexts.

By examining Edmonds's multitudinous roles in the music industry, alongside the discourses that chapter 1 engages, this chapter's analysis of cultural longings and destructive desires isolates three issues: (1) Edmonds's scoring and writing of the *Waiting to Exhale* soundtrack; (2) the autobiographical elements of his life that inform his lyrical production; and (3) his roles in creating opportunities for other artists, specifically through his music production (writing lyrics) and distribution (record label). By situating this argument within the emergence of black male feminist praxis, I demonstrate how Edmonds's work, including its radical, progressive, and traditional perspectives on black gender relations, calls for more nuanced understandings of how gender, gender roles, and their respective performances index the different possibilities for re(imagining) black subjectivities outside the normative face of destructive desires. I argue that Edmonds's cultural production, like Howard's (chapter 3), demonstrates the messiness of black sexual politics as he both contests and promotes destructive desires' investment in respectability politics and normative gender roles. This messiness, I maintain, reveals a politics of racial liberation that enjoins the renouncement of hegemonic masculinities as necessary for black thriving, even as the messiness at times reinforces hegemonic gender performances. Whereas chapter 3's examination focuses on black women's cultural production and black womanhood, this examination of black cultural production analyzes black men's cultural production to argue that hegemonic black masculinities reinforce the normative face of destructive desires. It finally contends that Edmonds's cultural production upends this face of destructive desires as he champions a masculinity that defies this norm, and that this rejection creates space to engender a more expansive set of possibilities for black life, black politics, and black culture (and solutions to black inequality).

TRACK 2

AN INTERLUDE: EDMONDS AND THE INDUSTRY, AND THE
SHAPING OF GENERATIONS

When the Songwriters Hall of Fame (2017) inducted Edmonds, his admission had been approximately forty years in the making, given that the music industry initially turned a spotlight on him because he had written several hits for groups during the 1980s. As a member of the group The Deele, Edmonds, alongside his soon to be business partner, L. A. Reid, co-wrote several songs that garnered attention. In addition to writing "Two Occasions" for The Deele, Edmonds also penned "Slow Jam" for the group Midnight Star. Both ballads, however romanticizing, imagine a more tender, less hegemonic black masculinity as necessary for black love and for black intimate relations to thrive. While Holland-Dozier-Holland, Teddy Riley, Terry Lewis, and Jimmy Jam had become household names in rhythm and blues production processes, by the late 1980s the upcoming Edmonds and Reid duo made inroads in the composing world. As David Adelson compares, "the two . . . have been a key force in shaping R&B music in the past few years, and rank with Teddy Riley and the team of Jimmy Jam and Terry

Lewis as top creative figures in the genre."[6] Their success at writing and producing not only shaped generations of performers and listeners, but their appeal garnered the attention of Clive Davis, the media mogul who empowered them to begin LaFace records, a subsidiary of Arista Records, that focused on rhythm and blues markets.

Although Arista provided Edmonds and Reid a substantial amount of autonomy to produce rhythm and blues music and select the artists whose careers they launched (or revived), racial (and gender) politics within the music industry circumscribed the reach of their cultural production. For example, chapter 4's analysis of Clive Davis's role in shaping Whitney Houston's persona specifically turns attention to the music industry's racialized, gendered politics; unless black cultural production explicitly had crossover appeal, industry executives thought it would appeal only to black markets. Similarly, the industry consigned black cultural producers and composers to black media, imagining them as lacking interest or talent to traverse nonblack racial markets. Although in 1996 black music consumption constituted 25 percent of the music market, and "R&B accounted for 12.1 percent of music sales," black executives did not constitute 25 percent of the industry's force because "one of the greatest barriers is that many Black executives often are pigeonholed by race and are locked out of areas in the industry other than Black music."[7] Edmonds's desire to circulate beyond the rhythm and blues classification and his desire to work with artists across musical genres brings to bear a set of interrelated concerns. First, it draws attention to how racial divisions within the music industry, the consignment of rhythm and blues production to "black division(s)," had the effect of "segregating Black artists; limiting airplay, promotional and publicity possibilities."[8]

The importance and desire for crossover appeal in an artist such as Whitney Houston position her in a different yet related category for black music. Yet the limiting of other black artists to rhythm and blues markets perhaps curtails their success, despite their success. Second, it explains why Edmonds desires a reputation that extends beyond the rhythm and blues label. On the one hand, *he understands* rhythm and blues culture's appeal as broader than black people and audiences. On the other, he recognizes that this perspective of rhythm and blues culture's particularity indexes a more pervasive sense of antiblackness that will also impact him financially. While chapter 4's analysis of Houston uncovers the contradictions and complications that postracial desires for America engender for post–civil rights era black cultural production, Edmonds's experiences with the entrepreneurial and business aspects of the music industry also clarify this challenge.

TRACK 3

THE TENDER LOVER INTERLUDE: BABYFACE AND THE RESHAPING OF BLACK
MASCULINITY IN THE CULTURAL IMAGINATION

Born in Indianapolis, Indiana, Face, which his friends affectionately call him, used music as an outlet to convey emotions that he otherwise could not articulate. Recollecting himself as a "painfully shy" kid, Edmonds found solace in writing, where he could, without the difficulty of verbal expression, convey his feelings. Often, these feelings pertained to love, and his inability to express those feelings verbally, coupled with his related inability to persuade his love interests, resulted in his writing love songs. As Edmonds explains, "writing songs was definitely comforting . . . it was kind of my voice. I was too shy to say something to the actual girl I was in love with so I just wrote it in a song. I didn't play it for her, but just put it in a song, it felt good to do it in that way."[9] Whereas these love songs ostensibly marked his unfulfilled longing for heterosexual love, these formative experiences ultimately shape Edmonds's ability to capture the complexity of love, and particularly its deferral, for both men and women. In other words, this reading insists that examining Edmonds's archive reveals a level of black masculine vulnerability that later becomes central to the nuanced perspectives on black gender relations that Edmonds's cultural production makes available. In *At Wit's End: Black Men and Vulnerability in Contemporary Satire*, Brandon Manning argues that vulnerability in black men's cultural production "foregrounds emotions to subvert how the interstice of patriarchy works with certain performances of blackness" and that vulnerability can provide a "site of catharsis, community building, and an embrace of being misunderstood."[10] For Manning, vulnerability in post–civil rights era black men's cultural production produces politics that disrupt performances of masculinity from previous eras which, in this book's argument, remain integral to the normative face of destructive desires.

To be more specific, Manning historicizes the avoidance of vulnerability as coinciding with sociopolitical movements, where one's status as a race man, for example, precluded him from exhibiting some of the perceived stigmas—weakness, uncertainty, and feminization/emasculation—associated with "vulnerability." The eschewal of vulnerability remains coextensive with the pursuit of mastery/sovereignty, a pursuit which makes sense in African American historical contexts, even as it proves problematic. Yet, as the post–civil rights era allows for more expansive ways to think about identities and their performances, vulnerability becomes an increasingly recurring trope in black men's cultural production such that we must investigate how it offers new masculine scripts. In his desire to "center the psychosocial potential of vulnerability for black men to subvert patriarchal formations," Manning considers how the feminization of this emotion undermines black men's thriving and thwarts black men's ability to empathize with and understand black women and themselves. In other words, hegemonic masculine scripts function as destructive desires, and my analysis of Edmonds's cultural production considers how it disrupts the normative face of destructive desires and thus provokes a consideration of the possibilities the nonnormative face may provide. I locate contexts that help us to understand Edmonds's articulation of vulnerability and sensitivity, for example, and examine how these articulations question the dominant masculine scripts that appear at odds with more capacious notions of black intimate relations.

The youngest of six brothers, Edmonds also situates the loss of his father, in his early adolescence, as having a profound impact on his understanding of himself (as a man), drawing attention to the constructedness of gender. He confesses to David Ritz, for example, "It took me a long time to grow into manhood. I couldn't relate to romance in traditional macho ways. I had to find ways of my own. Raw sex was never passion for me. Passion was love-making. And making love was the poetic idea of two minds, two hearts, two bodies interacting, actually creating love through sincere feelings."[11] Edmonds's rejection of the black macho, hypermasculine, oversexualized image of black masculinity helps him to divorce masculinity from sexual prowess, undermining a central tope of black masculinity in the popular imagination. While his father's death exacerbated his shyness, it strengthened his attachment to his mother, who also augmented his capacity to be vulnerable and attentive to women's plights (as he observed the toll it took for her to raise six young men). Whereas the trope of the black masculine "mama's boy" compels some black men to reject, in the words of Spillers, "the 'female' within," Edmonds effectively embraces it, to the degree that we understand the cultural construction of vulnerability as feminine (and therefore undesirable for men).

On the one hand, the sense that emotions can traverse gendered boundaries, and that one gender can imagine the emotions that another gender experiences, seems like a reasonable and obvious conclusion. On the other, given the persistence of gender essentialism, and the desire for African American men and women to occupy *proper* gender roles vis-à-vis respectability politics, and intraracial gender antagonisms, even emotional cross-gendering instigates problems within black intimate relationship discourses. Edmonds, however, resists this cultural trend, explaining, "When I wrote for female artists, I knew from being in relationships or having my heart broke, what the woman was feeling, because I would be feeling the same emotions. So when I wrote for a female, I could understand how to write from their female perspective, because it was from the heart."[12] That he and women experienced the *same feeling* turns attention to how the gendering of emotion does not foreclose the possibility for empathy, understanding, or relatability across genders. This empathy corroborates Danyel Smith's assertion that Edmonds possesses a "masculine serenity that is rare in today's black music," one that *Destructive Desires* maintains articulates expanded possibilities for imagining black heterosexual love, upending destructive desires' reliance upon rigid gender role constructions and performances.[13]

Whereas the image in the popular imagination of the brokenhearted forlorn teenager seeking unrequited love becomes gendered as woman and racialized as white (the imagination does not conceive of black teenagers as desiring or wanting love), Edmonds turns this image on its head, clearing space for a more complicated black masculine representation. As Edmonds notes, "If you lack the nerve to approach a girl in person, you do so in your dreams. Your songs fulfill your dreams, expressing all the frustrations and desires you're afraid to say out loud."[14] Edmonds's abilities and desires to tap into emotion, to show the romanticized and frustrating aspects of love, push the boundaries of black intimate relations insofar as his cultural production undermines some of the affective registers that inhibit black intimate relationships, and black men's emotional

availability in particular. By thinking about Edmonds's ability to articulate putatively feminized emotions, *Destructive Desires* demonstrates how patriarchy's
insistence on distinctly feminine and masculine emotions fails to thwart the
imagination. It argues that the imaginative creativity of Edmonds's entangled
networks in turn offers expanded possibilities for thinking about black intimate
relations, and those expanded notions in turn call forth different solutions to
black inequality. Here, thinking back to the argument chapter 1 outlines, I insist
that solutions to black inequality that call forth black intimate relations discourses summon normative hegemonic gender roles and masculinities that
ultimately impede black people's individual and collective abilities to thrive. By
displacing the centrality of these types of masculinities, Edmonds's thinking
around gender frustrates typical gender roles discourses in black intimate relations. By extension, this disruption upsets the traditional solutions to black
inequality that rely on traditional gender roles to buttress their case. Three
broader trends, the Clarence Thomas and Anita Hill debates, the O.J. Simpson
trial spectacle, and the Mike Tyson and Desiree Washington rape allegations,
as the next track explains, further contextualize the significance of Edmonds's
cultural production in gender discourses within black intimate relations debates.

TRACK 4
THE BLACK RENAISSANCE AND GENDER POLITICS IN THE 1990S

This chapter posits the centrality of *Waiting to Exhale* because both the movie
and the soundtrack emerge during a contested political, social, cultural, and economic milieu for African American men and women, as the last decade of the
twentieth century once again showcased African American advancement and
stagnation simultaneously. The 1990s indeed marked a profound moment for
black life in terms of the material and symbolic advances that emerge in black
cultural production and black politics. As a resonant example in black cultural
production, the hit television show *Living Single* (1993–1998) reflected the sense
that black women of the 1990s increasingly located personal and professional
success outside of the heteronormative cultural longings that society preferred
for women. Even as the characters resisted and sometimes willingly embraced
gendered destructive desires, the animating force of the show embraced the
ethos the show's theme song communicated: "In a nineties type of world, I'm
glad I got my girls. Keep your head up, what? . . . Whenever this life gets tough,
you gotta fight, with my homegirls standing to my left and my right."[15] Hip-hop
artist Queen Latifah, the sitcom's main character, sings the theme song; her roles
as artist, actor, and theme song lead singer create an entangled network that
emphasizes the politics of gender in 1990s black cultural production.

  Indeed, the sitcom reflected a broader inclination that encouraged black
women to champion women's independence, possess financial security and independence from men, live comfortably within their own skin, and pursue healthy,
mutually beneficial women-centered (intimate) relationships. On the show,
the desire for romantic couplings by way of heterosexual monogamy loomed

for most of the characters, even as they, too, pushed the boundaries of single sexuality by eschewing celibacy and instead embracing sexual vitality. Representations such as *Living Single* helpfully turn attention to the complicated, contrasting, and even contradictory ways that cultural production featuring black women construct, represent, and experience black womanhood. Even the most progressive ideas about black women's empowerment in mainstream black political discourses, black feminist thinking, and black modes of cultural expressivity sometimes fell short of encouraging a range of sanctioned sexual expressions that extended beyond respectability politics, compulsive heterosexuality, or compulsive monogamy (chapter 3's discussion of Howard will emphasize this point). Progressive politics may extend normativity but do not necessarily break its ties, and this chapter's reading of Edmonds keeps a keen eye on this point. Indeed, this cultural production expands the representational and imaginative possibilities for black life, culture, and politics. Nonetheless, insofar as it remains sutured to mainstream venues, it reinforced the very principles that ultimately undermine black thriving and black equality.

As black cultural production expanded, the politics of blackness also reinforced what Erica R. Edwards calls the black normal: "the constellation of narratives, images and state discourses that tie black freedom to the nation-to-empire-building project through images and imaginaries of everyday black empowerment within state institutions, an empowerment secured through both sanitizing and pathologizing representations of black sex and sexuality."[16] The normal thus turned attention further to black intimate relations and black sexual politics as behavioral explanations of inequality became increasingly more popularized. To propel these claims, public policy, politicians, and everyday citizens became increasingly invested in the idea that the legislative achievements of the modern civil rights era had indeed created equality and removed all obstructions to it. America had at last arrived in its postracial epoch, and the proliferation of black cultural production, and many black "firsts" further confirmed this notion. The cultural imaginary, for example, has read the appointment of Supreme Court Justice Clarence Thomas as evidence par excellence of postracial desires and successes. Yet, we must read the Clarence Thomas and Anita Hill debate within the context of the Rodney King beating, the O.J. Simpson murder trial, and the Mike Tyson rape of Desiree Washington. This contextualization foregrounds the conflicting and competing circumstances that facilitate our understanding of the destructive desires that are at play during Edmonds's rise and reign in rhythm and blues culture. These entangled networks matter even more when we try to understand the stakes of imagining and promoting less hegemonic black masculinities. Without a doubt, the era promoted the expansion of gender roles and opportunities and simultaneously reinforced the desire to contain black men and women within *proper* gender roles. As Edwards points out, *both* the sanitizing and pathologizing of blackness center black intimate relations discourses at the heart of black enfranchisement debates.

FIGURE 2.2. Demonstrators on Capitol Hill yell toward the Russell Senate Office Building in support of Supreme Court nominee Clarence Thomas in Washington, DC on October 15, 1991, as the Senate debated Thomas's nomination.

By the time McMillan published *Waiting to Exhale* in 1992 (track 8 discusses this), 1991 had offered a cultural trifecta that placed blackness, black intimate relations, and black intraracial gender strife on center stage for the public to advance conversations about blackness as it intersected with gender and sexuality. Whereas the early part of the year witnessed Desiree Washington accuse Mike Tyson of date rape, the second half of the year observed the Los Angeles Police Department's white police officers brutally beat the now deceased Rodney King. In the fall, Anita Hill called into question the fitness of Clarence Thomas to serve as a Supreme Court justice when she illuminated his pattern of sexual harassment (figure 2.2). Then, in 1994, the Los Angeles Police Department accused O.J. Simpson of murdering his ex-wife Nicole Brown Simpson (and Ronald Goldman), thus calling into focus more conversations about race, gender, and sexuality (intraracially and interracially). Signaling the cultural significance of the Hill–Thomas debate and Simpson murder trial, between 2014 and 2016, documentaries and other cinematic representations emerged that showed the continual cultural resonance of these incidents; they continue to shape discussions about black intimate relations and gender relations in black communities.[17]

The Anita Hill and Clarence Thomas debate captured this frustration because, unlike the other cases where, for a variety of reasons, publics had questioned the participants' respective integrities, Hill and Thomas provided access into a different population in black communities whose black intimate relations emerged in public discourses less frequently: the black middle class and seeming exemplars of respectability politics. As Nellie McKay writes of the debate: "Over the years, white Americans have grown accustomed to (and have taken for granted) the appalling statistics on black-on-black-crime among the least privileged group; never before had they had the chance to observe such a violent disagreement between so articulate a woman and a man from the privileged of the black race."[18] McKay's argument makes three points that bear elaboration. First, by introducing social class into the conversation, she foregrounds how black intimate relations discourses historically had focused on the presumed gender and sexual nonconformity of lower-class blacks (Daniel Moynihan, E. Franklin Frazier), yet turns attention to how those discourses include black people across classes; although the black middle class may espouse respectability politics, discipline other classes of blacks to espouse respectability politics, and distinguish themselves from black people who have yet to adopt them, society at large still views the majority of black people as ontologically outside gender and sexual normativity. Second, by contextualizing the case within the context of black-on-black crime, she usefully points out sexual harassment as a form of intraracial crime and violence, despite the tendency not to view it as either. Third, by turning attention to their respective forms of "privilege," she ultimately demonstrates how gender privilege for black men thwarts the possibility for the very racial allegiances that it would call and rely upon in order to render Hill's testimony inconsequential (as far as appointment to Supreme Court went).

That is, Justice Thomas's right-wing political leanings, harassment of Anita Hill, and spectacle of a confirmation hearing reflected the hypervisibility of blackness, intraracial gender and sexual schisms within black communities, and the potential for and (unintended) consequences of black incorporation into the State. This appointment of a black conservative represented a broader trend in which the State used black people to promote neoliberal politics, decrease the welfare state, and promote personal responsibility philosophies. Thomas, metonymically, represents how the incorporation of black people into the State functioned to exonerate accusations of racism even as neoliberal policies, practices, and logics disproportionately impacted black citizens' ability to thrive. If Thomas, or another black person, bore the responsibility of policy implementation, how could it then be racist? The example of Thomas importantly shows the limits of presumed racial allegiances and how the neoliberal State uses what Rosemary Ndubuizu calls "black disciplinarians" to maintain its policies that implicitly and explicitly thwart black thriving.[19]

Black disciplinarians, who historically have been predominantly black men, typically discipline blackness by locating aberrant and excessive black sexuality, and by extension, black intimate relations, as the cause of and explanation for black people's inequality. This cultural longing for black equality by normalized mechanisms (e.g., marriage, compulsory heterosexuality, and compulsory monogamy) produces destructive desires that this book examines. By focusing on the State's role in maintaining destructive desires, this argument clarifies how destructive desires actually work against implorations of the State to diminish inequality. The State, by regulating black intimate relations, shifts its responsibilities for providing for its citizens back to its citizens. These logics, too, avoid, as chapter 1 argues, addressing the superstructures that embed racism and that make inequality persist even when black people conform to these norms.

The debates over whether Tyson raped Washington too invoked a series of historical issues surrounding black intimate relations, including the idea (as critics of *Waiting* also insist) that black women should not publicly accuse black men of sexual misconduct. Even those who believed Tyson had raped Washington preferred that this conversation not emerge in the public lest it further stigmatize not only black people but, more representatively, "positive" black men role models. As Michael Awkward argues, the "racial responsibility to maintain silence is especially relevant in this case because Tyson, a successful black man, gives aid to the struggle against a white hegemony that seeks to deny Afro-American people widely celebrated, unassimilated, inspiringly heroic male examples."[20] Key to Awkward's analysis is the notion that Tyson represents what chapter 1 thinks of as *authentic* or *real* blackness and what chapter 4 characterizes as *too-black-blackness*. Both formulations think about how unassimilated, inspiringly heroic manhood also conjures up an interrelationship between race, gender, and sexuality. In other words, scripts about heterosexual black masculine ruggedness confirm Tyson's manhood and blackness simultaneously; the racial and gender discourses mutually constitute each other. Both definitions tie race to gender to sexuality and both invoke black intimate relations discourses by positing the struggle for racial equality as tantamount to performing normative gender roles and concealing any deviation from the norm.

The resistance toward acknowledging Tyson's rape thus also points toward a more general awareness of how black intimate relations function to explain black nonconformity and justify black exclusion from the body politic. In addition to questions of intraracial allegiances, and the politics of gender, this case also brought to question the fairness (i.e., the historical racism) of the American judicial system. The beating of Rodney King and the subsequent acquittal of the officers amplified this aspect of the debate, and the trial of O.J. Simpson, particularly his acquittal, presumably vindicated King and rebuked a racist judicial system. This Washington–Tyson saga representatively captured the tendency to elevate black men's interests, and revealed how privileging black men's perspectives and interests frustrates black gender relations; black men's heteropatriarchal interests demand a subordination of black women's calls for equality and this elevation of men's interests undermines black communities' abilities to collaborate to empower all of their members. Whereas critics, pundits, and everyday citizens have well rehearsed the particulars of the cases, *Destructive Desires* turns to their significances to contextualize the broader issues in which rhythm and blues cultural production becomes enmeshed because those discursive frameworks inform its production and interpretation. As important, rhythm and blues culture's repudiation of destructive desires' normative face challenges the politics of gender central to black intimate relations discourses and to solutions to black inequality.

TRACK 5

NEVER KEEPING SECRETS: BLACK MEN'S VULNERABILITY AND EMOTIONAL DEPTH, OR NOTES ON DE-ESSENTIALIZING GENDER AND GENDER ROLES

Scholarly examinations of (black) musical performances usefully distinguish between the *artist* and the *artistic persona* to disrupt the tendencies to reduce art to sociological realism and/or autobiographical reflection, and to call attention to the fact that musical performances reflect a stylized and constructed persona. This process, I argue, becomes useful in dismantling the gender essentialism that constitutes black intimate relations discourses and that perpetuates the normative face of destructive desires. Although I agree with Simon Frith's suggestion that the biography of the composer may become irrelevant in a song's interpretation, this point both echoes his claim and diverges from it. Frith argues, "In pop, biography is used less to explain composition (the writing of the song) than expression (its performance): it is in real, material, singing voices that the 'real' person is to be heard, not in the scored stylistic or formal devices."[21] My distinction troubles the boundaries between the autobiographical self and performing one to undercut the propensity for listening publics to examine artistic production *primarily* biographically, to use the performing artist's biography as the central explanatory framework. Rather than deny the ways that the autobiographical self influences the performing one, this perspective draws attention to the limitations of biographical criticism in music studies in order to eschew how an artist's biography *overdetermines* the meaning of *and* cultural significance for a song.[22] Although the discussion here focuses on the interpretations of songs, the general principle of hermeneutics applies more broadly to music culture as *Destructive Desires* conceives of its entangled networks. Put another way, the limitations of biography as the central interpretive force grow when we triangulate the relationship between the artist and the persona by adding the role of the song's composer, whose biography and identities may in fact matter.

If, for example, we were to analyze Toni Braxton's "Love Shoulda Brought You Home Last Night" as Braxton's lamentation of a series of unfulfilling heterosexual relationships, how does the fact that Edmonds penned the song complicate our analysis? If we come to understand Karyn White's "Superwoman" as embodying the black feminist ethic that Michele Wallace's *The Black Macho* proposes, how does the fact that Edmonds authored the song call into question the assumed relationship between biology and (black) feminism? If we insist that the *Waiting to Exhale* soundtrack captures a range of feminine and/or feminist ideas and perspectives, what does it mean for a black man to articulate that consciousness even as black women perform the sound and affect? These questions turn attention to the ways that black music culture figured prominently in contemporary questions about black feminism and black male feminism, in addition to rhythm and blues culture's broader engagement with gender roles and black intimate relations discourses. As important, they illuminate an underacknowledged role that rhythm and blues culture performed in reshaping discourses on gender and sexuality in the cultural imagination. By contesting hegemonic masculinities and femininities, rhythm and blues culture upstages the normative face of destructive desires to call for alternative black subjectivities.

In several ways, the questions demonstrate how rhythm and blues culture destabilized essential notions of gender (and sexuality) even while drawing attention to increased anxiety about *proper* gender roles and *normative* sexual couplings. This point notwithstanding, the questions also reflect the degree to which the performance of proper gender roles and normative sexualities captured an identification with and indifference to the regulation of black intimate relations. As chapter 3's examination of Adina Howard and chapter 4's of Whitney Houston clarify, market forces too contextualize why, for example, certain tropes of black love, black gender, and black sexuality resonated in the post–civil rights era cultural imagination. If in fact hip-hop's perceived verisimilitude to black lived abjection aided its ascent in the cultural imagination and marketplace, the "sad love songs" and "bullshit" of rhythm and blues would find a market to the degree that it promoted normative relationships, compulsory monogamy, and/ or compulsory heterosexuality. While compelling, this contextualization must also consider that the artistic production rejects the reduction of the music culture to sociological realism; it simultaneously insists that inasmuch as the music culture lends insights into dominant discourses it creates space to imagine alternatives. This imaginative space opens further when we equivocate the presumed relationships between the artists, personas, and song composers.

Thus the aforementioned questions that probe the relationships between Braxton's and White's performances and Edmonds's writing gesture toward why, in the words of Hortense Spillers, "at a time when current critical discourses appear to compel us more and more decidedly toward gender 'undecidability,' it would appear reactionary, if not dumb, to insist on the integrity of male/female gender."[23] Spillers makes this point, yet argues that we must first stabilize our understanding of black gender norms before we theorize black queerness. Similar to *Destructive Desires*, which does not privilege the nuclear family's organization, Spillers's argument requires that we first understand the scope and complexity of black gender norms and relations in order to upstage them. Spillers's discussion (1988), like much of the contemporary discussions about black intimate relations, invoked Moynihan's "Negro Family," but did so to reject its calls for black heteropatriarchy and normative couplings. In her seminal essay, "Mama's Baby, Papa's Maybe," Spillers explains how slavery displaced patriarchal law for black families and communities and thereby disrupted the gender relations that patriarchal law builds, protects, and perpetuates. Espoused by many scholars of black gender and sexuality studies, Spillers's formulations sever the relationship between biology and gender by turning attention to how slavery caused enslaved communities to adopt putatively *improper* gender roles. By tracing contemporary black gender relations to the institution of slavery, Spillers, similar to Ferguson, situates slavery's corruption of black familial systems as the main culprit for what is now assumed to originate in black people's own deviancies.

Spillers rejects the notion that black people's supposed nonconformity evidences an essential, biological difference, to instead posit a series of historically contingent and historically contextualized performances that mark gender itself.[24] Yet, given the insistence of patriarchal law, and the desire to resurrect "symbolic integrity" to the categorizations of "male" and "female," black communities have attempted to salvage normative gender roles. Rather than reject "the feminine within," Spillers suggests that the gender nondifferentiation that enslavement wrought might produce a harmony instead of an antagonism; that is, we might debunk the binary between the masculine and feminine, and, in the process, approximate a nonbinary, nonhierarchical set of gender relations. In historicizing the ways that black gender relations diverge from those of the dominant white culture, Spillers opines gender nonconformity as an opportunity by which we can reorganize gender relations, and, by extension, black intimate relations. This reorganization remains key to thinking more capaciously about solutions to black inequality insofar as the logics of gender and family at the heart of black intimate relations discourses would disintegrate, thus making room for alternatives.

By accepting the feminine within, for example, black men could resist the ways that (black) heteropatriarchy conceives of the feminine as devalued other that they must exorcise or otherwise suppress. By destigmatizing the feminine, black communities could also engender a broader paradigm shift in which (black) women's *presumed* value undercuts the institutionalized gender inequities that originate from and remain perpetuated by their *assumed* nonvalue.[25] While Moynihan's analysis of *inverted* gender roles, or what Spillers refers to as gender nondifferentiation, at times recognizes the racialized gender discrimination that necessitated these inversions, Moynihan ultimately reinscribes the normativity of patriarchal gender roles by recognizing the sociopolitical and economic benefits of adopting them. As he critiques racialized gender discrimination within American institutions, he still calls upon black people and black families to espouse the *correct* gender roles in order to succeed in American society. By contrast, Spillers's estimation identifies gender nondifferentiation as a starting point whereby to reimagine personal relationships and reconfigure the intersections of gender and race within institutions. Spillers's contention foregrounds institutional transformation as critical to the reimagining of black intimate relations, and this shift toward institutional reform, that originates from the self (the personal), upends conversations that pose black normativity as crucial to racial progress and uplift.

This turn to the "feminine within," as a basis for progressive or radical politics, lays at the heart of black male feminism, a theoretical imperative that articulates black men's relationship to feminism, provides methodological and practical questions with which the critical enterprise must grapple, and participates in a more expansive project of dismantling essentialism in black gender discourses. Instructively, Michael Awkward's paradigmatic essay, "A Black Man's Place in Black Feminist Criticism," situates Spillers as an important interlocutor from which he articulates the possibilities for, complexities of, and limitations within a black male feminist discourse, analysis, and praxis. Although contemporary understandings of black feminism emphasize its guiding principles of analysis and interpretation as crucial to a black feminist analysis or ethic, earlier formulations also bound the critical practice to the subject position of the interpreter. These critics conceived of black womanhood as necessary, though not necessarily sufficient, to offer an authentic black feminist critique. Awkward nimbly outlines the pitfalls of this thinking, particularly as he articulates how this point of view reasserts the logics of "essentialism" that black feminism desires to repudiate. Nonetheless, the thrust of his argument lies in the possibilities that a black male feminism can provide for black interpretive communities, and, I would add, black communities more generally. As Awkward explains, "To be of any sustained value to the feminist project, a [black male feminist] discourse must provide illuminating and persuasive readings of gender as it is constituted for blacks in America and sophisticated, informed, contentious critiques of phallocentric practices in an effort to redefine our norms of black male and female textuality and subjectivity."[26] The end goal will produce "an acknowledgement and celebration of the incontrovertible fact that 'the Father's law' is no longer the only law of the land."[27] Pointedly, the recognition of the Father's law as not the *only* law holds in tension the desire to disrupt the father's law with the recognition of the entrenchment of that law.

Awkward thinks through ways for men to navigate patriarchy even while calling forth the need to dismantle it and otherwise make space for nonpatriarchal models for gender relations to be less antagonistic. Whereas David Ikard asserts that Awkward's articulation of a black male feminism denies black women's agency, Awkward's argument actually forces a reconsideration of how we even understand the concept of agency itself within the context of a patriarchal society that rewards and incentivizes women's submission to and investment in patriarchal law.[28] Some critics outright dismissed the possibility for a black male feminism, while others would reject the categorization "black male feminist" to instead classify men who espouse feminist principles as "profeminists."[29] Yet Awkward's provocation, which he develops further in *Negotiating Difference: Race, Gender, and the Politics of Positionality*, offers an important intervention; to the degree that black heteropatriarchy constitutes *both* black men's and black women's understanding of gender roles and encloses their destructive desires for black intimate relations, both black women and black men must become equipped with the necessary tools to recognize destructive desires' limitations and to develop/adopt gender relationships that promote harmony.[30] Simone Drake argues that it is important to "begin to think about black men who are *making* choices through individual self-actualization, rather than understanding themselves as the victims of others' judgments" to underscore how black men resist (and reinforce) heteropatriarchal notions of black masculinity that position black men as perpetually in crisis and that position them as black women's primary oppressors in intimate relationships.[31] Drake believes black feminism provides theoretical frameworks wherein black men can understand themselves and their roles within and apart from the strictures of black heteropatriarchy. Her examination of representations of black men and black masculinity in post–civil rights era black cultural productions turns attention to how black men can divest from heteronormative masculinities.

TRACK 6
SOON AS I GET HOME: A BENEVOLENT, YET PROBLEMATIC BLACK HETEROPATRIARCHY?

Edmonds's role as hit maker, particularly for black women performers, evidences how rhythm and blues culture, implicitly and explicitly, participated in the project of reshaping black intimate relationship discourses, and by extension, discourses on gender relations and destructive desires. Whereas the previous track has rejected biographical realism as a primary mode of analysis for rhythm and blues culture, it also recognizes the biographical as an influential force, one that emerges as particularly useful in contextualizing Edmonds's role in providing more capacious possibilities for black intimate relationships. This claim becomes clearer when we consider Saidiya Hartman's insistence that autobiography helps us "to look to the historical and social process and one's own formation as a window onto social and historical processes, as an example of them."[32] Skeptics of this claim about Edmonds's *progressive* images might point toward a host of songs (see appendix A) that Edmonds has written, recorded, and performed that reproduce traditional gender roles, even as they provide a site to imagine *greater* intimacy, vulnerability, and emotional intelligence and depth for their persona, and, by extension, black men. Edmonds's song, "Soon as I Get Home," for example, paints the picture of a devoted (and doting) (black) man who is invested in a woman's economic, spiritual, and emotional well-being. By asserting that "it's not that you require a lot / Just need some tender love and care," the song's metacommentary about black intimate relations refutes the notions that black women's expectation for emotional and financial support and sexual fidelity elude black men's capacities. It simultaneously rejects the domineering matriarch and the oversexualized buck, two images within the cultural imaginary that strain black intimate relationships.

At the same time, the song binds the capacity for this level of intimacy to the persona's ability to adhere to the breadwinner model of heteronormative relationships, accentuating how, as chapter I explains, neoliberalism's financial markets shape black intimate relations in the post–civil rights era. Although the persona emerges as devoted, this devotion coincides with his access to economic stability that affords him the opportunity to take care of himself, "pay [her] rent," possess "lots of cash" and maintain "a stack of major credit cards."[33] If the persona's ability to remain a "faithful lover," who also becomes attuned to the emotional, financial, and sexual needs of his partner, hinges on his ability to access successfully the labor market, what does "Soon as I Get Home" intimate about black gender roles when we remember chapter 1's analysis of how institutional subordination continues to exclude black men from labor markets? In some respects, the song's portrait of black heteropatriarchy recasts the expectations for gender roles in black intimate relationships by also positioning black men as active and successful in both the private and the public spheres. Although he presumably already has worked a full-time job, he will also "cook [her] dinner." This expanded view of black men's roles, while still embedded within a broader patriarchal framework, pushes against the idea that patriarchy fully eclipses the potential to engage in actions that do not solely reinforce its oppressive logics (figure 2.3).

This point highlights the inroads that representations such as these make even if they fail to repudiate oppressive ideologies altogether. Further, it reflects the nuance of the argument that this book posits about the imaginative possibilities for black intimate relations; a transgressive and potentially radical politics can emerge *within* the very structure it desires to repudiate, and that these politics do not have to begin "as radical" to have a "radical end." Finally, by binding the probability of the relationship succeeding to access to and success within the labor market, "Soon as I Get Home" helps to think about how the eradication of institutional racism in the labor market emerges as a prerequisite before black intimate relationships can approximate the nuclear family model. The example here demonstrates the overarching claim that the nonnormative face of destructive desires, which here refers to contesting hegemonic racialized masculine and feminine social organization, assists in reimagining solutions to black inequality. On the one hand, we can read the song as a unique expression of one man's experience. On the other, we can think of the stakes of generalizing and particularizing the song. If we cannot extrapolate this personal narrative to have collectivist meaning, we must then concede this persona's exceptionality, acknowledging the intractability of the structural forces that elude him yet constrain others. Again, as chapter 1 argues, this point does not intend to assert the normativity of the nuclear family model, but rather it turns attention to how discourses, in the words of Roderick Ferguson, "have idealized heteropatriarchy as the essence of social relations and have presumed that heterosexual subjects and relations exist as absolute givens."[34] Yet this argument foregrounds the importance of emotional depth and intelligence as constitutive features of love and relationship discourses in the Edmonds era; they shape how black men and women construct gendered expectations for their romantic partners. It also more generally allows for a more expansive thinking about the eradication of discrimination in labor markets—for black men and black women—such that they can thrive economically within and outside of romantic couplings.

While emotional availability and vulnerability become crucial to the logics that classify rhythm and blues culture as apolitical, and that contribute to its marginalization in black music studies and African American studies, this turn to emotion reclaims a space for black intimacy as a site for politics and a politicized site. While Drake rightfully notes that "the expression and performance

FIGURE 2.3. Kenneth "Babyface" Edmonds performs during a taping of the NBC *Today* television program in New York, Thursday, December 6, 2007, for a show that aired on January 1, 2008.

of vulnerability so often return to the essence of patriarchal power," we can locate the ways that it defies the essence of patriarchal power and how vulnerability counters patriarchy in cultural production in addition to political and intellectual thought.[35] This examination of Edmonds thus considers how his cultural production becomes understood within this broader context, and probes how his refusal to let patriarchy eclipse his imagination and lived experience expanded ideas about black gender roles and gender relations in rhythm and blues culture. In particular, I want to turn our attention to Edmonds's distinct ability to capture so-called women's feelings and emotions or women's experience of love/relationships, which, in many ways remain tethered to his own experiences with love.

TRACK 7

BLACK SOUNDTRACKS, FILMS,
AND ECONOMIC CONSIDERATIONS IN THE 1990S

The 1990s served as a cultural renaissance for black cultural production, and the interrelationship (i.e., the entangled networks) between cultural media (film, music, television) and cultural producers (rappers, singers-turned-actors, black filmmakers) facilitated the distribution of cultural products and the construction of cultural aesthetics and cultural longings. This claim accounts for at least two types of relationships that emerge more prominently in black films during the 1990s, and accentuates the roles black music plays in constructing black cultural longings for and destructive desires about black intimate relations. Movies that cast singers (who have little acting experience or otherwise lack acting talent) and make the actors' "voice" central to the plot's development do so to increase the film's reception and marketability (Whitney Houston in *The Bodyguard* and *The Preacher's Wife*). Movies that cast singers (who have little acting experience or otherwise lack acting talent) and do not foreground the actors' "voice" as central to the plot's development still rely on their voice; their musical success facilitates their inclusion in the cinematic, and their inclusion on the soundtracks arguably propel the success of the movies and soundtracks (Whitney Houston in *Waiting to Exhale* and Queen Latifah in *Set It Off*).

As Yvonne Tasker explains, "the musical performer as movie star offers not necessarily a more extreme, but a specific instance of stardom, in part because they are already understood, and their images have been developed, in terms of an explicit and particular kind of performance. The body of the singer is defined through an elaborate and stylized performance that is often explicitly sexualized. She/he is also a figure of strength, controlling the image and compelling audiences with his/her voice."[36] The explicit sexualization of the singer/actor thus functions to promote ideas about gender, sexuality, gender roles, and black intimate relations to the extent that the performance taps into the cultural norms even as it (re)constructs its own. During the 1990s in particular, film and music, vis-à-vis the soundtrack, became increasingly tied together. This union relied upon corporate uneasiness concerning the marketability of black-oriented films.

The widely held view that black life and black interests lacked universal appeal or interest outside of niche black markets made risk-averse, economically driven production companies and studios less apt to invest in black films that did not have an apparent crossover appeal, or other type of financial support.[37] In the 1990s, the soundtrack became that support and helped to propel the cultural longings and destructive desires that the films put forth.

Undoubtedly, the blaxploitation era of the 1970s had produced a host of films that featured black actors and actresses, increased black people's presence in cinema, and produced soundtracks, yet those productions often presented blackness in stereotypical ways. The well-chronicled exploitative relationships between producers and actors and actresses; the flattening of the complexity of black life, politics, and aspirations; and the oversexualization of black people contextualize the complicated politics of classifying this era as a black *renaissance* in black cinema.[38] Although the number of films proliferated, the types of blackness on display did not. While Michael Gillespie rightfully contends that in black cinematic criticism there exists "a critical negligence and wish fulfilment that leaves black film as the fruit from the poison tree or the idea of race as quantifiably, fantastically whole," black cinema does in fact construct notions of blackness and black subjectivity.[39] Although similar critiques of 1990s black cinema emerged, thinking of this period as a renaissance, in the words of Gillespie, "does not and cannot satisfy identitarian fantasies of black ontology; it instead poses conceits, specificities, and contexts."[40] The classification thus centers upon and contextualizes the increased presence of black producers and directors, and the arrival of black films that, however problematic, did extend the parameters of black representation and attendant imaginings of black subjectivity.

The rise of hip-hop music, hip-hop studies in the academy, the persistence of realist aesthetics in African American cultural production, and the attraction of realism to consuming publics facilitated the box office success of movies such as *Boyz in the Hood* and *Menace II Society*.[41] Yet, in addition to these movies, the 1990s showcases films such as *Soul Food*, *Boomerang*, and *Waiting to Exhale*, where the movies' and soundtracks' rhythm and blues aesthetics forcefully tug at black intimate relations discourses and complicate the normative face of the destructive desires they posit and question. The 1990s thus witnessed an increase in the number of African American film producers, as well as in the number of films that starred African American actors and actresses and featured African American life. *Boomerang*, *Waiting to Exhale*, and *Soul Food*, for example, emerged as paradigmatic texts that (re)presented crucial themes and concerns about black life—romantic relationships and career development (*Boomerang*), family, romantic relationships, career development, and the opportunities for (un)encumbered black womanhood (*Waiting to Exhale*), and family and the importance of black familial traditions (*Soul Food*).

This argument does not ignore, for example, how a movie such as *The Preacher's Wife* calls upon the trope of the nuclear family or how *Soul Food* uses black matriarch tropes, and how both discursively reinforce some of the quite problematic ways that post–civil rights era appropriations of the black family misdirect the causes for and explanations of black inequality. While *Destructive Desires* maintains a skeptical eye toward these explanations, it resists abnegating the political and sociocultural values that these *black family* and black relationship–oriented films contribute to our understanding of black intimate relations. It is important to note, and these films help to make this point, that black intimacy and black love exist despite representations that characterize blackness solely as abject. When questioned about *The Preacher's Wife*'s appeal, and its presumable relatability to *authentic* (abject) blackness, Denzel Washington clarifies: "Don't look at us only as a group of people who are downtrodden, in despair. We have tremendous problems to overcome inside the community and from outside based on what's poured into it like drugs, guns, etc. We are the most resilient people, if not in the country, on this planet and we have a good time in our homes every day and on holidays."[42]

Washington turns attention to the ways institutions contribute to black dispossession, and does so to demonstrate that black communities alone cannot ameliorate their inequality. For example, by suggesting that external forces "pour" drugs into black communities, he upsets the notion that drug use among black people results from a cultural tendency or biological inclination (criminalization of blackness) to instead argue that the State has facilitated drug use in black communities. His emphasis on black joy undermines the perception that oppressed black people cannot imagine black thriving. Yet his invocation of black resilience also summons images of black strength that historically have functioned to diminish black suffering. These turns to intracommunal love and intimacy further reject the idea that both are out of reach or otherwise unimaginable or undesirable for black people for whom abjection becomes the sine qua non of black existence and desire.[43] Edmonds, too, confirms the persistence of black abjection in the cultural imagination when he explains the difficulty that he encountered in trying to market *Soul Food* and other projects; studios did not believe there would be *enough* demand for black romances, black dramas, or black (romantic) comedies.[44] More than possibly colluding to doom the production of this film and others, the perception of insufficient interest within and outside of black viewing publics reveals the degree to which the post–civil rights desire for postracialism always already called forth racial particularity as economic deficit.

Setting aside its thematic engagement with the politics of black intimate relationships, *Boomerang's* interrogation of gender roles, love, and monogamy in black middle-class relationships becomes tethered to the musical soundtrack, which necessarily constitutes the film's meaning-making matrix (figure 2.4). One could extrapolate the film's commentaries on black intimate relationships without the soundtrack, yet the soundtrack itself becomes a crucial link in the chain of meaning the film produces. And this meaning reaches past the film and soundtrack, gesturing toward the broader discursive field of rhythm and blues culture that *Destructive Desires* examines. The compact disc cover for the *Boomerang* soundtrack, for example, foregrounds the impending rise of rhythm and

FIGURE 2.4. A scene from the film *Boomerang* (1992) picturing Eddie Murphy (Marcus Graham), Halle Berry (Angela Lewis), Grace Jones (Helen Strange), Robin Givens (Jacqueline Broyer), Eartha Kitt (Lady Eloise), and John Canada Terrell (Todd).

blues artist Toni Braxton by centering "introducing TONI BRAXTON" on the bottom. The film and soundtrack serve as precursors to the release of *Toni Braxton*, which also features the song. Not only did this movie catapult Braxton into her Grammy-winning roles on LaFace Records by increasing her exposure and cultivating the listening public's interest, Braxton's *voice* in the film also becomes crucial to viewers' recollection and understanding of the scene and movie.[45] For many who have viewed *Boomerang*, the cinematic placement of the song constitutes its affective *and* sonic registers.

Braxton's Grammy-winning song, "Love Shoulda Brought You Home," calls to mind the scene in the movie where Marcus Graham's (Eddie Murphy) disinclination toward monogamy results in one of his love interests, Angela Lewis (Halle Berry), refuting his profession of love. Underscoring the centrality of the domestic space in contemporary black intimate relationships as an ur-sign of monogamy, Angela clarifies "love shoulda brought your ass home last night." Punctuated with a slap, the scene transitions as Braxton's voice laments "love shoulda brought you home last night." If film, as Julie Hubbert argues, "is conventionally considered as primarily a mode of viewing rather than listening," it becomes important to understand how "the impact that sound technologies have on the use of recorded music in film" becomes neglected in studies that consider how cinematic forms communicate meaning.[46] Hubbert's examination of the transformation of the *technologies* that produce sound recordings also invites an interrogation of the more general use of "recorded music in film."

Metonymically, this chapter uses this example to locate a set of meaning-making, entangled networks that relates specifically to, in this case, the relationships between the songwriter, the song's performer, the soundtrack, and the film. It considers how they function together, and independently, to produce cultural longings that may in fact be destructive desires.

TRACK 8

FOR THE LOVER IN YOU: *WAITING TO EXHALE* AND BLACK MEN

If the black women's literary renaissance of the 1970s opened a public debate about intraracial gender strife in black communities, the 1990s inaugurated a fresh return to these conversations by demonstrating how black heteropatriarchy, sexism, heterosexism, and homophobia continued to antagonize black intimate relationships. On the one hand, the publication of Toni Cade's *The Black Woman* (1970), Toni Morrison's *The Bluest Eye* (1970) and *Sula* (1973), Alice Walker's *The Third Life of Grange Copeland* (1970) and *Meridian* (1975), Gayl Jones's *Corregidora* (1975), Michele Wallace's *Black Macho* (1977), and the Combahee River Collective's "A Black Feminist Statement" (1977) called attention to how the intersections of racism, sexism, and classism in American society, public policy, and black interpersonal relationships complicated black women's abilities to thrive, develop a healthy sense of self, explore their sexualities in nonnormative ways, and experience communities in ways that benefited them. On the other, these texts served as calls to action to imagine black subjectivities outside of the gendered heterosexist racism that threatened the survival of black intimate relationships. In the terminology that *Destructive Desires* uses, they rejected the normative face of destructive desires to determine what possibilities, if any, the nonnormative face provided for black thriving. Critics, and black male critics in particular, viewed this body of literature and criticism as solely critical of black men, divorced from the texts' broader institutional critiques. They therefore condemned the texts as inappropriate racial laundry airing that betrayed racial allegiances to serve a (white) feminist movement (see chapter 3's discussion). This point of view, as track 4 contextualizes, remerges forcefully in response to the Clarence Thomas and Anita Hill debates of the era in particular, and also relates to debates about O.J. Simpson and Mike Tyson in noteworthy ways. Terry McMillan's return to black women–focused communities in *Waiting to Exhale* (1992) recalled these intraracial conversations about gender and sexuality in black communities that echoed those of the 1970s. Aneeka Henderson's *Wedding Bell Blues: Race and the Modern Marriage Plot* adeptly examines McMillan's broader corpus of work and the thematic and formal concerns of *Waiting to Exhale* as she theorizes the cultural significance of the author, the text, and the related debates.[47] These issues illuminate the broader intraracial gender debates and contextualize the stakes of Edmonds's involvement in the scoring of Forest Whitaker's cinematic adaptation of the text in 1995.

In 1995, producer Forest Whitaker oversaw the adaptation of Terry McMillan's novel into a motion picture, which grossed more than $67,000,000 in the United States and $81,000,000 worldwide.[48] Based on the screenplay that McMillan herself helped to produce, *Waiting* follows the lives of four black women, Bernadine Harris (Angela Bassett), Savannah Jackson (Whitney Houston), Robin Stokes (Lela Rochon), and Gloria Matthews (Loretta Devine), whose friendship does not simply explore the challenges that black women experience in terms of finding love, friendships, and healthy, productive, mutually fulfilling sexual relationships. Rather, *Waiting* equally imagines the conditions under which black women might thrive in a social and political system that seems determined to subordinate their personal happiness to societal norms, familial obligations, and career aspirations/successes.[49] By foregrounding the interrelationship between social norms, familial obligations, and career aspirations, *Waiting* reveals how social politics and culture become mapped onto the interpersonal, once again drawing attention to and emphasizing the feminist slogan, the personal is political and vice versa. *Waiting* appeals because of how realist aesthetics circumscribe African American artistic productions; the sense that *Waiting* provides access to the lived experiences—triumphs and struggles—of middle-class black women propels its success.[50] The movie arguably contests typical, negative, and reductive representations of black women during the 1990s by representing the complexity of black (women's) subjectivities.

Despite the film's emphasis on black women's relationships, the alleged priority the film gives to men's voices (within the film itself and in the adaptation process) contextualizes why some critics call into question readings of the film that overstate the degree to which we might read it as an exemplar of black women's agency and complex subjectivity. Monica Ndounou, for example, raises two points of contention regarding the cinematic adaptation that deserve consideration. First, Ndounou argues that the cinematic adaptation diverges from the literary text, revealing a "familiar pattern of narrative revisions to attract white audiences in hope of increasing revenue potential."[51] In particular, Ndounou takes exception to the view that the film did not include more substantive scenes from the book (a daughter tending to her ailing father), and argues that the elevation of more sensationalized scenes (sex and dysfunctional relationships) detracts from the film's black feminist politics. While Ndounou's consternation gestures toward the realist aesthetics for black cinema that Gillespie warns against, and suggests that cinematic adaptations must conform to the literary text, she also highlights how perceived consumer tastes and interests impact cultural production. What cultural longings, for example, make sexualized black women and black sex more attractive to viewing publics than a black woman caring for her father? If both types of scenes presumably represent black intimate relations and black families, what types of destructive desires increase the cultural longing for one type of representation instead of the other?

Ndounou seems to suggest that the cinematic production of McMillan's book dismantles the black feminist politic the written narrative possesses. Erica Edwards echoes a similar point in "Tuning into Precious," where she insists that the adaptation of *Waiting* "blurred the lines between a collective, insurgent black feminist critique of structures and a privatized, compensatory black women's empowerment narrative" and that "collectivist politics of black feminism often merged with and adapted to rhetoric of black self-help and individual success at the same time."[52] Together, Edwards and Ndounou force a consideration of how the economies of gender and race impact black cultural production, and the degree to which the cultural production pushes against and reinforces hegemonic structures and ideologies. Second, Ndounou notes the perception that "this is a film about black women told from black women's perspectives" ignores the fact "that the black male radio DJ's presence serves as a visual and aural reminder that black men, through the direction and music, control the perspective that is attributed to black women in the film."[53] While the politics of gender, and men's roles in the production process, require us to keep in mind the power and patriarchal dynamics at play, the inclusion of men does not necessarily foreclose the possibility to hear women's voices. In fact, part of what this chapter has argued has been for a more expansive notion of gendered collaboration, where awareness and intentionality can produce cross-gender allegiances that upset the antagonism that characteristically circumscribes black intimate relations.

While audiences can read *Waiting* as a metanarrative about black women's subjectivities, and a corrective to Hollywood's unsophisticated treatment of black women, the production of the soundtrack, as a related and separate unit, shifts debate about gender roles, gender identification, and gender essentialism in black intimate relations discourses away from the normative face of destructive desires. If *Waiting* narrates a black woman's subjectivity that, as black feminist arguments in the 1990s sometimes argued, becomes knowable only to and best by black women—Patricia Hill Collins's standpoint theory, for example—what does it mean that Edmonds, as the soundtrack cover prominently displays, wrote and produced the new music that the women artists perform? How, if at all, do Edmonds's roles as producer and/or composer of the fourteen tracks that constitute the soundtrack challenge the popular tendency to privilege biography and autobiography in the interpretive process that insists that the performer, performance, and song hold a predetermined relationship? While Edmonds understands the slippage among these terms, he also recognizes how, within the broader cultural imaginary, these distinctions simultaneously obtain and collapse. For instance, noting the ease with which *he* produced the album, Edmonds remarks, "The film was written from a female perspective, so it felt quite natural to have all the music written for and performed by women. Everyone falls in love. Everyone gets hurt. I just deal with how it works on both sides."[54] At play in Edmonds's response are the tensions that exist between essentialist ideas about gender that naturalize difference as biologically determined and therefore immutable, and the semioppositional claim that foregrounds putative differences as socially constructed. Socially constructed roles can become so embedded that, as Michel Foucault and Judith Butler suggest, people still do not necessarily possess greater agency to change them.[55] For example, Edmonds foregrounds the women's perspectives in the film and uses women's subject positions to explain why it is important (i.e., natural and/or essential) for the soundtrack to feature women.

Yet his assertion lacks a particular rigidity, and it slips when he notes the songs are "written for and performed by women" and when he later clarifies his ability to capture love (in all of its messiness) for both men and women. If, for example, Edmonds's naturalization promoted essentialist understandings of gender, it would have been "quite natural to have all the music written *by* and performed by women." Even as his actions destabilize gender binaries and their naturalization, his language points to the embeddedness of these ideas in American culture, and the anxieties that surround their destabilization. The normative face of destructive desires' forcefulness in black intimate relations discourses hinges on the naturalization of gender roles and the binary thinking that separates men's and women's social, political, and emotional spheres. Yet his ability to "tap into those deep emotions women feel and men rarely discuss," his industry status "as one of the few male singers who really knows what a woman feels and what a woman wants," and Whitney Houston's sentiment that he remains the "Only guy I know who can write about how a woman feels" collectively explain the significance of Edmonds's complicated roles in shaping black intimate relations; his work on the *Waiting* soundtrack emblematizes the multiple ways he shapes the cultural imaginary, at times revising and at times reinforcing destructive desires, through the cultural longings he generates.[56] This discussion of *Waiting* acknowledges that Edmonds's inspiration derives from preexisting texts (novel and adaptation), and insists that Edmonds's handling of and engagement with those texts remains noteworthy. By probing Edmonds's multifaceted positions, this argument makes a broader case for how gender, gender roles, and interpersonal relationships among African Americans during the 1990s underwent change. By examining the implications of Edmonds's role, it further rejects the tendency to conflate autobiography and biography (song's content), with composer (the song writer), with performer (the singer), and with performance (the singer's delivery). Each of these contexts matters, yet the critical and popular tendencies to a priori punctuate these relationships as necessarily correlative prematurely bankrupts the deeper imaginative possibilities of the music's composition and consumption.

If the popularity of McMillan's novel signaled the potential box office success of the cinematic adaptation, the soundtrack undoubtedly cemented the film's cultural significance by extrapolating poignant emotions, imaginative possibilities, and thematic concerns. In many ways, soundtracks *interpret* films by translating their narrative arcs into distilled audio clips that thus extend the cultural reach of the movie. *Extend* here functions in at least two ways; first, it gestures toward how soundtracks broaden a movie's scope to audiences that may not have viewed the film, and exposes them to its cultural pre-text. Second, it signals how the soundtracks participate in the circuit of meaning that moves beyond the cinematic adaptation, that pairs the sonic and the visual in creating affective and cognitive registers for a film. As Doane explains, "Music takes up where the image leaves off—what is in excess in relation to the image is the equivalent to what is in excess of the rational. Music has an anaphoric function, consistently pointing out that there is more than meaning, there is desire. To music is always delegated the task of pinpointing, isolating moments of greatest significance, telling us where to look despite the fact that the look is inevitably lacking."[57] If, as Doane contends, music functions to isolate great moments of significance, yet viewers cannot see them, its discursive references also summon the imagination in order to *understand* and *feel* that which the movie narrativizes but does not necessarily tell.

Although that imagination calls forth extant ideas about gender relations and black intimate relations, there also exists a space where the imagination exceeds that which it knows. Therein lays the possibility for imagining black intimate relations beyond the normative face of destructive desires. Because music becomes, as Heather Laing argues, "a central element of the way in which we actually understand emotion within the construction of gender," an examination of black intimate relations' discourses in this context should also consider how Edmonds's production—implicitly and explicitly—allows for more capacious thinking about black intimate relationship discourses.[58] While Edmonds can articulate and represent resonant emotions for black women subjects, this examination of his work also probes "whether and to what extent the soundtrack enforces compulsory heterosexual code, examining for instance how the soundtrack imposes normative gender roles and lines of sexual desire on the film's characters and our apprehensions of them."[59] Of course this argument recognizes the power dynamics at play and understands that Edmonds's representations of heterosexual unions participate in a larger system of patriarchy that remains inimical to black intimate relations' abilities to thrive. At the same time, it insists that the performances of Edmonds's representations call forth ways to reimagine black intimate relations within those strictures. It also remains receptive to the possibility that that reimagining sets forth the framework to imagine outside and beyond destructive desire's normative face. The soundtrack, the singing itself, thus imbues the lyrics with additional meaning and context that call forth emotion and meaning which the lyrics themselves, as a read representation, do not necessarily. For this reason, for example, Edmonds writes certain songs for specific artists.

For example, in Whitney Houston's "Exhale," the persona displaces the notion that women's lives become fulfilled when they find a man in whom they can make themselves whole, questioning what Banks refers to as the "ultimate merit badge" (marriage) and reinforcing Cobb's sense that the privileging of the couple dyad harms the individual within society (chapter 1). Houston croons, "If you're searching for a place you know / A familiar face, somewhere to go / You should look inside yourself / You're halfway there." *Halfway* here signals the process of looking inward instead of outward to locate joy and happiness. The song's emphasis on "friends who wish you well" helps listeners to think of community within homosocial bonds or noncathected relationships and displaces the primacy of heteronormative coupling as necessary for black women's thriving. It also calls forth several scenes in the movie that evidence this point. Mary J. Blige's "Not Gon Cry" advances a similar perspective by calling into question the payoff of black women deferring their dreams and career aspirations in an attempt to support their husband's dreams and raise a family. While the persona was both "lover and secretary / working every day of the week," and ostensibly had sacrificed "eleven years out of [her] life," ultimately he "leaves [her] at the drop of a dime." This song, by contrast, recalls a specific scene, where Angela Bassett cleans out her soon to be ex-husband's belongings, sets his car on fire with many of them inside, and hosts a yard sale (each item costs $1) for his remaining items.

Echoing Candi Staton's sense that "you'll get the babies / but you won't have your man," "Not Gon Cry" also elucidates how black heteropatriarchy demands black women's self-sacrifice and suggests that the self-sacrifice remains unreciprocated. It also questions whether, if not outright refutes that, the returns on those investments are worth the sacrifice. That the children become the main benefit of the relationship—"Besides the kids I have nothing to show"—invites listeners to consider whether the desire for children necessarily needs to be conjoined with marriage. As black intimate relations continue to emerge center stage as explanations for and solutions to black inequality, black cultural production that calls into question the usefulness of these destructive desires for specific types of families performs an important sociocultural and sociopolitical intervention as it relates to the politics of black familial organization; it decenters the nuclear family model and invites the opportunity to think of other forms of kinship (as chapter 1 intimates and chapter 4 explores in greater detail). Anticipating the argument chapter 3 advances about Adina Howard, the thinking here understands the messiness of sexual politics and recognizes radical politics as evolving and not necessarily wholly completed.

While the presence of the soundtrack's music within the film assists with "meaning making," the songs also possess a cultural life and interpretive field that exist in addition to their relationship to the film. Yet, because soundtracks and movies cohabitate, their respective discursive contexts collaborate to construct a soundtrack that best captures the film's deepest (though not necessarily most complicated or profound) thoughts, moods, and emotions. Thus, not only are the songs' lyrics as important as the artists who deliver them, but the sequencing of the songs, and the marketing of the artists and the songs (on the cover), constitute an interpretive entangled network that produces meaning. The flow of information, the communication circuit, as discourse, ideology, and materiality, crucially captures how discursive fields form, morph, and persist over time. That is, because production does "not constitute a closed discourse," production and reception "are differentiated moments within the totality formed by the social relations of the communicative process as a whole."[60] This totality of social relations also considers presumptions about the audiences' aesthetic and cultural tastes, and Hall's ideas can help us understand how entangled networks function more broadly in black cultural production.

When Edmonds collaborated on the *Waiting to Exhale* soundtrack, his introduction of Toni Braxton on the *Boomerang* soundtrack had already cemented his status as a perceptive, innovative, game-changing writer and producer whose creative genius articulated the emotional depths that the film attempted to convey. Unlike the *Boomerang* soundtrack, which had songs that extended beyond the rhythm and blues genre, and artists who were men and women, the *Waiting* soundtrack consisted solely of black women artists, who primarily performed rhythm and blues. TLC, Whitney Houston, Toni Braxton, Aretha Franklin, Patti Labelle, Chaka Khan, Mary J. Blige, and Sonja Marie, for example, performed decidedly within rhythm and blues genres, even if they also performed in additional ones.[61] Moreover, *Waiting to Exhale* not only had a black producer but was also a black movie that emphasized black women's interiorities, black intimacy, black family, and black strivings, as well as the politics of blackness in the post–civil rights era. By examining the soundtrack in light of the 1990s' broader cultural conversations around these issues, we can better understand how Edmonds (and the artists) intervene in these discourses to articulate alternative models of black intimate relations that simultaneously adopt, eschew, and modify the related gendered discourses around blackness. That is, beyond the love story, there is a story about love that, while not necessarily departing radically from normative ideologies, provides the possibility for thriving beyond destructive desires.

By writing the songs for and producing the *Waiting to Exhale* soundtrack, Edmonds unnerves the assumed relationship between writer, performer, and performance, as well as undermines gender essentialist ideologies in African American popular culture. Arguably, Edmonds has appealed and continues to primarily because his corpus of works—written and performed (by self and others)—idealizes and romanticizes heterosexual love. For Edmonds, love is self-sacrificing at its best, and the sacrificed self often serves the purpose of reinforcing notions about gender that are retrograde, difficult to sustain, or otherwise undesirable.[62] Critics thus might summarily dismiss my overarching claim as naive, or, even worse, as yet another black masculinist attempt to recuperate and reinforce black heteropatriarchy. Such an analysis provides an imbalanced view of Edmonds's role and reflects a more pervasive binary approach to African American gender studies. Furthermore, that type of analysis forestalls the ability to carve out the significance of radical moments when they occur within a seemingly nonradical event. By focusing on the particular moments where an artistic production offers cultural critique and revision, we better articulate the ways that indirect politics make their most acute intervention within the broader discursive field.

Collectively, these contexts converge to help frame how Edmonds's cultural production (i.e., his entangled networks) intervenes in black intimate relations discourses and how it provides space to imagine more expansive notions for gender roles that diminish the intraracial gender antagonism that became central to black politics, black life, and black intimate relations. In this way, Edmonds has disrupted the persistence of destructive desires' normative face, and his latest album, *The Return of the Tender Lover* (2015), continues to push the tropes that his second album, *The Tender Lover* (1989), inaugurated. As appendix A demonstrates, Edmonds has written songs for a host of black cultural producers that participate in this project of expanding black intimate relationship discourses, and this work evidences the aim of *Destructive Desires* to position him as a centripetal force in shaping this broader conversation about black intimate relations, particularly as it relates to the rhythm and blues culture's imagination for black gender and sexual politics. The reading of Edmonds thus considers the explicit, implicit, and discursive ways to interpret his roles in producing, constructing, reinforcing, and deconstructing cultural longings that engender destructive desires. As did chapter 1, this chapter, like the rest of this book, explores the nuance and complexity of black intimate relations in order to think through how, by turning these (il)logics on their head, we might better solve the problem of black inequality. Chapter 3's examination of Adina Howard considers how Howard's cultural influence provides additional ways to reimagine black intimate relations and probes what these imaginations reveal to us about solving black inequality and expanding our framework for black intimate relations in the process.

3

"Freak Like Me"

Reading Adina Howard

Boy you came, just in time / I'm feeling like, like I wanna ride / I still have some positions / That I still ain't done, let me have my fun.

—Adina Howard, *Second Coming*, "Nasty Grind"

Picture this I'm in my bed / Body's hot / Soaking wet / Thinking bout the things I like to do / I'm open wide when it comes to freaking you / Imagine me / Wet as can be / Between my legs / Ya tasting Me.

—Adina Howard, *Woo Soundtrack*, "T-Shirt and Panties"

You're a freak and you know it / You wanted to show it / You need it, you're feenin / Everyday and every night / You're a freak and you know it / You wanted to show it / And you need to Call Adina tonight.

—Adina Howard, *Fantasy Island*, "(Freak) and You Know It"

TRACK 1
INTERLUDE: HOWARD MEETS BLACK RESPECTABILITY POLITICS

In June 1995, the Michigan native Adina Howard had a certified platinum song, "Freak Like Me," and by 1996 she had amassed a certified gold record, *Do You Wanna Ride?* But in 1997, the record label shelved her second album, *Fantasy Island*, on which the preview song, "(Freak) And You Know It," Billboard reviewer Larry Flick described as "no sophomore slump" and "just too darn infectious to allow for much complaining."[1] Indeed *Fantasy Island*, as J. R. Reynolds noted, "has eased off sexually explicit content in favor of a more metaphoric approach."[2] *Vibe* magazine concurred, contending that "even though Adina isn't as wild as she once purported to be, freakiness *is* in the mind" when it characterizes this second album that intended to propel Howard's career even further.[3] When we contrast the success of her debut single and freshman album with the performance of the sophomore one, the lack of sales stuns. When we also note the popularity of the duet "T-shirt and Panties," which debuted the same year as *Fantasy Island*, the paucity of sales becomes enigmatic.

Of course, Howard would not have been the first rhythm and blues artist to become a "one-hit-wonder," to demonstrate exceptional promise in her debut but not follow through with a second, equally as promising/inspiring album.[4] From the rumor mill, to information that Howard herself has confirmed, personal disagreements, professional vendettas, and cultural expectations for black women's musical production coalesced to make the once hypervisible rhythm and blues artist less noticeable. Although many factors explain, contextualize, and clarify the disparate performances of Howard's albums, the tepid promotion, marketing, and, consequently, reception of Howard's post–"Freak Like Me" oeuvre epitomize how cultural longings, destructive desires, and entangled networks converged to demarcate the limits and possibilities for black women's cultural production. While supposition and speculation animated conversations about Howard's disappearance from stardom, more than a decade and a half following her initial meteoric rise, Howard began to narrate publicly the ascent and descent of her rhythm and blues career.

In October 2013, when Howard appeared on TV One's miniseries *Life After*, viewers had the opportunity to glimpse into what, as the episode's title alludes, had happened to Howard following her epic rise in and sudden disappearance from the rhythm and blues scene in the mid-1990s. By watching "Adina Howard: Life after 'Freak Like Me,'" viewers accessed Howard's own perspective to understand better the circumstances that rendered her first gold-selling album and platinum-certified single her only ones; that removed her from the visible, public role that she initially had in transforming the genre; and that instigated the listening public's desire for her to reoccupy a more central role in rhythm and blues culture. "Adina Howard" allowed fans, critics, pundits, and even scholars of rhythm and blues culture to uncover why she had disappeared, and perhaps as importantly, whether she planned to reappear. Did this episode, similar to the ones in the *Unsung* series, provide a possible venue for her return to rhythm and blues culture by raising awareness and increasing the listening public's desire for more music? Or, did the *Life After* episode provide public closure to a career that effectually had ended, or one that would not return to or approximate what it had been? What cultural longings for and about Howard (as individual, artist, and metonym) did the episode recall, and what did these longings intimate about black intimate relations? How did seeing Howard in the domestic space, as a married woman, contrast with the image of Howard on her *Do You Wanna Ride?* album cover, and what does this contrast suggest about destructive desires' two-facedness? How do we read the significance of these cultural longings and their related destructive desires historically and contemporarily, and how do entangled networks facilitate, complicate, and necessitate this analysis? To what degree does the specter of black intimate relations discourses and their role in improving black inequality govern these relationships? And what coexisting discourses and historical contexts help us to understand Howard's initial cultural iconography and later cultural obscurity? (See figure 3.1.)

Because Adina Howard produces music, performs concerts, conducts interviews, and actively engages with and in rhythm and blues culture still, it is

FIGURE 3.1. Adina Howard describes herself as "ladder leaning" in Phoenix, Arizona, in 2017. Photo courtesy of Adina Howard.

important to note that her career has transformed but certainly has not ended. Yet the trajectory of her career, to some degree, no longer appears in the *mainstream* how people hoped it would after her 1995 debut of *Do You Wanna Ride?*, where the lead song, "Freak Like Me," catapulted Howard into stardom *and* controversy. If, as Howard's website contends, her songs, and this one in particular, "were more than just chart-topping singles, they were anthems of liberation,"[5] part of Howard's appeal emerged from her ability to express ideas about gender and sexuality that imagined new possibilities for black subjectivity, life, and politics by extending black intimate relations discourses. Her age, comportment, looks, and physique, coupled with the lyrics she sang, music videos she produced, and live performances she gave, positioned Howard as an unabashed sex symbol that encouraged sex positivity. Howard embodied the young, vibrant, liberated '90s black woman who embraced sexuality and erotica as sources of pleasure and not sites of shame. As Howard notes in one interview, "The song describes me as an aggressive person who communicates what she wants. The whole album—the music and lyrics—are basically about who I am, an independent '90s woman."[6] (Recall chapter 2's discussion of *Living Single*.) Howard celebrated black women's sexuality, even if it required holding in tension a set of mutually constitutive *contrasts* that society deemed as mutually exclusive *contradictions*; Howard had a religious background, *and* lived as a single woman who promoted sensuality and sexuality; she celebrated women's sexual agency, expression, pleasure, and fulfillment, *and* remained sexually selective and discerning.[7] While the former example resists the tendency to pit religion's compulsory monogamy and/or compulsory celibacy against vibrant sexual expression, the latter refutes the propensity to equate sexual agency with sexual irresponsibility or promiscuity. The phrase "sexual irresponsibility or promiscuity" itself irks to the degree that it reinforces discourses surrounding monogamy and respectability politics that this book's engagement with black intimate relations desires to unsettle.

Howard's rejection of a particular type of respectability politics undoubtedly engendered a certain level of disdain for those invested deeply in the *performance* of respectability politics publicly, even if they did not cherish them personally or privately. For critics, Howard could be a "freak like me" in the privacy of her own bedroom, but she *should* not display it publicly. For her to celebrate the freak, to do so publicly, to do so unabashedly—seemingly without regard to the racial uplift workers who had deployed respectability politics as a method to eradicate these images—offended and undermined black political advancement. As a consequence of privileging respectability politics, as Mireille Miller-Young explains in *A Taste for Brown Sugar, Black Women in Pornography*, "the respectability-dissemblance framework has overwhelmed our ability to think of sex apart from the threat of harm to our womanhood and to our communities."[8] Miller-Young's contention rightfully attunes to the politicized ways that black women's sexuality remains tethered to racial uplift practices, and her scholarly project demands a dissociation of the two to better understand the political possibilities for sex and sexual pleasure for black women and their cultural production. Howard, however, divorces herself from the *solely* inhibiting aspects of this history, modeling how to acknowledge historical pasts without being bound to/by their logics. In this respect, she consistently calls into question which desires are in fact destructive, suggesting that normative ones do harm too. In making this intervention, Howard intimates that the nonnormative also provides possibilities for empowerment.

Black women indeed did try to detach black intimate relations from the cultural arsenal that used a putatively deviant black sexuality to justify and explain black inequality. But in recovering the physical and ideological violence that these logics, imageries, practices, and cultural narratives had rendered for black women, another type of violence emerged. This tendency to recover black women's images from violence has, in the words of Jennifer Nash, "reproduced another kind of violence, effectively rendering black female pleasures invisible."[9] Debates about Howard's cultural production thus emerge within the crosshairs of discussions about a cultural longing for life *after* respectability politics that becomes increasingly at odds with cultural longings for life *within* respectability politics. At the heart of both debates, as this chapter lays bare, black intimate relations discourses persist, as the presumption that they can shore up or retrench black inequality animates these conversations. Recall that *Destructive Desires* insists that life within respectability politics, where containment, concealment, and stigmatization circumscribe black intimate relations, does not thrive as it purports or intends. And that the double face of the phrase "destructive desires" points toward the fact that nonnormative sexual practices may in fact not be as destructive as characterizations of them suggest. Respectability politics also highlight how black sexuality exists within a glass closet, a phrase C. Riley Snorton uses to "describe how black sexualities are characterized by hypervisibility and confinement and subject to regulation and surveillance."[10] By masking respectability politics' deleterious effects, American culture reinforces the State's ability to regulate and surveil black sexuality and ignores the significance of sexual pleasure and freedom as necessary for black thriving. By not attending to the interwoven implications that respectability politics have for how the welfare state functions (chapter 1), proponents of this strategy provide the State with the opportunity to abdicate its responsibility to provide welfare and equality for its citizens.

This chapter thus advances how to read Howard's reimagining of black intimate relations outside of and beyond the scope of respectability politics as a point of entry to articulate new possibilities for black intimate relations and black equality. It argues that Howard's cultural production calls into question the normative face of destructive desires in order to destigmatize the assumed destructiveness of nonnormative desires, and does so to center black women's sexual pleasure as constitutive to black liberation and freedom. After a general discussion of Howard, it locates four representative aspects of Howard's career and life: (1) Howard's rise to stardom with her freshman album *Do You Wanna Ride?*; (2) respectability politics and its revisiting by way of her album cover, and subsequent "unsung" works; (3) her performances in the twenty-first century and the continued perceived threat of black women's sexuality; and (4) her personal branding and self-perceived role in rhythm and blues culture to demonstrate the interrelationship between the cultural longings and destructive desires to which they respond and that they articulate/make possible. It further examines how the entangled networks through which these articulations emerge become critical circuits through which to interpret the meaning and significance of Howard's work. Conversations and debates in black cultural production and black feminism—from the 1990s to the present—become crucial contexts for framing the questions at stake in the chapter, articulating the significance of the cultural longings, destructive desires, and entangled networks, and explaining the possibilities for black intimate relations and equality.

TRACK 2

HOWARD RESISTS RESPECTABILITY POLITICS

Since 1995, in academic and popular circles, Howard has emerged as a trend-setting, norm-defying, industry-reshaping artist whose *mediations on and representations of black intimate relations* have expanded opportunities available for black women's cultural production. Whether she also expanded the genre of what Charlotte Richardson Andrews terms "urban raunch pop" or set the stage for a warm reception to TLC's "Red Light Special," Howard's influence within mid-1990s black musical production merits attention.[11] Post-Howard rhythm and blues genealogies too have situated Destiny's Child and Beyoncé as artists who build and expand upon the ways that Howard redefined the terms by which black women's artistic production engages the topic of sexual pleasure and fulfillment. Acknowledging her influence beyond the genre, Howard identifies Lil Kim's rap career as parallel to hers, and I would add that Howard influences the artistic possibilities available to Kim. Of their similarities and differences, Howard surmises: "She was the rap version of me. But she was a lot more raw than I was. . . . I did wordplay in my music. I made it a little more appealing to the point where even though people opposed my music, the pill wasn't so jagged to swallow."[12] The respective genres in which Howard and Kim emerged also inform their reception, because black women rappers, while censured, did not experience respectability politics in the same ways that black women rhythm and blues artists did. Part of this distinction also relates to rap and hip-hop's realist aesthetics and the idea that sexualization of black women's bodies in those spaces made hard pills less difficult to swallow because of their presumed verisimilitude to black women's *real* lived experiences.

Notwithstanding her relatively brief tenure in the limelight, Howard thus remains a central figure who (re)positioned how black women artists within the industry and genre articulated more capacious notions of black women's subjectivity. As important, she shifted how listening publics who identified with her, the music, and culture came to understand their own subjectivities, lives, and politics in more expansive ways, also enhancing their abilities to thrive as black subjects. The suggestion here is that sexual freedom mutually constitutes racial freedom, a perspective that defies the repression of sexuality that figures prominently in respectability politics. Rhythm and blues artist David Tolliver notes that Howard allowed "women to be more open with their sexuality and more aggressive toward men," and that the song reached men, international audiences, and listening publics that extended the rhythm and blues target group.[13]

Brandi Wallace recalls that when "Freak Like Me" was released it helpfully shifted her mother's and grandmother's approach toward sex—don't talk about it, don't think about it, don't do it—to instead encourage dialogue, reflection, and sex positivity. Music such as Howard's encouraged teenage black women to think, in Wallace's own words, "maybe this isn't as taboo as my parents and grandparents told me."[14] Beyond thinking, they discussed, imagined, and experienced sex outside the parameters that their families and societies had set, and, in the process, understood black women's sexuality as evolving and complicated. In terms of sexual agency and pleasure, for example, Wallace notes that Howard challenged black heteropatriarchal understandings of the purpose of black women's sexuality; she encouraged women to have sex for their own enjoyment and not primarily because men wanted them to do it. Tolliver's point articulates the wide, crossover appeal of Howard's song, and the impact the song had on black women specifically and black gender relations more generally. Wallace compliments Tolliver's point to demonstrate more acutely how Howard pushed back against black respectability politics' hold on black intimate relations. Howard thus articulated imaginings of black women's sexuality that privileged women's sexual enjoyment and fulfilment, and provided a discursive space in which artistic production and artists capitalized on emerging cultural forms and aesthetics to represent enhanced political possibilities.

Whereas this chapter theorizes Howard's influence as advancing more capacious notions of black women's sexuality, it recognizes that dissent about her cultural influence persisted, and that these criticisms typically centered on Howard's refusal to espouse respectability politics. The refusal to do so threatens the "positive" image making that required sexual conformity and normativity (black behavior) in order for black people to make political progress. C. Delores Tucker, head of the National Congress of Black Women, for example, laments that Howard "signifies lost young people who stoop to such a low self-image to sell records."[15] An intern of Tucker's also blames Howard for obstructing black social and political progress, accusing that "the lyrics are nasty and vile. I'm striving to get an education and make something of myself. I have to constantly fight against catcalls and sexual harassment on the street and here comes Adina Howard."[16] And, in an editorial, "What We Sing, Why We Sing It," the author notes "those lyrics make me want to weep for our young people, weep for our future," suggesting Howard has corrupted current generation and future ones too.[17] Tucker's notion that Howard degrades and exploits herself for financial gain, the intern's suggestion that Howard's lyrics encourage patriarchy's threat to women's survival, and the editor's sense that women's unbridled sexuality will cause the downfall of civilization demonstrate how critics resist the potential for black life and sexuality to thrive beyond the parameters that respectability politics circumscribe for black intimate relations; they misattribute to black behaviors the causes of, and therefore miscalculate the solutions to, black inequalities.

Contemporary scholarship in black feminist studies thankfully continues to provide apertures through which to look critically at taboo, understudied, and underemphasized aspects of black women's cultural production (even and particularly in the context of black feminist analyses) by calling into question some of the premises, assumptions, methodologies, arguments, and archives that have constituted the predominant trends in black feminist thinking and scholarship about black women's sexuality. On the one hand, it remains dispositive that black feminist thinking prior to and during the 1990s provided a space for Howard to enter and upstage the current social milieu as it concerned black women's cultural production, the politics of race and gender within rhythm and blues culture, and the politics of gender and sexuality within respectability politics. On the other, recent turns in black feminist scholarship explicate further the fullness of the contrasts (and not contradictions) that constituted black women's cultural production. As *Destructive Desires* investigates and reads the ways that Howard opens additional possibilities to understand and imagine black intimate relations, recent scholarship that refocuses conversations about black women's (hyper)visibility and agency; participation in pornographic industries; interests in bondage, domination, sadism, and masochism; and movement across normative gender and sexual boundaries undoubtedly unpack the layers of Howard's cultural, musical, symbolic, and political significances.

By reexamining black women's agency and pleasure in the pornography industry, and refreshingly asserting that black women indeed can be agents and take pleasure in an industry that too often appears solely to disempower and exploit women, Jennifer Nash's *The Black Body in Ecstasy: Reading Pornography* contextualizes why people rejected and embraced Howard's calls for sexual fulfillment and pleasure. Indeed, Howard's freshman (semipornographic?) album cover stunned, and when Nicole Fleetwood analyzes what I am phrasing "the burdens and possibilities for representation" in *Troubling Vision: Performance, Visuality, and Blackness*, she clarifies the discursive paradigms that stigmatize the cover's portrayal of black womanhood, as well as envisions how it pushes back against that stigmatization. Arianne Cruz's careful consideration of the possibilities for sexual agency and pleasure in racialized schemas of presumably sexually exploitative scenarios, such as slavery or cuckold pornography, inform how the psychic hold of slavery still informs contemporary expressions of (racialized) sexuality and sexual normativity.[18] Cruz's *The Color of Kink: Black Women, BDSM, and Pornography* thus forces a consideration of the latent and historical factors that enable a contemporary reading of Howard that grasps the complexity, urgency, and depth of Howard's reshaping of black intimate relations discourses then and now.

Howard comes of age at a moment at which trailblazing black feminist discourses, which academia increasingly had institutionalized, expanded the representational, epistemological, and existential facts that black womanhood existed beyond the monolithic boundaries that historically had circumscribed it. By developing, theorizing, and archiving *a range* of experiences, histories, feelings, and thoughts that constituted black women's ways of being and existing across socioeconomic, sexual, and geographical boundaries, black feminist thinking and praxis compellingly demonstrated the existence of multiple black womanhood(s). These womanhoods, in many respects, unnerved the limiting and constricting stereotypical images of black women that had explained, justified, and maintained their presumed political, cultural, social, and economic inferiorities. Black women were not only, and certainly much more than, the neoliberal welfare queens whose sexual promiscuity and reliance on the welfare state evidenced a lack of personal responsibility and sexual control.[19] Neither were they the emasculating matriarchs who drove black men from their households, thus effeminizing their sons and leaving their daughters longing for father figures. This context explains why, even as black feminism called for expanded representations and conceptualizations of black womanhood, those expansions confined black women's sexuality within the boundaries of respectability politics (i.e., heteronormativity, compulsory heterosexuality, compulsory monogamy, or compulsory celibacy). If the limits of heteronormativity and compulsory heterosexuality, monogamy, and celibacy govern the terms of sexual expression, how, if at all, can black women's representational and existential possibilities move beyond or outside of these confining destructive desires? What are the stakes of this movement and what possibilities do these movements provide? And, as art makes these moves, how does it mold black politics, political expectations, and political possibilities?

Howard reveled in a woman-centered expression of sexuality—one that focused on black women's sexual pleasure, and that emphasized women securing the quality and quantity of sex that satisfied whatever appetites they possessed. Her celebration of sexual pleasure therefore shaped her image as a cultural norm rabble-rouser. More provocatively, it situates her (physical body and cultural production) at the disjunction between expansive and progressive politics and respectability politics. In black feminist politics and the political imagination, Howard's cultural production becomes a locus of possibility. This chapter examines Howard's transformative interventions in black feminist thinking and cultural production. Simultaneously, it acknowledges and wrestles with the cultural and political implications of her concurrent image as *cultural-retrograde*—as a black woman, who, through one song in particular, "Freak Like Me," putatively undermined the respectability politics that generations of black women had evoked to demand their civil, social-political rights. As Candace Jenkins has argued, cultural longings champion a salvific wish, or "the desire to rescue the black community from racist accusations of sexual and domestic pathology through the embrace of bourgeois propriety."[20] A constituent feature of respectability politics, the salvific wish responds to "a fiercely invasive body of myths that designate the African American community incapable of healthy intimate bonds" and the more general perception of black people "as sites of sexual excess and domestic ruin in U.S. cultural parlance."[21] The debate Howard's cultural production engenders thus calls attention to the two-facedness destructive desires signals, and demands, for example, what constitutes "healthy intimate bonds," "sexual excess," and "domestic ruin." By calling into question the logics that these phrases instigate and undercutting their normativity and naturalization, this turn to Howard once again thinks more energetically about which desires are in fact destructive.

These contexts help critics to insist that in one song, lasting four minutes and thirteen seconds, Howard had undone what they had labored all too hard to do: refute the idea that black women's sexuality remains unbridled, and therefore the cause of and explanation for their exclusion from and inequality within the American body politic. In other words, her display of sexuality—which her appearance and lyrics reinforced—provided yet another opportunity for intraracial and interracial scorn, especially at a time when black cultural production became increasingly called upon to explain and respond to more general assaults on black life, culture, and politics.[22] What cultural longings against respectability politics can analyses read in the desire for Howard to embody respectability politics? How does gender inflect the desire for respectability politics, and how do the emerging double standards between black men artists and black women artists align with and diverge from the broader cultural trends in black gender relations? As chapter 2 clarifies, possibilities emerge from these differences, and rhythm and blues culture facilitates the imagining and imbibing of those possibilities.

TRACK 3

HOWARD RECLAIMS THE FREAK AND OFFERS NEW POSSIBILITIES

The song, album cover, and music video compose a triad that reworks a host of tropes that had tethered black women's cultural production to abjection, and that circumscribed the possibilities available for sexual expression in a capitalistic and racist marketplace. More specifically, the triad forms an entangled network that turns the image of the freak upside down by detaching it from its history of abjection. Historically, the racialized use of the term *freak* intended to marginalize black women's sexual expression by characterizing it as excessive, nonnormative, uncontrollable, and otherwise outside the boundaries of decency and respectability. The cultural longings, for example, for a private "freak" butted against the public longings for a respectable lady; the cultural longings to be respectable ladies butted against the idea that black women were always and never more than freaks; the cultural longings for respectable womanhood too reflected the sense that respectability demonstrated worth, earned rights, and eschewed libidinal excesses.[23] From fifteenth-century travel narratives, to Saartjie Baartman's visual and physical exploitation in the nineteenth century, to contemporary black women whose expressions of sexuality social norms would hardly deem *modest*, the term *freak* in mainstream cultural appropriations distinguished white ladies from black women; reinforced notions that black people lacked the capacity to adhere to mainstream gender and sexual roles; and underwrote the need for sexual reticence.[24] If the jezebel stereotype demarcated black women with insatiable sexual appetites (quantity), the freak extended this framework to characterize sexual proclivities that included an unspeakable (at least publicly) range of sexual acts.

Within black culture, the term *freak* has also functioned to cauterize *respectable* black women who have adopted respectability politics and publicly displayed sexual decorum and modesty from hypersexual black women whose public display of unbridled sexuality undermines the possibility for racial progress.[25] Yet this particular interpretation of *freak* ignores a cadre of black women cultural producers and artists who have attempted to shift the paradigm on this term by embracing the freak as a site of possibility. Howard believes her work provides a framework to understand sexual expression as including sensuality and eroticism: "Make no mistake about it. This is me. . . . This is Adina. . . . I am not promiscuous, but I am not insecure at all. We are a sensual people . . . but when it comes to black people, the focus is always on the negative. . . . Everybody has a little freak in them. My definition of being a freak or being freaky is: with you an[d] that particular person anything goes in the bedroom."[26] Considering this remark alongside the lyrics of the songs on the album, anything goes can include women initiating and controlling the sexual interludes ("Do You Wanna Ride?"), oral sex ("Baby Come Over"), and a more general emphasis on women's sexual fulfillment and sexual experimentation ("Horny for Your Love" and "My Up and Down"). Although chapter 4's *reading* of Whitney Houston argues that Houston and Howard similarly become tethered to public expectations for *appropriate* expressions of black women's sexuality, Howard, unlike Houston, explicitly defies those entanglements to more generally embrace other modes of expression for black women's sexuality. The twenty-year-old Howard's response thus displays an awareness of the racialized double standard for black women's sexual expression—both in terms of the expressions of sexuality available without censure for white women, and, as she later reveals in subsequent interviews, those available for black men (figure 3.2).

Although Howard did not pen the single, she notes her involvement in the process; she and her manager met with the songwriters to describe Howard's attitude, values, and personality. Based on this information, they then wrote "Freak Like Me." In "Adina Howard," Howard recalls reading the lyrics and thinking "it embodies me," and her sister and long-time friend concurred that the song "is Adina."[27] Howard's use of the term *embodiment* also celebrates the sexuality of black women's bodies by detaching stigma and troublesome excess from the sexualized black woman's body. Her persona and her musical production become "sites where one would not expect to locate possibility" because "they are sites where black women's bodies have been represented not to engender political shifts."[28] By calling attention to how Howard's body does get read as a politicized site, this analysis offers two interventions. First, it reminds that when Howard gets censored that rebuke admits she does in fact instigate a political shift. The problem, however, is that critics presume she works *against* black political enfranchisement. Second, the critiques of Howard actually turn against themselves and uncover how her work embeds a politics of liberation that

FIGURE 3.2. Adina Howard performing at KMEL Summer Jam at Shoreline Amphitheater on August 12, 1995, in Mountain View, California.

empowers black sexuality by detaching it from a politics of abjection and respectability.

While freakiness certainly relates to sexual acts, her definition more broadly encompasses a boldness to resist the insecurity about sexual desire, expression, and fantasy that for too long had been bound by, and bound black women to, a larger history of denigration, exploitation, and commodification. As Howard expresses a more expansive understanding of sexuality, she emphasizes that she is not promiscuous, reflecting her understanding that compulsory celibacy and compulsory monogamy become paradigms through which the culture reads her. If she were sexually promiscuous, would that fact necessarily tie the term *freak* back to the history from which she tries to unbind it? Or, and this point seems to be critical to the broader discussion of black intimate relations—does the history tethered to the term *freak* pre- and overdetermine how culture imagines promiscuity?

Howard and cultural producers like her eschew the idea that the assignation *freak* only degrades, and the related notion that such a subject position undermines racial uplift projects by calling into question the efficacy of respectability politics as a racial uplift strategy. Arguments which suggest that women who embrace their inner freak, or, who, according to some, do not repress it, do not understand the relationships that exist between the political and the sexual, between individual sex acts and broader public discourses, or between commitments to racial and gender progress and practices that ostensibly subvert those efforts, underestimate the degree to which the unleashing of the inner freak becomes an act of cultural revision that can reshape the very norms that have delimited the freak's abject status. This vantage point implores citizens to, as Darieck Scott explains in *Extravagant Abjection: Blackness, Power, and Sexuality in the African American Literary Imagination*, "examine those deleterious effects not for the purpose of demonstrating their injurious outcomes but to see how the effects, indeed the injuries themselves, may themselves be tools that can be used to model or serve as a means of political transformation."[29] Howard, as do her predecessors, reveals this point by embracing freak as an identity that is replete with possibility and potential, one that allows her to more expansively embrace the multiple "uses of the erotic," to signify on Audre Lorde;[30] their deployment of the term *freak* invites the opportunity to imagine a sexuality and racial uplift project that extends beyond the white patriarchal, black heteropatriarchal, and conservative black feminist gazes. *Destructive Desires* articulates how that reimagining of black intimate relations "can be used to model or serve as a means of political transformation" as it relates to solutions to black inequality in the age of neoliberalism, the decline of the welfare state, and the rise of personal responsibility discourses.

In *Funk the Erotic: Transaesthetics and Black Sexual Cultures*, L. H. Stallings charts the development of freaks and freakery within black erotic culture to demonstrate the ways black women cultural producers resisted the denigrating characterizations the terminology imbibes, and also to elucidate the productive images and desires that this embracement has engendered across historical epochs. According to Stallings, even from the nineteenth century, "black narratives were creating a literary tradition of funk that would deploy the affects of sexual pleasure and corporeal displays to situate the freak at the crossroads of resistance, spiritual transcendence, freedom, and art and entertainment."[31] Exemplifying a broader practice within American culture, African American cultural practices, including the slave narrative tradition, typically excluded this counter image of freaks, freakiness, and freakery because nonnormative sexuality and sexual expression partially explained and fully justified the terrorism white racism wrought on black bodies. By tracing this history to the nineteenth century, Stallings usefully disrupts the tendencies, even in black cultural studies and black feminist studies, to treat the freak as always already and *only* tied to a history and discourse of exploitation. She instead offers an earlier genealogy for examining the cultural revision the term *freak* performs.

Regarding the broader theoretical intervention her project makes, Stallings remarks, "I am calling this literary tradition *funky erotixxx* . . . what I theorize as sacredly profane sexuality. . . . Sacredly profane sexuality ritualizes and makes sacred what is libidinous and blasphemous in Western humanism so as to unseat and criticize the inherent imperialistic aims within its social mores and sexual morality. I assert that cultural producers in this particular genre have been proposing a notably different understanding of sexual and erotic labor because they are also exploring new sensoriums and ways of being that cannot align with Western traditions of humanism."[32] Stallings's formulation does not, as cultural critics rightfully aver against, detach the term *freak* from its historical meanings and in turn use that detachment as a way to recuperate it into a revisionist *radical* tradition. Instead, Stallings provides an alternative and valuable history that runs alongside, and, in tandem with, the way Western epistemologies typically have used the term. This intervention thus upends the narratives that have governed freaks, freakiness, and freakery in American culture, Western thought, and black feminist criticism. It also charts a way for black people and cultural producers to imagine their subjectivity and futurity beyond the hegemonic binaries that delimit their personal and political options.

Neither Stallings, I, nor other critics ignore or underestimate the perceived dangers of this critical move as the language of freakery perpetuated the exploitation of Saartjie Baartman in the eighteenth and early nineteenth centuries, made black women the experimental objects on which modern gynecology made its medical advances in the nineteenth century, and made black women's bodies subject to state censure and medical control through forced sterilization in the mid- to late twentieth century. Each of these examples underscores the politicized historical ways that freak and freakery underwrote black women's dehumanization, suffering, and shame. Yet to go outside, and not necessarily beyond, these paradigms means to investigate how the counternarrative works against the dominant one as an oppositional force. As important, counternarratives also envision and innovate ontological and epistemological alternatives about and for black intimate relations, black life, and black politics. While newly developing notions of blackness and black identity may be mindful of their historical contexts, they too will inaugurate new histories. Scholarly inquiry must also move beyond the binaries that attachments to historical abjection often reproduce. As Jennifer Nash persuasively argues, "black feminism has yet to turn to the productive elements of racial fantasies, particularly the relationship between fantasy and freedom for black female subjects for whom there are too few representations of black bodies in pleasure."[33] This reading of Howard engages the work of articulating the possibilities that (sexual) empowerment might provide for the ongoing pursuit of gendered-racial-sexual freedoms, as it limns out the imaginative potential of a less encumbered epistemology of black intimate relations and remixes destructive desires.

TRACK 4

HOWARD AND THE FREAK(Y) IMAGINATION

On her freshman album, *Do You Wanna Ride?* Howard's lead song, "Freak Like Me," snatches listeners into this alternative archive for "the freak" and primes the listener for the ensuing collection of musical production that rebels against racial politics that situate black women's cultural expression and lived experience within Western notions of womanhood and blackness predicated on the circumscription and denial of their humanity and sexuality. Howard's freak trope extends at least twenty years as she samples it on her most recent album, *The Resurrection* (2017), in a song titled "Nasty," which remixes several songs—"Freak Like Me," "Nasty Grind," and "T-Shirt and Panties." By sampling this collection of songs that gave and sustained Howard's popularity, "Nasty" reveals how "Freak Like Me" created its own entangled network that propelled cultural longings for representations of black women that extended beyond the politics of respectability. Whereas progressive sexual politics still imbibe normativity, Howard may in fact be calling forth a sexual politic that is even more radical in its eschewing of normativity. The placement of "Freak Like Me" as the first sample song on an album entitled *Resurrection* sutures the initial ways that the song and artist transformed cultural expectations for black women artists and their artistic production to its ongoing cultural and political significances. "Freak Like Me" continues to inspire transformation not only for the genre but also of the artist. By associating her resurrection with "Freak Like Me," the listener can acknowledge the historical importance of the song, recognize its continued role in shaping the art, and view the new possibilities it opens by moving from freakery to nastiness. The "Adina Howard: Life after 'Freak Like Me'" clearly did not mark the end of a career, and the *Resurrection* marks a maturation that provides an even more capacious notion of black women's possible expressions of sexuality across time.

"Freak Like Me" thus also functions as an entangled network between the artist, her persona, the music video, previous black women artists, and other songs by the artist. Beginning with this album, Howard has resisted the notion that her expression of a vivacious, sensual, agency-oriented sexuality contradicts other social locations—wife—and cultural practices—spirituality—that constitute her social identity. As a resonant example, at the end of "Adina Howard," the recording crew films Howard preparing a shrimp dish to evidence her culinary interests and plans to write cookbooks and perhaps open a restaurant. While viewers might interpret the ending of the episode as signaling that the older Howard has matured out of the freak paradigm, embraced heterosexual marriage, and resigned herself to the domestic space, that understanding would presuppose that Howard sees those spaces as mutually exclusive or otherwise contradictory. In other words, Howard's life choices cohere within a broader perspective of black women's agency, their abilities to make choices, even when those choices seem circumscribed.

Howard furthers the case against the fact that these choices contradict when she concludes the episode by noting that "I've taught you how to be a freak like me; now you can be a cook like me."[34] If viewers read these statements conjunctively, "cook like me" adds "freak like me;" the cook does not supplant the freak, and the sampling of "Freak Like Me" on "Nasty" contextualizes this claim. Although the freak may have matured (and consequently become more "freaky"), it remains a central component of the artist's and artistic persona's personalities. By celebrating this aspect of her identity, she refuses to let the erotic life of racism control her eroticism by tethering her to respectability politics. If, as Sharon Holland argues in *The Erotic Life of Racism*, "so often our 'racist' culture is held as separate and apart from our desiring selves," we must take exceptional care and decisive action to ensure that racism does not eclipse how and with whom we express those sexual desires. Black intimate relations' primary role in explaining and justifying black inequality must be foreclosed upon in order for black sexual subjects to thrive.[35]

The album's cover centralizes Howard's corporeality by juxtaposing her well-proportioned figure against a BMW, and this representation of Howard rejects black women's respectability politics while championing a self-possessed, vibrant, sensual, and sexualized black womanhood. Black high-heeled boots, black fish-net stockings, and black booty-shorts grab the viewer as readily as do the white tank top and white bra strap on her left shoulder. With pinkish red lipstick, Howard looks matter-of-factly at eye level at her audience. ADINA HOWARD appears across the shoulder but below her face. Her face and her *gaze* remain unobstructed. This positioning allows Howard to hone her "look," her "stare" between the second *a* in ADINA and the *h* in HOWARD. This placement suggests that Howard intentionally commands the gaze insofar as she sets the stage for how people see her, displays awareness of how her multiple viewing publics might see her, and, as importantly, reveals how she views her role in specifying the grounds on which the former occurs. Under her name, upside down, in gold lettering, the album's title, "Do You Wanna Ride?" read from left to right appears subordinated in font size to ADINA HOWARD. The announcement clarifies that this compact disc states as much about the person and persona as it does about the music. This reading of the front side of the album cover understands that on the rear cover Howard's eyes remain partially closed as she looks down, that her leather jacket exposes her red bra on the left side, and that her right hand appears to be situated inside her pants and presumably in her crotch. While the juxtaposition of the front and back might suggest a more pornographic gaze on the rear cover, or call into question the degree of agency the front presents, Nash and Miller-Young's articulation of black women's pleasure allows a reading that recognizes the messiness of Howard's sexual politics; it considers how a seemingly objectifying/pornographic gaze may not foreclose the possibility for agency and pleasure.

As revealing, the second album, *Fantasy Island*, displays a snake adorning Howard's otherwise naked body as she lies on a desert, and the third, *Second Coming*, captures a braless Howard caressing a studio mic and looking at the audience. The fourth album, *Private Show*, uncharacteristically features only a red rose. The fifth album, *Resurrection*, shows Howard's long black hair head-crowned on the front, while the back displays her with a white afro, sitting in a chair with her legs spread and black high heeled boots and a bikini type outfit. With the exception of *Private Show*, each cover presents an image of Howard that pushes the limits of respectability politics' representation of black womanhood, and perhaps even broaches what some might call the pornographic. This constellation of images calls into question respectability politics' destructive desires, raising questions about what is in fact destructive. It suggests that sexual pleasure can be destructive only if we accept respectability politics' destructive desires as totalizing for black women's expressions of pleasure, sex, and desire. *Do You Wanna Ride?* stands out among the covers because it most prominently features Howard's command of the gaze, a metonym for how she navigates rhythm and blues culture throughout her career.

Visual culture, as theorists have argued, remains an important site for making meaning, and black people's particular relationship to the ocular and the Western gaze—vis-à-vis chattel slavery—positions it as a vexed and yet provocative site for examining how black cultural production might reinscribe and reject ideas about blackness. In *Troubling Vision* Nicole Fleetwood foregrounds the myriad ways that the visual field historically shaped black people's subjectivity, circumscribed their political choices, and delimited the responsibilities of black cultural production to "speak for black enfranchisement." Visual differences help to racialize sexism and sexualize racism by supplying the required ocular evidence to *prove* black deviance. Black art in general, and black women's art in particular, as chapter I recalls, has functioned under this premise, thus binding black art to racial uplift; it must always already be mindful of and work against the racial gaze. Black art, and by discursive extension, black people, become responsible for solving white racism by proffering "positive" images of black people. Positive imagery logics invoke respectability politics to the degree that they correlate how women display themselves corresponds to their potential to attain enfranchisement. Despite this burden of representation for black people in general and women in particular, black women's artistic production has resisted complete objectification. If the visual field tends to reduce black women to (stereo)types and to characterize them as deviant, to what degree can we also "acknowledge black women's resistance of the persistence of visibility"?[36]

Fleetwood thinks through the possibility of finding supplemental areas to locate meaning outside the visual field's predetermined ideologies. By reclaiming the freak, "Freak Like Me" gives access to these possibilities as it points toward tropes that black women cultural producers draw upon to complicate the histories attached to them, to deconstruct destructive desires.

The reluctance of Howard's photographer during the photoshoot and critics' disapprobation of the cover acknowledge the broader cultural forces at play between history, race, gender, sexuality, and social class and the racialized-gendered gaze. The reluctance and reactions further call attention to the tension between an artist's desire to provide representations that challenge the norms and the industry's recognition that those images circulate in a broader marketplace. Without a doubt, the cover pushes boundaries, although we cannot reduce its staging simply to a sexual provocation that reinforces stereotypes. Foregrounding her artistic control, Howard insists the idea for the cover was "totally my idea," and notes that the photographer "was a bit nervous about taking the picture."[37] She stated that "as soon as I struck the pose in that bent over position, [s]he started having second thoughts."[38] Recalling the incident in our interview in March 2018, Howard emphasized "you could hear a pin drop."[39] Because popular culture and the visual realm constitute discourses on gender, race, and sexuality, the photographer's uneasiness might reveal how such an image invoked histories of black abjection, and how commercial gazes have commodified black sexuality for public consumption. Recall Mapplethorpe's photographs of black men's genitalia in the mid-twentieth century as a poignant example of how visual culture continued to underwrite black sexuality as deviant and spectacular. Much remains at stake, albeit differently, in the photographer and Howard's respective participations in this part of her production.

As this chapter acknowledges the critiques and criticism that critics, fans, and pundits alike level at Howard, it reads them within the constellation of entangled networks that more broadly orchestrate how her aesthetics and cultural production challenge the cultural longings that (re)produce destructive desires. As the chapter moves beyond *Do You Wanna Ride?* (1995), to *Fantasy Island* (1997), to *The Second Coming* (2004), to *Private Show* (2007), to *Resurrection* (2017), it foregrounds how Howard's cultural production offers new ways of thinking about possibilities for black intimate relations that in turn imagine solutions for black equality that advance equality. Even though Howard has acknowledged that at the *outset* she had not used her music "to make any kind of statement" or "champion a feminist cause,"[40] the music "makes several statements" and gains meaning in the context of an expanding black "feminist discourse" and a developing "black masculinity studies." Howard here bears similarity to a genre foremother, Millie Jackson, who, in her 2016 *Unsung*, notes that she would not consider herself a feminist or women's activist.[41] The refusal of both women to adopt this moniker becomes noteworthy because, despite their insistences that they are not "feminists," both recognize how their music and, in the case of Jackson in particular, the musical performances, pioneered the way for other black women to navigate uncharted territories. Jackson identifies herself, for example, as the first black woman to sing about oral sex on stage in her song "Feelin Bitchy." (Chapter 4 will consider Oprah Winfrey's feminist commitments, using the phrase "de facto feminism" to capture one whose politics seem feminist even though that person does not identify as a feminist).

Given how race and racism functioned in the second-wave white feminist movement, and how the legacies of racism extended to the historical moment at which the second wave becomes more institutionalized, it is not surprising that neither Jackson nor Howard espouses this classification.[42] Yet black feminism *perhaps* provides critical language and discourses to expand how to think about and understand black intimate relations in particular and black gender and sexuality more generally (chapter 2's analysis of Edmonds). These contexts differentiate between Jackson's and Howard's respective roles in shifting conversations about black intimate relations. Beyond the significant epistemological work black feminism performs, and consistent with its goal of conjoining theory and praxis, black feminist readings and analyses of Howard and Jackson provide a space to imagine black life for those already living outside and/or beyond respectability politics *as well as* those who might.

TRACK 5
IT'S MILLIE, JACKSON IF YOU'RE NASTY, PRECEDES HOWARD

In one of her first interviews in *People Magazine* in 1995, Howard closes the discussion by noting, "The Lord created sex. He wouldn't be blessing me if he had a problem with it"[43] and, in the process, called into question the belief systems of detractors who censured her "Freak Like Me." In essence, she leveled a multipronged attack on black religious dogma, black conservative gender roles, and the arbitrary division between the black public and private spheres, in addition to respectability politics. In our recent interview, she extended this critique of religion, for example, noting that she is "spiritual" because religion functions more as a "dictatorship," whereas spirituality does so as a "democracy." In spirituality, Howard explains, "you have the freedom to choose and be as you are, and there's no restraint."[44] Howard foregrounds how religion has unduly hampered black intimate relationship discourses to provide unhealthy and stigmatized perspectives about black sexuality that undermine the development of more progressive black sexual politics. Although none of these phenomena, from respectability politics to public and private sphere divisions, became particularly novel to black culture in the 1990s, the desire to expand and constrict gender roles during the 1990s magnifies their manifestation (chapter 2, track 4). Howard's pushing of boundaries within rhythm and blues culture thus emerges within a broader genealogy of black women cultural producers and performers who have illuminated the two-facedness of destructive desires and chipped away at black intimate relations' regulatory roles.

Tracing a genealogy of neosoul black women artists from the late 1990s and early 2000s back to 1970, for example, Mark Anthony Neal argues "the profane (and gleefully so) music of Millie Jackson, whose 'Phuck u Symphony' from her

FIGURE 3.3. Millie Jackson performs onstage at The Dominion Theatre on
February 22, 1984, in London, England.

live recording *Live and Uncensored* (1981) would make Jay Z blush," offers a perti-
nent precursor of black women artists engaging in similar cultural and ideological contestations.[45] Howard, too, acknowledges Jackson's influence, recalling
how Jackson "commanded your attention," how Jackson remained "unconventional," and how Howard "always gravitated toward the unconventional."[46]
Jackson's entire corpus of music foregrounded black women's sexual agency,
liberation, and innovation. While she does not employ the term *freak* to describe
her artistic production, the song's messages cohere with the *liberated* usage of
freak this book champions (figure 3.3). In her song "Give it Up" (1979), she rebukes
"all you siddity bitches who've been listening to Linda Gifford telling you 'not to
give it up,' what you gone do, let it dry rot?" She then instructs, "Give it up right
now, goddamn, give it up." Similar to Howard's 1995 remarks that begin this
paragraph, Jackson too constructs sexuality as a blessing to be expressed (and
not repressed), and advises listeners to use and enjoy sexuality lest it dissipates.

Howard's expression of sexuality fits within a cadre of black women cultural
producers who had pushed the envelope of black sexuality vis-à-vis music, and
she specifically acknowledges Betty Wright, who one critic notes "is also known
to be bold, direct, and to the point," as an important musical influence.[47] While
these black women's thematic, performative, and aesthetic choices shape Howard's understandings of black cultural longings, destructive desires, and black
intimate relations, the advent of the music video during the 1980s transformed
the distribution, circulation, reception, and consumption of this genre of music.
Music videos draw into focus some of the ways that the sonic and visual

mutually constitute meaning, and the attention that music videos receive from broadcasting networks, particularly as these organizations use the politically and culturally determined aesthetic criteria of decency and morality to determine what can be shown, reinforces the visual field's privileged status in making meaning. This emphasis on the visual field, the ocular distinctions upon which it relies, and the discursive ideologies of Western domination that made the visual field a deadly one for black life, trouble its persistence as a vehicle for meaning making.

While any cursory Google or YouTube search can produce video footage of Millie Jackson's 1982 live performance, the 1982 performance itself, which produced a live record (as distinct from a compact disc), did not widely broadcast into people's living rooms, nor were any of the songs themselves subsequently accompanied by a music video. The rise of the music video during the 1990s, however, changed the ways the musical entangled networks functioned and how consumers gained a multisensory listening experience that elevated the visual field's role in meaning-making in a genre that previously primarily emphasized the aural. Regardless of how *explicit* her lyrics were or how many sexual *innuendoes* or double entendres she invoked, Jackson avoided censure from any broadcasting agency, and her music circulated without a "PARENTAL ADVISORY: EXPLICIT CONTENT" label appended.[48] Although Howard's early music does not carry this scarlet letter of sorts either, the propriety notions that govern black intimate relations and women's expected behaviors ultimately thwart the expansion of Howard's brand. Whereas Black Entertainment Television (BET) had requested a less titillating version of the "Freak Like Me" music video, it outright refused to play her other hit on the album—"My Up and Down." As critic Langston Hertz points out, Howard's video had striking verisimilitude to "the Miami-bass music videos that BET loves to show weekdays at II A.M. on 'Video Vibrations,' even though they refused to play the video on any of their music programs."[49] What ideas about black womanhood prevent BET from broadcasting Howard's video and how do these ideas pair "positive image-making" with black enfranchisement? How does this pairing reinforce destructive desires and miscalculate the ability of individual behaviors to remove structural impediments to black equality?

Although BET at the time had "uncut" videos that played in the late evening hours and provided an outlet for more (sexually) explicit videos, "My Up and Down" instead found a home on Box. This pay-per-view channel, for the price of $2.50, provided consumers the opportunity to experience Howard's "Up and Down," despite any mainstream network's unwillingness to play the video in *normal* broadcasting programming. The concession to play the video for a price, however, also signals how black intimate relations become regulated by and tied to economies of exploitation. That is, unlike BET, Box, for the right price, forewent the need to enforce respectability politics and profited on the sexuality BET intended to censure. At the same time, BET impugned Howard's sexuality as the cause of and explanation for her lack of exposure on its mainstream broadcasting. This trend aligns with the broader tendency to name black intimate relations as the cause and explanation for black inequality insofar as the decision not to play the video on mainstream programming reflects the belief that it threatens racial progress by confirming black sexual excess and nonconformity.

The debate about Howard's sexuality also illuminates how race, sex, and aesthetics not only inform the reception of black women's cultural production but also how race and sex continue to define aesthetic value. Music director Gregg Diggs laments, "Because she's a decent singer with a solid voice, I think it would have been wiser on her part if she had focused more of her energy on her talent and not her sexuality."[50] First, Diggs's claim presupposes that Howard's sexuality undermines her talent when in fact her sexuality enhances it. Second, Diggs suggests that by deemphasizing the sexual and focusing more on the "voice" Howard's talent might have overcome the obstacles her career later faced. His critique of Howard thus turns attention to her behavior and away from a broader cultural trend that pits sexuality against talent. The broader issue is patriarchy, which she acknowledges when she notes men's desires to "control black women." Describing how men think of women's assertions of sexual self-definition and self-possession, Howard explains, "If I do visualize you like that [sexually], I want the power and the control to be able to do that. I don't want you to have any freedom to even express yourself because then I've lost control and power over you."[51] In a 1995 interview with Howard on the acclaimed BET series *Video Soul*, interviewer Donny Simpson asks Howard, "Would you like to be remembered as a sex symbol or a good musician?" Rejecting the bifurcation between talent and sexuality, between sex symbol and good musician, Howard retorts, "I'd like to be remembered as both." Metonymically, Howard's response turns attention to the two-faced nature of destructive desires by calling into question what is in fact destructive, the norm or the nonnorm. Further, it situates sexual politics as central to the politics of black cultural production and suggests that a broader black liberation project will require a liberated black sexual politic too.

TRACK 6
HOWARD'S FREAK (EN)COUNTERS R. KELLY'S "BUMP AND GRIND"

Howard's rise in the mid-1990s occurs alongside the emergence of the talented and controversial rhythm and blues artist Robert Kelly (R. Kelly), whose debut album *12 Play*, was released approximately fifteen months prior to the debut of Howard's *Do You Wanna Ride?* Kelly's position in rhythm and blues culture informs Howard's understanding of her own role, despite the differing ways that the broader culture evaluates their respective cultural productions. Howard herself notes that she "represent[s] females for males the way (sexy male r&b singer) R. Kelly does for the ladies," confirming again her sense that women should be able to express sexuality in explicit ways without relinquishing public support.[52] She also nods to Kelly's fame making "Bump and Grind" in her own "Do You Wanna Ride," where the persona proclaims, "I ain't tryna hurt nobody, I'll be your Ms. Bump and grind ya, I just want to do you tonight." The significance of Howard's comparison becomes more striking when we consider how, despite controversy after controversy about Kelly's relationship to black intimate relations, he has remained a pretty stable cultural force in rhythm and blues culture. Unlike Howard, no label shelved one of his albums nor did any industry executive blacklist him.

If his lyrical genius were not enough to compel listening publics' interests in Kelly's music, his portrayal of black women in his music videos (and music) and treatment of black women in his personal life have engendered a noteworthy amount of controversy, debate, and discussion about Kelly within and outside of black communities. From dating and possibly marrying the then underage and now deceased Aliyah (R&B artist), to urinating on an underage woman (R&B artist Sparkle's cousin) as part of a sexual interlude (video footage emerged), to singing increasingly sexualized lyrics and producing corresponding music videos that seemingly objectify (black) women, to most recently holding (underage) black women in a sex cult at his residence, Kelly's musical repertoire and life experiences reveal many of the broader questions that have and continue to animate black cultural studies.[53] What relationship do black artists have to producing art that improves black people's political positions, and how do Kelly's lyrics, music videos, and "personal" choices propel and/or repulse this aim? How do we interpret listening publics' behaviors, and when a consumer purchases Kelly's work (albums and concert tickets) does that person necessarily condone or endorse Kelly's behavior or politics outside of and/or within his professional work? Can we abhor Kelly's racialized sexual politics as they relate to black intimate relations and yet enjoy the sonic properties of his music? If we can divorce those two issues, what implications does such a cleaving have for the relationships between the aesthetics of black cultural production and the political work black cultural production performs (or is expected to perform)? These questions undergird Kelly's controversial position in black cultural production, and the answers—for him and black cultural producers and production more generally—return to the roles black intimate relations have in shoring up, propelling, and justifying black inequality.

In recent years publics have more vociferously condemned Kelly's personal choices, reflecting the degree to which the personal and political mutually constitute each other. For example, the #MuteRKelly movement has urged the cancellation of at least ten of Kelly's concerts between 2017 and 2018, and more recently the movement has encouraged the music industry to sever ties with Kelly.[54] Yet to much academic and popular scorn, intrigue, frustration, and debate, nonacademic discussions of Kelly's *12 Play* (and other works) rarely lambast him for performing *outside of* the scripts of heteronormative black masculinity.[55] To the contrary, his enactments of black masculinist scripts, through various machinations of what Mark Anthony Neal theorizes as the soul man tradition, propel him forward as a sexually vibrant, needs-fulfilling man.[56] His *12 Play*, when coupled with his "Bump and Grind," could make, as Evelyn Champagne King might put it, a woman's "love come down" again and again.[57] In the 1990s, Kelly serves a specific purpose; Kelly's image provided a much lauded (and desired) masculinization of a genre that, as Neal reminds, broader culture had disparaged as a bunch of love songs (rhythm and bullshit). Kelly then sutures the desire for a dominant, harder masculinity with the sensuality of love to engorge a putatively flaccid genre.

Whereas other groups and individuals were crooning sexually explicit songs and expressing vulnerability (Jodeci, H-Town, Jagged Edge, Silk), and Ginuwine released his signature song "Pony" in 1996, Kelly's image (which the album cover helps to shape) makes him more of a bad boy in the tradition of Bobby Brown, than his contemporary crooners (figure 3.4). Unlike Ginuwine, whose lyrics too were explicit, but who also presented as a "pretty boy," Kelly becomes read as a symbol of sexuality, masculinity, and virility in ways the public did not read his contemporaries. L. H. Stallings's insightful analysis of the deep investment in black masculinity that propels the fetishizing of hip-hop studies during the 1990s contextualizes how respectability politics shape the reception of *both* Howard and Kelly. By promoting a black masculinity that is masculine (enough) but not too hypersexualized and a black femininity that is feminine (enough) but not too hypersexualized, respectability politics positions black men and black women in their *right* and socially acceptable places.

More recently, black popular culture and black music studies have critiqued Kelly for his reinforcement of black heteronormativity and masculine sexual prowess at the expense of *vulnerable* black women—in both his personal and his professional lives. Kelly is such a vexed figure in the cultural imagination that Mark Anthony Neal describes the difficulty of examining a "person who clearly offended [his] sensibilities as a feminist, as a father of two daughters, and ultimately as a human being."[58] But Neal ultimately chooses to examine Kelly in *Looking for Leroy: Illegible Black Masculinities* because Kelly's 2004 "*Trapped in the Closet* offers an exhumation of that tradition and its deep relationship to everyday black life—the proverbial soul closet, if you will—that helps contextualize Kelly's role as witness to and chronicler of black pathology and narratives of black respectability."[59] Whereas Neal rightfully situates Kelly and his work within broader discourses about black intimate relations, this chapter expands the historical scope to suggest that since Kelly became a staple within rhythm and blues culture in the 1990s black intimate relations and respectability politics have shaped discourses from and about him.

Although Kelly initially offered a more masculine masculinity to the rhythm and blues genre, he eventually became an exemplar of the problems of black masculine perversion that, in sociological discourses, threatened the formation of healthy black families, relationships, and communities. My reading of Bobby Brown's image relative to Whitney Houston's in chapter 4 echoes this claim too as it considers how racialization and sexualization mutually constitute each other. In many ways, well before his 2004 debut of *Trapped in the Closet*, Kelly's work and life fit in a broader tradition that, in the words of Jeffrey McCune, "illuminates the centrality and complexity of black sexual politics—particularly unmasking the creative possibilities and dangers that emerge at the site of sexual and gender regulation."[60] Kelly's sexual danger excites and intrigues as black sexuality's hypervisibility, vis-à-vis Snorton's "glass closet," historically has operated and continues to do so. At stake is how a figure like Kelly also

FIGURE 3.4. Ginuwine (Elgin Lumpkin Jr.) performs at the Motown Cafe in Las Vegas, Nevada, on Wednesday, June 25, 1997, and *Showtime* aired the performance live to promote pay-per-view's telecast of the Mike Tyson rematch against Evander Holyfield.

complements our understanding of destructive desires and what that revelation clarifies about black sexual politics.

This point goes beyond simply elucidating the double standard about the range of artistic expressions available to black men and black women, and situating that hypocrisy about sexual expressions within the broader patterns of black heteropatriarchy's enactment and enforcement. Instead, it compels a consideration of how the desire for putatively normative black masculine scripts works against the very premise on which black intimate relations' role in ameliorating black inequality operates. When the popular imagination neglects to consider Kelly *out of place* for enacting masculine scripts that historically have justified the extrajudicial killings and lynching of black men, one can wonder if the tacit championing of this role more perniciously recognizes a desire and plan to retrench black inequality. To champion it, while simultaneously censuring Howard because her ways of displaying womanhood position her *out of place* and as a threat to black advancement, advances an ideological, discursive, and philosophical dilemma that illuminates the illogic of respectability politics as a strategy and black intimate relations as primary sites for alleviating black suffering.

The celebration of Kelly's sexuality and simultaneous circumscription of Howard's perplexingly turn attention to how arguments that position black intimate relations as the cause of and solution to black inequality expose their own inconsistencies and faulty premises. When Howard comments to one interviewer that "if the guys can present sex in x terms, so can the woman," she draws attention to two persistent and relevant trends that inform the different ways that the public responds to her and Kelly; first, by turning attention to the history of black men's objectification of black women in black men's cultural production, she also calls into question what forms of cultural revision work against and outside of these parameters. To what degree does a song that champions women's sexual prowess and treats men *primarily* as objects of sexual satisfaction falsely attempt to undermine patriarchy by miscalculating the potential of the subject–object inversion? Second, if history and culture bind historical actors in predetermined ways such that historical actors' actions can be understood only or primarily through these predetermined formulas, what then is the political import of nonabstractionist aesthetics?

TRACK 7

HOWARD REMIXES THE FREAK

In Howard's late twentieth-century appropriation of the freak trope, listeners observe a usage of freak, freakery, and freakiness that continues to resist a history of abjection. In order for black subjectivities to move outside the strictures of representation, communities must concede that the argument that the album cover, songs, and music videos *primarily or only* hypersexualize black women by reinforcing the jezebel, sapphire, and other stereotypes has run its course. This turn to destructive desires' "other face" invites us to consider what it means for a black woman to be a freak in the United States in the late twentieth and early twenty-first centuries. How, for example, does Howard's art use the term *freak*, and what does her usage help us to envision about black women's personal and political desires beyond abjection? *Freak* here captures both the specific and implicit uses of the term to consider how its appropriations actually underscore the ways publics read her and her overall cultural production. I insist Howard and her art occasion a more robust discussion for the recuperative possibilities this term allows by showing very simply (and yet in a complicated way) that the freak appears aberrant only in a Western culture in which black women exist under an imperialistic Western gaze. In other words, on the one hand, her work, in complex ways, draws upon discourses and ideas—agency, pleasure, resistance, fulfillment—that underwrite Americanness. On the other, as a black woman, an object, she *is not supposed* to possess those tropes. The forthcoming analysis of one of Howard's performances of her signature freaky songs, "Nasty Grind," in Long Beach, California, in 2014 ponders ways she helps us to (re)conceptualize black intimate relations' possibilities by way of the freak trope.

From Saidiya Hartman's *Scenes of Subjection: Terror, Slavery, and Self-Making in Nineteenth-Century America* to Alexander Weheliye's *Habeas Viscus: Racializing Assemblages, Biopolitics, and Black Feminist Theories of the Human*, scholarship in African American studies has compelled scholars to offer more nuanced deployments of terms such as *agency*, *resistance*, *radical*, and *revolutionary* when discussing how black people historically have *responded to* disenfranchisement. Several concerns animate this admonishment, including a deep skepticism toward a presentism that obscures a historically, contextualized understanding of the terms. As Weheliye explains, "As modes of analyzing and imagining the practices of the oppressed in the face of extreme violence—although this is also applicable more broadly—resistance and agency assume full, self-present, and coherent subjects working against something or someone. Which is not to say that agency and resistance are completely irrelevant in this context, just that we might come to a more layered and improvisatory understanding of extreme subjection if we do not decide in advance what forms its disfigurations should take on."[61] Weheliye presupposes that oppression denies the possibility for a full, self-present, coherent subjectivity to form. Yet his admonition not to take for granted, *in any circumstance*, what *agency* should look like deserves consideration, particularly as we imagine how to locate it within destructive desires' other face. A predetermined point of view diminishes the possibility of identifying and locating agency (and resistance and revolutionary and/or radical politics) in unspoken, unfamiliar, unconventional, and unconceived of spaces.

This claim recognizes the ideological and discursive violence(s) that slavery leveled toward black women and their bodies and how this history informs contemporary production and reception contexts. In my interview with Howard, we discuss how slavery still informs how black people view themselves, and Howard insists: "I think even though slavery doesn't exist, so to speak, anymore, at least the outright, blatant, that history speaks about, I think we're still in the mindset of white people are looking. Master's looking and we have to be on our best behavior. And part of being on our best behavior is to do what they've trained us to do. We still have to be on our best behavior because we don't want them thinking we're this way, we don't want them thinking that we're that way and we're going to prove to them that we're good black folk."[62] From Howard's perspective, neither black behaviors nor the use of them to gain acceptance in American society will alone solve the more entrenched issue of antiblack racism. As Weheliye usefully encourages energetic thinking about the disfigurations (i.e., manifestations) resistance and agency take within specific contexts, the inability of behaviors to solve black inequality must contextualize Howard's attempts at cultural revision. This push in the late twentieth and early twenty-first centuries cautions against binary thinking that presumes she must either refute racially charged images—such as the jezebel—or be complicit in reinscribing them. *Destructive Desires* rejects claims that reinforce binary thinking, ignore the complexity of agency and representation, and miss the opportunity to investigate the cultural work performances such as Howard's render.

Images of hypersexualized *attractive* black women (jezebel) and those of desexualized *unattractive* black women (mammy) constitute two sides of the same coin insofar as both, albeit differently, function as controlling images that designate black women as nonnormative, limit black women's development of an empowered subjectivity, reinforce class distinctions as a way to inhibit black women's unification, and obfuscate the roles social institutions play in reproducing inequality. Controlling images, as Patricia Hill Collins notes, "are designed to make racism, sexism, poverty, and other forms of social injustice to appear to be natural, normal, and inevitable parts of everyday life."[63] This point usefully reminds us that the images become the scapegoat for inequality and unnerves the common argument that images cause it. For Collins, because they "are key in maintaining intersecting oppressions," controlling images continuously exercise their circle of domination, providing little, if any, possibility for transformation.[64] This practice becomes more salient as post–civil rights era explanations for black inequality will call upon black behaviors to explain it and ignore the persistence of structural racism.

In *Black Sexual Politics: African Americans, Gender, and the New Racism*, Collins further posits that popular culture, including music and music videos, remains an important site at which a complex negotiation transpires between controlling images and image control, between "representations of black women who are sexually liberated and those who are sexual objects."[65] In American society, which always already positions black women as sexual objects, and black intimate relations as the primary site for explaining and justifying black inequality, what possibilities exist for sexual liberation, and what contours do sexual liberation assume? *Destructive Desires*, as a book and as a concept, points to the need to probe these questions further to offer more complex nodules for thinking about black politics and black sexual politics outside of traditional black intimate relations discourses. However problematically, Shayne Lee's *Erotic Revolutionaries: Black Women, Sexuality, and Popular Culture* underscores the importance of these issues even as it narrows its theoretical sources outside the robust archive of black feminist thinking.[66] In other words, how do our critical faculties allow us to identify this liberation, and, when our conceptual maps become occluded, do our imaginative capacities enable us to envision sexual liberation beyond respectability politics?

TRACK 8
PERFORMANCE, POLITICS, AND A PATH FORWARD FROM HOWARD

Howard's reimagining of the possibilities for black intimate relations emerges not only in the entangled networks that her songs, album covers, interviews, and relationships with other cultural institutions make, but also instructively through her live performances (figure 3.5). A turn to this mode of cultural expressivity reveals how Howard's call and response conversations with her audiences emphasize her attempt to influence the cultural longings and destructive desires they have for and about black intimate relations. In 2014, at the Black Repertory Group Theater in Berkeley, California, Howard sings one of her signature songs, "Nasty Grind," from her third album, *The Second Coming* (2007). Prior to singing, Howard invites a willing participant to join her on the stage. Straddling him, she gyrates up and down and provides an aesthetic visualization that also self-consciously reveals a few ways this performance rethinks perspectives toward, and shifts away from, Western paradigms about monogamy, decency (racialized and gendered), spirituality, and/or religiosity.

The visualization is important because of the role the visual field has had in shaping black subjectivity, and because its aesthetics help to imagine new possibilities. In other words, as Soyica Colbert skillfully argues in *Black Movements: Performance and Cultural Politics*, "aesthetics' ability to engage with the impossible and unreasonable also allows the artist to illuminate the cross-purposes of desire and outcomes that perpetuate, crystallize, and transform racial categories."[67] When Howard's performance rejects the notion that the institution of marriage revokes her ability to enact eroticism and sensuality outside the confines of her monogamous marriage, she engages in the process of redefining and thereby "transforming [gendered] racial categories." For example, the institution of marriage fails to thwart Howard's expressions of sexuality insofar as she displays and embraces a black sexuality that thrives outside compulsory heterosexuality and black respectability politics' discourses. By intentionally weaving these perspectives into her performances, she also transforms how black women's subjectivity becomes understood.

While Howard recognizes the ways that the norms governing her own marriage diverge from those society more generally ascribes to black heterosexual marriages, she too understands that a broader discursive context remains in play and negotiates her performances to engage it. When Howard calls for audience participation, she explains, "I need a single man. I can't be dealing with somebody attached to stuff. You know. We don't need no women up in here acting foolish around these parts. You know. . . . This is why I love my job because I am married and can take advantage of somebody's son and not get in trouble because

FIGURE 3.5. Adina Howard wearing a white afro, dressed as she appears on the back cover of her 2017 album, *Resurrection*. Photo courtesy of Adina Howard.

my husband already knows how the show goes down."[68] Howard's observations call to mind the two-decade history both her music and her music persona have had in refashioning cultural expectations. In a society where interpersonal sexual relationships (i.e., marriage or other forms of heterosexual monogamous couplings) remap exploitative property relations (e.g., chattel slavery and the possessiveness of marriage) that have been detrimental to sociopolitical advancement, the call for single men draws attention to the possessive investment in couplings. By chiding the *foolish* women for subscribing to and being subscribed by monogamy's possessiveness, Howard gestures toward the need to rework property relations in interpersonal relationships. This reworking very much moves against how the State has reconstructed familial property relations and the role of the welfare state since Reconstruction (recall discussion of Ferguson's *Aberrations in Black* in chapter 1).

Through her playfulness, as her phrase "take advantage of" evidences, as well as her actions on the stage (she smiles, flirts, titillates, and teases), Howard rejects society's tendencies to restrict how married women—even as performers— express their sexuality. Her performance thus works to, in the words of Colbert, "evade the dehumanizing mandate of the black female as prototype for excessive embodiment."[69] She uses a sexualized body but rejects excess as problematic, thus exposing again the two-facedness of destructive desires. When her prefatory comments juxtapose herself with a husband who understands the show, she expands the ways people in relationships express sexuality within and outside of the dyad. This juxtaposition occurs against the foolish women, who become foolish precisely because of their investment in normative understandings of black intimate relations. Howard's admonition offers a model of patriarchal coupling that resists the possessive investment in couplings that dehumanizes black women by treating them as property. This possessive investment in couplings, among other injuries, thwarts the possibility for complex expressions of sexuality outside and within marriages because the logics that restrict black intimate relations to respectability politics, compulsive heterosexuality, and compulsive monogamy, also restrict its expression within these relationships too; property relations also reinforce the economic relationships central to neoliberal understandings of the family.

Overall, Howard's vision of black intimate relations pushes back against the ways that religious dogma, gender roles, gender essentialism, and histories of abjection bind contemporary black subjects, limiting their imaginations and lived experiences. If, as chapter 2 has suggested, an interrelationship between black men and black women's roles exists in black intimate relationship discourses, a shift for black women can instigate one for black men, within and outside of heterosexual relationships. If sexual pleasure and expanded notions of healthy sexual expression constitute black freedom dreams, this expanded vision ideally will turn on their head solutions to black inequality that center black intimate relations as *the solution* to black inequality. Although this book rejects black intimate relations' explanatory force, it concedes that as long as it remains central to public policy and discourses, new imaginings of black

intimate relations can "talk back" to the discourses and expand their capacities
to imagine actual solutions.

Artists such as Howard, as do Mtume and Cameo, provide alternative possibilities for black intimate relations that elucidate the pitfalls of respectability
politics, formulate new models for black intimate relationships, find solutions
to black inequality that extend beyond the marriage panacea thesis, and imagine possibilities under which black sexualized beings can thrive despite the vicissitudes of antiblack racism. As chapter 4 examines Whitney Houston, it will
further explore how post–civil rights era longing for postracialism produce
destructive desires and examine how Houston's persona, life, and career call for
more robust understandings of black life, black sexuality, and black politics to
ameliorate black inequality.

4

"Didn't We Almost Have It All?"

Reading Whitney Houston

I found out what I've been missing / Always on the run / I've been looking
for someone / Now that you're here like you've been before / And you
know just what I need / It took some time for me to see.

> —Whitney Houston, *Whitney Houston*, "You Give Good Love"

So many times that I want to just pick up the phone / And tell you, ooh
baby, baby I miss your love / And so I ain't holding back no more / Your
girl is coming home / And I want you to love me like I never left.

> —Whitney Houston and Akon, *I Look to You*, "Like I Never Left"

A few stolen moments is all that we share / You've got your family and
they need you there / Though I've tried to resist being last on your list /
But no other man's gonna do / So I'm saving all my love for you.

> —Whitney Houston, *Whitney Houston*, "Saving All My Love"

TRACK 1

"WHERE DO BROKEN HEARTS GO": INTRODUCTION AND BACKGROUND

In November 2011, *Access Hollywood*'s Shaun Robinson interviewed Whitney
Houston on the set of *Sparkle*, a twenty-first-century remake of the 1976 movie
that bears the same name, and traces a young black woman's pursuit of a music
career, despite her mother's misgivings, consternation, and admonitions. Prior
to *Sparkle* (2012), *The Preacher's Wife* (1996) had been the last major motion film
in which Houston had starred. For Houston, much had changed professionally
and personally within those sixteen years. In her return to acting, Houston
espoused a persona whom she had yet to play—a black mother whose eclipsed
opportunities, coupled with her religious beliefs and dogma, occlude her ability
to support her daughter's aspirations to become a singer. Arguably, the persona
(Emma) bears a striking resemblance to Houston's own mother, Cissy, whose
music career trailed Houston's, and whose religious austerity seemingly shaped
the destructive desires that animated Houston's life. The propensity to read

Houston's role in *Sparkle* biographically when she died gives this resonance more force. As suggestively, the foregrounding of motherhood gains greater significance when we consider the broader discourse in which black motherhood—as matriarch, mammy, or jezebel—supposedly threatens or otherwise hampers the development of children's opportunities. In the case of Houston, the maternal influence also becomes a crucial lens through which to examine Houston's own attitudes about marriage, motherhood, gender roles, sexuality, and black intimate relations.

Returning to the epigraphs that frame this chapter, we might ask, for example, how do the unfulfilled desires that "Saving All My Love" intimates gesture toward Houston's inability to fulfill her own sexual desires? And how does that denial inform the pathos with which she sings? On the one hand, the taboo subject of the song is an extramarital affair, as in the man's family "need[s] you there" thus rendering the persona only "a few stolen moments." On the other, does the song also force listening publics to consider how nonnormative familial configurations and destructive desires become deferred? Related, what does it mean (and feel like) to have someone give good love and never have public discourses recognize that love? How does this experience intensify or agonize, particularly when one's life, like Houston's, becomes fixed in public domains? And finally, in "Like I never left," how might we interpret "I am holding back no more," particularly as the song charts the persona's previous inability, but now willingness, to claim a love or express formerly concealed desire? While the film and song lyrics call attention to performances Houston rendered, they also reveal and construct sets of destructive desires. The juxtaposition of the movie and lyrics turns attention to how notions of family influence, and, further manufacture, destructive desires throughout Houston's life and career.

In the interview, Robinson discussed with Houston her roles in and with *Sparkle*, how Houston's own life has shaped those roles, Houston's attitudes about Jordin Sparks's talents, and Houston's own personal evolution. Although Robinson's graciousness prevented her from explicitly referencing Houston's public and ongoing challenges with drug addiction, it remained a subtext of the interview. At the beginning of the interview, Robinson beams "you look fantastic," drawing attention to both Houston's physical features and her forthright and pleasant demeanor. After Houston thanks her, Robinson adds, "you feel that too." Reserved in posture, Houston nonetheless radiates, "I do. I'm older. I'm matured."[1] This exchange points toward the myriad of controversies that had beleaguered Houston for the latter half of her career and extended well beyond the pleasantries of an interviewer flattering an interviewee. The *fantastic* look alludes to, and contrasts with, the emaciated image of Houston that, following her 2001 tribute to Michael Jackson, had heightened rumors, suppositions, and speculations that Houston indeed had a drug addiction and faced an imminent death.[2]

In a more metaphorical sense, the *fantastic* look suggested that Houston, contrary to popular belief, had achieved sobriety, and that, despite her recent reentrances into rehab, she had (finally) overcome what she, in her 2002 infamous interview with Diane Sawyer, referred to as her biggest devil.[3] Robinson underscored the public's investment in Houston's recovery, relaying to Houston a friend's sense of communal support: "I want Whitney to know she's got so many people rooting for her." Asking Houston if she knew that, Robinson's ebullience reflected a cultural longing for Houston to live and thrive because, for reasons that this chapter examines, Houston had become a cultural icon; Houston and her persona became sites of contestation and debate as conversations about black intimate relations, black politics, and black cultural expression depended on, and demanded much from, them. Those debates, demands, and dependencies fixed Houston within paradigms about black intimate relations (respectability politics) that, from the beginning of her career in 1983 until her death in 2012, thwarted her ability to thrive, and, arguably, may have informed her drug dependencies.

Approximately three months after Robinson's interview, on February 11, 2012, the people who had rooted for Houston began to mourn her death. At 3:55 P.M. PST, paramedics had pronounced Houston dead at the Beverly Hills Hilton in Los Angeles, California; a personal assistant had found her unconscious, submerged in scalding hot water approximately thirty minutes prior. While accidental drowning, as a consequence of cocaine use and atherosclerosis, ultimately emerged as the cause of death, speculation that her death involved drugs, illegal or prescription, emerged immediately.[4] That reputable newspapers, including the *New York Times* and *Los Angeles Times*, reported allegations that police and paramedics found a host of prescription drugs in Houston's hotel room, in addition to a spoon with crystal-like particles, and a white powdery substance, only fueled a sense that Houston had at last succumbed to her drug addiction. In the final week leading up to her death, several pieces of information emerged that painted the picture of an erratic Houston: (1) pictures surfaced of Houston leaving a night club with a disheveled look and blood running down her leg, (2) video footage showed her disrupting a live interview with Clive Davis and Monica and Brandy, (3) video footage revealed Houston uninvitedly joining a stage to perform an impromptu duet with Kelly Price, and (4) allegations circulated that she vociferously complained about diluted alcohol beverages at the bar inside the Beverly Hilton. For some, her behavior in this week alone confirmed that at last she had relapsed into drug use, and effectually killed the rest of her body as she had already done to her voice.[5]

Although the final autopsy had concluded that Houston's toxicology reports revealed cocaine and marijuana alongside other prescribed drugs, Los Angeles Chief Coroner Craig Harvey could not say *definitively* what had happened in Houston's final moments. Noting that Houston had not ingested a lethal dose of cocaine, Harvey proposed one of two scenarios: (1) cocaine had intoxicated Houston to the point of unconsciousness, thus causing her to collapse into the bathtub, where she drowned; (2) cocaine ingestion produced some type of heart episode (he does not say definitively whether it was a heart attack or arrhythmia) that incapacitated Houston and thus led to her drowning.[6] Either scenario leaves uncertainty as Harvey's conclusions still invite questions, making Houston, even after death, the subject of scrutiny and fascination. What actually happened to Houston on the afternoon of Saturday, February 12, 2012? And, had she not fallen into that bathtub, might she still be alive? Punctuating this uncertainty, pundits and other medical experts (Dr. Drew) disputed Harvey's conclusion that prescription drugs had not *contributed* to Houston's death.[7] Still, others would insist that the factors eventuating Houston's death began well before the afternoon of February 12, 2012. All of these debates attest to the cultural significance of Houston for any discussion about blackness, black intimate relations, destructive desires, and personal responsibility in the post–civil rights era.

This chapter identifies four generic "incidents" in Houston's life that form core discursive contexts, and uses them to think through the broader implications that Houston and those contexts have for helping us to understand post–civil rights era cultural longings about blackness, black aesthetics, and black women's sexuality. These roles include the ingénue-turned-superstar, the wife, the reality television spectacle, and the repentant confessor, each of which functions coextensively to understand the changing same politics of race, gender, sexuality, and class in the post–civil rights era. Whereas chapter 3's examination of Adina Howard foregrounds black feminist thinking to limn out the sexualized and gendered dimensions of racism in black women's cultural production and lived experiences, this chapter assumes those arguments to accentuate the changing dimensions of racism. It also recognizes the gendered and sexualized aspects of these morphing racial dynamics. An analysis of Arista's roles in molding Houston's image, the booing she experiences at the NAACP image awards (1989), her marriage to and divorce from Bobby Brown, her *Primetime* interview with Dianne Sawyer (2002), her participation in *Being Bobby Brown* (2005), her interview on the *Oprah Winfrey Show* (2009), and her death (2012) uncovers a more ubiquitous desire to regulate black intimate relations that originates within her family and career mentors. This desire to discipline extends into the public, where the image of Houston as American princess satisfies and repulses post–civil rights era aspirations for inclusion and normativity. Representatively, this animating force to control black intimate relations for Houston metonymically demonstrates a broader tendency to regulate black women's sexuality, including the mechanisms through which this disciplining occurs; how ideas about blackness and black aesthetics operate through gendered and sexualized discourses that gain particular meaning in the post–civil rights era; how discourses about personal responsibility undermine notions of community and communal accountability and support: how the effects of neoliberalism's restructuring of economies devastate black thriving; and how the general fascination with her exceptionally public struggles reveals a more pervasive desire and tendency to pathologize blackness. By reading Houston as both a unique and representative figure, I defamiliarize her celebrity-turned-drug-addict-gone-awry narrative to instead situate her iconography as interconnected to quotidian ideas about black people, black life, black politics, and black aspirations.

The risk of reading Houston as celebrity-turned-drug-addict returns us to behavioral explanations of black inequality, black failure, and black abjection that pin disparities for black individuals and communities on black people's behaviors, shortcomings, and poverties. Yet such explanations miss not only the ways that structural inequalities circumscribe behavior and choice but, as is the case for Houston, how entangled networks, including the music industry in particular, promote and sustain cultural longings that exploit even while bestowing material benefits. Undoubtedly, Houston has amassed a fortune, but Arista capitalizes on her labor, her image, and her brand—at her expense. Respectability politics shape how Arista (and Clive Davis in particular) markets Houston as a crossover artist. Black aesthetics and black listening publics' sense of soul, or essential blackness, factor into the infamous booing, as much as white desire for palatable blackness shapes Davis's portrayal of Houston. The obsession with Houston's personal life, including the desire to know the "true" identity of her *friend* Robyn Crawford, alongside the accusations that she did not perform an authentic blackness, inform, if not propel, Houston's decision to marry Bobby Brown, the so-called bad boy of rhythm and blues music/New Jack Swing. While this chapter examines other related concerns, it also emphasizes the multiple ways each of these factors stitches a larger fabric to which black intimate relations become increasingly tethered. In many respects, as it relates to the desire to regulate black women's sexuality vis-à-vis black intimate relations, Whitney Houston and Adina Howard become two sides of the same coin. Through this analysis, *Destructive Desires* continues to point toward more complex notions of black family, black familial configurations, and solutions to black inequality that move beyond the heteronormative nuclear family model.

TRACK 2
"ONE MOMENT IN TIME": THE BEGINNING OF A CAREER
AND POSTRACIAL DESIRES

Given the longevity of Houston's career, the significance of her role as a crossover artist, and the examinations of gender and sexuality in black popular culture and black women's cultural production, the paucity of scholarship that examines Houston remains curious. For example, in Daphne Brooks's "All That You Can't Leave Behind: Black Female Soul Singing and the Politics of Surrogation in the Age of Catastrophe," Brooks examines how Beyoncé Knowles's and Mary J. Blige's respective cultural productions respond to black women's sociopolitical marginalization and become sites to reimagine black women's subjectivities. Brooks insists that such an examination might reveal how "each artist's work creates a particular kind of black feminist surrogation, that is, an embodied cultural act that articulates black women's distinct form of palpable sociopolitical loss and grief" and how they "reinvent the politics of black female hypervisibility in the American cultural imaginary."[8] In tracing various musical, sonic, and cultural genealogies for Knowles in particular, Brooks references Houston's entangled networks (*Waiting to Exhale* and "It's Not Right But Okay"), yet does not identify Houston in the same thematic or sonic trajectory as Knowles.

Yet Houston becomes an ur-text for this hyperinvisibility that black women have, and in many respects, perhaps also articulates a sociopolitical loss around ideas of race, individuality, and intimacy that heighten perceived dangerous sexual and gender nonconformity in the post–civil rights era. While such a focus might have extended the purview of Brooks's argument, particularly as she focuses on how to read Knowles in light of Hurricane Katrina, her broader contention of Knowles's significance instructs: "her still vaulting iconicity represent[s] the extent to which the social, political, and cultural desires of R&B fans—especially female R&B music fans—still remain largely overlooked and under-theorized in popular music studies."[9] Brooks also rightfully concludes that "few critics have analyzed the ways that both female R&B performers and the fans who love them are actively and consistently producing a public record of cultural expressions that affirms the intersecting personal and political questions and concerns of women of color in the early twenty-first century."[10] Although scholarly attention has focused more on Knowles than Houston, Brooks's argument articulates the mutually constitutive relationship between the artists and fans, recognizing the potential for meaning making and the reimagining of politics as a shared site for both artists and fans (see the introduction's discussion of TV One's *Unsung* and *R&B Divas*). Moreover, Brooks's call for more scholarship of twenty-first-century black women's cultural production necessarily demands an interrogation of pre-twenty-first-century black women artists to the extent that tradition and artistic influence shape current cultural products. Accordingly, the absence of Houston from these conversations becomes increasingly peculiar, and the need to correct becomes more urgent (figure 4.1).

The release of *Whitney Houston* (1985) inaugurated Houston's music career, launched her into the celebrity limelight, and laid the foundation upon which she would earn a series of "firsts." From possessing the most-consecutive number of number one singles on the billboard charts, to selling the most albums of any woman in the late twentieth century, Houston without a doubt shattered expectations for women, African Americans, and African American women.[11] As Houston has revealed, she never imagined achieving the artistic success she did. Arista echoes this sentiment, noting that it too had expected *Whitney Houston* to sell approximately 300,000 units and not the twenty-two million that it did.[12] In breaking these barriers, Houston *proved* the Reagan era sense that hard work and personal responsibility allowed African Americans to compete and succeed within a post–civil rights era neoliberal marketplace. Although other record labels had competed for Houston's talent, in the end, Davis triumphed, and Arista remained the only label on which she produced music. More generous perspectives characterize Davis as a mentor and musical father who guided Houston through the music business, orchestrating her career moves to her benefit. Less generous views describe Davis as a Svengali, a term Houston herself had used, to connote Davis's manipulative and exploitative roles. Undoubtedly complicated, Davis's role, which cultural longings and entangled networks had driven, likely evinced each of these perspectives.

FIGURE 4.1. Whitney Houston poses backstage with her seven awards at the 21st annual American Music Awards in Los Angeles, California, February 7, 1994. Houston won favorite female artist, pop/rock; favorite female artist, soul/rhythm and blues; favorite single, "I Will Always Love You," soul/rhythm and blues; and the Award of Merit. The soundtrack for *The Bodyguard* won favorite album in the categories of pop/rock, soul/rhythm and blues, and adult contemporary.

Although Davis ultimately inked a deal with Houston in 1983, Arista kept Houston in the studio for almost two full years before releasing *Whitney Houston*, and did so to cultivate a racialized image of Houston that diminished the perceived threat of her unrefined race, class, and sexuality. Explanations differ as to why Houston had this two-year gap, yet financial, political, and cultural factors demanded that Davis mold Houston into a "respectable" black lady. As chapter 3 accentuates, the presumed mutual exclusivity of blackness and ladyhood meant the process of molding Houston's ladyhood also meant diminishing her blackness. Laden into this thinking are ideas about middle-class identity and heterosexual couplings. In other words, respectable ladyhood also conjures ideas about respectability politics more generally. Introducing her on the Merv Griffin show in 1983, where Houston sang "Home," Davis describes Houston as a woman who is "elegant, who's sensuous, who's innocent, and who's got an incredible range of talent . . . she's a beautiful girl and her poise doesn't hurt . . . but it's her natural charm. Either you've got it or you don't."[13]

To describe Houston's charm as "natural" ignores the degree to which, by all accounts, Davis laboriously constructs Houston's *public* persona in an attempt to write her into post–civil rights and post-riot era narratives of assimilation and acculturation.[14] Indeed, the perfection of talent, the shoring up of raw skills, reasonably explains the two-year gap. Yet the need to respond to perceived cultural tastes, which pecuniary interests inflect, creates an entangled network that also animates the *construction* of Houston as "innocent," "beautiful," and "elegant" that he inaugurates in 1983. Whereas Davis declares "either you've got it or you don't," his molding of Houston reveals that an individual and/or a record label can manufacture "it"; Davis's naturalization thus calls to mind the fictions of race that reinforce both essentialist notions and social construction ones simultaneously. It is well known that although she was the first black woman to appear on the cover of *Seventeen*, she preferred jeans and sneakers to dresses and heels. Although Houston's family had moved from Newark to a middle-class neighborhood in East Orange, New Jersey, following the 1967 riots, Houston's origins from Newark (the hood) consistently enter her biographical narrative to contextualize Houston's own tastes and behaviors as "naturally" different than those her performances required her to adopt. Whereas Houston could perform respectability politics, she primarily was, in the lyrics of one of L.L. Cool J's well-enjoyed songs, "an around the way girl."[15] Throughout the voluminous interviews that Houston had, interviewers consistently note their surprise at her informal, comfortable, everyday attire during their meetings. The amazement constantly reminds of the disjuncture between Arista's desired racial, gendered, and sexualized performances and Houston's preferred expressions.

At Houston's core existed a racial performance of identity that reflected racial, gender, and sexual *difference* and not racial acculturation and integration; her style of dress (jeans and T-shirts) read as tomboy and not well-respected black lady. Lurking beneath the surface of the tomboy assignation nonnormative sexual preference and identity lie. Because, as Madison persuades, "inherited gestural conventions from the way we sit, stand, speak, dress, [and] dance," carry gender, sex, racial, and class meanings, Houston's quotidian behaviors become sites to examine the meaning of her *difference*.[16] At the heart of Houston's racial difference, sexual, gender, and class variance lies. To sublimate her racial difference, Davis also had to eradicate her nonnormative gender, class, and sexual expressions. In order for Houston to be beautiful, innocent, and elegant, she had to embody and perform a regulated version of black intimate relations, a destructive desire, that integrated normative sexuality and espoused middle-class economic and cultural aspirations.

This move too revealed the benefits of espousing personal responsibility and hard work philosophies to advance black success. From the beginning, cultural longings about blackness, black women, and middle-class status calculatedly shaped Houston's career and increased her profitability for Arista Records. The Arista team, under Davis's leadership, manufactured an image of Houston that appropriated expressions of blackness that were black enough, but not "too black," in order to maximize economic profitability. Appealing to white aesthetic preferences meant they had to downplay certain elements of black musical production, including soul, for example, that rendered black music (too) black. Examples such as this one explain why Nelson George laments the death of rhythm and blues culture in the mid-1980s; integration would dilute the blackness of the genre as crossover appeal would drive the profitability of the records in ways it heretofore had not.

In the documentary *Whitney Houston: Can I Be Me?* (2017), former Arista marketing director Kenneth Reynolds recalls that the label (Clive Davis whom he does not name specifically) rejected any song for *Whitney Houston* that might have reflected what I am calling *too-black blackness*. This phrase captures lyrics, themes, expressions, logics, and sounds that management thought to be so particular to black culture, history, and experience they would not appeal outside of this niche market (similar to chapter 2's discussion of black films in the 1990s). Recalling his first introduction to Houston, he indicates that she struck him as "naive" and "insecure" and strikingly concerned about her image. These qualities, nonetheless, also made her "moldable" for the "foolproof vision" of a pop artist, which Davis sought, but could not yield from an artist like Warwick, whose more advanced career had fixed her image. To make this pop diva, Reynold explains, "her music was deliberately pop. Anything that was too black sounding was sent back to the studio. And to say black sounding, if you have a problem with that, is to say it's too George Clinton, it's too funkadelic, it's just too R&B. We want Joni Mitchell, we want Mariah Carey, we want Barbara Streisand. We want to achieve that sound more so than we want to achieve the R&B sound. We don't want a female James Brown."[17] There are very few ways to interpret "too R&B" other than as "too black." The explicit repudiation of a Brown-like figure, the quintessential black soul man, further focuses our attention toward an antiblack gendered blackness politics at play in Arista's construction of Houston's image and persona.

The sense that Houston's music diverged from listening publics' perceptions of blackness emerged not only in classifications of Houston's music but also in the critiques that appeared despite her successes. Questions about what we might think of as the *sound of blackness* emerge throughout Houston's career, extending well beyond the release of *Whitney Houston*, and persist even after she adopts a more definitive R&B sound in 1989. In 1985, Richard Defendorf, for example, classifies Houston's music as "pop-soul," noting that "the record places her breathy, stunning voice in glossy pop and soft rhythm 'n' blues settings."[18] In 1986, Stephen Holden notes "*Whitney Houston* is now the best-selling album by a black female vocalist in pop music history."[19] In 1987, Christopher Helm asserts, "her meticulously constructed urban pop is carefully designed to appeal to the widest audience. It is bright and cheerful and always about a universally popular and uncontroversial topic, love."[20]

Although *Destructive Desires* repudiates Helm's suggestion that love lacks controversy or even bears universal meanings, Helm's phrase "urban pop," when coupled with Defendorf's notion of "pop-soul," confirms the general perception that Houston's oeuvre extended the *traditional* boundaries of rhythm and blues. That five of Houston's six Grammy nominations were in rhythm and blues categories might undermine the assertion that Houston's repertoire circulated completely *outside* of rhythm and blues aesthetics. At the same time, it might also confirm the typical racism of the Grammy awards that would automatically assume that the black racial identity of the performer necessarily corresponded to the rhythm and blues genre.[21] Nina Serrianne asserts, "Pop culture in the 1990s represented an integration of social issues of marginalized communities into mainstream entertainment" and that "pop music of the 1990s provided a sense of comfort at the dawn of uncertainty."[22] While Serrianne rightfully articulates how pop music can offer sociopolitical critiques, Houston's crossover into pop also points toward the putative success of integration, symbolizing a post–civil rights era. In other words, Houston's crossover, which anticipates the 1990s' cultural phenomenon Serrianne describes, signals the perceived waning of social issues in marginalized communities rather than drawing attention to the ongoing needs those communities possess.

In *The Soundtrack of My Life: Clive Davis* (2013), Davis's thirty-three-page discussion of "Whitney" portrays himself primarily as a concerned businessman whose chief goal included discerning Houston's best interests, while incorporating Houston into decision-making processes. Collaboration and trust become foundational to and hallmarks of their relationship. He notes that his "creative partnership with Whitney had a storybook beginning," and this storybook reference highlights the romanticized image of Houston *Soundtrack* paints, in addition to his idealized recollection (and representation) of their relationship.[23] To parse out his vested interest in Houston's success, he quotes at length a *Rolling Stone* interview in which Houston confirms that she chose Arista and Davis precisely because Clive would indicate, "'Whitney, this song has potential. This song doesn't.'"[24] Houston's commentary thus authenticates Davis's role as a mentor whose animating motives advance Houston's career. Although Davis chronicles the production of the first album, noting that "the album would be two years in the making" and that "my A&R staff and I listened to and evaluated literally hundreds of songs," he excludes information regarding the criteria for selection and evaluation.[25] How, for example, did Arista's desire to make a black woman pop diva inform his selection of songs? What aspirations for acceptance and success compelled Houston to perform certain songs and reject others? How did Davis's selections and Houston's performances function to call forth destructive desires not only for Houston herself but for listening publics too?

Throughout his entire discussion of his relationship with Houston, Davis equally as curiously never refers to her as a pop or R&B artist, except when verifying that she won awards in both categories. Nor does he discuss his and/or the label's desire to construct a pop diva. We must wonder what animates Davis's decision to elide race, gender, and sexuality from his discussion of his relationship with Houston, given the centrality of the intersections of those identities to her persona, self, viewing publics, and the world more generally. Given the chapter's discussion of the racial implications of Houston's booing at the Soul Train awards, his acknowledgment of Aretha Franklin as the Queen of Soul in the preceding chapter, and his integration of LaFace into the production of "I'm Your Baby Tonight" and subsequent albums, it remains particularly striking that

Davis omits any discussion of the racial dynamics surrounding the criteria for song selection that needed Houston as not too-black black.

Although Davis resists explicitly discussing how race and antiblack racial discourses map onto his construction of Houston's public image, he vocalizes concerns that Houston might have been gay and intimates how this rumor might have impacted her cultural iconicity. By articulating this concern explicitly, Davis also invokes how not-too-black blackness also imbibes ideas about appropriate expressions of sex and sexuality. While the specific concerns about sexual expression for Houston differ from those about Howard, the desire to contain both of their sexualities and sexual expressions emerges from a contiguous discursive context that regulates black intimate relations. In fact, a broad range of scholarship in black sexuality studies confirms that in the popular imaginary blackness, as a discursive category, inherently denotes some level of sexual/gender alterity. In C. Riley Snorton's *Black on Both Sides: A Racial History of Trans Identity*, for instance, Snorton contends, "blackness and transness, with few exceptions, have been expressed in terms of disavowal."[26] Calling forth blackness simultaneously hails sexual "deviance," and calling forth sexual/gender deviance hails blackness; consequently, the repudiation of one symbolically repudiates the other. Clive Davis's desire to monitor Houston's sexuality grows from a broader cultural longing, on behalf of white and black audiences, to embrace a black woman artist whose perceived sexuality fits squarely within the parameters of respectability, thus reinforcing the normative face of destructive desires. Heteronormativity, compulsive heterosexuality, and compulsive monogamy have crossover appeal as each of these discourses and practices regulate black intimate relations. Recall that during the mid-1980s the illegal publication of nude photos caused Vanessa Williams, the first African American Miss America winner, to relinquish her title.[27]

Keenly aware that the music industry's norms toward sexuality aligned with those of the broader culture's, Davis admittedly took an active role to quell speculations that Houston resisted heteronormativity. He emphasizes his role in "introducing" Houston to Jermaine Jackson, and then immediately reveals that "[t]hey had become lovers and had an intense relationship during a time when rumors were swirling that Whitney was gay"[28] (figure 4.2). Like Houston's race, her sexuality, and questions surrounding it, haunted her career from its beginning. Davis's attempt to mold Houston into a respectable lady hinges upon disciplining her blackness, heterosexuality, womanhood, and middle-class performances. Emerging in an era where television shows such as *The Cosby Show* promoted black middle-class familial success and emphasized the importance of black middle-class nuclear familial thriving, Davis's tapping into broader cultural norms to facilitate Houston's success does not surprise. Davis capitalized on the cultural longings that would maximize Houston's crossover appeal, and, in the process, generated celebrity and wealth for Houston, Arista, and himself. This partnership reveals how cultural longings for racial, gender, sexual, and social-class normativity scripts enact destructive desires, which arguably underwrite Houston's death, as she conforms and simultaneously resists.

FIGURE 4.2. Whitney Houston performs with Jermaine Jackson at the Limelight in New York City, July 1, 1984.

Davis's desire for crossover appeal emerges within broader economic and cultural trends wherein black cultural performance frequently found itself at the economic crosshairs of racial innovation, racial curiosity, and racial exploitation.[29] As Stuart Hall admonishes, we must account for how economics structure race and how race structures economics in order to "connect together in a critical reflection different domains of life, politics, and theory, theory and practice, economic, political, and ideological questions and so on."[30] Hall's claim forces our analysis to attend to the entangled networks that shape Houston's promotion and reception, and to how pecuniary interests inform and are informed by racial discourses. This very conversation about crossover appeal, which extends to other cultural modes of expressivity, constantly turns our attention to the intersections of aesthetics, gender, race, and sexuality.

Although the 1980s had witnessed increased racial intermixing within musical genres, as *Destructive Desires'* introduction explains, the segregation of rhythm and blues, and other forms of black music, into "race records" helped to ensure that "the sonic color line" remained intact. As Jennifer Stoever explains in *The Sonic Color Line: Race & the Cultural Politics of Listening*, the sonic color line "describes the process of racializing sound—how and why certain bodies are expected to produce, desire, and live amongst particular sounds—and its product, the hierarchical division sounded between 'whiteness' and 'blackness.'"[31] The music industry was thus able to racialize sound by regulating listening practices of consumers by controlling the content distributed to respective racialized marketplaces (i.e., channeling black-sounding music to predominantly black audiences and white-sounding music to white ones). Content also played a role in segregated distribution practices to the degree that race records emphasized particular themes in addition to possessing formal qualities that marked them as black. Presumably, race records portrayed black cultural desires and aspirations, lambasted racial inequality and other forms of dispossession, and rejected narratives of racial progress and triumph. To cross over, one had to diminish, if not outright reject, both the formal and the thematic markers of blackness that had consigned some race records to black markets. The music industry's thinking aligned with the antiblack racism that existed throughout the nation: black experiences, black life, black culture, and black politics appealed most broadly when not obsessing over the *race issue*.

TRACK 3
"SAME SCRIPT, DIFFERENT CAST": MARKET FORCES AND
CROSSOVER RACIALIZED AND GENDERED APPEALS

During the 1950s, the music industry's desire to expand its financial returns and black artists' desire to amass more wealth collude and lay the foundation upon which Davis is able to build with artists such as Houston in the 1980s. As Brian Ward argues in *Just My Soul Responding: Rhythm and Blues, Black Consciousness, and Race Relations*, post–World War II economic strains helped major record labels to focus their interests on white [pop] music, yet the early crossover of R&B artists into pop inaugurated a traversing of the sonic color line. The entrance of R&B into pop music allowed white marketplaces to consume black cultural production, exposed white marketplaces to rhythm and blues music and culture, increased the consumption of rhythm and blues culture, and expanded the profit margins for artists and labels. As Ward explains, "By the end of 1954, income from r&b records and tours constituted a $25 million branch of the industry. A growing, if still relatively small, contingent of young white fans had combined with the black audience to double the market share claimed by r&b from 5 percent to 10 percent of the total industry gross."[32] While Ward labors to nuance the particular ways that independent labels and young white consumers cooperated to thrust rhythm and blues music into mainstream venues, three relevant arguments emerge: first, crossover artists inaugurated debates about authentic rhythm and blues music (i.e., *authentic* blackness) that persist in black cultural production even today; second, the transformation in black music forms from early rhythm and blues, to soul, to disco, to later rhythm and blues correspond with the politics of the civil rights movement, black power movement, integration, and anti–civil rights backlashes; third, to understand the aesthetic forms, we must consider how they align with and diverge from sociopolitical trends in which the music industry remained enmeshed (entangled networks). Houston's arrival at Arista in the 1980s gains further meaning, then, when we consider how these ongoing debates in the music industry operate through and alongside cultural longings for not-too-black blackness, as well as for respectability politics, and how the debates call forth the normative face of destructive desires.

Whereas Gordy's Motown had diligently scripted its crossover appeal in artists such as Smokey Robinson and groups such as *The Supremes*, Arista's crossover strategy for Houston more explicitly (even if not stated publicly) positioned Houston in at least two genres of music: one decidedly white (pop) and the other decidedly black (rhythm and blues). Motown's thriving, as Andrew Flory explains in *I Hear a Symphony: Motown and Crossover R&B*, depended on its ability to cross over, and this "success helps to illustrate the changing relationship between R&B and the mainstream, as different styles of representing the 'black division' of the American record business become popular outside of segregated R&B outlets."[33] Theoretically, this dual positioning gestures toward the possibilities for deconstructing racial essentialism and expanding the possibilities for black cultural production, black politics, and black life. By penetrating pop music and becoming a pop diva, Houston would embody a postintegration narrative of success, wherein the rise of a black woman to pop diva status signaled economic and social progress for African Americans and whites alike. Her success indicated that African Americans do in fact have access to opportunities. When they work hard and use their skills, white people accept them. For white people, accepting an artist such as Houston evidences their lack of white racial animus (except that it does not). This logic of course continues to position the onus of eradicating racism on black people. It also ignores how the fracturing of the economy during the Reagan administration disproportionately adversely impacted (economically vulnerable) black populations (in particular) by insisting everyone possesses equal access to equal opportunities. It does not, for example, account for whether that access, when it exists, will produce equal outcomes. This fiction of equal access diminishes the salience of race and racism in white imaginations by eliding the fact that antiblack racism makes not too-black blackness (and its corresponding politics) palatable for white people.

Although black audiences' critique of Houston's performance of not too-black blackness might reinforce essentialist notions of blackness, reaffirm the sonic color line, and circumscribe black performers' modalities of artistic expression, a more capacious analysis of the critique reveals a complexity of issues at play that center the relationships that aesthetics and politics have. In other words, while the criticism that Houston "lacks soul" and is "Whitey Houston" may reinforce, reaffirm, and circumscribe, that criticism also reveals cultural longings for blackness that move beyond abjection and acculturation. When black disc jockeys chided her for not "having soul" and "being too white" they called forth an essential yet nonessential soul.[34] That is, they were deeming necessary a nonessential (biologically racialized) quality of black music that we cannot quantify or describe precisely but that seems necessary for black musical performance.[35] Yet, to pin this desire on Houston and expect her to fulfill it creates another set of responsibilities for Houston that warrant examination. Houston's later decision to embrace more decidedly black cultural aesthetics, and then to conform to the social discourses that the aesthetic demands tether demonstrates the persistence of and possibility for black cultural production's relationship to black politics and black lives. It too reveals the dangers of both that possibility and that responsibility.

TRACK 4
"I'M YOUR BABY TONIGHT": RACE, SEXUALITY, AND MARRIAGE ASPIRATIONS

By many accounts, the 1989 Soul Train music awards marked a turning point in Houston's personal and professional lives because the demand that she performed an authentic blackness in her music coincided with increasing calls for her to perform authentic heteronormativity in her personal life. The confluence of these destructive desires arguably reframed the trajectory of Houston's life and career, situating her new *choices* within a predetermined set of socially acceptable options. The crowd's infamous booing when they heard Houston's name stunned Houston, and in interviews that follow the incident, Houston reveals her surprise and her abilities to perform within and beyond *authentic* racial scripts. For instance, in an interview with Byron Allen (1990), she renders an operaesque melody to intimate what singing *white* might sound like, and in an interview with Arsenio Hall, she notes that she too "grew up watching *Soul Train*," and that she has "soul."[36] Elsewhere, Houston clarifies that "blackness is not about the color of your skin" but rather "is where you come from. . . . It's an attitude. . . . It's understanding the Black Situation. . . . I've lived among my own people. And I understand their desires, and their cries."[37] Echoing Julian Mayfield's assertions in "You Touch My Black Aesthetic," Houston acknowledges that blackness extends beyond performative gestures to encapsulate shared histories, experiences, and geographies.[38]

In many ways, the debate surrounding Houston's sonic blackness transpires within a broader context of post–civil rights era performances of racial scripts where increased access to opportunities expand the contours of what constitutes black performances. Even her interviews demonstrated what Doreen St. Felix points out "was a witty version of white Hollywood's mid-Atlantic affectation: part Baptist gravity, part small-city charisma, at once assimilationist and easy."[39] In *Black Performances on the Outskirts of the Left: A History of the Impossible*, Malik Gaines theorizes "performance as a radical act" and examines "the possibility that performances of blackness have been capable, sometimes, provisionally, and contingently, of amending dominant discourses that manage representations and constrain the lives they organize."[40] The changing dynamics of the music industry, the expansion of black popular culture and black music into mainstream media, and the broader incorporation of black cultural production into mainstream culture during the 1980s augment the aesthetic and political possibilities available for black people and black culture. This debate nevertheless turns attention to the understandable worry that the incorporation of black cultural production into the mainstream also meant diluting and whitening black cultural production. Too, concerns about the financial exploitation of that culture at the literal expense of black people's material, spiritual, political, and social well-being persisted. Examining how constituents within the black arts movement fretted over the commercialization of black culture in the 1970s, Margo Crawford also posits that commercialization does not necessarily negate political and social value: "The most powerful part of black popular culture (in the midst of oppressive commercialism) is the zone where black people find a space to express love, happiness, and fantasy."[41] This reading of the cultural longings and destructive desires for Houston underscores the urgency for which we might locate love, happiness, and fantasy beyond the normal institutions that reinscribe antiblack racism while purporting to eschew it.

Obsessions with Houston's dating life, habits, and interests masked a more specific desire to reveal Houston's rumored nonheteronormative sexual practices and proclivities. This revelation would have undermined Houston's status as an exemplar of racial progress and reinforced black sexual deviance as constitutive to blackness. If the molding of Houston functioned to shore up gender-racialized anxieties, an openly and *public* nonheterosexual relationship would re-create these fears, damage Houston's brand, and undercut Arista's bottom line.[42] Houston's "fall from grace narrative" would invoke familiar arguments that posit nonconforming black sexuality as the cause of and explanation for a lack of progress; she would "have had it all" had she not been gay or bisexual (a behavioral choice). This logic posits nonheteronormativity as destructive, whereas *Destructive Desires* insists that the regulating and disciplining of black sexuality are the true destructive forces and desires. That is, it consistently calls into questions how we take for granted the normative face of destructive desires as not problematic, as it questions whether the nonnormative face necessarily causes dysfunction. This entangled network of the listening public's fascination, the record label's pecuniary interests, Houston's own investments in performing heteronormativity, the broader culture's misogynistic homophobia, and her mother's religious discourses about black sexuality explain the disjunction between Houston's public performances of heteronormativity and perhaps her private nonnormative ones. This chapter's interest in this disjuncture considers what the implications are for rhythm and blues culture, black women's sexuality, and black aesthetics and politics. That is, it does not intend to verify anything about Houston's specific sexual practices.

The desires to know and verify Houston's sexual practices encase Houston's life, and, with the release of the documentary *Can I Be Me*, persist in her death, inaugurating for Houston what we might call a queer afterlife. This phrase, "queer afterlife," draws attention to how discussions about Houston's life, sexuality, and cause of death might engender more robust thinking about normativity, black intimate relations, and sexual politics as usual, to reconsider which desires are in fact destructive. Personal assistant and former best friend Robyn Crawford's admission that Houston knew she would never have betrayed her "trust," ex-husband Bobby Brown's assertion that Houston married to clean up her image, mother Cissy Houston's verification that she would not have accepted Houston as (openly) gay, and long-time stylist Ellin LaVar's characterization of Houston as bisexual feed this desire to uncover Houston's *authentic/true* sexual practices.[43]

At the core of these discussions about racial authenticity lies a question about authentic sexual practices, and vice versa. *Destructive Desires* invokes these examples to argue that the tendency to regulate black intimate relations by promoting respectability politics stops short of its long-term goal; regulation ultimately fails to advance black thriving and political advancement despite its sometimes immediate appeal or incremental successes.

The racialization of sexism and the sexualization of racism contextualize for readers ways that the desire to regulate Houston's intimate relations circumscribed Houston's own view of herself, musical persona, and available dating pools. Moreover, this circumscription reproduced a set of destructive desires for and by Houston that arguably undermined her ability to thrive. Before 1989, questions about her sexuality ensnared interviewers and fans, and her responses to those questions vacillated. At times, Houston avoided direct answers to questions, suggesting the particulars of her sexuality remained her *private* business. When Lynn Norment questions her relationship with Crawford, Houston clarifies that Crawford is like an older sister, and that speculation about their romantic interests originate from Houston's more general privacy. Houston asserts speculation "has been fueled by the fact that I'm private with my life. I don't make it my business to expose my relationships; it's hard enough to just keep one. So I figured that since people didn't know who I was sleeping with, they just assumed I was sleeping with Robyn."[44] Houston reveals how celebrity further erodes the division between the public and private spheres as well as how *sexual privacy* becomes equated with *sexual deviancy*. Perceptively, her response also exemplifies how the desire to *know* and then contain black sexuality disciplines and regulates black intimate relations.

It also draws attention to how the cultural tendency to lesbianize black women's homosocial relationships serves patriarchy's desires to enact heteronormative masculine sexual fantasies and disrupt the possibility for the formation of women-centered relationships.[45] As Cheryl Clarke argues, "men at all levels of privilege, of all classes and colors, have the potential to act out legalistically, moralistically, and violently when they cannot colonize women, when they cannot circumscribe our sexual, productive, reproductive, creative prerogatives, and energies."[46] The political power of the label thus also lies in its ability to thwart intimate relations that potentially disrupt the existing order. Compounding this issue too is a slippage between the terms *gay* and *bisexual*, where *gay* signals all forms of nonnormative sexuality. Although Houston refutes being gay, she never broaches the issue of bisexuality directly, only insisting "I'm a mother. I'm a woman. I'm heterosexual. Period."[47] Perhaps Houston's "period" does more than end the discussion or dodge the issue; it actually calls attention to bisexuality's refusal to accede to normativity and nonnormativity. It can be read as both and as neither nor. Houston's declaration understands that any nonnormative sexual expression becomes read as "gay." It also resists the label *gay* but retains the possibility that she is bisexual, at once reinforcing and undermining the stigmatization of nonnormative sexualities, gesturing toward the two-faced meaning of destructive desires.

Houston thus becomes a cultural site through which a set of tensions and cultural longings become dramatized, her body, as metonym, bearing the tug of discourses that exceeded and bound her capacities. Not too-black blackness butts up against authentic, soulful blackness; the single woman who cherishes her homosocial bond bucks against the married woman who privileges the conjugal relationship; the desire for motherhood exposes respectability politics' confinement of motherhood to marriage; the desire to be an individual turns against the image of a representative black woman's narrative of exceptionality and racial progress. The booing at the Soul Train awards functions as a turning point for Houston, instantiating a destructive desire to resolve some of these tensions. Although not exhaustive, these pressures shape how to interpret the timing of when she meets Bobby Brown, the censuring she received from dating and later marrying Brown, and the postures she adopted to defend and sustain her marriage as questions about sobriety, domestic abuse, infidelity, and lavishness arose.[48]

Because Brown's blackness hinges on his performance of excessive heteronormative scripts, which the mainstream tropes of black masculinity always already assume, Houston's marriage to Brown could authenticate both her blackness and her heterosexuality. The sexualization of both Houston and Brown hinges on their racialization, and their racialization depends upon their sexualization; black intimate relations discourses bind Houston and Brown even as social class may divide them. Brown, too, falls outside of respectability politics' middle-class bourgeoisie sensibilities as his out-of-wedlock children and poverty roots (materially and culturally) mark him as outside the boundaries of black respectability (he embodies too-black blackness). The abjection upon which respectability politics builds its claims situate Houston and Brown in similar discourses, and by examining this parallel, this track foregrounds these cultural longings as recursive features of Houston's entire career rather than isolated ones.

TRACK 5
"ALL THE MAN I NEED": MARRIAGE AND THE REMAKING OF AN IMAGE

Conjoining the privileges that the State confers upon married couples, as well as the cultural capital conjugal relationships reinforce, Houston's July 1992 wedding provided her access to another set of opportunities for which she longed. Between meeting Brown in 1989 and marrying him in 1992, Houston had worked intentionally to eschew the American princess image. The wedding (and reception) reinforced this princess image of Houston as she publicly and lavishly took on what Ralph Banks refers to as the "ultimate merit badge," marriage, to mark her ascendancy into black heterosexual womanhood.[49] Whereas her decidedly *blacker* album, *I'm Your Baby Tonight*, was sanitizing Houston's racial image, the marriage would position her decidedly within the confines of heterosexuality. Together, the album and the marriage presumably allowed Houston to renounce

questions about racial authenticity and heterosexual nonconformity, and to fulfill her desired roles as wife and mother. By singing music that more explicitly
aligned with black musical aesthetics, and by marrying a black man who embodied *rugged* black masculinity and *undistilled* heterosexuality, Houston proved
her mutually constituted blackness and heterosexuality. The internalization of
destructive desires, particularly as they relate to the regulation of black intimate
relations vis-à-vis compulsory heterosexuality, monogamous marriage, and
motherhood proved as destructive personally as they are socially and politically.

Given the inner workings of their marriage, as well as some of the issues
that arose while they dated, one might rightly question what motivated Houston's decision to marry Brown, with whom she appeared unequally yoked. The
same year they marry, they release "Something in Common," an upbeat duet that
declares their mutual love and affection. Although a performance, the song par-
allels their lives, presumably scoffing at the idea that their marriage lacked
shared interests and values, and rejecting the popular belief that the union was
unsustainable.[50] It, too, acknowledges infidelity on behalf of the man persona
who admits, "I know I made my mistakes before" and recognizes, "A bird in the
hand beats two in the bush."[51] If the mistakes refer to engaging in extramarital
sexual relationships, the bird in the hand metaphor signals a newfound appreciation for the monogamous relationship despite the potential thrill of the extramarital liaisons. Moreover, Houston's persona allows for a man's vulnerability,
insisting that she "understands my man" and "I'll be strong when he is weak, I'll
hold his hand." No sooner than the song offers a more capacious image of black
gendered relations, it articulates a more traditional dynamic, declaring, "Now I
believe old fashioned rules, old fashioned ways, Courtesy, honor, like in the old
days."[52] The juxtaposition of these lines captures more broadly a tension that
undergirds Houston's life—a desire to move beyond categories that circumscribe
gender and sexual norms, and participation in activities that reinforce and capit-
ulate to the very categorizations she desires to escape.

Chapter 2 argues and this chapter maintains that we cannot conflate the
persona with the person and/or with the performance. Yet I also agree with Stuart Hall's contention that black life exists within the realm of representation.
As Hall reminds, "We tend to privilege experience itself, as if black life is lived
outside of representation. We have only, as it were, to express what we already
know we are. Instead, it is only through the way in which we represent and imagine ourselves that we come to know how we are constituted and who we are.
There is no escape from the politics of representation."[53] Accordingly, lived experiences equip us to read and understand representation, just as representations
prepare us to analyze and theorize lived experience. "Something in Common's"
explanatory force thus lies not primarily in how it imagines Houston and Brown's
relationship, or in how it wants others to envision their union, or even in how it
helps us to think about black intimate relations more generally. Its analytical
thrust emerges equally as powerfully in the commonalities it does not name. It
also provides a framework to uncover the hidden desires that are present yet not

(fully) articulated, not only in the song (representation) but also in Houston and Brown's relationship (lived experience).

Although Houston and Brown appear unequally yoked on the surface, their nonnormative sexual practices and proclivities, alleged, actual, or otherwise imagined, possibly give them common ground ("Something in Common") from the inception of their relationship. Houston repeatedly underscored their similarities, telling *Rolling Stone*, "You know, Bobby and I basically come from the same place. You see somebody, and you deal with their image, that's their image. It's part of them. . . . I am not always in a sequined gown. I am nobody's angel. I can get down and dirty too. I can get raunchy."[54] While the gendering of respectability politics presents a set of different political, personal, and pragmatic implications for black men and black women, Houston and Brown reside outside of black respectability politics to the degree that they both live outside of the confines of heterosexuality (Houston's possible same-sex relationships and desires) and respectability (sexual relations outside of marriage for both and Brown's out-of-wedlock children).[55] Houston's focus on their similarities, her disavowal of "sequined gowns" and an "angelic" image, purposefully resituates her in too-black blackness and heteronormativity.

TRACK 6
"YOU GIVE GOOD LOVE": MARRIAGE AND THE UNMAKING OF AN IMAGE

This reading posits that Houston (and Brown) may have used respectability politics to turn them on their head, and argues that the inability to do so also confirms Audre Lorde's contention that the master's tools will never dismantle (fully) the master's house.[56] To what degree did Houston see, in Brown, a way to upend respectability politics, to slip the yoke and change the joke, to circumvent respectability politics from reigning *entirely* over her intimate sphere? Imagine that Houston accepted Brown's sexual choices because she did not privilege monogamy as the sine qua non expression of sexuality in the marriage to him, and because she did not for *herself* either. They publicly declared fidelity and eschewed rumors of Brown's extramarital affairs, and throughout interviews following their union Houston deliberately characterized Brown as a *family man*.[57] Yet neither of these proclamations precludes the possibility for a more nuanced marital configuration. Robyn Crawford does not disappear when Houston marries, but instead holds the most socially significant and privileged role in wedding ceremonies besides those of bride and groom. A turn to Crawford's role in the marriage ceremony demonstrates how the marriage at once incorporates and rejects Crawford. This reading becomes especially illuminating in light of the new life that Crawford's role in Houston's marriage has experienced in the wake of Houston's death.

By electing Crawford to serve as maid of honor, for example, Houston affirms the importance of this homosocial bond, and simultaneously disavows its permanency because it threatens and is threatened by the heterosexual conjugal

FIGURE 4.3. Whitney Houston, Bobby Brown, Cissy Houston, and Robyn Crawford in New York City, prior to 2000.

bond. The attendees effectually witness a declaration of a heterosexual marriage wherein the ceremony itself symbolically and visually disrupts, displaces, and replaces a homosocial bond and potentially nonheterosexual relationship. Crawford's presence in the ceremony, however, calls into question whether the intent was to truly replace this bond or rather to display publicly a heterosexual bond (figure 4.3). In other words, what role, if any, did Crawford's presence contribute to the overall project of upstaging respectability politics? Whereas the analysis of Mtume's "You, Me, and He" in chapter 1 underscores how the song toys with the boundaries of patriarchy, it also insists that the song never altogether rejects heteropatriarchal principles. Similarly, Houston can push the boundaries of respectability politics and heterosexual marriage, even as she reaps the benefits from them and reinforces their cultural hegemony.[58] Although this argument grows within the tradition in which "feminists have critiqued monogamy" and "challenged its compulsory status" it aims not to "replicate the same naturalizing logics on which scientific claims that naturalize monogamy are founded: the human is fundamentally sexual, and sexuality is a naturally privileged organizing principle of relationships."[59] My emphasis here is on the socioconstruction of the mutually constitutive roles that desire and patriarchy play in shaping norms for sexual expression and not on the naturalness of sexuality. The reference to Mtume further returns us to the issue of monogamy, and its multiple possibilities within the Houston–Brown dyad. Both the song and the potential intrarelationship between Crawford and Houston within the Houston–Brown marriage center, in some respects, the woman's sexual desires as driving the relationship.

Houston's relationship falls short of upstaging heteronormativity, the master's tools fail to dismantle the master's house, and, in this context, respectability politics triumph. If Brown had, for example, conceded to Crawford's continued presence in their marriage, they may have provided an alternative model for marriage. Yet the inimical nature of patriarchy ultimately created a power struggle when Crawford's *influence* (and not solely presence) infringes upon Brown. Brown vocalizes this sentiment in *Every Little Step*, explaining why *he dismisses* Crawford: "You gotta get the fuck out. You gotta go. I can't take this no fuckin' more! This is my wife. You have to go."[60] Brown's possessiveness, "my wife," suggests a conflict existed for Houston's attention, and even her status as "spouse." A triangulated relationship in which a previous (or even ongoing) sexual relationship between Houston and Crawford created a power imbalance for Brown might contextualize why Crawford *could not* remain a part of Houston's life. Brown, at most, only intimates that Crawford and Houston's relationship had sexual underpinnings, and he curiously stops short of stating anything explicitly. Brown's sidestepping of this issue seems particularly striking given his lack of reticence on other issues that would uncover intimate details of Houston's life, and given his more general tendency to denigrate Houston in his belabored effort to elevate himself.[61] For example, he candidly discusses their drug use, attributes their divorce to her unwillingness to want sobriety, points out that everyone except for him exploited her financially, accuses her of poisoning his relationship with Bobbi Kristina, and concedes their parenting skills lacked coordination, consistency, and circumspectness.[62]

The public's desire coupled with Brown's newfound introspection and candor further bring into focus his coyness about Crawford. Does Brown refrain from explicitly naming a Crawford–Houston relationship because he harbors a disloyalty to heterosexism and homophobia? Does he refrain because he himself had agreed to the intra-marital relationship between Houston and Crawford, thus making it difficult to classify the relationship as "extramarital"? This reading recognizes the strength of the innuendo, and partially concurs with Michael Arceneaux's contention that "if Houston never felt compelled to share this part of her, it should stay buried."[63] On the one hand, nonexcavation further stigmatizes nonnormative sexual practices by equating secrecy with shame. On the other, Brown's excavation does not serve the purpose of providing a more robust conversation about black intimate relations that shows the two-facedness of destructive desires and/or calls into question what desires in fact destruct; it instead invited speculation, stigma, and judgment. How Brown discusses this particular issue provides an opening to imagine not only what he conceals but also to interpret the possible meanings of how he reveals what he shares. Either way, black intimate relations emerge center stage in conversations about Houston's rise, peak, fall, rebirth, descent, and death. Although Crawford refuses to address these rumors, a revelation from Brown could alter this quietness and compel her to offer a (counter) narrative that further contextualizes Brown's claims and explains his uncharacteristic reticence.

Finally, this information calls into question the assumed heteronormative readings of Houston's music, the conflation of the persona, artist, and autobiography. As my readings of the epigraphs at the beginning of the chapter suggest, a nonheteronormative reading of the music would upset and give new insights to the tendency to equate music performances with statements of biography. Such a reading would also demonstrate how within black intimate relationships imaginings of love and intimacy default to heteronormativity and, at the same time, would demonstrate how new insights into Houston's biography can reshape how we imagine the meanings of her cultural performances. Whereas chapter 2's discussion of Edmonds allows us to detach gender from biology, this aspect of Houston's life helps us to think more expansively about the attachments of heterosexuality to gendered musical performances too.

TRACK 7
"I WAS MADE TO LOVE HIM": SPLIT AFFINITIES AND
GENDER AND PATRIARCHAL LOYALTIES

In 2005, upon his release from jail, Bobby Brown began to film the reality television show, *Being Bobby Brown* (2005) to construct Brown as a family man, who, despite the physical distance between his family, prioritizes his children and his familial relationships. Executive Producer Tracey Baker-Simmons notes Brown "wanted his kids to have another public image of him besides being arrested and other things that the news was choosing to cover" because Brown is "someone's dad, someone's husband, someone's child."[64] This narrative of Brown as family man undermines the first two minutes of the episode, where clips from national television news stations report Brown's encounters with law enforcement that include "battery" against his wife, "pop-star Whitney Houston."[65] Although "editing, intra-diegetic repetition, camera angles, music, heightened conflict arcs, and inexpensive digital recording options" script, structure, and produce reality television shows, there simultaneously exists the sense that reality television still provides access to the real, essential self of its characters.[66] Neither the construction of reality-as-reality nor the performance of self-as-self necessarily undermines viewers' desire for and understandings of authenticity. This framework contextualizes the persistent thinking that Houston's authentic self, her real, indigenous, unrefined blackness (too-black blackness), which Davis had labored to contain, had spilled over for the public to really see on *Being Bobby Brown*.

Approximately seven minutes into the episode, the viewer sees Houston's televised *first* encounter with Brown, who, after introducing Houston to the camera crew, absconds with Houston to the (hotel) bedroom. Presumably among the first postjail coital experiences, Houston announces the presence of their daughter, Bobbi Kristina, thus deferring the encounter. Brown greets Bobbi Kris, introduces her to the camera crew, and then follows Houston's lead to the bedroom. Closing the door to the camera, Houston informs Bobbi Kristina (and viewers) that "daddy wants to make a baby." Bobbi Kristina fiddles with the door, protesting "no, no, no," with a teenager's playfulness and prescience. Devoted father and eager paramour, Brown uses the show to remake himself as devoted husband and father, talented artist, and savvy entrepreneur, who also enjoys alcohol, sex, and laughter (but not in a deviant, excessive way). Houston, by contrast, becomes the angry black woman, bad mother, and oversexualized woman all at once, one whose chain-smoking and cursing place her outside the limits of black respectability.

The *real* Houston emerged on the show, and this Houston further clarified her commonalities with Brown. Houston's *real* blackness becomes understood in the context of her performances of gender and sexuality, and the framing of her first encounter focuses our attention on the relationship among these discourses. Despite the show's title, it ultimately inveighs Houston's life, as Houston's life intrigues and interests, and her image incurs the most damage from its airing. Houston would later confess that her desire to be a *supportive wife* undergirds her decision to participate in the show. The effect the show had on her image attests to the ways that destructive desires in fact undermine her ability to thrive even as her decision to participate aims to help her marriage succeed.

Bravo Network reports that *Being Bobby Brown* increased its viewership within the 18 to 34 age range by 38 percent, yet the series canceled after one season, despite contentions that the producers had prepared footage for a second season.[67] Brown contends that Houston demanded to be in the show, and his brother Tommy insists that Houston's own team's mismanagement caused her untoward representations. Yet those explanations contravene common sense, more reliable testimony, and Baker-Simmons's claims. Clarence Avant, one of Brown's own agents, recalls that the show's production depended on Houston's participation: "I remember Bobby Brown calling me and saying 'You and Clive [Davis] and everybody has to get Whitney to do the show. . . . They won't give me the show without her.'"[68] Houston's confidant and stylist, Elin LaVar, adds that Houston valued privacy yet sacrificed it to once again support Brown: "She didn't want those cameras in her house or to be shown like that. But she went along for Bobby, and it cost her, I think. I think she felt that way too because she didn't like the way she came off at all."[69] Reviewer Alex Chadwick dismisses Brown's significance altogether, contending that "the camera always seems to be peeking over his shoulder at his more famous better half" and that "Bravo is just using Brown to get to Houston."[70] Whereas Houston's life since her marriage made her the subject of many interviews, controversies, and tabloids, Houston had in fact continued to perform and produce since marrying Brown. Her continued cultural production partially evidences why the public would be interested in her, and how her iconicity reproduced itself. We must question, too, what additional drives animated the public's desire to see Whitney Houston? How did her emaciated image at the 2001 Michael Jackson tribute show increase the public's fascination to *see* Houston's private space? What narratives about black womanhood would the broadcast contest and/or affirm? What cultural longings did the show fulfill and how did they produce destructive desires?

Like many reality television shows, *Being Bobby Brown* invades Houston and Brown's personal spaces and conversations, following them into what would otherwise be *private* meetings but for their national televising. The episodes arguably display Brown (and Houston) as ordinary people who laugh, drink, cook, joke, shop, and disagree. Neither wealth, fame, nor celebrity insulates them from the responsibilities and burdens of everyday living. *Being* displays a playfulness and silliness that might be common to many families and relationships off-camera. However, the camera's presence brought into focus the concerns that the public already had about Houston and Brown and intensified the imaginings of their seeming dysfunction. Viewers would question whether Houston's swift movements, propensity to reenact movies, and otherwise nonprovoked outbursts signaled *erratic* behavior that drug use produces. Or did they merely evidence a woman enjoying herself? By making the private public, reality television demonstrates how market forces hypervisualize blackness, regulate black behaviors and black intimate relations, and reinforce philosophies about personal responsibility as they relate to black inequality.

African American studies, film studies, and black feminist studies have well-documented histories of gendered-racial and racialized-gender exploitation in visual culture in general and television and film in particular.[71] Studies in reality television more recently have also begun to theorize how this cultural medium stages the performance of racial-gendered and gendered-racial scripts, and how social class and sexuality mutually constitute the staging and reception of these performances. Neoliberalism's emphasis on fiscal responsibility (free market) and personal responsibility (self-help and self-control) supplement our understanding of the impact that Houston's *performances* on *Being Bobby Brown* had on her career and the viewing public's perception of Houston. Whereas tabloids and other rumors had allowed the public to conjecture about Houston's drug habits and financial standing, *Being Bobby Brown* provided the necessary *evidence* and *confirmation* of Houston's general lack of discipline (erratic behavior), fiscal irresponsibility (shopping sprees for herself and Bobbi Kristina), and uneven disposition (testy conversations with Brown and others). As far as the viewing public believed, Houston had wasted both her talent and her purse, and this evaluation of Houston necessarily ties to neoliberal ideas about personal responsibility and economic self-sufficiency.

By the time *Being Bobby Brown* aired (2005) Houston had garnered a reputation for canceling events without notice during the mid- to late 1990s, and allegations of her drug use persisted. Designed to quell rumors about her addiction, health, marriage, and financial standing, and to promote the release of her *Just Whitney* album (2002), the now infamous "Diane Sawyer interview" on *Primetime* (2002) fueled speculation and supposition rather than allaying concerns (figure 4.4). Houston told Sawyer "crack is whack," contended she "makes too

FIGURE 4.4. Whitney Houston sits down with ABC News's Diane Sawyer (*Primetime Special Edition*) for a revealing one-hour interview at her home in suburban Atlanta, Georgia, broadcast on December 4, 2002, on ABC.

much money" to smoke crack, and demanded "receipts" about her putative hundred-thousand-dollar drug habit. By the end of the interview, viewers feared that not even Houston had escaped the crack-cocaine epidemic that skyrocketed with her generation. Framed as a prime-time tell-all interview, Houston remained taciturn, circumspect, and defensive in her responses to Sawyer's probing questions about her marriage, career, and drug use. Houston's faltering voice, which her unwillingness to answer Sawyer's questions compounded, cast doubts on her explanation of her hoarseness, and foreshadowed the ultimate decline of "the voice."[72] The interview gestured toward a troubled Houston, who only admitted "love-making" as her one addiction. Another commonality emerged; they were *codependent*. *Destructive Desires* raises these points because in an interview with Oprah Winfrey in 2009 (tracks 9 and 10), Houston amended and contextualized this narrative, providing insights about how cultural longings for heteronormativity fueled her destructive desires; she suggested that the toxicity of the desire, and/or unwillingness to achieve it, informed her decision-making processes. These incidents become significant within Houston's narrative and not simply additional examples of her putative deviance. They also contextualize public interest in *Being Bobby Brown*.

TRACK 8
AN INTERLUDE ON REALITY TELEVISION, PERSONAL RESPONSIBILITY,
AND OPRAH WINFREY

To understand Houston's choices, however, outside of the rise of neoliberalism's demands for personal and fiscal responsibilities, would further decontextualize how viewing publics, pundits, critics, and even supporters understand her marriage, addiction, and financial standing. Responses to Houston's performances on *Being Bobby Brown* direct attention to the ways that neoliberalism diminishes viewers' capacity to understand her life choices within a wider sociopolitical framework as well as the historical effects of racism, sexism, heterosexism, and classism (and their intersections) in the twenty-first century. In *Reality TV*, Mishka Kavka concedes the constructed(ness) of reality television and maintains that the moniker *reality* accentuates how reality television shows can engage, challenge, and inaugurate cultural norms. As Kavka clarifies, "the 'reality' of Reality TV is less about its claims to a privileged relation with reality . . . than about its capacity to intervene in a range of discourses about the self, the family, and community."[73] In Kavka's estimation, reality television, like other art forms, provides imaginative possibilities that shape viewers' own life choices. While Kavka rightfully turns attention to the art form of the show, the modifier *reality* continues to convey realist aesthetics. The desire to treat black reality television as unmediated life experience emerges as forcefully for *Being Bobby Brown* as it does for other forms of black cultural production. This conflation of the lived and represented, the experienced and imagined, the viewed and interpreted becomes increasingly vexed for Houston because the "neoliberal métier of Reality TV . . . mandates autonomously earned and privately financed self-empowerment as a condition of 'good' citizenship, all in the service of broader marketplace rewards."[74] These marketplace rewards gesture toward how the logics of neoliberalism, as Wendy Brown explains, shrink our political and cultural vocabularies and imaginaries into economic terms. At the same time, the marketplace rewards include continued contracts for the reality show, and, in the case of Houston and Brown, increased performance offers. They had also hoped to ameliorate their image in the public's view. The show, however, had the opposite of the intended effect.

In "When America's Queen of Talk Saved Britain's Duchess of Pork: Finding Sarah, Oprah Winfrey, and Transatlantic Self-Making," Brenda Weber argues that media mogul Oprah Winfrey's popular notion of living one's best life epitomizes "the neoliberal mandate of personal improvement," that one's best life coincides with one's ability to make *good* choices, and that one's inability to make good choices causes and explains one's standing in life. As Weber notes, "the best life/ best self proviso lays out a compelling causality, whereby all good things that come in a life (success, riches, fame) are perceived to be a reward for having developed a proper regard for and commitment to the cultivation of the self. Implied here is also the contrast: the failure to achieve success, riches, or fame can be attributed to the mismanagement of one's self-cultivation."[75] Winfrey becomes an important cultural producer not only because of her own network and *O* magazine, but also because the "neoliberal mandate of personal responsibility" "was *first* established on her long-running talk show," which began in the late 1980s. This turn to Winfrey anticipates how Winfrey, as cultural icon, gets juxtaposed to Houston, another cultural icon, and argues that this juxtaposition of neoliberalism's true success (Winfrey) and personal failure (Houston) becomes another important entangled network for articulating the deleterious effects that destructive desires have for Houston.

TRACK 9

"I LEARNED FROM THE BEST": OPRAH WINFREY,

AN AUTHENTIC INTEGRATION SUCCESS STORY?

As Winfrey relates to a discussion of Houston, her significance emerges not simply because of her 1995 interview with Houston and the cast of *Waiting to Exhale*, her 2009 interview with Houston, her tribute to Houston post–Houston's death, or her exclusive interviews with Houston's family members—Marion (Patricia) Garland Houston (sister-in-law), Cissy Houston (mother), Michael Houston (brother), or Bobbi Kristina Houston Brown (daughter)—after Houston's death. Rather, Winfrey, like Houston, symbolized the post–civil rights era success of integration and hard work, the potential for capitalistic thriving in an America in which the legislative gains of the civil rights movement had removed obstructions to equality. Whereas Houston's public performances of racial identity clashed with respectability politics, Winfrey's public persona, coupled with her espousal of hard work and personal responsibility discourses, embraced respectability politics. Arguably, Winfrey's crossover appeal, as her prime-time television slot and substantial white viewership evidence, depended largely upon her willingness to perform the racial scripts of not too-black blackness that Houston increasingly eschewed. Indeed, Winfrey's brand encouraged notions of postracialism that obfuscated the persistence of racial inequalities in the post–civil rights era by overemphasizing the degree to which individual behaviors determined outcomes irrespective of structural forces. This trend emerges in Winfrey's best-life, best-self ethos philosophies, both of which presuppose an equality of access to the opportunities that might make one's own responsibility as the primary determinant for his or her best life or best self more likely.

Winfrey's acknowledgment of racism as overt, individual, and conscious acts undermines the complexity of institutional racism that operates systemically and that cannot be overcome simply by individual successes that defy the ideologies of black inferiority on which racism thrives. Winfrey, for example, posits that "excellence is the best deterrent to racism or sexism or any sort of oppression."[76] For Winfrey, individuals can upend a racist, sexist, heterosexist society, and hold the responsibility to do so. Winfrey's estimation never clarifies whether oppressors and oppressive institutions possess any obligation or duty toward reparation. According to Weber, Winfrey's "best self is thus positioned as an undifferentiated but idealized classless, race-neutral, and in many ways sex-free signifier of global identity . . . this state of unified individualism bespeaks a neoliberal agenda that flattens differences of identity, race, power into a single concept of a self."[77] The appeal of sameness in the post–civil rights era functioned as a way to retrench inequality by discounting how difference (in terms of race, gender, and class) differentiates access and outcomes. Given Winfrey's celebrity in general and cultural influence, the turn to her demonstrates how she becomes situated within a set of discourses that she and her platforms in turn promulgate as necessary for success. They, too, inform Houston's appearance on the show in 2009.

If, as Weber further contends, "Winfrey's best life/best self ups the ante on neoliberal imperatives that seek marketplace rewards, since it is not only financial but emotional, physical, and spiritual dividends that announce one's success in the quest for the best life," Houston's final interview with Winfrey marks her last attempt to take control over her life by being personally responsible; by the time she appeared there, she had divorced Brown, acknowledged her drug addiction, sought treatment, completed her comeback album, and become financially solvent. On the one hand, the celebration of Houston's 2009 interview marks the public's desires to see *the voice* return to stage. On the other, it also tacitly reaffirms the desire to see her be personally responsible and to unmake the image that twelve years of tabloids and conjecture had implied, and that one season of performing on *Being Bobby Brown* had confirmed.

Neoliberalism provides a marketplace metaphor that permeates society, setting forth economies of exchange, including emotional and spiritual economies, that reward conformity and punish deviation, that, in essence, espouse the normative face of destructive desires. As Wendy Brown explains, "both persons and states are expected to comport themselves in ways that maximize their capital value in the present and enhance their future value, and both persons and states do so through practices of entrepreneurialism, self-investment, and/ or attracting investors."[78] While the 2009 interview with Winfrey signaled Houston's return to entrepreneurship and self-investment, her relapse to drug use would shift conversations to a deficient self, who had squandered talent, skill, and finance. Even analyses that attempt to contextualize her death and drug addiction veer toward personal responsibility philosophies by diminishing the significance of structural forces or overstating Houston's presumed resilience. How does focusing on Houston's drug use obfuscate the various ways that social institutions, including the destructive desire for a nuclear family, contributed to her death and/or drug use? How does turning attention to Houston's behavior engender a lack of sympathy for Houston, and how do Houston's performed social classes mediate those (racialized and gendered) responses? How does the lack of empathy for and sympathy toward Houston fit within a broader context in which black suffering, black abjection, and black humanity become illegible or otherwise inconsequential? As Nick Broomfield explains, "We're always looking for a reason not to give people a second chance, and I think she was so harshly judged for the drug addiction. There was very little attempt to understand where this was coming from or what it was about. I would like a lot of people to feel that there was a whole other way of looking at this."[79] *Destructive Desires* attempts to contextualize Houston's life by situating her destructive desires within competing and conflicting entangled networks. Although broader culture stigmatized Houston and read her as an aberration, her narrative seems rather mundane; Houston's dysfunctional marriage and the desires that propelled her to remain in it repositioned her within the discourse of an everyday black woman; despite access to opportunities, she cannot shake the yoke of black intimate relations' demand for normativity.

TRACK 10
"I'M EVERY WOMAN": FROM DIANE SAWYER TO OPRAH WINFREY,
A MEDITATION ON PERSONAL RESPONSIBILITY

The *Oprah Winfrey Show*, unlike Diane Sawyer's *Primetime*, targets women audiences, focuses on women's issues, and uses confessional interview tactics that cater to ways that American culture has socialized women to express themselves.[80] Despite Winfrey's refusal to accept the moniker *feminist*, the aforementioned aspects of the show, alongside Winfrey's investment in girls' leadership development, indebtedness to (black) women role models, and promotion of women-centered relationships, explain why some critics argue that Winfrey at minimum employs a de facto feminism. According to Jennifer Rexroat, "Oprah promotes a feminist ideology or practice without explicitly acknowledging the fact that she is endorsing either feminism or the United States' women's movement."[81] De facto feminism acknowledges that feminist politics do not require feminist identification, and recognizes that those feminist politics may fall on a spectrum from regressively conservative to radically liberal. Winfrey's politics arguably reinforce progressive *and* conservative politics by championing women's increased access, opportunities, and protections, but do not necessarily call into question the broader system of patriarchy. Nor do they connect patriarchy to other sources of exploitation, including neoliberalism, capitalism, and racism.

Just as some critics, for example, note Winfrey's eschewal of the term *feminist*, others have turned attention to how Winfrey's engagement with *racial* issues leaves intact the fundamental principles of antiblack racism. While Winfrey might call into question individual, conscious, overt episodes of racism, critics insist that she typically does not correlate them to systemic, institutional, unconscious, and covert manifestations.[82] Winfrey's engagement with (explicitly) *racial* issues positions Winfrey as someone who has *transcended* race, and this transcendence, which leads to discounting the persistence of systemic institutional racism, becomes "a principal reason for her show's success."[83] According to Peck, Winfrey "has been described as a comforting non-threatening bridge between black and white cultures" by "sometimes embracing, sometimes minimizing blackness."[84] An early symbol of post–civil rights era integration's success, Winfrey conjures in the viewing public's imagination the potential for postracialism (and not too-black blackness); the absence of racial animus presents equal opportunities and economic success for those who work hard, economize their talent, and remain personally responsible and disciplined. That she would later attribute her continued success as a global media giant to "inner strength and spirituality" perpetuates this cultural longing for black hard work and thrift. This reading focuses on the contexts that inform Winfrey's talk show and how we can understand her iconography in contemporary discourses about race, integration, and personal responsibility. It does not, more importantly, discount her commitment to black cultural production, black politics, and black life; rather it turns attention to the ways that hegemonic discourses eclipse the potential for a more radical imagination for black life, black culture, and black politics.[85]

As the "most anticipated music interview of the decade," Houston's two-part interview afforded Houston the opportunity to acknowledge her previous challenges, to illuminate the steps she had taken to overcome them, and to intimate her future plans.[86] In her first televised interview since 2002 (with Diane Sawyer), Houston emerged as a self-reflective woman whose (destructive) desire for marriage, family, and success had inadvertently gone awry. By framing her dreams and aspirations in this context, Houston rightfully suggests that despite her professional exceptionalism, her *desires* and *longings* remained common and relatable. Neither fame nor celebrity inured her from social pressure; to the contrary, they heightened these forces. Whereas earlier innuendo, rumor, and her own other admissions had characterized Houston as evidence par excellence of the dangers of insatiable material and physical desires, Houston's appearance on the *Oprah Winfrey Show* shifted attention to how previous analyses flattened the complexity of Houston's journey (figure 4.5). For example, while Winfrey's assignation "the voice" complimented Houston's unparalleled talent, Houston responded that it was "an overwhelming title." Houston then charted how her "life became the world's" and how she "had no normal 20s and 30s." In addition to absconding with her privacy, the persona of Whitney Houston had also become "too much to live up to, to try to be." The beginning of this interview instructively corroborates Houston's sense that Arista records created an image to sell, and, more importantly, illuminates the tenuous distinction between the artistic persona and the artist herself. The image of Houston needed to align with Houston's lived experience and vice versa, lest the viewing public disinvest in the artistic persona in addition to the artist. Indirectly, Houston's testimony anticipates what *Can I Be Me* reveals; in creating the image of Whitney Houston, Arista turned away from Houston's complex humanity, including her racial performances.[87]

In response, and not always in productive ways, Houston reasserted her self, her humanity, to distance the assumed persona from the *authentic* self. As Michael Awkward explains, "awareness of the self-perceptions and crafted images of recording artists is crucial when we attempt to understand their musical output, because, among other things, these constructed selves provide us with interpretive keys we can use to analyze their formulations of their songs' meanings."[88] Furthermore, Awkward admonishes, "we need also to be attentive to points of apparent dissonance between the purported selves, crafted

FIGURE 4.5. Whitney Houston and Oprah Winfrey discuss Houston's marriage, career, family, and drug addiction at Radio Hall in New York City for a two-hour season premiere of the *Oprah Winfrey Show* that aired on September 14 and 15, 2009, and coincided with the release of Houston's newest album, *I Look to You*.

images, and performed characters that come together, sometimes in quite problematic ways, in various public interpretation of the songs."[89] We can apply Awkward's methodology to interpret songs more generally to rhythm and blues culture because the *meaning* of their songs and cultural influences become tied to the music, "self-perceptions," "crafted images," and "performed characters." These images, perceptions, and characters exist beyond the musical performances into the entangled networks that they produce. For Houston, the tension between the persona and the artist engenders a loss of self, which informs other decisions, including her choice to marry Brown. Although Houston rejects the notion that her marriage to Brown was "strategic," she asserts that Brown "allowed me to be me," that Brown was "fun," and that their marriage was "passionate." Smiling, she reinforces for Winfrey what she had told Sawyer; although she avoided characterizing their passion as "an addiction to love making," she reminds viewers that their relationship had not been bereft of sex.

Houston's professional identity required an identity performance that diverged from her *authentic* self. Her marriage did too, albeit in different ways, signaling the ways marriage also required heteropatriarchal gender conformity. She reveals that she did enact certain gender performances in order to assuage Brown's aversion toward feeling like "Mr. Houston." Although she could be "black" with Brown, she does concede that dysfunction persisted early in the marriage, and attributes the marital strife to heteropatriarchal marriage's double-edged expectation; not only should men be heads of households, but women should subordinate themselves to their husbands. Her fame and economic prowess made this subordination all but impossible, despite her attempts to be *Mrs. Brown*. Houston had been famous at the time she married, yet her fame skyrocketed after her performance in *The Bodyguard* and the release of "I Will Always Love You." Houston correlates her success (economic and fame) following *The Bodyguard* to the decline in their marital bliss and the rise in their drug use and her addiction. Houston confides that, "something happens to a man when a woman has that much fame/control." By casting her marital discord as a function of imbalanced economic roles, for example, Houston taps into a history in black intimate relationships wherein black women's outearning of black men upset conventional gender role expectations and performances and caused relationship antagonisms.

TRACK 11
"I DIDN'T KNOW MY OWN STRENGTH": PERSONAL RESPONSIBILITY
AND GENDER POLITICS

Houston's example extends this argument to show how, even within upwardly mobile relationships that enjoy wealth, the incursion of patriarchal logics frustrates racialized gender roles. To accommodate, Houston admits that she downplayed her success, adopting her status as "Mrs. Brown."[90] Although "he's not gonna like this," she confirms Winfrey's suspicion that Brown was "jealous." Attributing her agreement to be a part of *Being Bobby Brown* to her desires to appease and support Brown, Houston remarks, "I just wanted people to know I was his wife. . . . I didn't quite know what to think. . . . I was hoping to be Mrs. Bobby Brown without shadowing the situation." Winfrey concludes this portion, reminding her that "it was after seeing you on that show that many people became worried about you." Houston's narration and self-presentation work coevally to contextualize her decision to participate on the show and to counteract the image that *Being Bobby Brown* had painted. Houston's deliberate, engaged, and focused narration here pushes back against the erratic, unkempt, and disengaged look each episode of *Being Bobby Brown* presented. Houston intimates that her love for Brown propelled her to make decisions that defied her thriving. *Destructive Desires* asserts that this love emerged within a broader discourse of destructive desires about black intimate relations.

Like most narratives, Houston's interview self-consciously allows her to construct an image of herself for the viewing public, and that context, alongside her desire to promote her new album, *I Look to You*, inform our interpretation of Houston's testimony. But her explanation pointedly demonstrates the degree to which, implicitly and explicitly, destructive desires shape her own expectations for her life, how she too had internalized some expectations for black intimate relations and respectability politics even as they undermined other desires (same-gender?) she may have possessed. While Houston undoubtedly conceals in her revelations, electing which parts of her history to tell and/or revise, her contextualization explains rather than absolves; in other words, Houston presents herself as someone who made a set of (bad) decisions. Yet she also reflects on the initial factors and contexts that motivated her to make them, and she examines the circumstances that compelled her to remake them. She effectively takes responsibility for the choices she has made rather than emerge as an agentless victim of black heteropatriarchy (wife) and white heteropatriarchy (music industry). This element of the interview proves necessary to stage the reception of the most-forthcoming admission from Houston—that she had in fact been addicted to drugs, had gone to rehab, and was drug free. Although Houston *verbalized* what many viewers felt they already knew, that confirmation generated a sense that Houston perhaps was ready to at last live her best life. As the "live your best life specialist," Winfrey facilitated the process, acting as a witness who, in the words of Dori Laub, "has to feel the victim's victories, defeats, and silences, know them from within, so that they can assume the form of testimony."[91]

In *accepting responsibility* for her drug use, Houston inadvertently tapped into and simultaneously resisted personal responsibility discourses that perpetuate drug use primarily as individualized choices that people make irrespective of institutions. Houston confirmed that during the "crack is whack" interview she had been addicted to drugs. Although she had resisted Sawyer's claim that she had spent $730,000 on drugs, she confides in Winfrey that "someone out there had made a lot of money." Her admission to sitting in her room for weeks at a time portrays someone suffering from depression, in addition to addiction. In other words, her testimony undermines an image of Houston as an addict without a reason or context. Neither confirming nor denying whether the *National Inquirer*'s picture of the "drug infested den" was her house, Houston demurs that she did not reside in the house when Brown's sister allegedly captured the photo. And, although she remained drug free at the time of the interview, Houston understands the complexity of addiction and the precariousness of sobriety; she told Winfrey, "I am taking it one day at a time."

While Houston acknowledges that early in her relationship she had done drugs recreationally and for enjoyment, she explains that drugs became a vehicle to mask pain, that she was "just trying to cover what you don't want people to know." She wanted to conceal the fact that although she had obtained the marriage, career, and child she *desired*, she did not feel fulfilled; she did not want the public to think it had been correct about her unequal yoking with Brown, thereby letting her relationship become another statistic to evidence the putative dysfunction of black intimate relationships. By staging Houston as *every woman*, the interview demystified her drug use as an example of excessive consumerism to instead recast it as a coping mechanism that quotidian desires and problems engendered. By connecting her drug use to her dysfunctional marriage, the interview demonstrated how black intimate relationship discourses circumscribe people's behaviors and produce destructive desires (and habits). By contextualizing Houston's *individual* behaviors within these broader contexts (institutions), the interview provides a discursive space to imagine conditions under which Houston could have thrived. By reimagining conditions under which Houston might have thrived, the interview turns attention to the interrelationship between the individual and the institutional, potentially noting the intimate ways they connect.

At the conclusion of the show, Houston performs "I Didn't Know My Own Strength," where the assertion, "I was not built to break," calls upon the "inner strength" the interview reveals Houston had developed in her postmarriage and postrehab lives. The conclusion of the show recalls the beginning and the parallel between the two functions as a part of the broader narrative arc. Tracing her move from the past to the present, the song, like the interview itself, charts Houston's descent, yet ends with an optimistic view toward the future. Although the temporality between the past, present, and future does not move linearly, the progression of the song demonstrates a fluidity between Houston and her persona. From her own accounts, Houston likened herself to the song's persona: "lost touch with my soul. . . . Lost sight of my dream / Thought it would be the end of me / I thought I'd never make it through." Even though she had "crashed down" and "tumbled," she did not "crumble" and "got through all the pain." Whereas the "lost" dream could reference the deferral of her professional and familial aspirations, the song conveys a more general sense of loss that extends beyond any specific objects. While the crashing and tumbling aptly describe the damage she, her persona, and image incur, it presages a more spiritual strength that these mishaps cannot unnerve. She sings: "My faith kept me alive / I picked myself back up / Hold my head up." Despite that she "wondered how I'd get through the night / Thought I took all I could take," Houston and her persona demonstrate they have indeed overcome despair; that she is there performing the song testifies to this fact. Yet it also forces us to think of overcoming as a process rather than a one-time act.

The importance of community contravenes the logics of singular strength that the song sometimes performs. The live performance itself affords Houston the opportunity to ad lib, where, at the end of the song, she nods toward the support networks that, beyond her faith, kept her alive. Houston interjects, "My mama said I was not built to break" [audience applause and cheering]. "Dionne [Warwick] said I was not built to break" [audience applause and cheering]. "Clive said come on back and sing, you're not built to break" [audience applause and cheering]. "Your love said" [audience applause and cheering] "your love said I was not built to break. Oprah said, girl do you know you're loved? Now I know my own strength." Houston's performance thus deprivileges the individualism that the song calls forth, instead positing community as central to her return. As important, the performance foreshadows the need for a continued support network; Houston's best life thus requires community not the self-help that neoliberal logics demand. Inasmuch as the interview and song stage individualism, they also posit a tension between it and community and other institutions beyond the self. This tension more symptomatically gestures toward and reflects a broader angst about the relationship between individuals and institutions in the

post–civil rights era. Even still, by the conclusion of the interview, Winfrey's assertion rings true: "you will certainly have a deeper appreciation for what she has
been through as a human being." The Houston that emerged in this interview and
the one that emerged on the set of *Sparkle* in 2011 would, on February 12, 2012, be
replaced by the one that *Being Bobby Brown* had cemented in 2005. The very
humanity that Winfrey helped Houston to restore vis-à-vis her interview in 2009,
Winfrey would be called upon to defend when Houston died in 2012.

TRACK 12

"I LOOK TO YOU": RACE, SEX, AND PERSONAL RESPONSIBILITY

IN RESPONSES TO ADDICTION

Although we may never know Houston's specific causes of death, the extent of
her drug use, and the degree to which long-term drug use may have contributed
to her death, broader culture magnifies her drug use, painting it, alongside her
personal choices, as the source of her death. For example, Rick Santorum's presidential campaign characterized Houston as a cautionary tale of the excesses of
drug use and poor personal choices. Chaka Khan pointed toward her death to
evidence the music industry's more pervasive problematic drug culture. These
discussions about Houston's death and drug use, often implicitly, called to
mind discourses about race and sexuality and tied them to black intimate relations discourses.[92] In "Celebrity Drug Scandals: Media Double Standards," for
example, Rebecca Tiger contrasts how the media portrayed Lance Armstrong's
drug addiction with its representation of Houston's to emphasize how racial and
gendered scripts influence responses to drug addiction and use. Tiger argues
that society distinguishes between *good* and *bad* drugs and that these distinctions occur along racial and gender lines. These differentiations become "codi-
fied in public policy" and "Houston's narrative conforms to the historic frame of
the degraded, immediately deviant addict, who is often pictured as black and
female."[93]

Whereas Armstrong, despite his repeated and ongoing use of drugs, retains
his other identities in addition to addict, "addict" overshadows Houston's other
identities.[94] Tiger's contention helps us to think about how characterizing Houston primarily as an addict calls upon and reinforces ideas about black people's
deviance and inability to conform to norms. It both indicts and disciplines as
debates about Houston's deviance (inability to mother effectively because of
drug use) tie Houston to a long history of black women's abjection within the
familial unit. What, for example, animates the desires to construct this narrative while ignoring the many ways that the Whitney Houston Foundation and
Houston herself fought against a range of social injustices, including those that
disproportionately affected black communities, or how she became an icon for
the arts (figure 4.6)?[95] *Destructive Desires* raises this point to demonstrate how
conversations that examine Houston's drug use persistently extrapolate it from
broader external forces that may inform our understanding of the usage and the
external forces themselves. In the terms of this book, it imagines whether drug

FIGURE 4.6. Whitney Houston poses in front of the newly renamed Whitney E. Houston Academy of Creative and Performing Arts, formerly the Franklin School, on June 12, 1997, in East Orange, New Jersey.

use has a relationship to the normative face of destructive desires, and the inability or unwillingness to meet its expectations. Post–civil rights era notions of personal responsibility that inform debates about Houston's death foreclose upon this type of analysis.

In *Sparkle* (track 1), for example, Houston's character, Emma, interrogatively admonishes her daughter, "Wasn't my life cautionary tale enough?" Critics have interpreted this remark/question as yet another cautionary tale for personal irresponsibility (using drugs). Reillustrating the permeability of the relationship between the persona and the artist, viewing publics analyzed this comment as foreshadowing; that Houston the artist envisioned her own life and career as a cautionary tale, and that her subsequent death made her own life one too. If Houston's life and career cautioned, *Destructive Desires* calls into question what they admonished, how, and why. It invites a careful consideration of the stakes of interpreting Houston's death as a *cautionary tale for humanity*, a warning against the lethal dangers of excessive drug use without contextualizing the usage within a destructive desires framework. Heath Deihl, for example, argues in "'Didn't [She] Almost Have it All? Being Whitney Houston/Performing Addiction/Imagining America" that critics and ordinary citizens cite Emma's warning "as a cautionary tale about the excesses of celebrity, the immorality of addiction, and the inevitability of a shameful and punitive death."[96] Within this framework, critics "cast addiction as a fault or wrong for which an addict can and must be held accountable through the punishment of death."[97] The lack of empathy that some had for Houston's death supports his assertion that American culture feels as if death rightfully punishes those who experience addiction and refuse to obtain treatment and/or maintain sobriety. In this line of thinking, Houston's testimony on the *Oprah Winfrey Show* betrayed itself.

Houston's own admission about the synchronicity between her increased drug use and her marriage further contextualizes why institutions, including ideas about family and community, call to mind black intimate relations discourses when we think about the debates surrounding Houston's death. In *Ezili's Mirrors: Imagining Black Queer Genders*, Omise'eke Natasha Tinsley argues that black intimate relations lie at the heart of the LGBTQI community's higher relapse rates because heteronormativity and homophobia decrease their access to the communal support necessary to maintain sobriety. In her discussion of Houston's potential nonnormative sexual practices and its relationship to her drug addiction, Tinsely observes, "Some speculate that Whitney's disintegration had less to do with the relationships that fame brought her than those it cost her."[98] Suggesting that fame cost Houston a public relationship with Crawford, for example, Tinsley further adds that "black women who love women grapple with addiction at rates up to three times those of their straight sisters," reinforcing how the normative face of destructive desires actually undermines black thriving.[99] While Houston's death invites us to question the destructiveness of compulsory heterosexuality, behavioral explanations of addiction that extrapolate her *choices* from heteronormativity, heterosexism, and homophobia reinforce the notion that Houston's behaviors cause her destruction. They also reinforce the normative face of destructive desires.

TRACK 13
"I LOVE THE LORD": AFTERLIFE AND THE POSSIBILITIES OF NEW LIFE

The focus on Houston's life since her death in 2012 has given Houston's life new life, and afterlife. The term *afterlife* calls attention to how discussions of Houston's life and career vacillate between the past, present, and future, and allows us to think energetically about how the cultural longings and destructive desires that animate her life and career return following her death. The many tributes at music award shows, articles in magazines, cinematic productions (a biopic, a documentary, and even TV One's *The Bobbi Kristina Story*), postdeath interviews, and books (by current and former family members, fans, and other "experts") invoke Houston not simply to pay homage to her past; as important, attempts to memorialize her simultaneously write new histories that resurrect her by enlivening her past and by posthumously bestowing new meanings to her life.[100] The persistence of necropolitics in black political and social life since slavery has made the boundary between life and death permeable, tenuous, and generative.

The flying African narrative in black culture embodies the many ways that members of the African diaspora have imagined the relationship between life and death. As Soyica Colbert argues, the flying African "narrative extends black life by demonstrating the interplay between the living and the dead and showing how the living may revive histories, narratives, and practices that seem to have passed on without leaving a trace."[101] Houston's afterlife clarifies the mutually constitutive role the dead play in the interplay between the living and dead and the crucial role the dead play in recovering and reviving known and unknown histories. Houston thus accentuates the role the dead play in this process of historical revision. Reading Houston's death allows us to consider ways to think about a more nuanced and complex set of black intimate relations discourses. Conversations about her life underscore the increasing political urgency to find more capacious notions of blackness. These more expansive notions of blackness must continue to foreground the crosscutting political issues that emerge at the intersections of race, gender, sexuality, and social class. They too must take into account how black familial organization and black intimate relations discourses impact destructive desires and solutions to black inequality.

The conjectures of whether Houston would still be alive had she been able to live an openly nonnormative sexual life bring into focus the continued need for a black sexual politics that foregrounds a range of black sexualities, black intimate relationships, and black sexual expressions as necessary for a thriving black futurity.[102] If we read Houston's wedding and afterlife as, in the words of Gershun Avilez, "an effective drama between contending forces that relies on demands of secrecy and public knowledge, questions of intimacy, and assertions of same sex-desire," we can view Houston's life within a continuum where the regulation of black intimate relationships becomes an important heuristic for understanding, constricting, and expanding black life and black political possibilities.[103] Yet, as chapter 1 argues, by tethering black intimate relations to black sociopolitical advancement, we reinforce the normative discourses that also prevent black people from thriving. The consequence of this practice is that nonnormative family structures escape both the limits of the political imagination and the capacities of public policy and the public imagination. *Destructive Desires* encourages, in the words of Susana M. Morris, "a fundamental reimagining of kinship to include examples of extended and fictive kin (as opposed to making the nuclear family the only legitimate model), platonic unions (such as Boston marriages), and queer families (such as same-sex unions and polyamory)."[104] If the solutions to black inequality remain increasingly tethered to black familial configuration, an expansion of what constitutes family might in turn elongate the solutions that emerge to ameliorate black inequality. Moreover, a more elastic definition of family can also move beyond the regulation of black intimate relations and allow black intimate relations the capacity to thrive outside of the strictures of discipline, regulation, and hypervisibility. Tinsley's contentions that we must examine texts that assert a "vision of creative gender and sexualities" and that we might locate those creative imaginings in *Ezili*, "a pantheon of lwa who represent divine forces of love, sexuality, prosperity, pleasure, maternity, creativity, and fertility," provide an additional framework for us to re(imagine) black intimate relations outside of normative, European-colonized perspectives.[105] As *Destructive Desires* turns toward the epilogue, it wants to stage how a figure like Toni Braxton helps us to continue to think about rhythm and blues culture, black intimate relations, and the challenges and possibilities for black political advancement.

Epilogue
"It's Just Another Sad Love Song"

Reading Toni Braxton

And boy I hope you know it / That no one could love you like I could / Lord knows I want to trust you / And always how I'd love you / I'm not sure if love is enough.

–Toni Braxton, *Toni Braxton*, "You Mean the World to Me"

Love was always something magical / But the feeling is so tragic for / And all I know is in love / The thing that I want most / I can't possess / There's only emptiness.

–Toni Braxton, *Secrets*, "In the Late of Night"

"Long as I live (long as I, I can live) / I'll never get over (you getting over me) / It's killing me (it's killing me, killing me) / I'll never get over you (you getting over me).

–Toni Braxton, *Sex and Cigarettes*, "Long as I Live"

In March 2018, Toni Braxton released her latest album, *Sex and Cigarettes*, where the song, "Long as I Live," articulates a point about love and relationships that her two-and-a-half decades' worth of cultural production emphasizes: romanticized notions of love fall short of grasping love's complexity, incompleteness, emptiness, unevenness, and limits. More pointedly, if the song's persona assumes the identity of heterosexual (black) women, her musical production further suggests that love's failures disproportionately affect black women, who, as a result of their romantic partner's infidelity, disinterest, or otherwise unavailability, all too often discover the shortcomings of romantic love. Yet, despite this ambivalent tone toward love, Braxton's corpus of music, which also explores other themes, still paints love as desirable. Her portrayal essentially invites listeners to imagine the circumstances under which black intimate relations might thrive in the absence of destructive love desires; or, the conditions under which love proves not to present destructive desires to black intimate relations. From her debut on the *Boomerang* soundtrack to her latest CD, Braxton's cultural production has toyed with love, imagining and reimagining its personal and political possibilities. As the persona of "Long as I live" croons it, inasmuch as individuals possess love, love possesses them; hence, "Long as I live (long as I can live), I'll never get over (you getting over me)." Recalling Lauren Berlant's theory of cruel optimism, the juxtaposition of the parenthetical refrains in both verses suggests that the absence of love threatens the persona's well-being as does the desire for it and its presence. In a heteropatriarchal society in which structural racism invades black intimate relations, love, too, can become a destructive desire.

As Braxton has revealed, this fascination originated from her desire to show love's complications rather than its romanticized aspects: "I wanted to sing about love. Not the corny television side of love, but the realistic side. That it is not always 'Baby, I love you,' but 'Why you didn't call me last night?' and 'if you love me, why don't you show me you love me?'"[1] As the second epigraph of this epilogue suggests, love, in and of itself, is not always enough, and Braxton's willingness to call into question what love is and how it manifests itself pushes against the broader cultural trend in the 1990s that promotes marriage for black communities to the degree that love becomes a prerequisite for romantic couplings. If, as "In the Late of the Night" laments, the inability to possess the one the persona loves usurps love's magic and replaces it with emptiness, what prospects for love and mutually fulfilling relationships do black couples have? Braxton's repertoire thinks energetically about the definitions in and of themselves (e.g., what constitutes love) as well as the conditions under which (personal and structural) love can thrive. Her cultural production, in this regard like Edmonds's, shapes cultural longings, destructive desires, and black intimate relations discourses for her listening publics and black cultural production more broadly.

Braxton's shaping of rhythm and blues culture also hinges on her voice, aesthetic, and body image insofar as her sound, hair, and dress pushed the boundaries of black women's cultural representations within the rhythm and blues genre. In challenging these expectations, she called into question governing norms about black women's *proper* spaces in the public and private spheres. That listening publics would situate Braxton in a genealogy that included Anita Baker remains important for two reasons. First, when Edmonds (and Reid) produced "Love Shoulda Brought You Home Last Night" and "Give You My Heart," they intended for Baker to sing the songs. Consequently, they composed the songs for an artist whose voice carries a lower vocal register, which both Baker and Braxton have. Braxton's performance of the song on the lower register then echoes Baker's voice. At the same time, it invites listening publics to expand how they equate sounds with the bodies that produce them. Whereas the lower register distinguished Braxton as a sultry singer, a contralto, it also, according to Braxton, caused listeners to mistake her for a man.[2] Whereas chapter 4 discusses Stover's notion of a sonic color line, Braxton's recollection reinforces how the sonic color line remains gendered. Yet her disruption of that line once again speaks to how black rhythm and blues artists and cultural production consistently

FIGURE E.1. Toni Braxton performs during a LaFace Records party to celebrate the Recording Industry Association of America certifying platinum her first record, *Toni Braxton* (July 1993), in Atlanta, Georgia, on October 14, 1993.

blurred essentialist ideas about gender identity, expression, and performances lurking in the cultural imagination.

More importantly, conversations about Braxton's voice and others like it reveal how market forces reshaped the circulation of rhythm and blues sounds in the post-1990s era, making Braxton one of the last figures to emerge in the rhythm and blues contralto tradition. Whereas prior to the mid-1990s, rhythm and blues culture championed the range of its artists' voices, "where singers with a mastery of clean, high tones—from Patti Labelle to Deniece Williams to Ralph Tresvant to Usher—flourished next to singers who favored lower, rougher registers, artists like Barry White, Chaka Khan, Anita Baker and Toni Braxton," the rise of hip-hop and rap changed this phenomenon.[3] As rap and hip-hop artists expanded and "took over the vocal ranges that once belonged to R&B," and music stations also began to play less R&B, the changes "limited the avenues of exposure for all R&B singers but especially hurt those who favor low, throaty intonations."[4] The music industry and the listening public's desires thus constitute an entangled network that propelled Braxton's career, and made her one of the last artists to benefit from this exposure. This distinction has contributed to Braxton's multiplatinum records and the honors and awards they have garnered; when Braxton's voice appears, listeners readily recognize its distinctiveness (figure E.1).

Whereas Braxton's voice carved out the sonic component of her aesthetic, her short-crop haircut, petite figure, and fitted dresses made her an icon for black sensuality and sexuality. Like Howard, Braxton too championed a sensual and sexualized presentation for black women. With the exception of "You're Making Me High," from *Secrets*, which emphasizes women's sexual pleasure, including masturbation, Braxton's sex appeal draws less ire than does Howard's. This difference arguably pertains to the different ways their entangled networks read their physical presentation, song lyrics, and album covers. Even still, Braxton's performances and dress invited criticism that centered on respectability politics and the need to contain black sexuality and sexual expression. The critiques, evidencing the normative face of destructive desires, reveal the continuous trappings of racial stereotypes as the primary framework through which to understand black identity and blackness.[5] But, unlike Howard, Braxton's songs themselves insulate her from censure and public reprimand. Whereas Braxton does garner iconic status, that iconicity does not call to mind "a sexual revolution" in ways that Howard's iconicity does.

Although Braxton never became a symbol for post–civil rights era notions of postracial success, post–civil rights era notions of neoliberalism, particularly as they relate to fiscal and personal responsibilities, invade Braxton's personal and professional lives. With the exception of Braxton's *More Than a Woman* (2002), her album sales flourished, and arguably should have amassed her ample wealth. Why then, in 1997, did the first lady of LaFace Records have to file for bankruptcy? And, following her first filing, why did she have to file again a second time ten years later? Because of the gag order that Braxton signed as a part of a lawsuit against Arista records, she could not defend herself against the accusations of personal irresponsibility that insisted she had wasted her finances. For example, in her *VH1 Behind the Music*, she recalls how Winfrey had been "so friggin mean" when she appeared on Winfrey's show in 1996, where Winfrey chastised her for excessive spending.[6] Rather than focus on the ways that Arista Records, and other labels, exploited their artists, Braxton's critics instead focused on her behaviors, citing excessive consumerism as the cause for and explanation of her bankruptcy.[7] While Braxton's spending habits may have contributed to her financial woes, Winfrey privileged her choices and spending habits (her behaviors) as causing her bankruptcy; her excessive consumerism, and her misplaced values (depreciating items over appreciating ones) caused her downfall; Winfrey did not vocalize publicly that the recording industry, by redistributing costly services to the artists, and by augmenting its profit line from the revenue the artists generate, caused the bankruptcy or even shared the responsibility/blame.[8] In 2000, *JET* magazine echoed the importance of taking control of one's life and of taking responsibility for one's actions in thinking about Braxton's bankruptcy.[9] These ideas gel alongside the developing philosophies of neoliberalism, hard work, and postracial political responses to economic disparities in general. Although Braxton's second bankruptcy filing resulted because she had to cancel scheduled concert performances as a result of unexpected illness, this first bankruptcy still colored the public's perception of her as fiscally irresponsible. In this way, like Houston, she remains responsible for purging her finances, and, therefore undeserving of sympathy. She must take responsibility by admitting

FIGURE E.2. Toni Braxton and Kenneth "Babyface" Edmonds perform their Grammy-winning "Hurt You" at the UNCF Evening of Stars Show at Boisfeuillet Jones Atlanta Civic Center on April 12, 2015, in Atlanta, Georgia.

her mistakes and curtailing her spending habits. Given that her second bankruptcy resulted from medical bills, it is worth noting that medical bills and other related medical expenses remain a primary cause for filing bankruptcy. As we continue to consider how broader structures impact individual choice, we must also note that loopholes within insurance laws allowed her insurance not to cover the contracts she canceled.

Given Braxton's tumultuous relationship with the business side of the music industry, it became disappointing, although not necessarily surprising, that she decided to retire from singing in 2013. The announcement stunned fans, yet Edmonds soon allayed their fears by completing a duet album, *Love, Marriage and Divorce*. Although the album itself fittingly suits their collaborations over the course of their careers, another set of important entangled networks coalesced to precede the retirement and to facilitate her coming out of it. First, as Braxton shares, and artists like Howard concur (and Houston too would likely agree), the business components of the music industry exhaust. In addition to this point, the industry had changed, as the aforementioned discussion suggests. Braxton battled with the fact that people told her "she was dated, that 'the old Toni Braxton' is played out," presumably reflecting the changing sound of rhythm and blues culture.[10] Edmonds, however, admonished, "You've stopped believing in yourself. Why have you stopped playing the piano on your albums? Stop thinking like a record company—I need you to remember you're an artist."[11] For Braxton, she had to reconstruct her artistic identity in light of how the industry had transformed and in light of what she valued in her cultural production. Both the duet and the latest CD show that Braxton's cultural aesthetic and thematic concerns about black intimate relations resound. Recognizing her ongoing influence, Soul Train honored Braxton with a Living Legend Award in 2017. In the same year, the Song Writer Hall of Fame inducted Kenneth "Babyface" Edmonds. Although Braxton has referred to Edmonds as her industry husband, both have insisted their relationship remains professional, platonic, and familial (figure E.2). The synchronicity of their achievements gestures toward their mutually constitutive influence on black intimate relations vis-à-vis their cultural production in rhythm and blues culture.

Braxton's writing of *UnBreak My Heart*, executive producing of the biopic, and starring in the WETV show *Braxton Family Values* also inform her retirement and reentrance. First, the narrative and the biopic allowed Braxton the opportunity, as *Life After* does for Howard, to finally give her perspective on why she had sued the record labels and filed bankruptcies. Her participation on *Braxton Family Values* also allowed viewers the opportunity to learn about interior aspects of Braxton's life, which she intentionally had kept private. Whereas the memoir and biopic allowed Braxton to provide closure to what she perceived as unfinished business of her music career, *Braxton Family Values* reinvigorated interest in her music production (as the TV One music shows did for others). Combined, Braxton received closure and new beginnings simultaneously. These platforms have allowed her to extend her meditations on black intimate relations and destructive desires while creating new ones (particularly in the representations of family and intimate relations on *Braxton Family Values*).

By ending *Destructive Desires* with this discussion of Braxton, this epilogue charts the implicit and explicit ways that cultural longings, destructive desires, and entangled networks facilitate how we imagine black intimate relations. By focusing on the imagination, this book underscores the need to look beyond what we currently *may know* to develop innovative models for organizing black intimate relations *and* for developing solutions to black inequality. By shifting cultural paradigms about black intimate relations, the discussion calls for a more nuanced structural analysis of black inequality while acknowledging that current conversations bind black inequality to black intimate relations. By calling for more nuanced solutions, *Destructive Desires* demands remedies that *also* look away from/beyond black intimate relations; it emphasizes the need to innovate structural solutions that replace black inequality with black equity. *Destructive Desires* insists that the eradication of structural inequality can offer reparation to black communities.

APPENDIX A

SELECT LIST OF KENNETH "BABYFACE" EDMONDS'S SONGS

Title[1]	Artist(s)	Year
Crazy Bout 'Cha	The Deele	1983
Slow Jam	Midnight Star, Usher and Monica	1983
Don't Keep Me Waiting	The Whispers	1984
Some Kinda Lover	The Whispers	1984
All I've Ever Known	The Deele	1985
I'll Send You Roses	The Deele	1985
Let's Work Tonight	The Deele	1985
Stimulate	The Deele	1985
Suspicious	The Deele	1985
Sweet November	The Deele/ Troop	1985/1992
I'd Still Say Yes	Klymaxx/The Braxtons	1986/1996
Circumstantial Evidence	Shalamar	1987
Dry Your Eyes	The Deele	1987
Girlfriend	Pebbles	1987
I Want You (to Be My Playthang)	Shalamar	1987
In the Mood	The Whispers	1987
Let No One Separate Us	The Deele	1987
Rock Steady	The Whispers	1987
So Many Thangz	The Deele	1987
Two Occasions	The Deele	1987
Cruel Prelude	Bobby Brown	1988
Days Like This	Sheena Easton	1988
Dial My Heart	The Boys	1988

[1] Note: List includes songs that Edmonds has (co)written for himself and other artists and/or groups.

Title[1]	Artist(s)	Year
Don't Be Cruel	Bobby Brown	1988
Don't Mess with Me	Karyn White	1988
Every Little Step	Bobby Brown	1988
Family Man	Karyn White	1988
Follow My Rainbow	Sheena Easton	1988
Jealous	The Mac Band	1988
Knocked Out	Paula Abdul	1988
A Little Romance	The Boys	1988
Love Saw It	Karyn White	1988
The Lover in Me	Sheena Easton	1988
Lucky Charm	The Boys	1988
No Deposit, No Return	Sheena Easton	1988
One Love	Sheena Easton	1988
Roni	Bobby Brown	1988
Roses Are Red	The Mac Band	1988
Secret Rendezvous	Karyn White	1988
Stuck	The Mac Band	1988
Superwoman	Karyn White	1988
The Way You Love Me	Karyn White	1988
Can't Stop	After 7	1989
Heat of the Moment	After 7	1989
It's No Crime	Babyface	1989
Let's Be Romantic	Babyface	1989
Love's Been So Nice	After 7	1989
My Kinda Girl	Babyface	1989
Nothin' (That Compares 2 U)	The Jacksons	1989
On Our Own	Bobby Brown	1989
One Night	After 7	1989
Ready or Not	After 7	1989
Rock Wit'cha	Bobby Brown	1989
Sayonara	After 7	1989
Soon As I Get Home	Babyface	1989
Sunshine	Babyface	1989
Tender Lover	Babyface	1989

Title[1]	Artist(s)	Year
Where Will You Go	Babyface	1989
Whip Appeal	Babyface	1989
Anymore	Whitney Houston	1990
Backyard	Pebbles	1990
Don't Wear It Out	Mary Davis	1990
Fairweather Friend	Johnny Gill	1990
Feels So Much Better	Johnny Gill	1990
Giving You the Benefit	Pebbles	1990
Give It to Me	Pebbles	1990
Good Thang	Pebbles	1990
I'm Your Baby Tonight	Whitney Houston	1990
Love Hurts	Ralph Tresvant	1990
Love Makes Things Happen	Pebbles	1990
Miracle	Whitney Houston	1990
My, My, My	Johnny Gill	1990
Never Know Love	Johnny Gill	1990
Say a Prayer for Me	Pebbles	1990
Why Do I Believe	Pebbles	1990
Don't Remind Me	Damian Dame	1991
Don't You Deserve Someone	Jermaine Jackson	1991
Exclusivity	Damian Dame	1991
Gotta Learn My Rhythm	Damian Dame	1991
I Dream, I Dream	Jermaine Jackson	1991
A Lovers Holiday	Jermaine Jackson	1991
Rebel (With a Cause)	Jermaine Jackson	1991
Right Down to It	Damian Dame	1991
Secrets	Jermaine Jackson	1991
Slave to the Rhythm	Michael Jackson	1991
Treat You Right	Jermaine Jackson	1991
True Lovers	Jermaine Jackson	1991
Trumpet Man	Damian Dame	1991
We're Making Whoopee	Jermaine Jackson	1991
Whack It on Me	Damian Dame	1991
When I'm Crying	Damian Dame	1991

Continued

Title[1]	Artist(s)	Year
You Said, You Said	Jermaine Jackson	1991
Baby-Baby-Baby	TLC	1992
Don't Wanna Love You	Shanice	1992
End of the Road	Boyz II Men	1992
Give U My Heart	Babyface and Toni Braxton	1992
Good Enough	Bobby Brown	1992
Ho of My Own	Highland Place Mobsters	1992
Humpin' Around	Bobby Brown	1992
Love By Day, Love By Night	After 7	1992
Love Shoulda Brought You Home	Toni Braxton	1992
Pretty Little Girl	Bobby Brown	1992
Queen of the Night	Whitney Houston	1992
Reversal of a Dog	The LaFace Cartel	1992
Shock Dat Monkey	TLC	1992
Somethin' You Wanna Know	TLC	1992
There U Go	Johnny Gill	1992
Tonight Is Right	Keith Washington	1992
Truly Something Special	After 7	1992
Always in My Heart	Tevin Campbell	1993
And Our Feelings	Babyface	1993
Another Sad Love Song	Toni Braxton	1993
A Bit Old-Fashioned	Babyface	1993
Breathe Again	Toni Braxton	1993
Can We Talk	Tevin Campbell	1993
For the Cool in You	Babyface	1993
I'll Always Love you	Babyface	1993
Illusions	Babyface	1993
I'm Ready	Tevin Campbell	1993
Lady, Lady	Babyface	1993
Long Way from Home	Johnny Gill	1993
Never Forget You	Mariah Carey	1993
Never Keeping Secrets	Babyface	1993
Rock Bottom	Babyface	1993
Saturday	Babyface	1993

Title[1]	Artist(s)	Year
Seven Whole Days	Toni Braxton	1993
Something in Your Eyes	Bell Biv DeVoe	1993
Tell Me How U Want It	Johnny Gill	1993
Well Alright	Babyface	1993
When Can I See You	Babyface	1993
With All My Heart	Walter & Scotty	1993
You Mean the World to Me	Toni Braxton	1993
Betcha Never	Vanessa Williams	1994
Can I Stay with You	Karyn White	1994
Diggin' on You	TLC	1994
Have I Never	A Few Good Men	1994
Here Comes the Pain Again	Karyn White	1994
Honey	Aretha Franklin	1994
I Don't Want to Know	Gladys Knight	1994
I'll Make Love to You	Boyz II Men	1994
Let's Do it Again	TLC	1994
Red Light Special	TLC	1994
Southern Girl	A Few Good Men	1994
Take a Bow	Madonna	1994
Water Runs Dry	Boyz II Men	1994
Where Is My Love	El DeBarge and Babyface	1994
Willing to Forgive	Aretha Franklin	1994
You Can't Run	Vanessa Williams	1994
Young Girl	A Few Good Men	1994
All Night Long	SWV	1995
And I Gave My Love to You	Sonja Marie	1995
Count On Me	Whitney Houston and CeCe Winans	1995
Cryin' for It	After 7	1995
Exhale (Shoop Shoop)	Whitney Houston	1995
How Could You Call Her Baby	Shanna	1995
How Do You Tell the One	After 7	1995
It Hurts Like Hell	Aretha Franklin	1995
Kissing You	Faith Evans	1995

Continued

Title[1]	Artist(s)	Year
Let It Flow	Toni Braxton	1995
Love Will Be Waiting at Home	For Real	1995
Melt Away	Mariah Carey	1995
My First Night with You	Deborah Cox/ Mya	1995/1998
My Love, Sweet Love	Patti LaBelle	1995
Not Gon Cry	Mary J. Blige	1995
Pretty Girl	Jon B.	1995
Sittin' Up in My Room	Brandy	1995
Someone to Love	Jon B.	1995
This Is How It Works	TLC	1995
Til You Do Me Right	After 7	1995
Wey U	Chanté Moore	1995
Why Does It Hurt So Bad	Whitney Houston	1995
All Day Thinkin	Babyface	1996
Care for Me	Az Yet	1996
Could You Learn to Love	Tevin Campbell	1996
The Day (That You Gave Me a Son)	Babyface	1996
Every Little Bit of My Heart	Az Yet	1996
Every Time I Close My Eyes	Babyface featuring Mariah Carey and Kenny G	1996
Find Me a Man	Toni Braxton	1996
How Come, How Long	Babyface and Stevie Wonder	1996
I Don't Want to Be Lonely	Az Yet	1996
I Said I Love You	Babyface	1996
In the Late of Night	Toni Braxton	1996
Last Night	Az Yet	1996
Let's Get the Mood Right	Johnny Gill	1996
My Heart Is Calling	Whitney Houston	1996
The Power of the Dream	Celine Dion	1996
Sadder than Blue	Az Yet	1996
Saved for Someone Else	Az Yet	1996
Seven Seas	Babyface	1996
Simple Days	Babyface	1996
Talk to Me	Babyface featuring Eric Clapton	1996

Title[1]	Artist(s)	Year
Tell Me Where	Tevin Campbell	1996
That Somebody Was You	Kenny G featuring Toni Braxton	1996
That's All I Want	Az Yet	1996
There's No Me Without You	Toni Braxton	1996
When Your Body Gets Weak	Babyface	1996
Why Should I Care	Toni Braxton	1996
You Bring the Sunshine	Gina Thompson	1996
You're Makin' Me High	Toni Braxton	1996
Baby I	Tenderoni	1997
Bedtime	Usher	1997
The Best of Love	Michael Bolton	1997
Boys and Girls	Tony!	1997
Girl in the Life Magazine	Boyz II Men	1997
I Care 'Bout You	Milestone	1997
Just Hold On	Boyz II Men	1997
Missing You	Mary J. Blige	1997
Never	Boyz II Men	1997
Pride & Joy	Jon B.	1997
Say What's in My Heart	Aaron Neville	1997
A Song for Mama	Boyz II Men	1997
We're Not Making Love No More	Dru Hill	1997
Whatever	En Vogue	1997
Why Me	Michael Bolton	1997
You Are the Man	En Vogue	1997
Never Gonna Let You Go	Faith Evans	1998
These Are the Times	Dru Hill	1998
Until You Come Back	Whitney Houston	1998
When You Believe	Whitney Houston and Mariah Carey	1998
Your Eyes	Xscape	1998
Ain't Got No Remedy	Shanice	1999
A Girl Like You	Kevon Edmonds featuring Babyface	1999
Baby Come to Me	Kevon Edmonds	1999

Continued

Title[1]	Artist(s)	Year
Can't Help Myself	Destiny's Child	1999
Dear Lie	TLC	1999
Dreamin	Shanice	1999
Fall for You	Shanice	1999
Fly Away	Shanice	1999
How Can I Not Love You	Joy Enriquez	1999
How Often	Kevon Edmonds	1999
I Miss You So Much	TLC	1999
If Only in Heaven's Eyes	NSYNC	1999
Love Will Be Waiting at Home	Kevon Edmonds	1999
Never Love You	Kevon Edmonds	1999
So Sexual	Sisqô	1999
Fairy Tale	Toni Braxton	2000
Gimme Some	Toni Braxton featuring Lisa Lopes	2000
Most Girls	P!nk	2000
Split Personality	P!nk	2000
When Men Grow Old	Babyface	2000
Baby's Mama	Babyface featuring Snoop Dogg	2001
Don't Take It So Personal	Babyface	2001
Grown Thangs	Luther Vandross	2001
How Can U Be Down	Babyface	2001
I Keep Callin	Babyface	2001
If I Want To	Usher	2001
Losin' the Love	Joy Enriquez	2001
Lover and Friend	Babyface	2001
Outside In/ Inside Out	Babyface	2001
Situation	Joy Enriquez	2001
Someday	Joy Enriquez	2001
Still in Love with U	Babyface	2001
Stressed Out	Babyface	2001
There for Me (Baby)	Tyrese Gibson	2001
There She Goes	Babyface	2001
This Time Next Year	Toni Braxton	2001

Title[1]	Artist(s)	Year
U Should Know	Babyface	2001
What If	Babyface	2001
Wish U Was My Girl	Babyface	2001
With Him	Babyface	2001
Work It Out	Babyface	2001
You Are My Life	Michael Jackson	2001
And I Love You	Toni Braxton	2002
The Color of Love	Boyz II Men	2002
Hands Up	TLC	2002
Hovi Baby	Jay-Z	2002
Love That Man	Whitney Houston	2002
Tell Me No	Whitney Houston	2002
Try It on My Own	Whitney Houston	2002
Woman Don't Cry	Boyz II Men	2002
Thankful	Kelly Clarkson	2003
You Thought Wrong	Kelly Clarkson	2003
Ain't Nothing Wrong	Houston	2004
Like You Used to Do	Anita Baker	2004
Smile	Tamia	2004
Thinkin' Bout My Ex	Janet Jackson	2004
Can't Stop Now	Babyface	2005
Drama, Love & 'Lationships	Babyface	2005
The Gettin' to Know U	Babyface	2005
God Must Love U	Babyface	2005
Going Outta Business	Babyface	2005
Good to Be in Love	Babyface	2005
Grown & Sexy	Babyface	2005
I Hate You	Toni Braxton	2005
The Loneliness	Babyface	2005
Mad, Sexy, Cool	Babyface	2005
She	Babyface	2005
She's International	Babyface	2005
Sorry for the Stupid Things	Babyface	2005
Tonight It's Goin' Down	Babyface	2005

Continued

Title[1]	Artist(s)	Year
We Belong Together	Mariah Carey	2005
Best of Me	Chrisette Michele	2007
Everywhere I Go	Katharine McPhee	2007
Your Joy	Chrisette Michele	2007
Broken-Hearted Girl	Beyoncé	2008
Comfortable	Lil Wayne featuring Babyface	2008
Mother	Ashanti	2008
Cried Me a River	Kristinia DeBarge	2009
Doesn't Everybody Want to Fall in Love	Kristinia DeBarge	2009
It's Gotta Be Love	Kristinia DeBarge	2009
Make It Last	Tyrese Gibson featuring Jewel	2009
There Goes My Baby	Charlie Wilson	2009
No Place Like Home	Kenny G featuring Babyface	2010
Best Thing I Never Had	Beyoncé	2011
Dreaming	Beyoncé	2011
Pray for Me	Anthony Hamilton	2011
Woo	Anthony Hamilton	2011
Catching Feelings	Justin Bieber	2012
That's When I Knew	Alicia Keys	2012
Baby I	Ariana Grande	2013
Change Your Mind	Fantasia Barrino	2013
Honeymoon Avenue	Ariana Grande	2013
Love Is Everything	Ariana Grande	2013
Lovin' It	Ariana Grande	2013
Snow in California	Ariana Grande	2013
Tattooed Heart	Ariana Grande	2013
Where It Hurts	Tamar Braxton	2013
You'll Never Know	Ariana Grande	2013
The D Word	Babyface and Toni Braxton	2014
Game Changer	Johnny Gill	2014
Heart Attack	Babyface and Toni Braxton	2014
Hurt You	Babyface and Toni Braxton	2014

Title[1]	Artist(s)	Year
I Hope That You're Okay	Babyface	2014
I'd Rather Be Broke	Toni Braxton	2014
Just Like That	Colbie Caillat	2014
Land Called Far Away	Colbie Caillat	2014
Let's Do It	Colbie Caillat	2014
Never Gonna Let You Down	Colbie Caillat	2014
One	Babyface and Toni Braxton	2014
Reunited	Babyface and Toni Braxton	2014
Roller Coaster	Babyface and Toni Braxton	2014
Sweat	Babyface and Toni Braxton	2014
Take It Back	Babyface and Toni Braxton	2014
Try	Colbie Caillat	2014
Where Did We Go Wrong	Babyface and Toni Braxton	2014
Every Day Is Christmas	The Braxtons	2015
Exceptional	Babyface	2015
Fight For Love	Babyface	2015
I Want You	Babyface featuring After 7	2015
Love and Devotion	Babyface	2015
Our Love	Babyface	2015
Shake That	Samantha Jade featuring Pitbull	2015
Solid	Ty Dolla $ign featuring Babyface	2015
Something 'Bout You	Babyface	2015
Standing Ovation	Babyface	2015
They Don't Give	Jordin Sparks	2015
Walking on Air	Babyface featuring El DeBarge	2015
We've Got Love	Babyface	2015
Who's Gonna (Nobody)	Chris Brown	2015
Be That Dude	Jaheim	2016
If I	After 7	2016
Jam	Kevin Gates featuring Trey Songz, Ty Dolla $ign and Jamie Foxx	2016

Continued

Title[1]	Artist(s)	Year
Let Me Know	After 7	2016
Loving You All My Life	After 7	2016
More Than Friends	After 7	2016
Running Out	After 7	2016
Scar	Foxes	2016
Something New	Zendaya featuring Chris Brown	2016
Stronger Together	Jessica Sanchez	2016
Too Good To Say Goodbye	Bruno Mars	2016
All Night Long	Kat Graham	2017
Call da Police	Kat Graham	2017
Can't Get Enough	Kat Graham	2017
Fool for Ya	Kat Graham	2017
Koolaid Man	Kat Graham	2017
Magic	Kat Graham	2017
Sometimes	Kat Graham	2017
Time = $	Kat Graham	2017
What the Funk	Kat Graham	2017

APPENDIX B

SELECT AWARDS AND HONORS

Whitney Houston

1985

The 18th NAACP Image Awards: *Outstanding New Artist*
Billboard Number One Awards: *New Pop Artist and New Black Artist*

1986

The 13th American Music Awards:
  Favorite Soul/R&B Single: "You Give Good Love"
  Favorite Soul/R&B Video: "Saving All My Love for You"
The 28th Grammy Awards: *Best Pop Vocal Performance, Female: "Saving All My Love for You"*
NARM Best Seller Awards:
  Best-Selling Album By a New Artist and Best-Selling Black Music
  Album by a Female Artist
The 3rd MTV Video Music Awards: *Best Female Video: "How Will I Know"*
The 38th Emmy Awards: *Outstanding Individual Performance in a Variety or Music Program*
Billboard: The Year in Music & Video:
  Top Pop Artist of the Year
  Top Pop Album
  Top Pop Album Artist
  Top Pop Album Artist—Female
  Top Black Album
  Top Black Album Artist

1987

1. The 14th American Music Awards:
   a. *Favorite Pop/Rock Female Artist*
   b. *Favorite Pop/Rock Album*
   c. *Favorite Soul/R&B Female Artist*
   d. *Favorite Soul/R&B Album*
   e. *Favorite Soul/R&B Video Single: "Greatest Love of All"*
2. BRIT Awards: *Best International Solo Artist*
3. 13th People's Choice Awards: *Favorite Female Musical Performer*
4. 9th American Black Achievement Awards: *The Music Award*
5. Billboard: The Year in Music & Video: *Top Pop Album Artist—Female*

1988

1. 15th American Music Awards:
   a. *Favorite Pop/Rock Female Artist*
   b. *Favorite Pop/Rock Single: "I Wanna Dance with Somebody (Who Loves Me)"*
2. 30th Grammy Awards: *Best Pop Vocal Performance, Female: "I Wanna Dance with Somebody (Who Loves Me)"*
3. 14th People's Choice Awards: *Favorite Female Musical Performer*
4. The 2nd Soul Train Music Awards: *Best R&B Album of the Year, Female: "Whitney"*
5. National Urban Coalition: *Distinguished Artist/Humanitarian Award*
6. Grambling State University: *Honorary Doctorate of Humane Letters*
7. American Dental Hygienists' Association: *America's Greatest Smiles*
8. The 1st Garden State Music Awards:
   a. *Best Female Vocalist, Rock/Pop*
   b. *Best Album, Rock/Pop: "Whitney"*
   c. *Best Single, Rock/Pop: "So Emotional"*
   d. *Best Female Vocalist, R&B/Dance*
   e. *Best Album, R&B/Dance: "Whitney"*
   f. *Best Single, R&B/Dance: "I Wanna Dance with Somebody (Who Loves Me)*
9. Bravo Magazine's Bravo Otto: *Best Female Singer*
10. Rennbahn Express Magazine's Starwahl: *Goldender Pinguin Award*
11. Billboard of the Year in Music & Video: *Top Pop Singles Artist—Female*

1989

1. 16th American Music Awards:
   a. *Favorite Pop/Rock Pop Artist*
   b. *Favorite Soul/R&B Female Artist*
2. 15th People's Choice Awards: *Favorite Female Musical Performer*

1990

1. The 46th United Negro College Fund Awards: *The Frederick D. Patterson Award*
2. The Points of Light Institute (George Bush): *Appointed by George Bush as the first Point of Light Contributing Leader*
3. The 21st Songwriters Hall of Fame Induction & Awards: *Howie Richmond Hitmaker Award*
4. The 4th Essence Awards: *The Essence Award for Performing Arts*

1991

1. The 8th American Cinema Awards: *The Musical Performer of the Year*
2. The 13th American Black Achievement Awards: *The Music Award*
3. The 2nd Billboard Music Awards:
   a. *Top R&B Artist*
   b. *Top R&B Album: "I'm Your Baby Tonight"*
   c. *Top R&B Album Artist*
   d. *Top R&B Singles Artist*

1992

1. The 13th CableACE Awards: *Performance in a Music Special or Series*
2. The 8th Carousel of Hope Ball (The Children's Diabetes Foundation): *Brass Ring Award*

1993

1. The 7th Soul Train Music Awards: *Best R&B Performance, Female: "I Belong to You"*
2. The 19th People's Choice Awards:
   a. *Favorite Female Musical Performer*
   b. *Favorite New Music Video: "I Will Always Love You"*
3. The 2nd MTV Movie Awards: *Best Song From A Movie: "I Will Always Love You"*
4. The 5th Billboard Music Awards:
   a. *Hot 100 Singles Artist*
   b. *Hot 100 Single: "I Will Always Love You"*
   c. *Hot R&B Singles Artist*
   d. *Hot R&B Single: "I Will Always Love You"*
   e. *Top Billboard 200: The Bodyguard Soundtrack*
   f. *Top R&B Album: The Bodyguard Soundtrack*
   g. *Top Soundtrack Album: The Bodyguard Soundtrack*
   h. *Album Most Weeks at #1 (20 weeks): The Bodyguard Soundtrack*
   i. *Single Most Weeks at #1 (14 weeks): "I Will Always Love You"*
   j. *#1 World Artist*
   k. *#1 World Single*
   l. *Hot 100 Singles Artist—Female*
   m. *Hot 100 Singles Sales: "I Will Always Love You"*
   n. *Hot R&B Singles Sales: "I Will Always Love You"*
5. Smash Hits Poll Winners Party: *Best Female Artist*
6. BRAVO Magazine's Bravo Otto:
   a. *Best Actress—Silver Otto Award*
   b. *Best Female Singer—Silver Otto Award*
7. The 7th Japan Gold Disc Awards:
   a. *Album of the Year, International: The Bodyguard Soundtrack*
   b. *Compilation Album of the Year, International: The Bodyguard Soundtrack*
   c. *Single of the Year, International: "I Will Always Love You"*

1994

1. The 26th NAACP Image Awards:
   a. *Entertainer of the Year*
   b. *Outstanding Female Artist: The Bodyguard Soundtrack*
   c. *Outstanding Album: The Bodyguard Soundtrack*
   d. *Outstanding Soundtrack Album, Film or TV: The Bodyguard Soundtrack*
   e. *Outstanding Music Video: "I'm Every Woman"*
2. The 21st American Music Awards:
   a. *Favorite Pop/Rock Album: The Bodyguard Soundtrack*
   b. *Favorite Pop/Rock Song: "I Will Always Love You"*
   c. *Favorite Pop/Rock Female Artist*
   d. *Favorite Soul/R&B Album: The Bodyguard Soundtrack*
   e. *Favorite Soul/R&B Single: "I Will Always Love You"*

    f. *Favorite Soul/R&B Female Artist*
    g. *Favorite Adult Contemporary Album: The Bodyguard Soundtrack*
    h. *Award of Merit*
3. BRIT Awards: *Best Soundtrack/Cast Recording: The Bodyguard Soundtrack*
4. The 36th Grammy Awards:
    a. *Album of the Year: The Bodyguard Soundtrack*
    b. *Record of the Year: "I Will Always Love You"*
    c. *Best Pop Vocal Performance, Female: "I Will Always Love You"*
5. The 8th Soul Train Music Awards:
    a. *Sammy Davis Jr. Award as Entertainer of the Year*
    b. *Best R&B Song of the Year: "I Will Always Love You"*
6. The 24th Juno Awards: *Best Selling Album: Foreign or Domestic: The Bodyguard Soundtrack*
7. The 10th Communications Awards Dinner: *Entertainer of the Year*
8. The NARM 1993–1994 Best Seller Awards: *Best-selling Soundtrack: The Bodyguard Soundtrack*
9. The 6th World Music Awards:
    a. *World's Best Selling Overall Recording Artist*
    b. *World's Best Selling Pop Artist of the Year*
    c. *World's Best Selling R&B Artist of the Year*
    d. *World's Best Selling American Recording Artist of the Year*
    e. *World's Best Selling Female Recording Artist of the Era*
10. The 8th Japan Gold Disc Awards:
    a. *Special Award, International: The Bodyguard Soundtrack*
    b. *Special Award, International: "I Will Always Love You"*

1995

1. The 2nd VH1 Honors: *VH1 Honors Award*
2. The Soul Train 25th Anniversary Hall of Fame Special: *Soul Train Hall of Fame Inductee*
3. The 2nd International Achievement in Arts Awards: *Distinguished Achievement in Music and Film/Video*

1996

1. The 10th Soul Train Music Awards: *Best R&B/Soul Single, Female: "Exhale (Shoop Shoop)"*
2. The NARM 1995–1996 Best Seller Awards: *Best-Selling Soundtrack Recording: Waiting to Exhale Soundtrack*
3. 27th NAACP Image Awards:
    a. *Outstanding Motion Picture: Waiting to Exhale*
    b. *Outstanding Female Artist: "Exhale (Shoop Shoop)"*
    c. *Outstanding Song: "Exhale (Shoop Shoop)"*
    d. *Outstanding Soundtrack Album: Waiting to Exhale Soundtrack*
    e. *Outstanding Album: Waiting to Exhale Soundtrack*
4. The 2nd BET Walk of Fame: *Walk of Fame Inductee*
5. The 12th Carousel of Hope Ball: *The Davises' High Hopes Award*
6. The 7th Billboard Music Awards: *Soundtrack Album of the Year: Waiting to Exhale Soundtrack*

1997

1. The 24th American Music Awards:
   a. *Favorite Adult Contemporary Artist*
   b. *Favorite Soundtrack Album: Waiting to Exhale Soundtrack*
2. The 28th NAACP Image Awards:
   a. *Outstanding Lead Actress in a Motion Picture: The Preacher's Wife*
   b. *Outstanding Gospel Artist (with Georgia Mass Choir): The Preacher's Wife Soundtrack*
   c. *Outstanding Album: The Preacher's Wife Soundtrack*
3. The NARM 1996–1997 Best Seller Awards: *Best-Selling Gospel Recording: The Preacher's Wife Soundtrack*
4. The 3rd Blockbuster Entertainment Awards: *Favorite Female, R&B: The Preacher's Wife Soundtrack*
5. The 10th Essence Awards: *The Triumphant Spirit Award*
6. The 28th Dove Awards (The Gospel Music Association): *Outstanding Mainstream Contribution to Gospel Music*
7. The 12th ASCAP Film & Television Music Awards: *Most Performed Songs Motion Pictures (with Michael Houston): "Count on Me"*
8. The 14th ASCAP Pop Awards: *ASCAP Pop Award (with Michael Houston): "Count on Me"*
9. The Franklin School in East Orange: *Houston's former grammar school was renamed "The Whitney E. Houston Academy for Creative and Performing Arts"*
10. The 8th Billboard Music Awards: *Top Gospel Album: The Preacher's Wife Soundtrack*

1998

1. The 24th People's Choice Awards: *Favorite Female Musical Performer*
2. The 6th Trumpet Awards: *The Pinnacle Award*
3. The 12th Soul Train Music Awards: *The Quincy Jones Award—for outstanding career achievements in the field of entertainment.*
4. The 29th Dove Awards (The Gospel Music Association): *Best Traditional Gospel Recorded Song: "I Go to the Rock"*

1999

1. The 30th NAACP Image Awards: *Outstanding Duo or Group: "When You Believe" (Duet with Mariah Carey)*
2. Deidre O'Brien Child Advocacy Center: *Child Advocate of the Year*
3. Recording Industry Association of America:
   a. *Top-Selling R&B Female Artist of the Century*
   b. *Top-Selling Soundtrack Album of the Century: The Bodyguard Soundtrack*
4. 1999 MTV Europe Music Awards: *Best R&B*
5. 1999 Bambi Verleihung: *Pop International*

2000

1. The 1st NRJ Music Awards: *International Album of the Year: My Love Is Your Love*
2. The 42nd Grammy Awards: *Best Female R&B Vocal Performance: "It's Not Right But It's Okay"*
3. The 31st NAACP Image Awards: *Outstanding Female Artist: "Heartbreak Hotel"*
4. The 14th Soul Train Music: *The Artist of the Decade—Female*

5. The 15th International Dance Music Awards: *Best Pop 12th Dance Record: "It's Not Right But It's Okay"*
6. The 1st HMV Harlem Walk of Fame: *Walk of Fame Inductee*

2001

1. Meteor Ireland Music Awards: *Best International Female*
2. 1st BET Awards: *BET Lifetime Achievement Award*
3. The 16th Japan Gold Disc Awards: *Pop Album of the Year (International): Whitney: The Greatest Hits*

2004

1. The 1st Women's World Awards: *World Arts Award for Lifetime Achievement*
2. The 6th CCTV-MTV Music Honors: *International Outstanding Achievement*

2006

1. The New Jersey Walk of Fame: *Inductee*
2. Guinness World Records:
   a. *Most Consecutive US No. 1 Singles*
   b. *Most Awarded/Popular Female Artist of All Time*

2009

1. The 37th American Music Awards: *International Artist Award*

2010

1. The 3rd BET Honors: *The BET Honor for Entertainment*
2. The 41st NAACP Image Awards: *Outstanding Music Video: "I Look to You"*

2012

1. Billboard Music Awards: *Billboard Millennium Award*
2. Guinness World Records: *Most Simultaneous Hits in the United Kingdom*
3. MTV Europe Music Awards: *Global Icon Award*
4. 2012 Soul Train Music Awards: *Best Gospel/Inspirational Performance: "Celebrate" (Duet with Jordin Sparks)*

2013

1. 2013 R&B Music Hall of Fame: *Inductee*
2. Grammy Awards: *Grammy Hall of Fame*
3. The 44th NAACP Image Awards:
   a. *Best Song: "I Look to You"*
   b. *Best Outstanding Album: I Will Always Love You: The Best of Whitney Houston*
4. 2013 Barbados Music Awards (BMA): *International Icon Award*
5. The Singers Hall of Fame: *Inductee*
6. Georgia Music Hall of Fame: *Posthumous Award*
7. ABC Greatest Women in Music: *Rank No. 1*

2014

1. New Jersey Hall of Fame: *Inductee*
2. Rhythm and Blues Music Hall of Fame: *Inductee*
3. The Official Charts Pop Gem Hall of Fame: *Inductee No. 80: "I Wanna Dance with Somebody (Who Loves Me)"*

Toni Braxton

1994

1. American Music Awards:
   a. *Favorite Adult Contemporary New Artist*
   b. *Favorite Soul/R&B New Artist*
2. End of the Year Billboard History:
   a. *Top R&B Artist—Female (Singles & Albums)*
   b. *Top R&B Album Artist—Female*
3. The Grammy Awards:
   a. *Best New Artist*
   b. *Best Female R&B Vocal Performance: "Another Sad Love Song"*
4. The Soul Train Music Awards:
   a. *Best R&B/Soul Single, Female: "Breathe Again"*
   b. *Best R&B Album of the Year, Female: Toni Braxton*

1995

1. American Music Awards: *Favorite Soul/R&B Album: Toni Braxton*
2. The Grammy Awards: *Best Female R&B Vocal Performance: "Breathe Again"*

1996

1. Billboard Music Awards: *Best R&B Single: "You're Makin' Me High"*

1997

1. American Music Awards:
   a. *Favorite Soul/R&B Female Artist*
   b. *Favorite Soul/R&B Album: Secrets*
2. Billboard Music Awards:
   a. *R&B Artist of the Year, Female*
   b. *Adult Contemporary Single of the Year: "UnBreak My Heart"*
3. End of the Year Billboard History:
   a. *Top Hot 100 Singles Artist—Female*
   b. *Top R&B Artist—Female (Singles & Albums)*
   c. *Top Hot R&B Singles Artist—Female*
   d. *Top Hot Dance Club Play Artist*
   e. *Top Hot Dance Club Play Single: "UnBreak My Heart"*
   f. *Top Hot Adult Contemporary Artist*
   g. *Top Hot Adult Contemporary Track: "UnBreak My Heart"*
4. The Grammy Awards:
   a. *Best Female Pop Vocal Performance: "UnBreak My Heart"*

    b. *Best Female R&B Vocal Performance:* "*You're Makin' Me High*"
5. The NAACP Image Awards: *Outstanding Female Artist*
6. The Soul Train Music Awards:
    a. *Best R&B/Soul Single, Female:* "*You're Makin' Me High/Let It Flow*"
    b. *Best R&B Album of the Year, Female: Secrets*

1998

1. Echo Awards: *Best International Pop/Rock Female Artist*

2000

1. Billboard Music Awards: *R&B Artist of the Year, Female*
2. End of the Year Billboard History
    a. *Top R&B/Hip-Hop Artist—Female*
    b. *Top R&B/Hip-Hop Album Artist—Female*
    c. *Top Hot R&B/Hip-Hop Singles & Tracks Artist—Female*

2001

1. American Music Awards:
    a. *Favorite Soul/R&B Female Artist*
    b. *Favorite Soul/R&B Album: The Heat*
2. The Grammy Awards: *Best Female R&B Vocal Performance:* "*He Wasn't Man Enough*"

2013

1. Soul Train Awards: *Best Collaboration.* "*Hurt You*" *shared with Kenneth* "*Babyface*" *Edmonds*

2015

1. The Grammy Awards: *Best R&B Album: Love, Marriage & Divorce*

2017

1. Soul Train Awards: *Living Legend Award*

Kenneth "Babyface" Edmonds

1990

1. BMI Film & TV Awards: *Most Performed Song from a Film:* "*On Our Own*" *in Ghostbuster II*

1993

1. The 36th Annual Grammy Awards:
    a. *Producer of the Year (Non-Classical):* "*For the Cool in You*"
    b. *Best R&B Song:* "*End of the Road*"
2. BMI Film & TV Awards: *Most Performed Song from a Film:* "*End of the Road*" *From the film Boomerang*

1994

1. The 37th Annual Grammy Awards: *Album of the Year (As a Producer): The Bodyguard Soundtrack*

1995

1. The 38th Annual Grammy Awards: *Producer of the Year*
2. The America Music Awards: *Favorite Soul/R&B Male Artist*

1996

1. The 39th Annual Grammy Awards: *Producer of the Year: Slow Jams*
2. BMI Film and TV Awards:
   a. *BMI Film Music Award: "Waiting to Exhale"*
   b. *Most Performed Song from a Film: "Exhale (Shoop Shoop)"*

1997

1. The 40th Annual Grammy Awards:
   a. *Record of the Year: "Change the World"*
   b. *Producer of the Year: "Change the World"*
   c. *Best R&B Song: "Exhale (Shoop Shoop)"*
2. The BET Awards: *Walk of Fame Award for Hot R&B Songwriter: "When You Believe" shared with Stephen Schwartz*
3. BMI Film & TV Awards: *Songwriter of the Year: "When You Believe"*
4. GQ Men of the Year Awards: *GQ Men of the Year Award Solo Artist of the Year: "How Can I Not Love You"*
5. MTV Video Music Awards:
   a. *Best Male Video: "Every Time I Close My Eyes"*
   b. *Best R&B Video: "How Come, How Long"*

1998

1. The NAACP Image Awards
   a. *Outstanding Album: Soul Food*
   b. *Outstanding Song: "A Song for Mama"*
   c. *Outstanding Male Recording Artist: Soul Food*
   d. *Outstanding Motion Picture as Producer: Soul Food*
2. The Image Awards: *Entertainer of the Year Award*
3. The American Music Awards: *Favorite Rock/Pop Male Artist*
4. The Billboard Music Awards: *Hot R&B Songwriter: "When You Believe" shared with Stephen Schwartz*
5. The Grammy Awards: *Producer of the Year (Non-Classical): How Come, How Long*

1999

1. The America Music Awards: *Favorite Soul/R&B Male Artist*

2000

1. ASCAP Award: *Most Performed Songs From Motion Picture: "The Prince of Egypt"*
2. AMI Award: *Best United States Song: "You're Makin' Me High"*

2001

1. Emmy Awards: *Emmy Outstanding Main Title Theme Music for "Soul Food"*

2006

1. BMI Urban Awards: *Icon Award for "On Our Own"*

2013

1. Walk of Fame: *Star on the Walk of Fame*
2. Soul Train Awards: *Best Collaboration: "Hurt You" shared with Toni Braxton*

2015

1. The 57th Annual Grammy Awards: *Best R&B Album: Love, Marriage & Divorce*
2. The Soul Train Awards: *The Soul Train Music Legend Award*

2017

1. Inductee: *Song Writer Hall of Fame*
2. The Leo Awards: *Best Television Movie: Toni Braxton*

Adina Howard

1995

1. "Freak Like Me" hits number 2 on Billboard Hot 100

1996

1. "What's Love Got to Do with It" (w/Warren G) hits number 2 on the UK charts.

2013

1. "Switch" wins Best Dance/Club Single of the Year at UB Honors

As chapter 3 discusses, the industry marginalized Howard, which decreased her exposure and limited the number and types of awards she could earn.

APPENDIX C

ROBERT J. PATTERSON
INTERVIEWS ADINA HOWARD

March 6, 2018
Phoenix, Arizona

RP: You fundamentally changed the face of rhythm and blues culture in the 1990s. I look forward to our conversation, and thinking about songs, different moments in your life, your broader ideas about R&B, your influences, and people you've influenced. How did you get started in R&B?

AH: My mother used to force me on a consistent basis to sing when I was a little girl. I don't know what she heard because I sounded like crap. She was like, "Dina, sing, Dina, sing." I was shy but had the church solos and had to sing in front of company. That's really where it started.

RP: Can you speak about how the sex-positive environment your mother and grandmother provided gave you the courage to sing lyrics that really transformed how people thought about black women's gender and sexuality?

AH: It wasn't until after the success that my grandmother was supportive. Keep in mind my dad's mother did not approve at all. Grandma Lee was like, "That is disrespectful. No good Christian woman is going to say stuff like that." My mother's mom, Grandma Thelma, who's 91, used to just, even to this day, say "Baby, shake your booty. I want to see you shake your booty." And she'll tell me before a show, "You better shake it and let them know, it started with me." It was very interesting about me doing what I do or what I did back then. I was raised in the church, Baptist and Pentecostal, and could not listen to secular music on Sundays. If we did listen to music, of course, it was what my mother wanted to listen to. I grew up listening to her genre and era of music. I remember there were certain songs that I gravitated toward. My mother loved Minnie Riperton. And there was a song that she did that was very sensual. Somehow I came across it and it moved me and I didn't know why, but I liked it. It sounded very dark and there was just something about the mood that it set that intrigued me. And I would always gravitate toward people who sang provocative music, Madonna, Vanity Six—Prince. Anybody that had that type of energy. I didn't know what they were singing about, but it was something that made me like that a lot.

RP: Your album cover for "Do You Wanna Ride" definitely pushed the envelope in a positive way because part of living is about sex and its enjoyment. What was the photographer's reaction when you bent over that BMW?

AH: When I did that pose, you could hear a pin drop and you could also hear the gasps. Somebody that worked for Elektra said, "Okay. Okay, enough, enough."

RP: When "Freak Like Me" came out, BET requested an edited version and when "My Up and Down" released they refused to play it. Although listeners could access it on Box, it didn't reach as many people nor did you reap as many royalties. R. Kelly's 12 *Play*, however, did not get censured similarly? What kind of message did your treatment send artists about pushing the envelope, about the ability for black women to express themselves outside of sexual norms?

AH: I never focused on it in that moment. And I really don't even focus on it now. However, there's always a double standard. Women are supposed to be more pure, more obedient, and not be sexual beings. But we have desires just like men do. And we want to express them just like men do. We want the freedom to be able to speak our minds and really get into what sex is about because God made man and woman in its image. And I don't believe that God is a man or woman; I just believe that the divine is what it is. But we are made in its image. How is it that it's okay for men to do it and women not? The only reasoning is that it's a patriarchal society. Men don't want you to have any freedom to even express yourself because then they've lost control and power over you. And how dare men not have that rope around your neck, or the ball and chain around your ankle. When it comes to sex, though, we're equal. And it's just something that society just continues to want to put us in a box or on a pedestal, and say, "No, no. We want you to be pure. We want to look at you that way but we don't want you to express yourself that way." It's bullshit. And I've always had the mentality of, "If you can do it, I can do it. And watch me."

RP: One of the troubling issues for me is that black people internalize these stereotypes and we police each other when someone acts outside the norms.

RP: I really appreciate that your whole repertoire, and "Freak Like Me" in particular, turns these stereotypes on their head, especially when you think historically of the connotations the term *freak* has had. That work is tremendously important because black people are always thought of as freaks. Whether you are—or not. But there's sort of this notion that our sexuality is always thought of outside of what's "normal," right?

AH: It's more heathens than freaks. It's animalistic. Uncouth. Untrained.

RP: Yes, it's all of that. Some criticisms of your music, for example, have suggested you're responsible for this larger system of patriarchy and racism and sexism, and that you don't have any agency against it. Your work, however, pushes back against these notions. Why do you think critics, and black ones in particular, take exception to your lyrics and performances?

AH: We already talked about a double standard and when it comes to our people—even though slavery doesn't exist, we're still in the mindset that white people are looking. Master's looking and we have to be on our best behavior. And part of being on our best behavior is to do what they've trained us to do. We still have to be on our best behavior because we don't want them thinking we're this way, we don't want them thinking that we're that way and we're going to prove to them that we're good black folk.

RP: One of the key issues that the book pushes back against is the idea that black behaviors necessarily cause black inequality or black suffering. Black people should not have to prove our deservedness of being treated as full citizens. Yet a lot people think, "Well if we act this way, we'll get more." That thinking seems incorrect because it ignores the system of antiblack racism and how it uses gender and sexuality to conceal its operation.

AH: You can be the good black negro. Go to church every Sunday, give your tithes and offering, and read the good book on the regular, and step off the curb when a white person's coming or whatever. It's still not going to make a bit of difference. You're still a black person. And why is it that we're judge and jury with our own people? And if you look at them just as close as you look at us, you'll realize that they're heathens too. They sit there and call us savage, but we wouldn't know savagery if it weren't taught by the savages.

RP: Any form of black music that's helping us think about sex, sexuality, and intimacy provides this space to open up conversation of how we might look at these ideas differently. Your performances, too, particularly of "Nasty Grind" in the last few years, suggest to me that your lyrics align with your values. Does that congruence contribute to your success?

AH: I'm in alignment with what I was supposed to do. I truly, genuinely believe that if the divine had an issue with what I do and how I do it, I wouldn't be able to do it. One of the things that I tell individuals is, "I did not choose the music industry, it chose me." I've come to recognize, because I've walked away from the industry multiple times, that this platform serves a purpose. And I need to use this platform for that purpose. Liberation, restoration, deliverance. Set them free from all of this false doctrine that seduces them into believing that what's natural is a curse, is of the devil. For me to be who I am is to express myself through my music and my performances, and have the freedom to just do me.

RP: I think that point reflects such a developed understanding and articulation of spirituality, religion, or whatever you want to call it.

AH: I'm a spiritual person, not a religious person. Religion, to me, religion is like a dictatorship. Spirituality is a democracy where you have the freedom to choose and be as you are, and there's no restraint. We, for the most part, know right from wrong because there's an internal thing with us. When we do something wrong, we don't have to be taught to feel guilty, even though we're taught to feel guilty about certain things. Sexuality is one of those things that we're taught to feel guilty. I remember dating this gentleman when I was 16. And I remember my mom looking at me and asking, "Are you having sex?" "Yes." And then the next thing I hear is, "I'm just so disappointed. I'm so disappointed. We're putting you on birth control, but I'm so disappointed." It's like, so what are we saving it for? and who?

RP: Right, saving it for whom and what? In "Give it Up," Millie Jackson wonders whether you are saving it to let it "dry rot."

RP: "Nasty" is the next single and it samples key moments in your career and in your legacy. Why did you sample those or were they your favorites?

AH: I've had so many people approach me about "Freak Like Me," and it has been re-created, re-recorded, umpteen times. So many people say "Adina, we want you to sing 'Freak Like Me.' We're remixing. We're doing whatever and want you to be a part of it." And I always say, "Nah, I'm good." There's only two other times I've recorded "Freak Like Me." But when it came to "Nasty," the producer King Nas, he's a young king out of Las Vegas, was hesitant on getting me the song, but said "I wrote it for you." And I listened to it and then when the "Freak Like Me" kicked in, I was like, "I like this one. This is it." Because it's fresh, it incorporates the songs from back in the day, but it does it in a new way where it doesn't sound like I'm trying to stay relevant. "Nasty" came about and the lyrics just flowed. But the young king that I worked with, he's just amazing talent, and we just connect in such a manner where all I could do was just give him an idea, and he just knows. And so, when he did "Nasty," it was like, "This is a no-brainer." It's like even though I'm not a fan of singing "Freak Like Me," I'd be foolish to pass on this one. And so we moved forward with it. And it just so happened to have the "T-shirt and Panties," and so on and so forth.

RP: In many ways, this book tells a story about rhythm and blues culture, artists, movies, and soundtracks. Although the book has chapters on you, Babyface, Whitney, and a short epilogue on Toni Braxton, I'm working on a journal article that'll be thinking about Ginuwine, Kenny Lattimore, and maybe a third man. When you think of key figures in rhythm and blues culture in the 1990s, who are they and why?

AH: Jodeci. If I were to be in a male group, Jodeci would have been the group. One of the reasons why I like Jodeci was they looked like they got a lot of ass. And they could just do whatever the hell they want and they also were authentic in their representation. Lil' Kim is another. I think she's the epitome of '90s. She was the rap version of me. But she was a lot more raw than I was. There was no beating around the bush, no biting the tongue. I did wordplay in my music. I made it a little more appealing to the point where even though people opposed my music, the pill wasn't so jagged to swallow. Lil' Kim, I don't know if you could swallow the pill. I loved her because she had no filter. And I'm so very proud of what she's accomplished as a female rapper in that time because she was a liberator too. For some reason Boyz II Men comes to mind because as much as I love Boyz II Men, and I love the talent of Boyz II Men, I think they did more harm than good in the sense that romanticizing love creates this false perception of relationships and how a person really can think and feel about you. I love their music and it made me feel all good inside and made me think that one day somebody's going to love me. "I'll make love to you." It's like, "Oh my gosh. That's sweet. Yes he is and I'm looking forward to it." And this shit never happens. I've just to this day have yet to really experience that but it created this false perception of relationships and what love is. When I think about *The Notebook* and those types of movies. And *Titanic*. How they have done so much damage to a little girl's psyche. That she's looking for this man in this world that really, honestly, does not exist. Because, in my experience of living, I haven't met Boyz II Men men—opening doors, bringing flowers, and just doing all of this stuff that you see in the movies.

RP: That stuff also comes with other ideas that don't necessarily help or empower individuals within relationships. I'm being chivalrous, but I also think of you as being less than I am. I do, though, think Boyz II Men and other artists are trying to show this other side of black masculinity that can love, that can do all these other things too.

AH: I do believe that our kings are able to love. But it is interesting because that's really not the thing that you run into. It's not common. Not to say that love isn't common, but everybody has a different definition of what love is. How you express love also depends on your upbringing.

RP: R&B now. What do you think its challenges are? What do you think is optimistic about it?

AH: R&B now has become very male dominated. When you look at the '90s, though, there were just as many women artists as there were men. They're doing a lot of '90s shows, performances, a lot of '90s concerts, but most of the '90s concerts are majority guys. But there were so many women groups and solo artists that were out. It's become crasser. It definitely has the sexuality part, but the sensuality is missing. The one thing about R&B that really made it what it was, was sensuality. It added a softness to it. It made you feel a certain way. It made you feel sexy. It made you want to prepare a room with candle lights. You knew you were going to get some ass, but you didn't mind putting up with everything.

RP: Do you think part of that is because they're also trying to compete with hip-hop? Do you think that part of that is because they feel the need to stay relevant?

AH: No. My perception of it is that there's just something lacking in their perception of what sexuality is. This younger generation lacks a filter. So being 44 years young, and listening to my mother's music, and listening to Gladys Knight & the Pips, and listening to even Prince, we incorporated that into our music. This generation grew up listening to our music and 2 Live Crew. We grew up with filters. They grew up with none. And so their music is a reflection of not having a filter.

RP: Evelyn Champagne King sang "You make my love come down." Now they'll just say, "You get my pussy wet." Before (in some cases), you'd have to figure out what love coming down means, but now your imagination doesn't have to work as hard.

RP: What do you think about Whitney Houston's influence on black music?

AH: Her influence has been indelible. You can't erase Whitney Houston. I remember growing up and listening to this woman's incredible voice, and I did not know that somebody could sing like that. Her voice was just—really there are no words. It was just gorgeous, the power in it. There's no one to this day that can sing like her. The passion that she had. She's just untouchable. There are other—just like there are young ladies out there who can mimic Beyoncé's voice but it's like that's really not your style. You can do it, but it doesn't have the same feeling, doesn't have the same passion, doesn't have that spirit. Because whatever her experiences were . . .

RP: . . . they contributed to that sound and how she sang. What about Toni Braxton?

AH: I like Toni. I have a thing for women who have this lower register. Lalah Hathaway has it, and so does Gladys Knight. There's a raw realness in—to me, that tone that just is soothing for me. It's very hypnotic. And, when it comes to Toni, Toni just—to me, Toni had this grown-ass woman's voice. She had this home girl next door like, what? I'm going to sing all of this to you and I'm going to give it to you. But she also got this attitude like, "Fuck with me if you want to." They also they tried to put her in a female Babyface type vibe.

RP: When she and Babyface did the *Love, Marriage & Divorce* CD in 2014, she had to remind him she had become her own artist. Although he had begun her career, she rightfully demanded an equal voice in that collaboration. It's also funny what you said about Babyface because he considers the impact he has had on other artists as his biggest influence.

AH: The beautiful thing about him is he was able to use his gift to be able to be those different people that he couldn't physically be. He was able to be those people through his music and his alter egos. Johnny Gill might have been an alter ego, Bobby Brown might have been an alter ego, Toni Braxton may have been an alter ego. And he was able to say, "You know what? I want this person to sing my song," or, "I want this person—" because he could see himself. He couldn't do it himself, but he knew he had somebody that—yeah, if I could be this person, my song would be this.

ACKNOWLEDGMENTS

In some respects, writing a first monograph prepared me to write the second, although writing the second one provided me with tremendous satisfaction and joy. On the one hand, my love for black music made the investigation of rhythm and blues culture a sheer pleasure. On the other hand, the persistence of black inequality made the analysis sometimes painful and other times optimistic. The music, and, as this book examines more broadly, rhythm and blues culture, provided great hope, inspiration, and consolation, notwithstanding the ever-increasing entrenchment of black inequality. As I noted when I published my first monograph, *Exodus Politics: Civil Rights and Black Leadership in African American Literature and Culture* (2013), one incurs many debts when writing a book. In this book, rhythm and blues culture, artists, and music engendered my largest debt. For once, I remain grateful for a debt I cannot repay, and remain hopeful that the analysis herein pays forward what I owe.

Two research assistants provided invaluable support, at different stages of this project, that facilitated my ability to complete *Destructive Desires*. In its earlier stages, Linda M. Blair completed a variety of tasks that provided me the necessary archive to begin constructing the book's preliminary arguments, artists, and sources. After Linda graduated, Sebastien Pierre-Louis eagerly accepted the baton, and provided research and administrative support that allowed me to concentrate my energies on thinking, writing, and thinking more. Both Linda and Sebastien proved to be conscientious, reliable, and thorough investigators, and I am grateful for their participation in this project.

The Georgetown University Main Campus Research award committee took consistent interest in this project, and the summer academic grants allowed me to concentrate my energies primarily on conducting the research and writing necessary to complete this book. My Senior Faculty Research Fellowship, too, recognized the project's scholarly contribution, and I am grateful for this institutional aid from Georgetown University. I thank the Department of African American Studies, the Department of English, and the College Dean's Office for the resources they made available. Institutional support can make or break a book's completion, and I appreciate that Georgetown University aided this book's completion.

Access to Adina Howard added another element that this project could not have possessed without the direct interview so I appreciate her graciousness in affording me the opportunity and privilege to conduct a live interview with her. While the extant archive allowed me to think broadly about her influence, the interview focalized her legacy within the context of *Destructive Desires'* narrative arc. For her grace, time, insights, and artistic production, I thank Adina Howard, living legend, whose "Freak Like Me," "T-shirt and Panties," and "Nasty Grind" have indelibly shaped (and arguably helped to produce) at least one generation (see appendix C). I also appreciate her generosity in providing two of the images that appear in chapter 3.

Jason Ryan, the manager for rights, clearances, standards, and practices at TV One facilitated my access to *Life After* episodes that were no longer available to the public. These archives contained a robust set of information and enriched the arguments this book makes. I appreciate TV One's investment in black cultural production more generally, and Jason's willingness to grant me access to these episodes in particular. Also, I thank the editorial staff of the *Journal of Popular Music Studies*, which published an earlier version of chapter 1, thus providing a preliminary audience for the ideas this manuscript further developed. The article, "Marriage Panacea: Black Music (Re)imagines Sociological Explanations of Black Inequality," appears in 2017;29:e12244.

The editorial staff at Rutgers University Press deserves high praise for their consistency, professionalism, and excellence. Leslie Mitchner, whose commitment to expanding African American studies remains commendable, first took interest in *Destructive Desires*, noting its suitability to the Rutgers University Press list. I appreciate her sustained work in building the African American studies list, as well as her desire to make *Destructive Desires* a part of the Rutgers family, and I wish her the best during retirement. Following Leslie's departure, Lisa Banning continued to shepherd the book, and I thank her for standing in the gap before Nicole Solano added the book to her portfolio. I thank Nicole for the seamless transition as well as her enthusiasm for and leadership with *Destructive Desires*. Thank you, too, to Jasper Chang, an editorial assistant whose conscientiousness and efficiency ensured the successful production of this project. For the two anonymous readers of the manuscript, I appreciate the thoroughness of their feedback, and how their suggestions helped me to accentuate and clarify arguments *Destructive Desires* offered.

In Toni Morrison's dedication in *Song of Solomon*, she notes that it is good fortune to miss someone before he or she leaves you. Equally as good, I'd argue, are the abilities to think and write in community, especially in a profession where writing and thinking occur in solitude or even solitary confinement. My appreciation for my colleagues, interlocutors, family, and friends captures my beliefs that I am not an island unto myself, and that conversation, debate, and disagreement sharpen arguments and provoke precise articulation of ideas. While writing *Destructive Desires*, I have had a range of conversations and debates that have clarified my arguments and helped me to think energetically about the stakes of this project and what it contributes to African American studies, black music and popular culture studies, and black life, black politics, and black interpersonal relationships. Additionally, several colleagues and friends graciously and generously have taken the time to read various aspects of this manuscript and to provide thoughtful feedback. I offer sincere gratitude to Michael Awkward, Soyica Colbert, Leslie Hinkson, LaMonda Horton-Stallings, and Susana Morris for their conscientious readings and subsequent conversations about the manuscript. I send a special thanks to Margo Crawford and Aida Levy-Hussen, both of whom read early drafts of the project and provided crucial feedback that reshaped the book's scope.

I have also had a community of believers and supporters—friends, family, and colleagues—whose interest in and support of my work have encouraged me throughout the writing process. Our conversations, too, about the artists, culture, and themes have nuanced my thinking as well. For your *consistent* engagement, enthusiasm, and support, thank you: Paul Butler, Robert "Bob" Caldwell Sr., Toya Carmichael, Tiffany Craig, Erica Edwards, Brett Gadsden, Ramonda Horton, Brandon Manning, Johnathan McGriff, Angelyn Mitchell, Sherry Nielsen, Crystal Nwaneri, Christopher Powell, Christina Sharpe, Charles Shedrick, Scott Taylor, Maurice Wallace, and Anthony Williams.

I am thankful, too, for the support of my family, a term that, for me, also includes family I have chosen. My mother, Doris Patterson, and her musical tastes and interests cultivated my love for music as did my sister's, Marcilyn Patterson. Both remain constant champions and supporters, and I thank them for the gifts of life, love, and laughter. My aunts, Glenda Patterson and Shirley ("Shirley Ann") Williams continue to support my endeavors and celebrate my accomplishments. Carla Frett, Pauline Patterson Greer, Nigel Kelly, Karla Benson Rutten, Jason Simmonds, Anjulet Tucker, Ebony Walden, Michelle Wallace and I share a love for black music culture, and our affinities for music, conversation, and laughter show up throughout this book. I have welcomed their voices, enthusiasm, and energy.

In the end, peace, love, music, and the Spirit abided and helped bring *Destructive Desires* to fruition. May they continue to abide, inspire, and transform.

Robert J. Patterson
October 2018
Washington, DC

NOTES

PREFACE

1. Atlantic Starr, "Secret Lovers," *As the Ballad Turns*, 1985, Mp3 file, downloaded, December 7, 2008, iTunes.
2. Michael Awkward, *Soul Covers: Rhythm and Blues Remakes and the Struggle for Artistic Identity* (Durham, N.C.: Duke University Press, 2006).
3. In chapter 1, I explain this argument in greater depth. An earlier version of it appears in "Marriage Panacea: Black Music (Re)imagines Sociological Explanations of Black Inequality," *Journal of Popular Music Studies* 29 (2017): e12244.
4. Although Columbia House now maintains a movie and television division, its cassette and compact disc departments are now defunct. As did the movie and television division, the music division functioned as a membership subscription service that offered its members discounted compact discs and cassettes when they agreed to purchase a set amount of music within the agreed-upon time period. BMG Music Service, which, in the 1990s, competed against Columbia House, acquired Columbia House's music division in 2005. Prior to the mass digitization of music in the twenty-first century, these businesses provided mass access to contemporary music and artists.

INTRODUCTION

1. Lisa Duggan, *The Twilight of Equality?: Neoliberalism, Cultural Politics, and the Attack on Democracy* (Boston: Beacon Press, 2004), xxii.
2. Michel Foucault, *The Archaeology of Knowledge and the Discourse on Language* (New York: Pantheon Books, 1972), 59.
3. *The Souls of Black Folk* remains a key text in the study of black life and culture insofar as DuBois's analyses rely on a wide range of data, discourses, and cultural forms to evidence and buttress their claims. In terms of both form and content, DuBois offers a methodology for thinking about and thinking through black cultural production and politics, and this book builds upon that interdisciplinary "model" in its deployment of entangled networks. W.E.B. DuBois, *The Soul of Black Folk* (New York: Barnes and Noble, 2011).
4. Alexander Weheliye, *Phonographies: Grooves in Sonic Afro-Modernity* (Durham, N.C.: Duke University Press, 2005), 199.
5. Ibid.
6. Ibid, 200.
7. Shana Redmond, *Anthems: Social Movements and the Sound of Solidarity in the African Diaspora* (New York: New York University Press, 2013), 1.
8. Ibid., 141.
9. Gene Jarrett, *Representing the Race: A New Political History of African American Literature* (New York: New York University Press, 2011), 9.
10. Toni Braxton, *UnBreak My Heart: A Memoir* (New York: Dey Street Press, 2015).

11. Stuart Hall, "Encoding, Decoding," in *The Cultural Studies Reader*, ed. Simon During (London: Routledge, 1993), 93.

12. As a paradigmatic text, see Mae Henderson and E. Patrick Johnson's *Black Queer Studies: A Critical Anthology* (Durham, N.C.: Duke University Press, 2007).

13. E. Patrick Johnson, "'Quare Studies, or (Almost) Everything I Know about Queer Studies I Learned from My Grandmother," *Text and Performance Quarterly* 21, no. 1 (2001): 3.

14. Ibid.,10.

15. Roderick Ferguson, *Aberrations in Black: Toward a Queer Color of Critique* (Minneapolis: University of Minnesota Press, 2004), 3, 4.

16. Michael Awkward, *Soul Covers: Rhythm and Blues Remakes and the Struggle for Artistic Identity* (Durham, N.C.: Duke University Press, 2006), xxiii.

17. In chapter 10 of *Just My Soul Responding*, Ward argues that James Brown's protest politics transition between the 1960s and 1970s and the broader incorporation of black people into mainstream politics informs the less pronounced critique that emerges in Brown's music. See Brian Ward, "'Get Up, Get Into It, Get Involved': Black Music, Black Protest, and the Black Power Movement," in *Just My Soul Responding: Rhythm and Blues, Black Consciousness, and Race Relations* (Oakland: University of California Press, 1998), 388–416.

18. Nelson George, *The Death of Rhythm and Blues Music* (New York: Penguin Books, 1988), 183.

19. See Patricia Dixon, *African American Relationships, Marriages, and Families: An Introduction* (New York: Routledge, 2006) and Stephanie Coontz, *Marriage, a History: How Love Conquered Marriage* (New York: Penguin Books, 2006) for historiographical analyses of how marriage has evolved and how cross-cultural comparisons of marriage demonstrate its variations and specific histories.

20. In *Unprotected Texts: The Bible's Surprising Contradictions about Sex and Desire*, Jennifer Knust compellingly argues that the Bible presents conflicting messages about sex and desire to unsettle biblical authority as a primary source for arguments that promote monogamy, reject same-sex relationships, and characterize contemporary North American marriage as having forever existed as it does. See Jennifer Knust, *Unprotected Texts: The Bible's Surprising Contradictions about Sex and Desire* (New York: HarperOne, 2012). For debates about same sex marriage, see: Barack Obama, "Barack Obama Supports Gay Marriage in Interview with Robin Roberts of ABC News," May 9, 2012. Accessed June 1, 2016. http://abcnews.go.com/Politics/transcript-robin-roberts -abc-news-interview-president-obama/story?id=16316043; Otis Moss III, "Letter Supporting Gay Marriage by Pastor Otis Moss III of Trinity UCC," May 13, 2012. Accessed June 1, 2016. http://www.huffingtonpost.com/2012/05/28/otis-moss-iii-challenges-on -marriage-equality_n_1550449.html. Anthony Evans, "The Hypocrisy of the Gay Community: Why Do They Want Marriage." Accessed June 1, 2016. http://www .naltblackchurch.com/pdf/marriage-opposition.pdf. Dwight McKissic Sr, "Response to President Obama's Decision to Endorse Same-Sex Marriages," May 9, 2012. Accessed June 1, 2016. https://dwightmckissic.wordpress.com/2012/05/09/response-to-president -obamas-decision-to-endorse-same-sex-marriages/. Al Sharpton, Julian Bond, et al., "Open Letter Embracing President Obama's Position on Equality for Gay and Lesbian Individuals," May 11, 2012. Accessed June 1, 2016. http://nationalactionnetwork.net /press/open-letter-embracing-president-obamas-position-on-equality-for-gay-lesbian -individuals/.

21. Mark Anthony Neal, *Songs in the Key of Life: A Rhythm and Blues Nation* (New York: Routledge, 2003), 2, 3.

22. In *Know What I Mean?: Reflections on Hip Hop*, Dyson contends "As Tupac understood and as cultural theorist Michel Foucault argued, one's very life can be a work of art. Hence authenticity didn't consist so much in relating one's work to oneself, but in relating one's life to creative activity" (13). Beyond evidencing his claim that hip-hop

is indeed an art form and offering a more layered understanding of authenticity, Dyson's juxtaposition of rapper Shakur with theorist Foucault positions Shakur as a parallel theorist and hip-hop as an extension. Even this more robust understanding privileges hip-hop vis-à-vis Shakur over rhythm and blues music. In Michael Eric Dyson, *Know What I Mean?: Reflections on Hip Hop* (New York: Basic Cavitas Books, 2007).

23. Imani Perry, *Prophets of the Hood: Politics and Poetics in Hip Hop* (Durham, N.C.: Duke University Press, 2004) and Dyson, *Know What I Mean?*

24. In "Criteria for Negro Art," DuBois rejects the notion of "art for art's sake" by demonstrating that art is often politicized, and by arguing that African American art must be used to uplift the social and political positions of African Americans. See "Criteria for Negro Art," in *Within the Circle: An Anthology of African American Literary Criticism: From the Harlem Renaissance to the Present*, ed. Angelyn Mitchell (Durham, N.C.: Duke University Press, 1994), 60–68.

25. Tracey Sharpley-Whiting, *Pimps Up, Ho's Down: Young Black Women, Hip Hop and the New Gender Politics* (New York: New York University Press, 2007).

26. Phillip Brian Harper, *Abstractionist Aesthetics: Artistic Form and Social Critique in African American Culture* (New York: New York University Press, 2015), 2.

27. Stuart Hall, "What Is This 'Black' in Black Popular Culture?" in *Black Popular Culture*, ed. Gina Dent (Seattle: Bay Press, 1992), 30.

28. Imani Perry, *Prophets of the Hood*, 3.

29. While a range of black feminist thought has considered the complexities of hip-hop in terms of its aesthetic forms and ideological content, here I reference Gwendolyn Pough's "Seeds and Legacies: Tapping the Potential in Hip-Hop" and Kyra Gaunt's "Translating Double-Dutch to Hip-Hop: The Musical Vernacular of Black Girl's Play." Whereas Pough's essay provides a more layered examination of hip-hop's gender and sexual politics, Gaunt's reorients our understanding of the archive from which we might construct black women's interventions into and positions within hip-hop. See Gwendolyn Pough, "Seeds and Legacies: Tapping the Potential in Hip-Hop" in *That's the Joint! The Hip-Hop Studies Reader*, ed. Murray Forman and Mark Anthony Neal (New York: Routledge, 2004), 283–290. See Kyra Gaunt, "Translating Double-Dutch to Hip-Hop: The Musical Vernacular of Black Girl's Play," in *That's the Joint!*, 251–263.

30. See Langston Hughes, "The Negro Artist and the Racial Mountain" in *Within the Circle: An Anthology of African American Literary Criticism: From the Harlem Renaissance to the Present*, ed. Angelyn Mitchell (Durham, N.C.: Duke University Press, 1994), 55–59.

31. Richard Wright, "Between Laughter and Tears," *New Masses* (October 5, 1937), 22–23.

32. Regarding the protagonist Bigger Thomas in Wright's famed *Native Son*, Baldwin remarks, "For Bigger's tragedy is not that he is cold or black or hungry, not even he is American, black; but that he has accepted a theology that denies him life, that he admits the possibility of his being subhuman and feels constrained" (155). For Baldwin, this despair exemplifies the failure of the protest novel to imagine black humanity and life outside the limits social constructions pose. See James Baldwin, "Everybody's Protest Novel," in *Within the Circle: An Anthology of African American Literary Criticism: From the Harlem Renaissance to the Present*, ed. Angelyn Mitchell (Durham, N.C.: Duke University Press, 1994), 149–155.

33. See Zora Neal Hurston, "Characteristics of Negro Expression," in *Within the Circle: An Anthology of African American Literary Criticism: From the Harlem Renaissance to the Present*, ed. Angelyn Mitchell (Durham, N.C.: Duke University Press, 1994), 79–94.

34. See Larry Neal, "The Black Arts Movement" and Addison Gayle "Cultural Strangulation: Black Literature and the White Aesthetic," in *Within the Circle: An Anthology of American American Literary Criticism: From the Harlem Renaissance to the Present*, ed. Angelyn Mitchell (Durham, N.C.: Duke University Press, 1994), 184–198; 207–212.

35. Madhu Dubey argues that black women writers of the 1970s respond to these nationalist demands to contest the black heteropatriarchal logics that support the claims

and to demonstrate how black women writers were proposing alternative models. See Madhu Dubey, *Black Women Novelists and the Nationalist Aesthetic* (Indianapolis: Indiana University Press, 1994).

36. Gershun Avilez, *Radical Aesthetics and Modern Black Nationalism* (Urbana-Champaign: University of Illinois Press, 2016), 8.

37. Roderick Ferguson, *Aberrations,* 140.

38. Margo Natalie Crawford, *Black Post-Blackness: The Black Arts Movement and Twenty-First—Century Aesthetics* (Urbana-Champaign: University of Illinois Press, 2017), 2.

39. L. H. Stallings, *Funk the Erotic: Transaesthetics and Black Sexual Cultures* (Urbana-Champaign: University of Illinois Press, 2015), 73.

40. Paul Gilroy, *The Black Atlantic: Modernity and Double Consciousness* (Cambridge, Mass.: Harvard University Press, 1993), 75.

41. See Michael Awkward, *Soul Covers,* Mark Anthony Neal, *Songs in the Key of Life: A Rhythm and Blues Nation* (New York: Routledge, 2003); Mark Anthony Neal, *What the Music Said: Black Popular Music and Black Public Culture* (New York: Routledge, 1998); Mark Anthony Neal, *Looking for Leroy: Illegible Black Masculinities* (New York: New York University Press, 2013); Nelson George, *The Death of Rhythm and Blues* (New York: Penguin Books, 2003); Craig Werner: *A Change Is Gonna Come: Music, Race, and the Soul of America* (Ann Arbor: University of Michigan Press, 2006); Brian Ward, *Just My Soul Responding: Rhythm and Blues, Black Consciousness, and Race Relations* (Oakland: University of California Press, 1998).

42. Suzanne Smith, *Dancing in the Street: Motown and the Cultural Politics of Detroit* (Cambridge: Harvard University Press, 2001); Nelson George, *Where Did Our Love Go? The Rise and Fall of the Motown Sound* (Urbana-Champaign: University of Illinois Press, 1987).

43. Mark Anthony Neal, *Soul Babies: Black Popular Culture and the Post-Soul Aesthetic* (London: Routledge, 2004), 17.

44. Hall, "What Is This,"30.

45. See Sharpley-Whiting *Pimps.*

46. Thelma Golden, "Post-Black," in *Freestyle,* ed. Christine Y. Kim and Franklin Sirmas (New York: Studio Museum of Harlem, 2001), 14.

47. Awkward, *Soul Covers,* xv.

48. Hall, "What Is This," 32.

49. W.E.B. DuBois, *Souls of Black Folk* (New York: Barnes and Noble, 2009).

50. Lauren Berlant. *Cruel Optimism* (Durham, N.C.: Duke University Press, 2013).

51. See https://urban1.com/. Accessed October 10, 2018

52. See "TV One's 2009–10 Season the Highest in Network's Six-Year History," *Target Market News: The Black Consumer Market Authority* (October 1, 2010). Accessed June 6, 2016. http://www.targetmarketnews.com/storyid10251002.htm.

53. See http://tvone.tv/show/unsung-4/. Accessed June 6, 2016.

54. Carlton Hargro, "Unsung Producer Shares Recipe for TvOne's Soul/R&B Show," January 2, 2012. *Crib Notes: Atlanta Music Blog.* Accessed July 12, 2016. http://archive.is /7rgqM.

55. William McClatchy, "TV Series Puts 'Unsung' Black Music Stars Back in the Spotlight," June 6, 2011. *Pittsburgh Post-Gazette.* Accessed June 4, 2016. http://www.post-gazette .com/ae/tv-radio/2011/06/06/TV-series-puts-Unsung-black-music-stars-back-in-the -spotlight/stories/201106060128.

56. Ibid.

57. Brenda Weber, "Introduction—Trash Talk: Gender as an Analytic on Reality Television," in *Reality Gendervision: Sexuality & Gender on Transatlantic Reality Television,* ed. Brenda Weber (Durham, N.C.: Duke University Press, 2014), 6.

CHAPTER 1   READING RACE, GENDER, AND SEX

1. See Michele Wallace, *The Black Macho and the Myth of the Superwoman* (New York: Verso, 1999). For a recent discussion that explains the cultural significance of Wallace's text, see Terrion Williamson, *Scandalize My Name: Black Feminist Practice and the Making of Black Social Life* (New York: Fordham University Press, 2017).

2. The culture of poverty, as a move away from biological racism, suggested that black people's culture, including their misplaced values, prevented them from thriving. This concept reinforced racism and failed to think about how institutions thwarted black success. As a resonant example, particularly from the late 1960s, see Oscar Lewis, "Culture of Poverty," in *On Understanding Poverty: Perspectives from the Social Sciences*, ed. Daniel P. Moynihan, 187–220 (New York: Basic Books, 1969).

3. See Robert J. Patterson, 'Do You Want to Be Well?' The Gospel Play, Womanist Theology, and Tyler Perry's Artistic Production," *Journal of Feminist Studies in Religion* 30, no. 2 (Fall 2014): 41–56.

4. Michael Awkward, *Soul Covers: Rhythm and Blues Remakes and the Struggle for Artistic Identity* (Durham, N.C., Duke University Press, 2007), 176.

5. See Brian Ward, *Just My Soul Responding: Rhythm and Blues, Black Consciousness, and Race Relations* (Oakland: University of California Press, 1998).

6. Whereas texts such as Frazier's *The Black Family* precede Moynihan's publication, several also emerge afterward. See Robert Staples, *The Black Family: Essays and Studies*, 6th ed. (Boston: Cengage Learning, 1998).

7. Julius Wilson (with Kathryn Neckerman), "Poverty and Family Structure: The Widening Gap between Evidence and Public Policy Issues" in *The Truly Disadvantaged: The Inner City, the Underclass, and Public Policy* (Chicago: University of Chicago Press, 2012), 63.

8. Roderick Ferguson, *Aberrations in Black: Toward a Queer of Color Critique* (Minneapolis: University of Minnesota Press, 2005), 146–147.

9. Daniel P. Moynihan, *The Negro Family: The Case for National Action* (Washington, DC: Office of Planning and Research, US Department of Labor, 1965), section v.

10. Wilson, "Poverty and Family Structure," 73.

11. Moynihan, *Negro Family*, section v.

12. Dixon explains how the sexual revolution, the feminist movement, and the gay and lesbian movement coalesced to generate an overall decline in marriage rates. See Patricia Dixon, *African American Relationships, Marriages, and Families: An Introduction* (New York: Routledge, 2006), 5–7.

13. As Coontz explains, the breadwinner model, which foregrounded men as the primary economic earners in households, increased its prominence between the 1920s and 1950s in American marriage discourses. See Stephanie Coontz, *Marriage, a History: How Love Conquered Marriage* (New York: Penguin Books, 2006).

14. Dixon, *African American Relationships*, 7.

15. Melvin Oliver and Thomas Shapiro, *Black Wealth, White Wealth: A New Perspective on Racial Inequality* (New York: Routledge, 1997), 118.

16. Ibid., see pages 119–125 for a complete explanation.

17. Helene Slessarev, *The Betrayal of the Urban Poor* (Philadelphia: Temple University Press, 1997), 16–17.

18. In Ava DuVernay's *13th*, the documentary describes the southern strategy as Reagan's way of invoking racial and economic fears to attract poor Democrats to the Republican Party. Although they did not use race explicitly, they relied on racial tropes and metaphors to solidify investments in whiteness even if those interests defied their own class interests. The criminalization of crack (in ways that cocaine was not), which affected black communities, also contributed to the devastation of black communities and removal of black men. See Ava DuVernay, *13th* (2016).

19. Yascha Mounk, *The Age of Responsibility: Luck, Choice, and the Welfare State* (Cambridge, Mass.: Harvard University Press, 2017), Kindle version, page 5, location 104.

20. Ibid., page 25, location 409.

21. Jodi Melamed, "The Spirit of Neoliberalism: From Racial Liberalism to Neoliberal Multiculturalism," *Social Text* 24, no. 4 (Winter 2006): 1.

22. Ibid., 4.

23. Ibid., 8.

24. Ibid., 15.

25. Ibid., 15.

26. http://www.songfacts.com/detail.php?id=5589 and http://www.rollingstone.com/music /lists/the-500-greatest-songs-of-all-time-20110407/the-beatles-eleanor-rigby -20110526.

27. Simon Frith, *Performing Rites: On the Value of Popular Music* (Cambridge, Mass.: Harvard University Press, 1998), 9.

28. Candace Jenkins identifies this practice of desiring a black male patriarch to save black communities as the salvific wish in *Proper Lives: Proper Relations: Regulating Black Intimacy* (Minneapolis: University of Minnesota Press, 2007). Susana Morris articulates the crippling effects that respectability politics have on the development of healthy black relationships and communities in *Close Kin and Distant Relatives: The Paradox of Respectability Politics in Black Women's Literature* (Charlottesville: University of Virginia Press, 2014).

29. Tyler Perry's film *Madea's Family Reunion* emphatically and didactically confirms a parallel point not only by using this song as a part of the movie but also by having actress Cicely Tyson engage in a monologue wherein she encourages—at the family reunion—black men and women to assume their rightful positions. Tyler Perry, *Madea's Family Reunion* (Santa Monica, Calif.: Lionsgate, 2006).

30. The O'Jays (Performer), "Family Reunion" (1975).

31. See Rolland Murray's *Our Living Manhood: Literature, Black Power, and Masculine Ideology* (Philadelphia: University of Pennsylvania Press, 2007).

32. Quoted in Neal, *Soul Babies: Black Popular Culture and the Post-Soul Aesthetic* (New York: Routledge, 2002).

33. See Charles V. Hamilton, "Federal Law and the Courts in the Civil Rights Movement" in *The Civil Rights Movement in America*, ed. Charles Eagles, 97–126 (Jackson: University of Mississippi Press, 1986); Jacquelyn Dowd Hall "The Long Civil Rights Movement and Political Uses of the Past," *Journal of American History* 91, no. 4 (2005): 1233–1263; Bayard Rustin, "From Protest to Politics," in *Time on Two Crosses: The Collected Writing of Bayard Rustin*, ed. Devon Carbado and Donald Weise, 214–267 (San Francisco: Cleis Press, 2003); and Manning Marable, *Race, Reform, and Rebellion: The Second Reconstruction and Beyond in America, 1945–2006* (Jackson: University of Mississippi Press, 2007).

34. The persona takes exception to the fact that she is not the *only* other woman, noting that she can love a married man, though not one who has multiple partners besides his wife. Thus the persona rejects monogamy and simultaneously calls for it.

35. L. H. Stallings, *Funk the Erotic: Transaesthetics and Black Sexual Culture* (Champaign: University of Illinois Press, 2015).

36. Coontz, *Marriage, a History*, 220–245.

37. Ralph Banks uses this phrase to capture the explicit and implicit ways that marriage bestows cultural capital onto individuals who opt in to the institution. See Banks *Is Marriage for White People? How the African American Marriage Decline Affects Everyone* (New York: Plume, 2012).

38. L. H. Stallings, *Funk*, 122.

39. http://www.allmusic.com/album/single-life-mw0000189389/awards.

40. See David Ikard, *Breaking the Silence: Toward a Black Male Feminist Criticism* (Baton Rouge: Louisiana State University Press, 2007).

41. Michael Cobb, *Single: Arguments for the Uncoupled* (New York: New York University Press, 2012), 18.
42. See Mark Anthony Neal's discussion of R. Kelly in *Looking for Leroy: Illegible Black Masculinities* (New York: NYU Press, 2013), 117–125.
43. Angela Willey, *Undoing Monogamy: The Politics of Science and the Possibility of Biology* (Durham: Duke University Press, 2016), 8.
44. Michael Cobb, *Single*, 18.
45. Ibid., 31.
46. Willey, 7.
47. Quoted in Awkward, *Soul Covers*, 15.
48. As Coontz explains, the breadwinner model, which foregrounded men as the primary economic earners in households, increased its prominence between the 1920s and 1950s in American marriage discourses. See Coontz, *Marriage, a History*.
49. Anastasia Curwood, *Stormy Weather: Middle-Class African American Marriages between the Two World Wars* (Chapel Hill: University of North Carolina Press, 2010), 50.
50. Roderick Ferguson, *Aberrations*, 203.
51. Ibid., 86.
52. See Kevin Gaines, *Uplifting the Race: Black Leadership, Politics, and Culture in the Twentieth Century* (Chapel Hill: University of North Carolina Press, 1996).
53. Ferguson, *Aberrations*, 86.
54. In *Cruel Optimism* (Durham, N.C.: Duke University Press, 2011), Lauren Berlant uses the phrase "cruel optimism" to theorize the process under which people desire objects that are in fact detrimental to their thriving, or *perceive* said detrimental objects as necessary for their survival.

CHAPTER 2 "WHIP APPEAL"

1. Carolyn Bingham, "'Waiting to Exhale': Babyface Produces Entire Soundtrack," *Los Angeles Sentinel*, January 18, 1996, B5.
2. Although Laura Sinagra's "Pop Review: Swinging Sounds for Lovers by Babyface, All Grown Up," references a Babyface aesthetic, it falls short of mapping out the contours of that aesthetic. While this task extends the purview of this project, it is worth noting that Edmonds has a range of sounds, styles, and musical properties that constitute his oeuvre that this task would be at best partial if undertaken. Sinagra in *New York Times*, December 12, 2005, E4.
3. In an interview with David Ritz, for example, Edmonds notes that he never intended to sing and that his specialty was songwriting. See "The Soul Behind the Face," *Rolling Stone*, December 1, 1994, 103. Edmonds's songwriting talents made his way into the industry, and Dennis Hunt noted in 1988 that his works were "dominating the black music charts." See Hunt, "L.A. and Babyface: Heatin' up the Charts," *Los Angeles Times*, September 18, 1988, L88. And, in 1995, he received his fourth consecutive songwriter of the year award at the BMI (Broadcast Music Industry) awards. See "'Breathe Again': Babyface Named Top Songwriter," *New Pittsburgh Courier*, June 10, 1995, 7.
4. Kimberly Roberts, "Babyface Releases New Best of CD," *Philadelphia Tribune*, December 29, 2000, 5E.
5. Although track 6 will discuss in more detail Edmonds's influence outside of rhythm and blues culture, here it is worth noting that he has collaborated with Madonna, Eric Clapton, and Olivia Newton-John, and Edmonds also attributes his diverse musical interests to the variety of music forms he listened to growing up and his interest in the acoustic guitar.
6. David Adelson, "L.A. Reid and Babyface May Dissolve R&B Reign," *Los Angeles Times*, July 25, 1993, F73.

7. Lynn Norment, "Top Black Executives in Music Industry: 14 African-American Men and Women are Among the Movers and Shakers in the Lucrative World of Recording," *Ebony*, 52, no. 9 (July 1997), 88.

8. Charles Rogers, "L.A. and Babyface Sign $10M Arista, Deal," *New York Amsterdam News*, October 29, 1989, 26.

9. Kenneth Edmonds in Dale Kawashima, "Special Interview with Kenneth 'Babyface' Edmonds, Legendary Songwriter and Artist, and New Songwriters Hall of Fame," March 20, 2017. Accessed October 7, 2018. https://www.songwriteruniverse.com /babyface-interview-2017.htm

10. Brandon Manning, *At Wit's End: Black Men and Vulnerability in Contemporary Satire* (Manuscript, in progress), introduction.

11. Kenneth Edmonds in "Babyface: Notes from a Tender Lover," *Essence*, 26, no. 4 (August 1995), 64.

12. Kenneth Edmonds in Dale Kawashima, "Special Interview."

13. Danyel Smith, "Babyface Is Tangy Sweet on Love and Relationships," *New York Times*, August 15, 1993, H25.

14. In David Ritz's "Not Just a Pretty Face" *Essence*, 21, no. 5 (September 1990), 74.

15. By using this show's theme song, I am drawing attention to a move in black cultural production that centered black women's narratives, that adhered to the principle that black women telling their own stories was an important and central claim to a sense of black women becoming empowered and having more capacious views of self. See *Living Single,* produced by Yvette Lee Bowser. Hollywood: Fox Broadcasting Company, 1993–1998.

16. Erica R. Edwards, "Sex after Normal," *Differences: A Journal of Feminist Cultural Studies*, 26, no. 1 (2015), 142.

17. See *The People v. O.J. Simpson: American Crime Story,* directed by Ryan Murphy, Anthony Hemingway, and John Singleton. Los Angeles, Calif.: FX, February 2016; and *Anita: Speaking Truth to Power*, directed by Freida Lee Mock. New York: Goldwyn Films, 2014, DVD.

18. Nellie McKay, "Remembering Anita Hill and Clarence Thomas: What Really Happened When One Black Woman Spoke Out," ed. Toni Morrison, *Race-ing Justice, En-gendering Power: Essays on Anita Hill, Clarence Thomas, and the Construction of Social Reality* (New York: Pantheon Books, 1992), 271.

19. Ndubuizu argues that black disciplinarians become instruments of the state to enforce the curtailment of welfare benefits, and that the black disciplinarians are typically men who are enforcing policies that disproportionately impact black women, whose gender and sexuality often are the sources of stigma. Black disciplinarians often police black intimate relations and champion behavioral solutions to black inequality. Rosemary Ndubuizu, "(Black) Papa Knows Best: Marion Barry and the Appeal to Black Authoritarian Discourse," *National Political Science Review* 16, no. 1 (2014): 31–48.

20. Michael Awkward, "You're Turning Me On: The Boxer, the Beauty Queen, and Rituals of Gender," in *Black Men on Race, Gender, and Sexuality,* ed. Devon Carbado (New York: New York University Press, 1999), 137.

21. Simon Frith, *Performing Rites: On the Value of Popular Music* (Cambridge, Mass.: Harvard University Press, 1996), 185.

22. The issue here is one of degree because the chapter will argue that aspects of Edmonds's background become important aspects of the interpretive matrix. It specifically refuses the collapsing of biography onto the artistic project when unearthing the meaning.

23. Hortense Spillers, "Mama's Baby, Papa's Maybe: An American Grammar Book," *Diacritics* 17, no. 2 (1987): 66.

24. Although Judith Butler typically gets the credit for thinking about the performativity of gender in *Gender Trouble*, Spillers's contention here thinks about the racialized

contexts for gender performance and becomes an ur-text for thinking about these issues in African American and black diasporic contexts. Judith Butler, *Gender Trouble: Feminism and the Subversion of Identity* (London: Routledge, 1990).

25. Cedric Robinson points out that the more general black desire to espouse American principles of the American Dream (and I would add the nuclear family) forgets that America's founding myths are predicated on the exploitation of black bodies and that black elites espoused these ideas without ever calling into question this fact. This argument agrees and foregrounds how black women become further marginalized within these narratives, and destructive desires for American ideals. See chapter 9 in particular in Cedric Robinson's *Black Marxism: The Making of the Black Radical Tradition* (Chapel Hill: University of North Carolina Press, 2000).

26. Michael Awkward, "A Black Man's Place in Black Feminist Criticism," in *Black Men on Race, Gender, and Sexuality*, ed. Devon Carbado (New York: New York University Press, 1999), 379.

27. Ibid.

28. Ikard contends that Awkward does not analyze black women's agency in his reading of *Sula* and that this misstep occurs because of Awkward's attention to black men. See pages 20–23 in particular. David Ikard, *Breaking the Silence: Toward a Black Male Feminist Criticism* (Baton Rouge: Louisiana State University Press, 2007).

29. For a discussion of profeminist, "[a] male advocate for women's equality," see Joy James, "Profeminism and Gender Elites: W.E.B. DuBois, Anna Julia Cooper, and Ida Wells-Barnett," in *Next to the Color Line: Gender, Sexuality, and W.E.B. DuBois*, ed. Susan Gillman and Alys Weinbaum (Minneapolis: University of Minnesota Press, 2007), 69–95. For a discussion of how black men might engage in the black feminist project, see Valerie Smith's "Gender and Afro-Americanist Literary Theory and Criticism," in *Within the Circle: An Anthology of African American Literary Criticism from the Harlem Renaissance to the Present*, ed. Angelyn Mitchell (Durham, N.C.: Duke University Press, 1994), 482–498. For a discussion of men's roles in black womanism, see Sherley Williams, "Some Implications for Womanist Theory," *Callaloo* 27, no. 9 (1986): 303–308.

30. Awkward suggests that an awareness of one's subject positions and the power dynamics inherent in them can help one to engage in informed, critical, and useful analyses of race and gender, even if one does not hold membership in the respective groups. This type of awareness and critical practice seems crucial for black intimate relationships, particularly to the degree that black heteropatriarchy compromises the development of productive relationships. Michael Awkward, *Negotiating Difference: Race, Gender and The Politics of Positionality* (Chicago: University of Chicago Press, 1995).

31. Simone Drake, *When We Imagine Grace: Black Men and Subject Making,* (Chicago: University of Chicago Press, 2016), xiii–xiv (emphasis mine).

32. Saidiya Hartman in Patricia J. Saunders, "Fugitive Dreams of Diaspora: Conversations with Saidiya Hartman," *Anthurium: A Caribbean Studies Journal* 6, no. 1 (2008): 7.

33. Kenneth Edmonds (writer and performer), "Soon as I Get Home," (1989).

34. Ferguson, *Aberrations in Black: Toward a Queer Color of Critique* (Minneapolis: University of Minnesota Press, 2002), 140.

35. Drake, *When We Imagine*, 28.

36. Yvonne Tasker, *Working Girls: Gender and Sexuality in Popular Cinema* (London: Taylor and Francis, 1998), 181.

37. The issue of crossover appeal, or the need to appeal to wider racial audiences to increase the production's financial backing, was not particularly novel to the 1990s. Yet the increase in black cultural production and increased focus on black life across cultural media brought to bear these conversations in multiple contexts. For a through discussion of this issue in television and film, for example, see Monica W. Ndounou, *Shaping the Future of African American Film: Color-Coded Economics and the Story Behind the Numbers* (New Brunswick, N.J.: Rutgers University Press, 2014).

38. For a discussion of these issues, see Manthia Diawara's collection *Black American Cinema* (New York: Routledge, 1993). See chapter 3 in particular of Edward Guerrero's *Framing Blackness: The African American Image in Film* (Philadelphia: Temple University Press, 1993). See Paula Massood's *Black City Cinema: African American Urban Experiences in Film* (Philadelphia: Temple University Press, 2003). See Mia Mask's *Divas on Screen: Black Women in American Film* (Urbana-Champaign: University of Illinois Press, 2009).

39. Michael Boyce Gillespie, *Film Blackness: American Cinema and the Idea of Black Film.* (Durham, N.C.: Duke University Press, 2016), 6.

40. Ibid., 7.

41. Massood presses these issues further in chapter 3 of *Black City Cinema*, but my point here emphasizes again how black abjection becomes a focal point for how black life becomes imagined and contextualizes the difficulty Edmonds and others have in trying to secure backing for films that defy these images. The argument, too, acknowledges how soundtracks function for those films.

42. Denzel Washington in Veronica Mixon's "'The Preacher's Wife' is Gentle and Feels Good: Denzel and Whitney Stress the Importance of Positive Images," *Philadelphia Tribune*, December 13, 1996, 4E.

43. Even in a review of one of Edmonds's albums, *The Day*, the reviewer Amy Linden notes that it is difficult for white reviewers to deal with black love and intimacy, specifically declaring "it's easier for critics, in particular white ones, to jump on the latest roughneck's bandwagon than it is to settle into silky, polished, slick, and yes, commercial groove that Babyface offers up." *The Village Voice*, November 26, 1996, 54.

44. See Richard Natale, "Black Power in Hollywood: A Few African-Americans Have Parlayed Success in Another Field into Power in Movies. But It Isn't Easy-Even for the Decade's Most Successful R&B Figure," *Sun Sentinel*, August 30, 1998, 10.

45. Jason King argues that Braxton becomes one of the most frequently described "sultry" artists in the 1990s, and I attribute her lyrics, staging, and performances as central to this characterization of Braxton. Her singing on the soundtrack for *Boomerang* and its overlaying onto Berry's performance contribute to this imagery, which shapes Braxton's entire career. See "Toni Braxton, Disney, and Thermodynamics," *Drama Review*, 46, no. 3 (T175), Fall 2002, 54–81.

46. Julie Hubbert, "The Compilation Soundtrack from the 1960s to the Present," in *The Oxford Handbook of Film Music Studies*, ed. David Neumeyer (Oxford: Oxford University Press, 2014), 294.

47. See Aneeka Henderson's forthcoming *Wedding Bell Blues: Race and the Modern Marriage Plot* (Chapel Hill: University of North Carolina Press). 2020

48. See http://www.boxofficemojo.com/movies/?id=waitingtoexhale.htm. Accessed July 18, 2016.

49. While Daphne Brooks rightfully points out that romantic distrust and material disillusionment factor deeply into the film's narrative, the film also provides ways to think about the aforementioned issues too. See page 183 in Brooks, "'All That You Can't Leave Behind': Black Female Soul Singing and the Politics of Surrogation in the Age of Catastrophe," *Meridians* 8, no. 1 (2008), 180–204.

50. Tina M. Harris and Patricia Hill emphasize the importance of the accuracy of portrayals and attempt to situate their discussion in black feminist thinking. See "'Waiting to Exhale' or 'Breath(ing) Again': A Search for Identity, Empowerment, and Love in the 1990s," *Women and Language* 11, no. 2 (1998): 9–20.

51. Monica W. Ndounou, *Shaping the Future*, 121.

52. Erica R. Edwards, "Tuning into Precious: The Black Women's Empowerment Adaptation and the Interruptions of the Absurd," *Black Camera: An International Film Journal* 4, no. 1 (Winter 2012): 75.

53. Ndounou, *Shaping the Future*, 121.

54. Edmonds in Bingham's "Waiting."

55. See Judith Butler, "Imitation and Gender Insubordination" in *Literary Theory: An Anthology*, ed. Julie Rivkin and Michael Ryan (Malden, Mass.: Blackwell Publishing, 2017), 955–962. See Michel Foucault, "Method" in *History of Sexuality. An Introduction*, Vol. I (New York: Vintage Books 1990), 92–113.

56. See Aldore Collier's "Babyface Explains the Inspiration for His Hot New Album 'Grown & Sexy,'" *Jet*, August 1, 2005. 56–62 Houston quoted in Laura Randolph's "Babyface and Tracey Edmonds Talk about Life, Love and Launching Their New Adventures," *Ebony*, June 1998, 37.

57. Mary Anne Doane, *The Desire to Desire: The Woman's Film of the 1940s* (Bloomington: Indiana University Press, 1987), 97.

58. Heather Laing, *The Gendered Score: Music in 1940s Melodrama and the Woman's Film* (Burlington: Ashgate, 2007), 7.

59. James Buhler, "Gender, Sexuality, and the Soundtrack," in *The Oxford Handbook of Film Music Studies*, ed. David Neumeyer (New York: Oxford University Press, 2014), 370.

60. Hall, "Encoding, Decoding," in *The Cultural Studies Reader*, ed. Simon During (London: Routledge, 1993), 93.

61. Here I am thinking of Whitney Houston as pop-star or pop-musician and Chaka Khan in the funk tradition.

62. In Ritz's "Not Just a Pretty Face," Edmonds laments the decimation of the black family and argues that strong families set the foundation for success.

CHAPTER 3   "FREAK LIKE ME"

1. Larry Flick, "Adina Howard: (Freak) and You Know It," *Billboard* 109, no. 24 (June 14, 1997), 79.

2. J. R. Reynolds, "Howard Gets Less Graphic: Mecca Don Set More Sensual Than Explicit," *Billboard* 109, no. 27 (July 5, 1997), 15.

3. Cristina Verán, "Voices of Theory," *Vibe*, August 1997, 154.

4. In "Howard Get Less Graphic," Reynolds also reports that the promotion company relied on Howard's existing fan base and had released the single without any other major promotional tactics. This strategy ultimately may have undermined the expectation that Howard's existing fan base would support the new album and that she would also increase her base. That the album was never released officially further complicates its reception.

5. https://www.adinahoward.com/bio. Accessed July 24, 2017.

6. Howard in J. R. Reynolds, "Howard Takes Fans on Steamy 'Ride,'" *Billboard* 107, no. 3 (January 21, 1995), 20 and 24.

7. In an interview with Jean Wiggins, Howard notes that "freakiness" does not necessarily equate with "promiscuity." Howard's declarations demonstrate a tension between promoting sexual liberation while being attentive to cultural norms. While Dossie Easton and Janet Hardy's *The Ethical Slut: A Practical Guide to Polyamory, Open Relationships, and Other Adventures* echoes a similar claim, L. H. Horton rightfully demonstrates how the introduction of ethics into discussions of polyamory, for example, reinforces the normalcy of marriage and monogamy, which I correlate with Howard's comments as doing as well. See Williams's "Howard Brings Bold Tone, Strong Voice to Special R&B Act," *Chicago Sun-Times*, August 18, 1995, 13. See Easton and Hardy, *The Ethical Slut* (Berkeley: Celestial Arts: 2009), 3–26, and L. H. Stallings, *Funk the Erotic: Transaesthetics and Black Sexual Cultures* (Urbana-Champaign: University of Illinois Press, 2015), 124.

8. Mireille Miller-Young, *A Taste for Brown Sugar: Black Women in Pornography* (Durham, N.C.: Duke University Press, 2014), 279.

9. Jennifer Nash, *The Black Body in Ecstasy: Reading Race, Reading Pornography* (Durham, N.C.: Duke University Press, 2014), 149.

10. C. Riley Snorton, *Nobody's Supposed to Know: Black Sexuality on the Down Low* (Minneapolis: University of Minnesota Press, 2014).

11. In "10 of the Best," Andrews outlines the influence that ten black musical artists and/ or groups had in the 1990s. The article usefully demonstrates how the coexistence of each of the artists/groups created an entangled network in black musical production to produce more aesthetic or thematic choices for black artists to engage. See "10 of the Best: 90s R&B—Hip-hop Soul, Machine-Tooled Funk, Sexually Charged New Jack Swing—Here's Your Whistlestop Tour of One of Pop's Great Eras," *Guardian*, February 26, 2014. Accessed July 15, 2017. https://www.theguardian.com/music/musicblog /2014/feb/26/10-of-the-best-90s-r-and-b. In "Until the Day, Until the Dawn: The Legacy of Adina Howard's 'Freak Like Me,'" Jackson Howard compellingly argues for the ways that Howard's production made possible the acceptance of other women's cultural production, including TLC. Accessed July 28, 2017. http://notmad.us/2015/02 /until-the-day-until-the-dawn-the-legacy-of-adina-howards-freak-like-me.

12. Adina Howard, "Conversation with Robert J. Patterson," March 6, 2018 (appendix C, this volume).

13. *Adina Howard 20: A Story of Sexual Liberation* (Rebel Life Media, 2015). Accessed June 15, 2017. https://www.youtube.com/watch?v=mjyhffW6alc.

14. Quoted in *Adina Howard 20*.

15. Delores Tucker, quoted in Lonnae Parker, "The Body of Her Work: Singer Adina Howard's Sexy Ways Stir up a Fuss," *Washington Post*, September 5, 1995, D1.

16. Quoted in Lonnae Parker, "The Body of Her Work."

17. Author unknown, "What We Sing, Why We Sing," *Daily Hampshire Gazette*, June 16, 1995, para. 3.

18. Cruz deploys the phrase "politics of perversion" to think about "what ways can perversion open up new modes of being in the world for black women while at the same time accounting for the historical bondage (literally and symbolically) associated with black women's bodies" (11). In other words, Cruz, too, looks at typically ascribed sites of sexual exploitation to think about how black women's cultural production reworks those power dynamics. See *The Color of Kink* (New York: New York University Press, 2016).

19. Nixon's invocation of the welfare queen as an example of the State subsidizing black women became a resonant example in the public imaginary of the excesses of black sexuality and the need to regulate it. Although the image had existed before, the post– civil rights era deployment of it as an excuse to curtail the scope of the welfare state sharpened during Nixon's retrenchment of inequality and contextualizes the push in black culture to embrace respectability politics.

20. Candace Jenkins, *Private Lives, Proper Relations: Regulating Black Intimacy* (Minneapolis: University of Minnesota Press, 2007), 43.

21. Ibid., 44.

22. See Patricia Hill Collins, *Black Sexual Politics: African Americans, Gender, and the New Racism* (London: Routledge, 2005), 126.

23. See Lisa Thompson, *Beyond the Black Lady: Sexuality and the New African American Middle Class* (Urbana-Champaign: University of Illinois Press, 2012). Thompson argues how middle-class black ladies espouse respectability politics vis-à-vis the image of the respectable lady in order to rebuff "dominant presentation of black womanhood in the public imagination, where one-dimensional images of them as promiscuous, seductive, and sexually irresponsible circulate" (7).

24. See Beverly Guy-Sheftall, "The Body Politic: Black Female Sexuality and the Nineteenth-Century Euro-American Imagination" (13–33) and Anne Fausto-Sterling, "Gender, Race, and Nation: The Comparative Anatomy of 'Hottentot' Women in Europe, 1815–17" (66–95) in *Skin Deep, Spirit Strong: The Black Female Body in American Culture*, ed. Kimberly Wallace-Sanders (Ann Arbor: University of Michigan Press, 2002).

25. In *Beyond Respectability Politics*, Cooper also argues that respectability politics also aimed to keep black women safe in the public sphere, where their bodily integrity was especially in jeopardy in the post- Reconstruction era. Here she turns attention to black women's modest dressing practices in particular to underscore this point, and I insist that this continued emphasis on propriety and modesty extends beyond protection to the related moral chastising attributed to respectability politics. See Brittney Cooper, *Beyond Respectability Politics: The Intellectual Thought of Race Women* (Urbana-Champaign: University of Illinois Press, 2017).

26. Parker, "The Body of Her Work," D1.

27. Adina Howard, "Adina Howard: Life After Freak Like Me" in *Life After*, Season 5, Episode 5 (TV One, 2013).

28. Nash, *Black Body in Ecstasy*, 147.

29. Darieck Scott, *Extravagant Abjection: Blackness, Power, and Sexuality in the African American Imagination* (New York: New York University Press, 2014), 11.

30. In "Uses of the Erotic: The Erotic as Power," Lorde compellingly contends that the erotic, while denigrated, serves as a source of untapped power upon which women should capitalize. In this power, women possess the ability to reshape the world, and my use here turns our attention to how these imaginings might reshape black intimate relations and responses to black inequality. See Audre Lorde, *Sister Outsider: Essays and Speeches* (Freedom: Crossing Press, 1979).

31. L. H. Stallings, *Funk the Erotic*, 34.

32. Ibid., 11.

33. Nash, *The Black Body in Ecstasy*, 150.

34. Adina Howard, "Adina Howard: Life After."

35. Sharon Holland, *The Erotic Life of Racism* (Durham, N.C.: Duke University Press, 2012), 9.

36. Nicole Fleetwood, *Troubling Vision: Performance, Visuality, and Blackness* (Chicago: University of Chicago Press, 2010), 106.

37. Janice Malone, "The Scoop: Adina Howard Representing Aggressive Sistas," *Columbus Times*, September 12, 1995, A5.

38. Ibid.

39. Adina Howard, "Conversation with Robert J. Patterson," March 6, 2018 (appendix C, this volume).

40. See Jo-Carolyn Goode, "Adina Howard Reflects on Changing the Face of Sexual Liberation and New Projects 20 Years After 'Freak Like' Me, *Houston Style Magazine*, May 14, 2015, where Howard notes that she did not set out to start a movement yet was grateful for the work's impact.

41. Millie Jackson in *Unsung: Millie Jackson*, aired on TV One, February, 6, 2012.

42. Even in a 2016 interview with Aaron Foley, Howard notes that she is not a feminist and that she doesn't like the dictionary definition of *feminism*. Foley also notes that Millie Jackson, whom he identifies as her forbear, resisted this classification too. See "R&B Pioneer Adina Howard Talks Feminism and New Music," *BLAC Detroit*, March 2016. Accessed April 6, 2016. http://www.blacdetroit.com/BLAC-Detroit/March-2016/R-B-Pioneer-Adina-Howard-talks-feminism-and-new-music/

43. Adina Howard, "Naughty by Nature: R&B Temptress Adina Howard Scores Big," *People Magazine* 4, no. 5 (1995). Accessed October 8, 2018. https://people.com/archive/naughty-by-nature-vol-44-no-5/.

44. Adina Howard in "Conversation with Robert."

45. Mark Anthony Neal, *Songs in the Key of Black Life: A Rhythm and Blues Nation* (New York: Routledge, 2003), 4.

46. Howard, in Foley, "R&B Pioneer Adina."

47. Janice Malone, "Adina's a Freak and Proud of It," *Philadelphia Tribune*, September 12, 1995, 5. She also notes Patti Labelle as an influence in Helen Birch's "Wanna Get Freaky With Me?" *Independent*, London, April 28, 1995.

48. Although the effort to censor explicit music began in the mid-1980s, the actual label-ing of the affected material did not happen until the early 1990s, when "Explicit Lyrics" was used from 1990 until 1996 when it became "explicit content." This trend persists, and, even in 2016, on iTunes, songs with explicit lyrics, which include profanity, carry the assignation "E."

49. Langston Wertz, "Is Howard Video Too Nasty to Air?" *Charlotte Observer*, October 15, 1995, 2E.

50. Quoted in Parker, "The Body of Her Work." In "The Music All Sounds the Same," David Person echoes a similar claim, arguing that "talented folks like Sister Adina readily succumb to substituting not so subtle sexual themes for real musical ideas." *Hunts-ville Times*, July 27, 1995, D3.

51. Adina Howard in "Conversation with Robert."

52. Adina Howard in Fred Shutter, "'Boy Toy,' Yes, but Who's Doing the Toying? Singer Adina Howard Is in Full Command of Her Sexuality," *Kansas City Star*, March 28, 1995, E5. In "Top to Bottom, the Appeal Is Clear—Adina Howard's Gotta Have It—Stardom, That Is," Jim Farber characterizes Howard as the woman version of R. Kelly as well. *New York Daily News*, March 20, 1995, 33.

53. Although Neal documents the first three incidents, the sex cult allegations occurred in 2017. See Elias Leight, "R. Kelly Faces New Allegations of Underage Sex, Physical Abuse," *Rolling Stone*, August 22, 2017. Accessed August 22, 2017. http://www.rollingstone.com /music/news/r-kelly-faces-new-allegations-of-underage-sex-physical-abuse-w498861.

54. The #MeToo and Time's Up movements that bring to public attention sexual assault have vociferously protested Kelly, including constructing a website (https://www .muterkelly.org/) to promote their cause. Kelly, via a lawyer, continues to assert his innocence, and drawing on historical tropes of the State's violence against black men, have referred to these campaigns as a lynching. See https://www.muterkelly.org/. Accessed April 28, 2018. See Alana Vagianos, "Time's Up Demands Investigation into R. Kelly Sexual Abuse Allegations," *Huff Post*, April 30, 2018. Accessed October 7, 2018. https://www.huffingtonpost.com/entry/times-up-demands-investigation-into-r-kelly -sexual-abuse-accusations_us_5ae73480e4b04aa23f259f6a.

55. R. Kelly, in many ways, is a vexing figure for what he symbolizes about black masculinity—its oversexualization and pathology—and the desire for a sexualized masculinity (that remains contained to the private sphere and normative gender relations).

56. In *Looking for Leroy*, Neal argues that the soul-man tradition, which includes Luther Vandross and Sam Cooke, "can easily be acknowledged as embodying the knowledge produced in name of black masculinity, firmly planted at the cross-roads of desire and fear; secular and scared; blackness and Americanness; deviance and innocence" (125). Despite Kelly's particular personal challenges, he emerges from within a broader tradition of black men soul singers whose musical production reflects and touches the depths of black identities and politics. See Mark Anthony Neal, *Looking for Leroy: Illegible Black Masculinities* (New York: New York University Press, 2013), 117–142.

57. Evelyn Champagne King's "Love Come Down" invoked the sense of a lover's sexual prowess and attentiveness that could bring immense sexual pleasure.

58. Neal, *Looking for Leroy*, 10.

59. Ibid., 11

60. Jeffrey McCune, *Sexual Discretion: Black Masculinity and the Politics of Passing* (Chicago: the University of Chicago Press, 2014), 5.

61. Alexander Weheliye, *Habeas Viscus: Racializing Assemblages, Biopolitics, and Black Femi-nist Theories of the Human* (Durham, N.C.: Duke University Press, 2014), 2.

62. Adina Howard in "Conversation with Robert."

63. Patricia Hill Collins, *Black Feminist Thought: Knowledge, Consciousness, and the Politics of Empowerment* (New York: Routledge 1990), 69.

64. Ibid.

65. Patricia Hill Collins, *Black Sexual Politics: African Americans, Gender, and the New Racism* (London: Routledge, 2005), 126.

66. Shayne Lee, *Erotic Revolutionaries: Black Women, Sexuality, and Popular Culture* (Lanham, Md.: Hamilton Books, 2010).

67. Soyica Colbert, *Black Movements: Performance and Cultural Politics* (New Brunswick, N.J.: Rutgers University Press, 2017), 16.

68. Adina Howard, performance at Repertory Theater, 2014.

69. Colbert, *Black Movements*, 88.

CHAPTER 4   "DIDN'T WE ALMOST HAVE IT ALL?"

1. Whitney Houston in "Reflecting on 30 Years in Hollywood," interview with Shaun Robinson, *Access Hollywood*, November 15, 2011. Accessed November 30, 2017. http://www.accessonline.com/videos/whitney-houstons-final-access-interview-reflecting-on-30-years-in-hollywood-30999.

2. Speculation about Houston's drug use and general health became intensified when Houston appeared on the Michael Jackson tribute show in 2001. See "Michael Jackson 30th Anniversary Tribute," September 7, 2001. It is reported that she was thinner than she appears in photographs from the event, as publishing venues airbrushed the photographs to add weight. Her stylist later reported that Houston's handlers enabled her, telling her she looked healthy, and that at that moment, her stylist reinforced that death might be imminent.

3. In her *Primetime* interview with Diane Sawyer, Houston contests the idea that Bobby Brown has corrupted her or that drugs beset her. She instead saw herself as her largest obstruction. See interview, Diane Sawyer, "Primetime: Whitney Houston," *Primetime*, December 4, 2002.

4. See "Whitney Houston Autopsy Report" in www.autopsyfiles.org. Accessed June 5, 2015.

5. These series of incidents, particularly in the aftermath of her death, became read as parts of larger evidence of Houston's presumed descent into a drug overdose. See Casey Schwartz, "Whitney Houston's Death: Xanax and Alcohol, Lethal Duo," *Daily Beast*, February 13, 2012. Accessed October 9, 2018. https://www.thedailybeast.com/whitney-houstons-death-xanax-and-alcohol-lethal-duo; See "Celine Dion on Houston: Drugs Took over Her Dreams." *CNN Entertainment*, February 12, 2012.

6. In a series of interviews, Harvey would not say definitively what caused Houston's death and leaves open multiple possibilities. See Alan Duke, "Cocaine, Heart Disease Contribute to Houston's Drowning, Coroner Says," March 23, 2012, www.cnn.com. In the Associated Press's reporting, they emphasize how Harvey also does not name the other drugs present as contributing factors to her death. See "Whitney Houston Coroner's Report Details Drug Signs, Liquor, Drowning," CBS News, April 5, 2012.

7. Also see "Whitney Houston's Death: 9 Surprising Details in Coroner's report," where other "experts" debate Harvey's conclusions about the causes of death and the influence other drugs make. ABC News, April 5, 2012.

8. Daphne Brooks, "'All That You Can't Leave Behind': Black Female Soul Singing and the Politics of Surrogation in the Age of Catastrophe," *Meridians: Feminisms, Race, and Transnationalism* 8, no. 1 (2008): 183.

9. Ibid., 201.

10. Ibid., 201.

11. Richard Defendorf notes that Houston also spent 29 weeks on the top of Black Album charts; see "Whitney Houston Takes Fame in Stride," in *Orlando Sentinel*, October 20, 1985, 1. See Audrey Edwards, "Revlon Salutes: Whitney Houston," *Essence* 28, no. 1 (May 1997), 96.

12. Clive Davis, *The Soundtrack of My Life* (New York: Simon & Schuster, 2013), 323.

13. Clive Davis on *The Merv Griffin Show*, June 23, 1983. Accessed October 9, 2018. https://www.youtube.com/watch?v=Dw2hjXDCM6k.

14. *Can I Be Me* posits that this construction of Houston precedes her entrance into celebrity and locates its origins with her family. See Jim Farber, "Nick Broomfield on His Damning Whitney Houston Film: 'She had Very Little Control Over Her Life,'" *Guardian*, April 26, 2017, 16. Accessed May 1, 2017. https://www.theguardian.com/film/2017/apr/25/nick-broomfield-on-his-damning-whitney-film-she-had-very-little-control-over-her-life.

15. L.L. Cool J, "Around the Way Girl," on *Mama Said Knock You Out* (New York: Def Jam Recordings, 1990).

16. D. Soyini Madison, "Foreword" in *Black Performance Theory*, ed. Thomas DeFrants and Anita Gonzalez (Durham, N.C.: Duke University Press, 2014), viii.

17. Kenneth Reynolds, *Can I Be Me*, dir. Nick Broomfield (New York: Lafayette Films, 2017), film.

18. Richard Defendorf, "Whitney Houston Takes Fame in Stride," *Orlando Sentinel*, October 20, 1985, 1.

19. Stephen Holden, "Houston: A Composite of Her Predecessors," *Daily Breeze*, June 6, 1986, E3.

20. Chris Helm, "Whitney Houston Charms with Pizazz," *Chicago Tribune*, 1987, A14.

21. Whitney Houston is nominated for favorite rhythm and blues female vocalist, favorite rhythm and blues single ("You Give Good Love"), favorite rhythm and blues female video artist, and favorite rhythm and blues video single ("Saving All My Love for You). Her only pop nomination was for favorite pop female artist. See Associated Press reporting in the *Baltimore Sun*, January 6, 1986, 2B.

22. Nina Serrianne, "Pop Culture," in *America in the Nineties* (New York: Syracuse University Press, 2015), 141, 148.

23. Clive Davis, *Soundtrack of My Life*, 308.

24. Ibid., 309.

25. Ibid., 312.

26. C. Riley Snorton, *Black on Both Sides: A Racial History of Trans Identity* (Minneapolis: University of Minnesota Press, 2017), 8.

27. *Penthouse* published photos of Williams in its September 1984 issue, and the first Miss Black America then became the first to relinquish her title due to this scandal.

28. Davis, *Soundtrack of My Life*, 311.

29. In "Whitney Houston: More than Top Talent," *Sun*, July 20, 1986, 1E and 3E, Paul Grein notes that changes in adult contemporary music also aided in Houston's crossover appeal.

30. Stuart Hall, "Cultural Studies and Its Theoretical Legacies," in *Stuart Hall: Critical Dialogues in Cultural Studies* (New York: Routledge, 1995), 265.

31. Jennifer Stoever, *The Sonic Color Line: Race and the Cultural Politics of Listening* (New York: New York University Press, 2016).

32. Brian Ward, *Just My Soul Responding: Rhythm and Blues, Black Consciousness, and Race Relations* (Los Angeles: University of California Press, 1998), 20.

33. Andrew Flory, *I Hear a Symphony: Motown and Crossover R&B* (Ann Arbor: University of Michigan Press, 2017), 12.

34. Lynn Norment, "Whitney Talks about the Men in Her Life—and the Rumors, Lies, and Insults That Are the High Price of Fame," *Ebony*, May 1991,110.

35. In an interview with ABC news, Houston notes her desire to have audiences who "truly hear someone singing from their soul, their heart." On the one hand, this attachment of soul to voice suggests that the performance calls forth some inner quality (biological) that is authentic (true to one's self) that critics had argued was missing from Houston's performances, aside from the racial soul. See "Whitney Houston on

Childhood, Her Voice" ABC News, December 9, 2002. For criticism about the stiltedness of her performances in the early part of her career, see Anthony Tranfa, "Second Houston Album Disappointing," *Daily Breeze*, June 26, 1987, E15; Mike Boehm's "Whitney in Need of Fairy Godmother," *Providence Journal*, July 10, 1987, A-19.

36. Whitney Houston, *The Arsenio Hall Show* (Los Angeles: Paramount Studios, 1990).

37. Whitney Houston, "The Three Faces of Whitney Houston," *Black Collegian*, 22, no. 2 (November 1991), 129. In "The Soul of Whitney Houston," *Essence* 21, no. 8 (December 1990) with Joy Cain, Houston notes she has been trying to figure out how to sing white or black and posits that, "Music is not a color line. It's an art" (55). This attempt to deracialize reflects her conflicted expressions of race's importance and how it operates in the post–civil rights era.

38. In Julian Mayfield, "You Touch My Black Aesthetic and I'll Touch Yours," in *The Black Aesthetic*, ed. Addison Gayle (New York: Doubleday, 1972), 24–31, Mayfield expresses dismay over what he perceives as superficial markers of blackness and calls for a more complicated set of definitions that cannot be co-opted through performance and that eschew the oversexualization of black people.

39. Doreen St. Felix, "The Two Voices of Whitney Houston," *New Yorker*, September 14, 2017. Accessed September 21, 2017. https://www.newyorker.com/culture/culture-desk/the-two-voices-of-whitney-houston.The issue of race, its performance in speech, from accent, to word choice, permeated Houston's aesthetics and career; she was at once hyperracialized even as she functioned to show the waning significance of race as an obstruction to postracialism—the il(logics) of assimilationist thinking.

40. Malik Gaines, *Black Performances on the Outskirts of the Left: A History of the Impossible* (New York: New York University Press, 2017), 1.

41. Margo Crawford, *Post-Black Blackness: the Black Arts Movement and Twenty-First Century Aesthetics* (Urbana-Champaign: University of Illinois Press, 2017), 173.

42. Reportedly, Arista's "annual gross profit had jumped from $35 million, when Houston first signed, to $400 million, and Houston's record sales were largely credited with boosting that number." See David Browne, "Whitney Houston: The Diva and Her Dark Side," *Rolling Stone*, 115, 2, March 15, 2012, 32.

43. Brown in Bobby Brown, *Every Little Step: My Story* (New York: Dey Street Books, 2016); Houston *Oprah's Next Chapter* 2.221, January 28, 2013 (West Hollywood: OWN); Lavar in *Can I Be Me*, dir. Nick Broomfield (New York: Lafayette Films, 2017), film. Crawford, "Whitney Elizabeth Houston, 1963–2012: A Look Back at a Star From One of Her Closest Friends," *Esquire*, February 12, 2012. Accessed February 15, 2012. https://www.esquire.com/entertainment/music/a12753/whitney-houston-6654718/.

44. Whitney Houston in "Whitney Houston Talks about the Men in Her Life—and the Rumors, Lies, and Insults That Are the High Price of Fame," *Ebony*, May 1991, 114.

45. Tricia Romano charts the ways that the lesbian assignation follows Houston, noting that even when she marries, she has to say, "I'm not gay." See "Whitney Houston: Anatomy of a Lesbian Rumor," *Daily Beast*, February 13, 2012. Accessed October 10, 2018. https://www.thedailybeast.com/whitney-houston-anatomy-of-a-lesbian-rumor.

46. Cheryl Clarke, "Lesbianism: An Act of Resistance," in *Words of Fire: An Anthology of African-American Feminist Thought*, ed. Beverly-Guy Sheftall (New York: New Press 1995), 242.

47. Whitney Houston quoted in Noah Michelson "Bobby Brown Claims Whitney Houston Was Bisexual," *Huffington Post*, June 8, 2016. Accessed July 2, 2016. https://www.huffingtonpost.com/entry/bobby-brown-whitney-houston-bisexual_us_57586Ia1e4b00f97fba6f786.

48. See Jacob Bernstein's "Production of a Lifetime: Whitney Houston and Clive Davis," *New York Times*, September 20, 2017. Accessed September 21, 2017. https://nyti.ms/2fFEYZF.

49. Recall from chapter 1 that Ralph Banks uses this phrase to capture the explicit and implicit ways that marriage bestows cultural capital onto individuals who opt in to

the institution. See Banks, *Is Marriage for White People? How the African American Marriage Decline Affects Everyone* (New York: Plume, 2012).

50. Widespread interest in their marriage was fueled by the sense that they lacked common ground, which increased the public's interest in seeing if and how long the marriage would last.

51. Whitney Houston and Bobby Brown "Something in Common" on *Bobby* (Santa Monica: MCA Records, 1992).

52. Ibid.

53. Stuart Hall, "What Is This 'Black' in Black Popular Culture? In *Black Popular Culture*, ed. Gina Dent (New York: New Press, 1998), 30.

54. Whitney Houston in Anthony DeCurtis, "Whitney Houston: Down and Dirty." *Rolling Stone*, June 10, 1993, 46.

55. Bobby Brown Jr., for example, was born in 1992, the same year in which Brown and Houston got engaged (April) and married (July). The timing of these events all but assures that Brown was having sex with at least one other woman while Houston was reporting their exclusivity.

56. See Audre Lorde "The Master's Tools Will Never Dismantle the Master's House" in *Sister Outsider* (New York: Ten Speed Press, 2007), 110–113. Although I do not want to discount the important ways that work within a system can challenge it, I too want to underscore the complexity of retrenchment. This navigation, I think lies at the heart of the more fascinating work in black gender and sexuality studies currently.

57. See Lynn Norment, "Whitney at 35!" *Ebony* 54, no. 2 (1998), pages 160–162 in particular.

58. Houston notes that she wanted to experience family and motherhood, and both desires emerge post-1989. Crawford shares that Houston wanted something more in life and the next stage of marriage would provide that. See Crawford in *Can I Be Me*.

59. Angela Willey, *Undoing Monogamy: The Politics of Science and the Possibility of Biology* (Durham, N.C.: Duke University Press, 2016), 76.

60. Brown, *Every Little Step*, 154, location 1880.

61. This claim emerges from a host of interviews Brown completes to promote *Every Little Step* and discuss the death of Bobby Kristina. See Zach Seemayer, "Bobby Brown Addresses Whitney Houston 'Crack is Whack' interview, Says He 'Should Have Been Better,'" *ET Online*, July 7, 2016. Accessed July 10, 2016. https://www.etonline.com/news /190541_bobby_brown_addresses_whitney_houston_crack_is_whack_interview; see Dave Quinn's "Bobby Brown Claims He Has Sex with a Ghost—and Other Bombshells from His Upcoming Interview," *People*, June 7, 2016. Accessed June 10, 2016. https:// people.com/celebrity/bobby-brown-bombshells-from-2020-interview-sex-with-ghost /; see also Bobby Brown interview with Robin Roberts, "Bobby Brown: Every Little Step Special Edition," *Primetime*, June 7, 2016.

62. Brown makes these points not only in *Every Little Step: My Story*, but also in a series of interviews he gives to promote the book, as noted in the previous footnote.

63. Michael Arceneaux, "The Rumors of Whitney Houston's Same-Sex Relationship Is Not Bobby Brown's Business to Tell," *VH1*, June 9, 2016. Accessed June 10, 2016. http://www .vh1.com/news/267241/bobby-brown-whitney-houston-same-sex-love/

64. Quoted in Alen Block's "The Buzz about 'Bobby,'" *Television Week Chicago* 24, no. 33 (August 2015), 12.

65. *Being Bobby Brown, Bravo*, S1 E1, July 2005 (New York: Bravo Network).

66. Weber, "Introduction" *Reality Gendervision: Sexuality and Gender on Transatlantic Reality Television*, ed. Brenda Weber (Durham, N.C.: Duke University Press, 2014), 4.

67. Block, "The Buzz," 12.

68. Ibid.

69. Alison Samuels, "Whitney Houston's Protective 'Baby Girl' Daughter Bobbi Kristina," *Daily Beast*, February 13, 2012. Accessed October 9, 2018. https://www.thedailybeast .com/whitney-houstons-protective-baby-girl-daughter-bobbi-kristina.

70. Alex Chadwick, "Review: New Reality TV Series 'Being Bobby Brown,'" *NPR*, Los Angeles, June 30, 2005, 1.

71. Donald Bogle's *Toms, Coons, Mulattoes, Mammies, and Bucks: An Interpretive History of Blacks in American Films* (New York: Bloomsbury, 2016), Manthia Diawara's edited collection *Black American Cinema* (New York: Routledge, 1993), Nicole Fleetwood's *Troubling Vision: Performance, Visuality, and Blackness* (Chicago: University of Chicago Press, 2010), and Michael Gillespie's *Film Blackness: American Cinema and the Idea of Black Film* (Durham, N.C.: Duke University Press, 2016) demonstrate the scholarly tendencies to historicize racial representation in the context of visual aesthetics and racial/racist iconography and to articulate how black cultural production resisted one-dimensional representations of blackness. Gillespie and Fleetwood further question the degree to which black cultural production can meet the expectations for representation to reconfigure blackness outside of abjection, while demonstrating how representations of blackness can in fact produce more capacious notions about blackness.

72. Although Clive Davis would later attribute her inability to quit smoking to her voice's decline, Alexandra Coghlan would note that her continued straining of her vocal cords destroyed her voice, and voice coach Gary Catona would assert that vocal exercises were restoring her voice, this hoarseness metonymically signified an irreparable damage to Houston's voice, image, career, and personhood. See Alexandra Coghlan's "Whitney Houston: A Voice that Destroyed Itself," *NewStatesmanAmerica*, February 17, 2012. Accessed February 20, 2012. https://www.newstatesman.com/music /2012/02/houston-voice-pop-records; Davis, *Soundtrack*, 338; Catona in Mark Seal's "The Devils in the Diva," *Vanity Fair* (June 2012). Accessed June 20, 2012. https://www .vanityfair.com/hollywood/2012/06/whitney-houston-death-bathtub-drugs-rehab.

73. Misha Kavka, *Reality TV* (Edinburgh: Edinburgh University Press, 2012), 113.

74. Laura Ouellette and James Hay, *Better Living through Reality TV: Television and Post-Welfare Citizenship* (Malden, Mass.: Blackwell, 2008), 7.

75. Weber, "When America," in *Reality Gendervision: Sexuality and Gender on Transatlantic Reality Television*, ed. Brenda Weber (Durham, N.C.: Duke University Press, 2014), 98.

76. Oprah Winfrey, quoted in Weber, "When America," 100.

77. Weber, "When America," 100.

78. Wendy Brown, *Undoing the Demos: Neoliberalism's Stealth Revolution* (Cambridge: Massachusetts Institute of Technology Press, 2015), 65.

79. See David Konow, "New Whitney Houston Doc Takes Deeper Look at Addiction Battle," *The Fix*, August 29, 2017. Accessed September 4, 2017. https://www.thefix.com/new -whitney-houston-doc-takes-deeper-look-addiction-battle.

80. See Kimberly Springer, "Introduction: The Contours of the Oprah Culture Industry," in *Stories of Oprah: The Oprahfication of American Culture*, ed. Trystan Cotton and Kimberly Springer (Jackson: University of Mississippi Press, 2010), vii–xix.

81. Jennifer Rexroat, "'I'm Everywoman:' Oprah Winfrey and Feminist Identification," in *Stories of Oprah*, 19.

82. This definition of racism shifts away from the individual, conscious, and overt explanations that detach from systemic (institutional), unconscious, and covert to turn attention to the pervasiveness of racism and racial ideology and its embeddedness in typically unacknowledged places. See Gerald Sue, "The Invisible Whiteness of Being," in *White Privilege: Essential Readings on the Other Side of Racism*, ed. Paula Rothenberg (New York: Worth Publishers, 2014), 19–28.

83. Rexroat, "'I'm Everywoman,'" 21.

84. Janice Peck, "Talk About Racism: Framing a Popular Discourse on Race and Oprah Winfrey," *Cultural Critique* 27 (1994), 90–91.

85. My point here is that Winfrey fits within a larger pattern in the post–civil rights era where increased access to American institutions alters the ways that black people

form allegiances or demonstrate a commitment to black communities' interests and draws attention to the range of interests those communities might have.

86. "Oprah Announces Upcoming Interview of Whitney!" Accessed January 17, 2018. http://www.whitneyhouston.com/news/oprah-announces-upcoming-interview -whitney/.

87. Richard Huff argues that the interview allows us to appreciate Houston's experiences as a human being, and recenters her humanity instead of her celebrity. "Whitney Houston Dishes to Oprah on Marriage, Drugs," *New York Daily News*, September 8, 2009. Accessed January 17, 2018. http://www.nydailynews.com/entertainment/tv-movies /oprah-winfrey-calls-whitney-houston-interview-best-diva-dishes-marriage-drugs -article-1.402815.

88. Michael Awkward, *Soul Covers: Rhythm and Blues Remakes and the Struggle for Artistic Identity* (Durham, N.C.: Duke University Press, 2006), 5.

89. Ibid., 5.

90. In *Can I Be Me?* former bodyguard David Roberts insists that even Houston's drug use was part of her mechanism to adjust to the social discrepancy that existed between her and Brown.

91. Dori Laub, "Bearing Witness or the Vicissitudes of Listening," in *Crises of Witnessing in Literature, Psychoanalysis, and History*, ed. Shoshana Felman and Dori Laub (New York: Taylor and Francis), 221.

92. See Chaka Khan on *Piers Morgan Tonight*, February 12, 2012. Accessed February 12, 2012. https://www.youtube.com/watch?v=Wr-0PSB6Uow; see Rick Santorum on *Piers Morgan Tonight*, February 15, 2012. Accessed February 17, 2012. https://www.youtube .com/watch?v=6XbCWl2YpbA.

93. Benjamin Chavis, "Beloved Whitney Houston," *Chicago Defender*, February 15–21, 2012, 10.

94. Rebecca Tiger, "Celebrity Drug Scandals: Media Double Standards," *Contexts* 12, no. 4 (2013), 37.

95. In "Whitney Houston Dead at 48: Remembering Her Charity Work," *Ecorazzi*, February 12, 2012, China Despain reminds us that Houston was socially conscious and had a sense that racial injustice was problematic. She refused, for example, to work in South Africa because of apartheid. The Associated Press notes in 2004 that she received a humanitarian award for her charitable work and foundation. See "Whitney Houston Honored as a Humanitarian," *Today*, June 10, 2004. In "Happy Birthday Whitney Houston: A Look at Whitney Houston's Great Charity Work; She Was a True Humanitarian!" *BCG*, August 9, 2012, the BCG staff lays out the range of charities with which Houston engaged. The tendency to exclude this aspect of Houston's life serves a broader narrative to criminalize black women's supposed excess.

96. Heath Deihl, *Wasted: Performing Addiction in America* (New York: Routledge, 2016), 134.

97. Ibid. Also, see Allison Samuels, "Whitney's Private Hell: I Have Nothing," *Newsweek* 159, no. 19 (May 7, 2012), 28–32. Although Samuels attempts to contextualize the many factors that precipitated Houston's death, the article and its respondents ultimately cast blame on Houston herself.

98. Omise'eke Natasha Tinsley, *Ezili's Mirrors: Imagining Black Queer Genders* (Durham, N.C.: Duke University Press, 2018), 137.

99. Ibid.

100. In terms of cinematic examinations, I am referring to *The Bobbi Kristina Story*, the *Whitney* biopic (Lifetime), and the estate authorized documentary, *Whitney*. See *The Bobbi Kristina Story*, dir. Ty Hodges (Silver Spring, Md.: TV One, 2017); *Whitney*, dir. Angela Bassett (New York: Lifetime Movies, 2015); and *Whitney*, dir. Kevin MacDonald (Los Angeles, Calif.: Miramax and Roadside Attractions Film, 2018). A host of books have also examined Houston. Whereas Ian Harper's *Whitney and Bobbi Kristina: The Deadly Price of Fame, an Unauthorized Biography* centers Houston's drug addiction as

points of departure, Mark Bego's *Whitney Houston! The Spectacular Rise and Tragic Fall of the Woman Whose Voice Inspired a Generation* additionally considers Houston's influence on a musical tradition. See Ian Halperin, *Whitney and Bobbi Kristina: The Deadly Price of Fame, an Unauthorized Biography* (New York: Gallery Books, 2015); and Mark Bego, *Whitney Houston! The Spectacular Rise and Tragic Fall of the Woman Whose Voice Inspired a Generation* (New York: Skyhorse Publishing, 2012). In terms of biography, both texts extend this historical frame of Kevin Ammons and Nancy Bacon's unauthorized and often sensationalized biography, *Good Girl, Bad Girl: An Insider's 1996 Biography of Whitney Houston* (Hertford, N.C.: Crossroads Press, reprinted 2016). While Cissy Houston's *Remembering Whitney: My Story of Love, Loss, and the Night the Music Stopped* (New York: HarperCollins Publishers, 2013) details Cissy Houston's perspectives and feelings about Houston's life and death, and complements other extant narratives about Houston, her family, and her struggles, it does not offer any new biographical insights per se. It does, however, and importantly, paint a more complex picture of Houston's feelings as a woman who, outside of the public eye, was as ordinary as her talents were extraordinary, and was as vulnerable as she was strong.

101. Soyica Colbert, *Black Movements: Performance and Cultural Politics* (New Brunswick, N.J.: Rutgers University Press, 2017), 24.

102. See Irene Monroe, "Would Whitney Houston Still Be Alive If She Had Come Out? Family, Career and Church Kept Her in the Closet—Pushing Her into a Downward Spiral of Drug Abuse," *GayStarNews*, October 12, 2017. Accessed October 24, 2017. https://www.gaystarnews.com/article/whitney-houston-still-alive-come. See Michael Arceneaux "A New Whitney Houston Documentary Argues That Love Could Have Saved Her," *Elle*, August 24, 2017. Accessed September 4, 2017. https://www.elle.com/culture/movies-tv/a47614/whitney-houston-can-i-be-me-documentary/

103. Gershun Avilez, *Radical Aesthetics and Modern Black Nationalism* (Urbana-Champaign: University of Illinois Press, 2016), 158.

104. Susana Morris, *Close Kin and Distant Relatives: The Paradox of Respectability in Black Women's Literature* (Charlottesville: University of Virginia Press, 2014), 4.

105. Tinsley, *Ezili's Mirrors*, 4.

EPILOGUE "IT'S JUST ANOTHER SAD LOVE SONG"

1. Toni Braxton in Manuel Mendozza, "Toni! Toni! Toni! Brash, Young Braxton Takes R&B by Storm," *Dallas Morning News*, December 17, 1993, 32.

2. Toni Braxton, *VH1 Behind the Music*, October 29, 2012.

3. Elias Leight, "R&B's Changing Voice: How Hip-Hop Edged Grittier Singers Out of the Mainstream," *Rolling Stone*, October 13, 2017. Accessed November 8, 2017. https://www.rollingstone.com/music/features/how-hip-hop-edged-grittier-rb-singers-out-of-the-mainstream-w504678.

4. Ibid.

5. See Bill Maxwell, "Toni Braxton Stimulates Debate on Blacks and Sex," *Press of Atlantic City*, June 13, 1997, A13. Braxton also notes that Edmonds intentionally does not write sexually explicit songs that they perceive as sexually exploitive. This framework informs the types of songs Braxton sings too. See Ken Parish Perkins, "Toni Braxton: Red-Hot R&B Act Is a Beautiful Bundle of Contradictions," *Fort Worth Star*, March 7, 1997, 24. In a review, another reviewer makes claims about Braxton's performances that parallel ones made against Howard. Perhaps the perception that Braxton's approach remains subtle explains the different degree of critique they experience. See Jean Williams, "Braxton Adds Sexy Look to Solid Songs," *Chicago Sun-Times*, January 20, 1997, 28.

6. Toni Braxton, *Behind the Music*."

7. See "Superstar Singer Toni Braxton Tells Why She Filed for Bankruptcy," *JET*, March 23, 1998, 58. See Joy Bennett, "The Rise and Fall and Rise of Toni Braxton," *Ebony*, December 2000, 164–170.

8. See "Toni Braxton Shocked and Hurt after Oprah Interview," *Entertainment Examiner*, October 30, 2012, para. 1.

9. See "Toni Braxton Back on Top after Bankruptcy," *JET*, July 17, 2000, 56–60.

10. Toni Braxton in Alex Macpherson, "Toni Braxton: I Feel Like I've Been Given a Third Chance," *Guardian*, February 28, 2014. Accessed October 7, 2018. https://www.theguardian.com/music/2014/feb/28/toni-braxton-kenneth-babyface-edmonds-interview.

11. Kenneth Edmonds in "Toni Braxton: I Feel."

BIBLIOGRAPHY

#MuteRKelly. https://www.muterkelly.org, accessed April 28, 2018.

13th, directed by Ava DuVernay. Los Gatos, Calif.: Netflix, 2016.

"500 Greatest Songs of All Time." *Rolling Stone.* http://www.rollingstone.com/music/lists/the -500-greatest-songs-of-all-time-20110407/the-beatles-eleanor-rigby-20110526. Accessed June 6, 2016.

Adelson, David. "L.A. Reid and Babyface May Dissolve R&B Reign." *Los Angeles Times,* July 25, 1993, F73.

Adina Howard 20: A Story of Sexual Liberation. Rebl Life Media, 2015. Accessed June 15, 2017. https://www.youtube.com/watch?v=mjyhffW6alc.

Ammons, Kevin, and Nancy Bacon. *Good Girl, Bad Girl: An Insider's 1996 Biography of Whitney Houston.* Hertford, NC: Crossroads Press, 2016.

Andrews, Charlotte Richardson. "10 of the Best: 90s R&B—Hip-Hop Soul, Machine-Tooled Funk, Sexually Charged New Jack Swing—Here's Your Whistlestop Tour of One of Pop's Great Eras." *Guardian,* February 26, 2014. Accessed July 15, 2017. https://www .theguardian.com/music/musicblog/2014/feb/26/10-of-the-best-90s-r-and-b.

Anita: Speaking Truth to Power, directed by Freida Lee Mock. New York, NY: Goldwyn Films, 2014. DVD.

Arcenaux, Michael. "A New Whitney Houston Documentary Argues That Love Could Have Saved Her." *Elle,* August 24, 2017. Accessed September 4, 2017. https://www.elle.com /culture/movies-tv/a47614/whitney-houston-can-i-be-me-documentary/.

"Around the Way Girl." Performed by LL Cool J. 1990.

Avilez, Gershun. *Radical Aesthetics and Modern Black Nationalism.* Urbana-Champaign: University of Illinois Press, 2016.

Awkward, Michael. "A Black Man's Place in Black Feminist Criticism." In *Black Men on Race, Gender, and Sexuality,* edited by Devon Carbado, 362–382. New York: New York University Press, 1999.

———. *Negotiating Difference: Race, Gender and the Politics of Positionality.* Chicago: University of Chicago Press, 1995.

———. *Soul Covers: Rhythm and Blues Remakes and the Struggle for Artistic Identity.* Durham, N.C.: Duke University Press, 2007.

Baldwin, James. "Everybody's Protest Novel." In *Within the Circle: An Anthology of African American Literary Criticism: From the Harlem Renaissance to the Present,* edited by Angelyn Mitchell, 149–155. Durham, N.C.: Duke University Press, 1994.

Banks, Ralph Richard. *Is Marriage for White People? How the African American Marriage Decline Affects Everyone.* New York: Plume, 2012.

Bego, Mark. *Whitney Houston! The Spectacular Rise and Tragic Fall of the Woman Whose Voice Inspired a Generation.* New York: Skyhorse Publishing, 2012.

Being Bobby Brown. Episode 1, season 1. Bravo. July 1, 2005. Directed by Bobby Brown.

Bennett, Joy. "The Rise and Fall and Rise of Toni Braxton." *Ebony,* December 2000, 164–170.

Berlant, Lauren. *Cruel Optimism.* Durham: Duke University Press, 2013.

Bernstein, Jacob "Production of a Lifetime: Whitney Houston and Clive Davis." *New York Times*, September 20, 2017. Accessed September 21, 2017. https://nyti.ms/2fFEYZF.

Bingham, Carolyn. "'Waiting to Exhale': Babyface Produces Entire Soundtrack." *Los Angeles Sentinel*, January 18, 1996, B5.

Birch, Helen. "Wanna Get Freaky with Me?" *Independent*, April 28, 1995, 26.

Block, Alen. "The Buzz about 'Bobby.'" *Television Week*, August 2015.

Bobbi Kristina Story, The, directed by Ty Hodges. Silver Spring, MD: TV One, 2017.

Boehm, Mike. "Whitney in Need of Fairy Godmother." *Providence Journal*, July 10, 1987, A-19.

Bogle, Donald. *Toms, Coons, Mulattoes, Mammies, and Bucks*. New York: Bloomsbury Academic, 2016.

Braxton, Toni. *UnBreak My Heart: A Memoir*. New York: Dey Street Press, 2015.

"'Breathe Again': Babyface Named Top Songwriter." *New Pittsburgh Courier*, June 10, 1995, 7.

Brooks, Daphne. "'All That You Can't Leave Behind': Black Female Soul Singing and the Politics of Surrogation in the Age of Catasrophe." *Meridians* 8, no. 1 (2008): 180–204.

Brown, Bobby. *Every Little Step: My Story*. New York: HarperCollins, 2016.

Brown, Wendy. *Undoing the Demos: Neoliberalism's Stealth Revolution*. Cambridge: Massachusetts Institute of Technology Press, 2015.

Browne, David. "Whitney Houston: The Diva and Her Dark Side." *Rolling Stone*, March 15, 2012, 30–37.

Buhler, James. "Gender, Sexuality, and the Soundtrack." In *The Oxford Handbook of Film Music Studies*, edited by David Neumeyer, 366–382. New York: Oxford University Press, 2014.

Butler, Judith. *Gender Trouble: Feminism and the Subversion of Identity*. London: Routledge, 1990.

———. "Imitation and Gender Insubordination" in *Literary Theory: an Anthology*, edited by Julie Rivkin and Michael Ryan, 955–962. Malden: Blackwell Publishing, 2017.

Cain, Joy. "The Soul of Whitney Houston." *Essence*, December 1990, 54–56.

"Celine Dion on Houston: Drugs Took over Her Dreams." *CNN Entertainment*, February 12, 2012. Accessed October 10, 2018. http://marquee.blogs.cnn.com/2012/02/13/celine-dion-on-houston-drugs-took-over-her-dreams/.

Chadwick, Alex. "Review: New Reality TV Series 'Being Bobby Brown.'" *NPR*, June 30, 2005.

Chavis, Benjamin. "Beloved Whitney Houston." *Chicago Defender*, February 15–21, 2012, 10.

Clarke, Cheryl. "Lesbianism: An Act of Resistance." In *Words of Fire*, edited by Beverly Guy-Sheftall, 242–252. New York: New Press, 1995.

Cobb, Michael. *Single: Arguments for the Uncoupled*. New York: New York University Press, 2012.

Colbert, Soyica. *Black Movements: Performance and Cultural Politics*. New Brunswick, N.J.: Rutgers University Press, 2017.

Collier, Aldore. "Babyface Explains the Inspiration for His Hot New Album 'Grown & Sexy.'" *JET*, August, 1, 2005, 56–62.

Collins, Patricia Hill. *Black Feminist Thought: Knowledge, Consciousness, and the Politics of Empowerment*. New York: Routledge 1990.

———. *Black Sexual Politics: African Americans, Gender, and the New Racism*. London: Routledge, 2005.

Confirmation, directed by Rick Famuyiwa. New York: HBO Films, 2016.

Coontz, Stephanie. *Marriage, a History: How Love Conquered Marriage*. New York: Penguin Books, 2006.

Cooper, Brittney. *Beyond Respectability Politics: The Intellectual Thought of Race Women*. Urbana-Champaign: University of Illinois Press, 2017.

Crawford, Margo Natalie. *Black Post-Blackness: The Black Arts Movement and Twenty-First-Century Aesthetics*. Urbana-Champaign: University of Illinois Press, 2017.

Crawford, Robyn. "Whitney Elizabeth Houston, 1963–2012: A Look Back at a Star from One of Her Closest Friends." *Esquire*, February 12, 2012. Accessed February 15, 2012. https://www.esquire.com/entertainment/music/a12753/whitney-houston-6654718/.

Cruz, Ariane. *The Color of Kink*. New York: New York University Press, 2016.

Curwood, Anastasia. *Stormy Weather: Middle-Class African American Marriages between the Two World Wars*. Chapel Hill: University of North Carolina Press, 2010.

Davis, Clive. *The Soundtrack of My Life*. New York: Simon & Schuster, 2013.

Defendorf, Richard. "Whitney Houston Takes Fame in Stride." *Orlando Sentinel*, October 20, 1985, 1.

Deihl, Heath. *Wasted: Performing Addiction in America*. New York: Routledge, 2016.

Despain, China. "Whitney Houston Dead at 48: Remembering Her Charity Work." *Ecorazzi*, February 12, 2012. Accessed October 10, 2018. http://www.ecorazzi.com/2012/02/11/whitney-houston-dead-at-48-remembering-her-charity-work.

Diawara, Manthia. *Black American Cinema*. New York: Routledge, 1993.

Dixon, Patricia. *African American Relationships, Marriages, and Families: An Introduction*. New York: Routledge, 2006.

Doane, Mary Anne. *The Desire to Desire: The Woman's Film of the 1940s*. Bloomington: Indiana University Press, 1987.

Dolak, Kevin, and Sheila Marikar. "Whitney Houston's Death: 9 Surprising Details in Coroner's Report." ABC News, April 5, 2012. Accessed April 8, 2012. http://abcnews.go.com/Entertainment/whitney-houston-death-surprising-details-coroners-report/story?id=16076589.

Drake, Simone. *When We Imagine Grace: Black Men and Subject Making*. Chicago: University of Chicago Press, 2016.

Dubey, Madhu. *Black Women Novelists and the Nationalist Aesthetic*. Indianapolis: Indiana University Press, 1994.

DuBois, W.E.B. "Criteria for Negro Art." In *Within the Circle: An Anthology of African American Literary Criticism: From the Harlem Renaissance to the Present*, edited by Angelyn Mitchell, 60–68. Durham, N.C.: Duke University Press, 1994.

———. *The Soul of Black Folk*. New York: Barnes and Noble, 2011.

Duggan, Lisa. *The Twilight of Equality? Neoliberalism, Cultural Politics, and the Attack on Democracy*. Boston: Beacon Press, 2005.

Duke, Alan. "Cocaine, Heart Disease Contribute to Houston's Drowning, Coroner Says." *CNN*, March 23, 2012. Accessed March 23, 2012: https://www.cnn.com/2012/03/22/showbiz/whitney-houston-autopsy/index.html.

Dyson, Michael Eric. *Know What I Mean? Reflections on Hip Hop*. New York: Basic Cavitas Books, 2007.

Easton, Dossie, and Janet W. Hardy. *The Ethical Slut: A Practical Guide to Polyamory, Open Relationships, and Other Adventures*. Berkeley: Celestial Arts: 2009.

Edmonds, Kenneth. "Babyface: Notes from a Tender Lover." *Essence*, August 1995, 62–64

———. In Alan MacPherson, "Toni Braxton: I Feel Like I've Been Given a Third Chance." *Guardian*, February 28, 2014. Accessed October 7, 2018. https://www.theguardian.com/music/2014/feb/28/toni-braxton-kenneth-babyface-edmonds-interview.

———. "Soon as I Get Home." (Writer and performer). Recorded 1989.

Edwards, Audrey. "Revlon Salutes: Whitney Houston." *Essence*, May 1997, 96.

Edwards, Erica R. "Sex after the Black Normal." *Differences: A Journal of Feminist Cultural Studies* 26, no. 1 (2015): 141–167.

———. "Tuning into Precious: The Black Women's Empowerment Adaptation and the Interruptions of the Absurd." *Black Camera: An International Film Journal* 4, no. 1 (Winter 2012): 75.

Evans, Anthony. "The Hypocrisy of the Gay Community: Why Do They Want Marriage?" *National Black Church*, n.d. Accessed June 1, 2016. http://www.naltblackchurch.com/pdf/marriage-opposition.pdf.

Farber, Jim. "Nick Broomfield on His Damning Whitney Houston Film: 'She Had Very Little Control Over Her Life.'" *Guardian*, April 26, 2017. Accessed May 1, 2017. https://www .theguardian.com/film/2017/apr/25/nick-broomfield-on-his-damning-whitney-film -she-had-very-little-control-over-her-life.

———. "Top to Bottom, the Appeal Is Clear—Adina Howard's Gotta Have It—Stardom, That Is." *New York Daily News*, March 20, 1995, 33.

Fausto-Sterling, Anne. "Gender, Race, and Nation: The Comparative Anatomy of 'Hottentot' Women in Europe, 1815–17." In *Skin Deep, Spirit Strong: The Black Female Body in American Culture*, edited by Kimberly Wallace-Sanders, 66–95. Ann Arbor: University of Michigan Press, 2002.

Felix, Doreen St. "The Two Voices of Whitney Houston." *New Yorker*, September 14, 2017. Accessed September 21, 2017. https://www.newyorker.com/culture/culture-desk/the -two-voices-of-whitney-houston.

Ferguson, Roderick. *Aberrations in Black: Toward a Queer of Color Critique*. Minneapolis: University of Minnesota Press, 2003.

———.*The Reorder of Things: The University and Its Pedagogies of Minority Difference*. Minneapolis: University of Minnesota Press, 2012.

Fleetwood, Nicole. *Troubling Vision: Performance, Visuality, and Blackness*. Chicago: University of Chicago Press, 2011.

Flick, Larry. "Adina Howard: (Freak) and You Know It." *Billboard*, June 14, 1997, 79.

Flory, Andrew. *I Hear a Symphony: Motown and Crossover R&B*. Ann Arbor: University of Michigan Press, 2017.

Foley, Aaron. "R&B Pioneer Adina Howard Talks Feminism and New Music." *BLAC Detroit*, March 2016. Accessed April 6, 2016. http://www.blacdetroit.com/BLAC-Detroit/March -2016/R-B-Pioneer-Adina-Howard-talks-feminism-and-new-music.

Foucault, Michel. *The Archaeology of Knowledge and the Discourse on Language*. New York: Pantheon Books, 1972.

———. "Method" in *History of Sexuality: Volume 1 an Introduction*. New York: Vintage Books 1990, 92–113

Frith, Simon. *Performing Rites: On the Value of Popular Music*. Cambridge, Mass.: Harvard University Press, 1998.

Gaines, Kevin. *Uplifting the Race: Black Leadership, Politics, and Culture in the Twentieth Century*. Chapel Hill: University of North Carolina Press, 1996.

Gaines, Malik. *Black Performances on the Outskirts of the Left: A History of the Impossible*. New York: New York University Press, 2017.

Gaunt, Kyra. "Translating Double-Dutch to Hip-Hop: The Musical Vernacular of Black Girl's Play." In *That's the Joint! The Hip-Hop Studies Reader*, edited by Murray Forman and Mark Anthony Neal, 251–263. New York: Routledge, 2004.

Gayle, Addison. "Cultural Strangulation: Black Literature and the White Aesthetic." In *Within the Circle: An Anthology of African American Literary Criticism: From the Harlem Renaissance to the Present*, edited by Angelyn Mitchell, 207–212. Durham, N.C.: Duke University Press, 1994.

George, Nelson. *The Death of Rhythm and Blues Music*. New York: Penguin Books, 1988.

———. *Where Did Our Love Go? The Rise and Fall of the Motown Sound*. Urbana-Champaign: University of Illinois Press, 1987.

Gillespie, Michael Boyce. *Film Blackness: American Cinema and the Idea of Black Film*. Durham, N.C.: Duke University Press, 2016.

Gilroy, Paul. *The Black Atlantic: Modernity and Double Consciousness*. Cambridge, Mass.: Harvard University Press, 1993.

Golden, Thelma. "Post-Black." In *Freestyle*, edited by Christine Y. Kim and Franklin Sirmas, 14–15. New York: Studio Museum of Harlem, 2001.

Goode, Jo-Carolyn. "Adina Howard Reflects on Changing the Face of Sexual Liberation and New Projects 20 Years After 'Freak Like Me.'" *Houston Style Magazine*, May 14, 2015.

Accessed July 15, 2016. http://stylemagazine.com/news/2015/may/14/adina-howard
-reflects-changing-face-sexual-liberat/?page=2.

Grein, Paul. "Whitney Houston: More than Top Talent." *The Sun*, July 20, 1986, 1E and 3E.

Guerrero, Edward. *Framing Blackness: The African American Image in Film*. Philadelphia:
Temple University Press, 1993.

Guy-Sheftall, Beverly. "The Body Politic: Black Female Sexuality and the Nineteenth-Century
Euro-American Imagination." In *Skin Deep, Spirit Strong: The Black Female Body in
American Culture*, edited by Kimberly Wallace-Sanders, 13–33. Ann Arbor: University
of Michigan Press, 2002.

Hall, Jacquelyn Dowd. "The Long Civil Rights Movement and Political Uses of the Past." *Journal of American History* 91, no. 4 (2005): 1233–1263.

Hall, Stuart. "Cultural Studies and Its Theoretical Legacies." In *Critical Dialogues in Cultural
Studies*, 262–275. New York: Routledge, 1995.

———. "Encoding, Decoding," in *The Cultural Studies Reader*, edited by Simon During,
90–98. London: Routledge, 1993.

———. "What Is This 'Black' in Black Popular Culture?" In *Black Popular Culture*, edited by
Gina Dent, 21–33. Seattle: Bay Press, 1992.

Halperin, Ian. *Whitney and Bobbi Kristina: The Deadly Price of Fame, an Unauthorized Biography*. New York: Gallery Books, 2015.

Hamilton, Charles V. "Federal Law and the Courts in the Civil Rights Movement." In *The
Civil Rights Movement in America*, edited by Charles Eagles, 97–126. Jackson: University
of Mississippi Press, 1986.

"Happy Birthday Whitney Houston: A Look at Whitney Houston's Great Charity Work; She
Was a True Humanitarian!" *Black Celebrity Giving*, August 9, 2012. Accessed June 7,
2014. http://www.blackcelebritygiving.com/rip-whitney-houston-a-look-at-whitneys
-great-charity-work-she-was-a-true-humanitarian/.

Hargro, Carlton. "Unsung Producer Shares Recipe for TvOne's Soul/R&B Show." January 2,
2012. *Crib Notes: Atlanta Music Blog*. Accessed July 12, 2016. http://archive.is/7rgqM.

Harper, Phillip Brian. *Abstractionist Aesthetics: Artistic Form and Social Critique in African
American Culture*. New York: New York University Press, 2015.

Harris, Tina M., and Patricia Hill. "'Waiting to Exhale' or 'Breath(ing) Again': A Search for
Identity, Empowerment, and Love in the 1990s." *Women and Language* 11, no. 2 (1998):
9–20.

Helm, Chris. "Whitney Houston Charms with Pizazz." *Chicago Tribune*, July 22, 1987, A-14.

Henderson, Aneeka. *Wedding Bell Blues: Race and the Modern Marriage Plot*. Chapel Hill:
University of North Carolina Press, 2019.

Henderson, Mae, and E. Patrick Johnson (eds). *Black Queer Studies: An Anthology*. Durham,
N.C.: Duke University Press, 2017.

Holden, Stephen. "Houston: A Composite of Her Predecessors." *Daily Breeze*, June 6, 1986,
E-3.

Holland, Sharon. *The Erotic Life of Racism*. Durham: Duke University Press, 2012.

Houston, Cissy. *Remembering Whitney: My Story of Love, Loss, and the Night the Music Stopped*.
New York: HarperCollins Publishers, 2013.

Houston, Whitney. "Reflecting on 30 Years in Hollywood." Interview by Shaun Robinson.
November 15, 2011. Accessed November 30, 2017. http://www.accessonline.com/videos
/whitney-houstons-final-access-interview-reflecting-on-30-years-in-hollywood-30999
/.

———. "The Three Faces of Whitney Houston," *Black Collegian* 22, no. 2 (November 1991):
128–130.

———. "Whitney Houston Talks about the Men in Her Life—and the Rumors, Lies, and
Insults That Are the High Price of Fame." *Ebony*, May 1991, 110–118.

Howard, Adina. "Adina Howard: Life after 'Freak Like Me.'" *Life After*, Episode 5, season 5.
TV One, 2013.

———. "Biography." *Adina Howard*. Accessed July 24, 2017. https://www.adinahoward.com /bio.

———. "Nasty Grind." Performed by Adina Howard. Repertory Theater. Long Beach, Calif. April 26, 2014.

Howard, Jackson. "Until the Day, Until the Dawn: The Legacy of Adina Howard's 'Freak Like Me.'" *NotMad*, n.d. Accessed July 28, 2017. http://notmad.us/2015/02/until-the-day -until-the-dawn-the-legacy-of-adina howards-freak-like-me/.

Hubbert, Julie. "The Compilation Soundtrack From the 1960s to the Present." In *The Oxford Handbook of Film Music Studies*, edited by David Neumeyer, 291–319. Oxford: Oxford University Press, 2014.

Huff, Richard. "Whitney Houston Dishes to Oprah on Marriage, Drugs." *New York Daily News*, September 8, 2009. Accessed January 17, 2018. http://www.nydailynews.com /entertainment/tv-movies/oprah-winfrey-calls-whitney-houston-interview-best-diva -dishes-marriage-drugs-article-1.402815.

Hughes, Langston. "The Negro Artist and the Racial Mountain." In *Within the Circle: An Anthology of African American Literary Criticism: From the Harlem Renaissance to the Present*, edited by Angelyn Mitchell, 55–59. Durham, N.C.: Duke University Press, 1994.

Hunt, Dennis. "L.A. and Babyface: Heatin' Up the Charts." *Los Angeles Times*, September 18, 1988, L88.

Hurston, Zora Neal. "Characteristics of Negro Expression." In *Within the Circle: An Anthology of African American Literary Criticism: From the Harlem Renaissance to the Present*, edited by Angelyn Mitchell, 79–94. Durham, N.C.: Duke University Press, 1994.

Ikard, David. *Breaking the Silence: Toward a Black Male Feminist Criticism*. Baton Rouge: Louisiana State University Press, 2007.

Jackson, Millie. "Unsung: Millie Jackson." *Unsung*, Episode 41, season 4. TV One, February 6, 2012.

James, Joy. "Profeminism and Gender Elites: W.E.B. DuBois, Anna Julia Cooper, and Ida Wells-Barnett." In *Next to the Color Line: Gender, Sexuality, and W.E.B. Du Bois*, edited by Susan Gillman and Alys Weinbaum, 69–95. Minneapolis: University of Minnesota Press, 2007.

Jarett, Gene. *Representing the Race: A New Political History of African American Literature*. New York: New York University Press, 2011.

Jenkins, Candace. *Proper Lives: Proper Relations: Regulating Black Intimacy*. Minneapolis: University of Minnesota Press, 2007.

Johnson, E. Patrick. "'Quare Studies, or (Almost) Everything I Know about Queer Studies I Learned from My Grandmother." *Text and Performance Quarterly* 21, no. 1 (2001): 1–25.

Kavka, Misha. *Reality TV*. Edinburgh: Edinburgh University Press, 2012.

Kawashima, Dale. "Special Interview with Kenneth 'Babyface' Edmonds, Legendary Songwriter & Artist, and New Songwriters Hall of Fame Inductee." *Songwriter Universe*, March 20, 2017. Accessed October 8, 2018. http://www.songwriteruniverse.com /babyface-interview-2017.htm.

King, Jason. "Toni Braxton, Disney, and Thermodynamics." *Drama Review* 46, no. 3 T175 (Fall 2002), 54–81.

Knust, Jennifer. *Unprotected Texts: The Bible's Surprising Contradictions about Sex and Desire*. New York: HarperOne, 2012.

Konow, David. "New Whitney Houston Doc Takes Deeper Look at Addiction Battle." *The Fix*, August 29, 2017. Accessed September 4, 2017. https://www.thefix.com/new-whitney -houston-doc-takes-deeper-look-addiction-battle.

Laing, Heather. *The Gendered Score: Music in 1940s Melodrama and the Woman's Film*. Burlington: Ashgate, 2007.

Laub, Dori. "Bearing Witness or the Vicissitudes of Listening." In *Crises of Witnessing in Literature, Psychoanalysis, and History*, edited by Shoshana Felman and Dori Laub, 57–74. New York: Taylor and Francis, 1992.

Lee, Shayne. *Erotic Revolutionaries: Black Women, Sexuality, and Popular Culture.* Lanham, Md.: Hamilton Books, 2010.

Leight, Elias. "R&B's Changing Voice: How Hip-Hop Edged Grittier Singers Out of the Mainstream." *Rolling Stone*, October 13, 2017. Accessed November 8, 2017. https://www.rollingstone.com/music/features/how-hip-hop-edged-grittier-rb-singers-out-of-the-mainstream-w504678.

———. "R. Kelly Faces New Allegations of Underage Sex, Physical Abuse." *Rolling Stone*, August 22, 2017. Accessed August 22, 2017. http://www.rollingstone.com/music/news/r-kelly-faces-new-allegations-of-underage-sex-physical-abuse-w498861.

Lewis, Oscar. "Culture of Poverty." In *On Understanding Poverty: Perspectives from the Social Sciences*, by Daniel Moynihan, 187–220. New York: Basic Books, 1969.

Linden, Amy. "When a Man Loves a Woman." *Village Voice* New York, November 26, 1996, 54.

Living Single. Fox TV. Hollywood: Fox Broadcasting Company, 1993–1998.

Lopez, Ian. *White by Law: The Legal Construction of Race.* New York: New York University Press, 2006.

Lorde, Audre. *Sister Outsider: Essays and Speeches.* New York: Ten Speed Press, 2007.

Macpherson, Alex. "Toni Braxton: I Feel Like I've Been Given a Third Chance." *Guardian*, February 28, 2014. Accessed October 7, 2018. https://www.theguardian.com/music/2014/feb/28/toni-braxton-kenneth-babyface-edmonds-interview.

Madea's Family Reunion, directed by Tyler Perry. Santa Monica, Calif.: Lionsgate, 2006. DVD.

Madison, D. Soyini. "Foreword." In *Black Performance Theory*, edited by Thomas DeFrantz and Anita Gonzalez, vii–ix. Durham, N.C.: Duke University Press, 2014.

Malone, Janice. "Adina's a Freak and Proud of It." *Philadelphia Tribune*, September 12, 1995, 5.

———. "The Scoop: Adina Howard Representing Aggressive Sistas." *Columbus Times*, September 12, 1995, A5.

Manning, Brandon. *At Wit's End: Black Men and Vulnerability in Contemporary Satire.* n.p, n.d.

Marable, Manning. *Race, Reform, and Rebellion: The Second Reconstruction and beyond in America, 1945–2006.* Jackson: University of Mississippi Press, 2007.

Mask, Mia. *Divas on Screen: Black Women in American Film.* Urbana-Champaign: Illinois University Press, 2009.

Massood, Paula. *Black City Cinema: African-American Urban Experiences in Film.* Philadelphia: Temple University Press, 2003.

Maxwell, Bill. "Toni Braxton Stimulates Debate on Blacks and Sex." *Press of Atlantic City*, June 13, 1997, A-13.

Mayfield, Julian. "You Touch My Black Aesthetic and I'll Touch Yours." In *The Black Aesthetic*, edited by Addison Gayle, 24–31. New York: Doubleday, 1972.

McClatchy, William. "TV Series Puts 'Unsung' Black Music Stars Back in the Spotlight." *Pittsburgh Post-Gazette*, June 6, 2011. Accessed June 4, 2016. http://www.post-gazette.com/ae/tv-radio/2011/06/06/TV-series-puts-Unsung-black-music-stars-back-in-the-spotlight/stories/201106060128.

McCune, Jeffrey. *Sexual Discretion: Black Masculinity and the Politics of Passing.* Chicago: University of Chicago Press, 2014.

McKissic Sr., Dwight. "Response to President Obama's Decision to Endorse Same-Sex Marriages." *Dwight McKissie*, May 9, 2012. Accessed June 1, 2016. https://dwightmckissic.wordpress.com/2012/05/09/response-to-president-obamas-decision-to-endorse-same-sex-marriages/.

Melamed, Jodi. "The Spirit of Neoliberalism: From Racial Liberalism to Neoliberal Multiculturalism." *Social Text* 24, no. 4 (2006): 1–24.

Mendozza, Manuel. "Toni! Toni! Toni! Brash, Young Braxton Takes R&B by Storm." *Dallas Morning News*, December 17, 1993, 32.

The Merv Griffin Show. NBC. June 23, 1983. Directed by Dick Carson. Accessed October 9, 2018. https://www.youtube.com/watch?v=Dw2hjXDCM6k.

Michael Jackson 30th Anniversary Celebration. Episode 1. CBS. September 7, 2001. Accessed October 9, 2018. https://www.youtube.com/watch?v=eLlkSQb8NE8.

Miller-Young, Mireille. *A Taste for Brown Sugar: Black Women in Pornography*. Durham, N.C.: Duke University Press, 2014.

Mixon, Veronica. "'The Preacher's Wife' Is Gentle and Feels Good: Denzel and Whitney Stress the Importance of Positive Images." *Philadelphia Tribune*, December 13, 1996, 4E.

Monroe, Irene. "Would Whitney Houston Still Be Alive If She Had Come Out? Family, Career and Church Kept Her in the Closet—Pushing Her into a Downward Spiral of Drug Abuse." *GayStarNews*, October 12, 2017. Accessed October 24, 2017. https://www.gaystarnews.com/article/whitney-houston-still-alive-come.

Morris, Susana. *Close Kin and Distant Relatives: The Paradox of Respectability Politics in Black Women's Literature*. Charlottesville: University of Virginia Press, 2014.

Moss II, Otis. "Letter Supporting Gay Marriage by Pastor Otis Moss III of Trinity UCC." *Huffington Post*, May 13, 2012. Accessed June 1, 2016. http://www.huffingtonpost.com/2012/05/28/otis-moss-iii-challenges-on-marriage-equality_n_1550449.html.

Mounk, Yascha. *The Age of Responsibility: Luck, Choice, and the Welfare State*. Cambridge, Mass.: Harvard University Press, 2017.

Moynihan, Daniel P. *Negro Family: The Case for National Action*. Washington, DC: Office of Planning and Research, US Department of Labor, 1965.

Murray, Rolland. *Our Living Manhood: Literature, Black Power, and Masculine Ideology*. Philadelphia: University of Pennsylvania Press, 2007.

Nash, Jennifer C. *The Black Body in Ecstasy: Reading Race, Reading Pornography*. Durham, N.C.: Duke University Press, 2014.

Ndounou, Monica. *Shaping the Future of African American Film: Color-Coded Economics and the Story Behind the Numbers*. New Brunswick, N.J.: Rutgers University Press, 2014.

Ndubuizu, Rosemary. "(Black) Papa Knows Best: Marion Barry and the Appeal to Black Authoritarian Discourse." *National Political Science Review* 16, no. 1: 31–48.

Neal, Larry. "The Black Arts Movement." In *Within the Circle: An Anthology of African American Literary Criticism: From the Harlem Renaissance to the Present*, edited by Angelyn Mitchell, 184–198. Durham, N.C.: Duke University Press, 1994.

Neal, Mark Anthony. *Looking for Leroy: Illegible Black Masculinities*. New York: New York University Press, 2013.

———. *Songs in the Key of Black Life: A Rhythm and Blues Nation*. New York: Routledge, 2003.

———. *Soul Babies: Black Popular Culture and the Post-Soul Aesthetic*. London: Routledge, 2004.

———. *What the Music Said: Black Popular Music and Black Public Culture*. New York: Routledge, 1998.

Norment, Lynn. "Top Black Executives in Music Industry: 14 African-American Men and Women Are Among the Movers and Shakers in the Lucrative World of Recording," *Ebony*, July 1997, 88–92.

———. "Whitney at 35!" *Ebony*, December 1998, 156–162.

———. "Whitney Talks about the Men in Her Life—and the Rumors, Lies, and Insults That Are the High Price of Fame" *Ebony*, May 1991, 110–118.

Obama, Barack. "Barack Obama Supports Gay Marriage in Interview with Robin Roberts of ABC News." ABC News, May 9, 2012. Accessed June 1, 2016. http://abcnews.go.com/Politics/transcript-robin-roberts-abc-news-interview-president-obama/story?id=16316043.

O'Jays, The. (Performers) "Family Reunion." 1975.

Oliver, Melvin, and Thomas Shapiro. *Black Wealth, White Wealth: A New Perspective on Racial Inequality*. New York: Routledge, 1997.

"Oprah Announces Upcoming Interview of Whitney!" *Whitney Houston*. Accessed January 17, 2018. http://www.whitneyhouston.com/news/oprah-announces-upcoming-interview-whitney/.

Oprah's Next Chapter. Oprah Winfrey Network. http://www.oprah.com/app/oprahs-next
    -chapter.html.

Ouellette, Laura, and James Hay. *Better Living through Reality TV: Television and Post-
    Welfare Citizenship.* Malden: Blackwell, 2008.

Parker, Lonnae O. "The Body of Her Work: Singer Adina Howard's Sexy Ways Stir Up a Fuss."
    Washington Post, September 5, 1995, D1.

Patterson, Robert J. "Do You Want to Be Well? The Gospel Play, Womanist Theology, and Tyler
    Perry's Artistic Production." *Journal of Feminist Studies in Religion* 30, no. 2 (2014):
    41–56.

Peck, Janice. "Talk About Racism: Framing a Popular Discourse on Race and Oprah
    Winfrey." *Cultural Critique* 27 (1994): 89–126.

The People v. O.J. Simpson: American Crime Story, directed by Ryan Murphy, Anthony
    Hemingway, and John Singleton. Los Angeles, Calif.: FX, February 2016.

Perkins, Ken Parish. "Toni Braxton: Red-Hot R&B Act Is a Beautiful Bundle of Contradic-
    tions." *Fort Worth Star,* March 7, 1997, 24.

Perry, Imani. *Prophets of the Hood: Politics and Poetics in Hip Hop.* Durham, N.C.: Duke
    University Press, 2004.

Person, David. "The Music All Sounds the Same." *Huntsville Times,* July 27, 1995, D3.

Piers Morgan Tonight. CNN, February 13, 2012. Accessed February 12, 2012. https://www
    .youtube.com/watch?v=Wr-oPSB6Uow.

Pough, Gwendolyn. "Seeds and Legacies: Tapping the Potential in Hip-Hop." In *That's the
    Joint! The Hip-Hop Studies Reader,* edited by Murray Forman and Mark Anthony Neal,
    283–290. New York: Routledge, 2004.

Randolph, Laura. "Babyface and Tracey Edmonds Talk About Life, Love and Launching Their
    New Adventures." *Ebony,* June 1998, 36–40.

Redmond, Shana. *Anthems: Social Movements and the Sound of Solidarity in the African Dias-
    pora.* New York: New York University Press, 2013.

Rexroat, Jennifer. "'I'm Everywoman': Oprah Winfrey and Feminist Identification." In *Sto-
    ries of Oprah: The Oprahfication of American Culture,* edited by Trystan Cotton and
    Kimberly Springer, 19–32. University: University of Mississippi Press, 2010.

Reynolds, J. R. "Howard Gets Less Graphic: Mecca Don Set More Sensual Than Explicit."
    Billboard, July 5, 1997, 15.

———. "Howard Takes Fans on Steamy 'Ride.'" *Billboard,* January 21, 1995, 13.

Ritz, David. "Not Just a Pretty Face" *Essence,* September 1990, 72–74.

———. "The Soul Behind the Face." *Rolling Stone,* December 1, 1994, 103–105.

Roberts, Dorothy. *Killing the Black Body: Race, Reproduction, and the Meaning of Liberty.* New
    York: Vintage, 1998.

Roberts, Kimberly. "Babyface Releases New Best of CD." *Philadelphia Tribune,* December 29,
    2000, 5E.

Robinson, Cedric. *Black Marxism: The Making of the Black Radical Tradition.* Chapel Hill: Uni-
    versity of North Carolina Press, 2000.

Rogers, Charles. "L.A. and Babyface Sign $10M Arista, Deal." *New York Amsterdam News,*
    October 29, 1989, 26.

Romano, Tricia. "Whitney Houston: Anatomy of a Lesbian Rumor." *Daily Beast,* February 12,
    2012. Accessed October 10, 2018. https://www.thedailybeast.com/whitney-houston
    -anatomy-of-a-lesbian-rumor.

Rustin, Bayard. "From Protest to Politics." In *Time on Two Crosses: The Collected Writing of
    Bayard Rustin,* edited by Devon Carbado and Donald Weise, 116–129. San Francisco:
    Cleis Press, 2003.

Samuels, Alison. "Whitney Houston's Protective 'Baby Girl' Daughter Bobbi Kristina." *The
    Daily Beast,* February 13, 2012. Accessed October 9, 2018. https://www.thedailybeast
    .com/whitney-houstons-protective-baby-girl-daughter-bobbi-kristina.

———. "Whitney's Private Hell: I Have Nothing." *Newsweek,* May 7, 2012, 28–32.

Saunders, Patricia J. "Fugitive Dreams of Diaspora: Conversations with Saidiya Hartman." In *Anthurium: A Caribbean Studies Journal* 6, no. 1 (2008): 1–17.

Sawyer, Diane. "Primetime: Whitney Houston." ABC News, *Primetime*, December 4, 2002. Accessed March 15, 2015. https://www.dailymotion.com/video/x2hhajc.

Schwartz, Casey. "Whitney Houston's Death: Xanax and Alcohol, Lethal Duo." *Daily Beast*, February 13, 2012. Accessed October 9, 2018. https://www.thedailybeast.com/whitney -houstons-death-xanax-and-alcohol-lethal-duo.

Scott, Darieck. *Extravagant Abjection: Blackness, Power, and Sexuality in the African American Imagination*. New York: New York University Press, 2014.

Seal, Mark. "The Devils in the Diva." *Vanity Fair*, June 2012. Accessed June 20, 2012. https:// www.vanityfair.com/hollywood/2012/06/whitney-houston-death-bathtub-drugs-rehab.

Seemayer, Zach. "Bobby Brown Addresses Whitney Houston 'Crack is Whack' interview, Says He 'Should Have Been Better.'" *ET Online*, July 7, 2016. Accessed July 10, 2016. https:// www.etonline.com/news/190541_bobby_brown_addresses_whitney_houston_crack _is_whack_interview.

Serrianne, Nina. "Pop Culture." In *America in the Nineties*, 141–171. New York: Syracuse University Press, 2015.

Sharpley-Whiting, Tracey. *Pimps Up, Ho's Down: Young Black Women, Hip Hop and the New Gender Politics*. New York: New York University Press, 2007.

Sharpton, Al, Julian Bond, et al. "Open Letter Embracing President Obama's Position on Equality for Gay and Lesbian Individuals." *National Action Network*, May 11, 2012. Accessed June 1, 2016. http://nationalactionnetwork.net/press/open-letter-embracing -president-obamas-position-on-equality-for-gay-lesbian-individuals/.

Shutter, Fred. "'Boy Toy,' Yes, But Who's Doing the Toying?" *Kansas City Star*, March 28, 1995, E5.

Sinagra, Laura. "Pop Review: Swinging Sounds for Lovers by Babyface, All Grown Up." *New York Times*, December 12, 2005, E4.

"Single Life." *All Music*. http://www.allmusic.com/album/single-life-mw0000189389/awards.

Smith, Danyel. "Babyface Is Tangy Sweet on Love and Relationships." *New York Times*, August 15, 1993, H25.

Smith, Suzanne. *Dancing in the Street: Motown and the Cultural Politics of Detroit*. Cambridge, Mass.: Harvard University Press, 2001.

Snorton, C. Riley. *Black on Both Sides: A Racial History of Trans Identity*. Minneapolis: University of Minnesota Press, 2017.

———. *Nobody's Supposed to Know: Black Sexuality on the Down Low*. Minneapolis: University of Minnesota Press, 2014.

"Something in Common." (Performers) Whitney Houston and Bobby Brown. Recorded 1992. *Song Facts*. Accessed July 3, 2015. http://www.songfacts.com/detail.php?id=5589.

Spillers, Hortense. "Mama's Baby, Papa's Maybe: An American Grammar Book." *Diacritics* 17, no. 2 (1987): 66.

Springer, Kimberly. "Introduction: The Contours of the Oprah Culture Industry." In *Stories of Oprah: The Oprahfication of American Culture*, edited by Trystan Cotton and Kimberly Springer, vii–xix. University: University of Mississippi Press, 2010.

Stallings, L. H. *Funk the Erotic: Transaesthetics and Black Sexual Culture*. Urbana-Champaign: University of Illinois Press, 2015.

Staples, Robert. *The Black Family: Essays and Studies*. Boston: Cengage Learning, 1998.

"State Senate GOP Rejects Request to Honor Whitney Houston." *Culvert Chronicles*, February 16–22, 2012, 3.

Stoever, Jennifer. *The Sonic Color Line: Race and the Cultural Politics of Listening*. New York: New York University Press, 2016.

Sue, Gerald. "The Invisible Whiteness of Being." In *White Privilege: Essential Readings on the Other Side of Racism*, edited by Paula Rothenberg, 19–28. New York: Worth Publishers, 2014.

"Superstar Singer Toni Braxton Tells Why She Filed for Bankruptcy." *JET*, March 23, 1998, 58.

Tasker, Yvonne. *Working Girls: Gender and Sexuality in Popular Cinema.* London: Taylor and Francis, 1998.

Tiger, Rebecca. "Celebrity Drug Scandals: Media Double Standards," *Contexts* 12, no. 4 (2013): 36–41.

Tinsley, Omise'eke Natasha. *Ezili's Mirrors: Imagining Black Queer Genders.* Durham, N.C.: Duke University Press, 2018.

Thompson, Lisa. *Beyond the Black Lady: Sexuality and the New African American Middle Class.* Urbana: University of Illinois Press, 2012.

"Toni Braxton Back on Top after Bankruptcy." *JET*, July 17, 2000, 55–60.

"Toni Braxton Shocked and Hurt after Oprah Interview." *Entertainment Examiner*, October 30, 2012 (page unavailable).

Tranfa, Anthony. "Second Houston Album Disappointing." *Daily Breeze*, June 26, 1987, E15.

"TV One's 2009–10 Season the Highest in Network's Six-Year History." *Target Market News: The Black Consumer Market Authority.* Last modified October 21, 2010. Accessed June 6, 2016. http://www.targetmarketnews.com/storyid10251002.htm.

TV One. Accessed June 6, 2016. http://tvone.tv/show/unsung-4/.

Urban One Website. https://urban1.com, accessed October 10, 2018.

Vagianos, Alana. "Time's Up Demands Investigation into R. Kelly Sexual Abuse Allegations," *Huff Post*, April 30, 2018. Accessed October 7, 2018. https://www.huffingtonpost.com /entry/times-up-demands-investigation-into-r-kelly-sexual-abuse-accusations_us _5ae73480e4b04aa23f259f6a.

Verán, Cristina. "Voices of Theory." *Vibe*, August 1997.

VH1 Behind the Music. Episode 238, season 1. VH1. Performed by Toni Braxton.

"Waiting to Exhale." Box Office Mojo. Accessed July 18, 2016. http://www.boxofficemojo.com /movies/?id=waitingtoexhale.htm.

Wallace, Michele. *The Black Macho and the Myth of the Superwoman.* New York: Verso, 1999.

Ward, Brian. *Just My Soul Responding: Rhythm and Blues, Black Consciousness, and Race Relations.* Oakland: University of California Press, 1998.

Weber, Brenda. "Introduction—Trash Talk: Gender as an Analytic on Reality Television." In *Reality Gendervision: Sexuality & Gender on Transatlantic Reality Television*, edited by Brenda Weber, 1–34. Durham, N.C.: Duke University Press, 2014.

———. "When America." In *Reality Gendervision: Sexuality & Gender on Transatlantic Reality Television*, 97–122. Durham, N.C.: Duke University Press, 2014.

Weheliye, Alexander. *Habeas Viscus: Racializing Assemblages, Biopolitics, and Black Feminist Theories of the Human.* Durham, N.C.: Duke University Press, 2014.

———. *Phonographies: Grooves in Sonic Afro-Modernity.* Durham, N.C.: Duke University Press, 2005.

Werner, Craig. *A Change Is Gonna Come: Music, Race, and the Soul of America.* Ann Arbor: University of Michigan Press, 2006.

Wertz, Langston. "Is Howard Video Too Nasty to Air?" *Charlotte Observer*, October 15, 1995, 2E.

"What We Sing, Why We Sing." *Daily Hampshire Gazette*, June 16, 1995 (page unavailable).

Whitney, directed by Angela Bassett. New York: Lifetime Movies, 2015.

Whitney, directed by Kevin MacDonald. Los Angeles: Miramax and Roadside Attractions Film, 2018.

"Whitney Houston Autopsy Report." *Autopsy Files.* Accessed June 5, 2015. http://www .autopsyfiles.org/reports/Celebs/houston,%20whitney_report.pdf.

Whitney Houston: Can I Be Me?, directed by Nick Broomfield. BBC. 2017.

"Whitney Houston Coroner's Report Details Drug Signs, Liquor, Drowning." CBS News, April 5, 2012. Accessed April 5, 2012. https://www.cbsnews.com/news/whitney-houston -coroners-report-details-drug-signs-liquor-drowning/.

"Whitney Houston Gets 6 Nominations." *Baltimore Sun*, January 6, 1986, 2B.

"Whitney Houston Honored as a Humanitarian." *Today,* June 10, 2004. Accessed July 15, 2017. https://www.today.com/popculture/whitney-houston-honored-humanitarian -wbna5183450.

Wiggins, Jean A. "Howard Brings Bold Tone, Strong Voice to Special R&B Act." *Chicago Sun-Times*, August 18, 1995, 13.

Willey, Angela. *Undoing Monogamy: The Politics of Science and the Possibility of Biology.* Durham, N.C.: Duke University Press, 2016.

Williams, Jean. "Braxton Adds Sexy Look to Solid Songs." *Chicago Sun-Times*, January 20, 1997, 28.

Williams, Sherley. "Some Implications for Womanist Theory." *Callaloo* 27, no. 9 (1986): 303–308.

Williamson, Terrion. *Scandalize My Name: Black Feminist Practice and the Making of Black Social Life.* New York: Fordham University Press, 2017.

Wilson, Julius. "Poverty and Family Structure: The Widening Gap between Evidence and Public Policy Issues." In *The Truly Disadvantaged: The Inner City, the Underclass, and Public Policy*, 63–92. Chicago: University of Chicago Press 2012.

Wright, Richard. "Between Laughter and Tears," *New Masses*, October 5, 1937, 22–24.

INDEX

Photographs are indicated by page numbers in italics.

ABOUT THE AUTHOR

ROBERT J. PATTERSON is an associate professor of African American studies at Georgetown University, where he also serves as the inaugural chair of the Department of African American Studies. He is the author of *Exodus Politics: Civil Rights and Leadership in African American Literature and Culture* (UVA Press), co-editor of *The Psychic Hold of Slavery: Legacies in American Expressive Culture* (Rutgers University Press), and editor of the forthcoming *Black Cultural Production after Civil Rights* (University of Illinois Press). Currently, he is working on a book titled *Black Equity, Black Equality: Reparation and Black Communities*.